– TREASURES OF THE SAN JUANS SERIES –

VOLUME I

FORTRESS SAN JUANS

1803-1874

True Stories of Grit, Gumption and Gambles that Transformed America

BY DON BOOHER

ISBN 979-8-9934766-1-2

Second Edition
Printed in the United States

Cover and Text Design by Laurie Casselberry
Laurie Goralka Design

Cover photo © Michael Underwood

booherbookorders@gmail.com

Fortress San Juans *is dedicated to my loving wife Lana,*

both supportive and patient beyond measure.

Lana, boundless thanks for your encouragement, prayers,

and willingness to sacrifice time required to research

and write this book.

Contents

Acknowledgments

History is not written, but rewritten.
— Alpheus H. Favour —

*F*ortress San Juans is a factual narrative often featuring improbable accomplishments of everyday people. Cited eyewitness testimonies and primary sources unmask the social and cultural dynamics of the times. Meaningful focus and context also benefit from extensive contemporary scholarship. For this notable writers well-recognized in their areas of expertise are referenced. For some, their accomplishments are so extraordinary that special recognition is called for here.

Fortress San Juans, in many respects a collection of vignettes, in some cases quotations and profiles that open up colorful people or circumstances to fuller understanding, relies on lengthy excerpts to preserve the flow of ethos and authenticity they reveal. The origin of these excerpts may be daily entries from a trail journal or stagecoach trip, a compilation of pioneer recollections, or assessments eloquently stated by journalists and scholars that have been mined throughout careers of experience and research. Endnotes document these sources, but the following contributors warrant heightened recognition. Overstating the central role of their research and writings to the understanding of this time period would be difficult —their skillful weaving of raw material with insightful analysis is masterful. Their combined bibliographies alone could dominate the typical library. My sincerest gratitude and thanks is extended to every contributor to this work, but especially to the following writers for underpinning critical *Fortress San Juans* topics.

Will Bagley's *Overland West* series, *So Rugged and Mountainous* (Vol. I) and *With Visions Bright Before Them* (Vol. II), has no equal. His work is enriched throughout with accounts of score after score of first-hand testimonies and original sources that draw the reader into experiences and circumstances that could not be appreciated otherwise. Both his sources mined from historical literature and archives across the West and his commentary are unmatched. Neither should be overlooked in any way if one is interested in who emigrated west and why.

Immeasurable gratitude is extended to him for his brilliant treatment of epic topics and the comprehensive roadmap of primary sources he provides.

Steven G. Baker not just researched and wrote *Juan Rivera's Colorado, 1765*, he walked Rivera's 1765 walk. Complementing his extensive historical and geological research with personal on-the-ground insights adds a dimension of understanding that brings life to Rivera's centuries-old exploration. Every San Juans historian, writer, and curious reader will benefit greatly from his diligent search for truth, pursuit of where it led, and the illustrations that support this fast-paced adventure through the Spanish southwest.

Allen Nossaman's *Many More Mountains* is an incredibly thorough treatment of people and events that led to the discovery and development of the San Juan Mountain Range and the Animas River watershed. He has no equal. No discussion of this region should shy away from heavy reliance on the extensive and comprehensive research found in this and two subsequent volumes. His depth and scope of sources and analysis is truly spectacular.

Rodman W. Paul's *The Far West and the Great Plains in Transition, 1859-1900*, and *Mining Frontiers of the Far West, 1848-1880*, provide rare insight into what became mass western migrations. Paul's writings rise to the rare rank of western history classics. His ability to explain the global sweep of this period of American expansionism in terms of common people with everyday aspirations brings the march of momentous events to life.

Marshall Sprague's writing style and ability to captivate his readers begins with the title of *The Great Gates*. "Gates," mountain passes in customary terms, are discussed in terms of a multi-century adventure. His perspective is a combination of hiker's guide, geology, exploration and history. What makes Sprague's research particularly valuable to *Fortress San Juans* is the essential context it provides for one of its central themes, namely that the San Juan Range is a natural fortress that delayed [along with the threat of Ute attacks] mineral exploitation of the region until well into the 1870s. There is no better example of weaving multiple disciplines unified by a common theme [mountain passes] into an action-packed history. Clearly a regional classic in a broader sense, it should be seen as a strong pillar underpinning any narrative focused on the Colorado Rockies San Juan Range.

Elliott West's *The Contested Plains, Indians, Goldseekers, and the Rush to Colorado* stands out as another foundation stone for *Fortress San Juans*. It too is a Western history classic that has special relevance to any attempt to describe the character and motivations of the men and women who first crossed the Great Plains in search of the means to a better life. Testimony to Elliott West excellence is the credit given by so many others found in history's hall of fame.

In addition, reliance on the following primary sources warrants additional attention and a cautionary note.

Lewis H. Garrard's *Wah-to-yah* serves as an excellent source of examples of the customs and conversations associated with the 1840s frontier. Thought was given to expressing his observations in socially acceptable vernacular, but little action was taken in this direction—the desired outcomes are insights into Native American culture and frontier attitudes rarely found in more genteel quarters. Retaining this aspect of a given period of history, a general goal of *Fortress San Juans*, is greatly aided by Garrard. Like Garrard, "I have naught set down in malice, and it is no more my prerogative to exclude than to add."

LeRoy R. Hafen in his role of editor of a number of eye-witness accounts of the Colorado gold rush and guidebooks intended to assist those undertaking the journey provides a rich source of testimonies and drama. Living and writing as close in time to the events in question as he did can be risky but provides access and insights unattainable by those who succeeded him.

Frank Hall's *History of the State of Colorado* is another example of the benefits and risks of living close to the action. Criticized for relying too heavily on eyewitness accounts, for the most part his rendering of events and dialogs contributes greatly to understanding of the times.

Ovando James Hollister's *The Mines of Colorado* is unique in the sense that it is broad-based history written from the perspective of a "mining engineer" in close temporal proximity to his subject matter. His work offers many opportunities to capture the intangible characteristics of American exceptionalism, "manifest destiny," and westering through the application of extensive quotations and raw insights.

Hubert Howe Bancroft's *History of Colorado*, first published in 1890 in Vol. XX of *History of the Pacific States of North America*, conveys unmistakable authenticity also best achieved by proximity to the subject. Bancroft contributes a valuable sense of the human condition as well as a mundane march of circumstances. His writings, often embellished with collections of letters and other primary sources, include details not addressed in many other works.

Albert D. Richardson's *Beyond the Mississippi* also achieves "classic status" for different reasons. By virtue of A.D.R.'s witty journaling of his travels west, his adventurous nature, and his gifts as a journalist willing to "live his storyline," his writings are a treasure trove of insightful quotations and observations conveying the excitement and mystery of the 1860s "American Experience."

Robert Edmund Strahorn's autobiography and remembrances in *Gunnison and San Juan* provide hard-to-find insight and authenticity concerning a final phase of the "White Man/Red Man" battles over the West and the development of the mineral resources of the San Juans. Like Garrard, Hollister and Uncle Dick Wootton, Strahorn did not concern himself with gentrifying his choice of language. The consequence for subsequent readers is a source rich in color if not good taste.

Richens Lacy Wootton's *Uncle Dick Wootton* is the life story of one of the Rocky Mountain's last mountain men. It is unique in scope and content that reaches far beyond mountain-man status. It is told to Howard Louis Conard and edited by M.M. Quaife. It ranks high on the list of resources filled with first-hand insight into the life and times of the men and women that settled the West. First-hand insight, however, should not be equated with first-hand writings or the fidelity of memory. Uncle Dick was not a writer and he told his story late in life to a professional chronicler. That said, both Conard and Quaife claim Uncle Dick's memory was sharp and their rendering of his accounts in print is faithful to his narrative. Such assurances should suit the general reader, scholars maybe not so much. For the purpose of appreciating the challenges of early Denver, and describing the role of the Ute and Plains tribes in the transformation of the West and the San Juans, Conard and Quaife versions of Uncle Dick's activities and explanations are consistent with other valued sources and are relied on here. As a cautionary note, M.M. Quafe's observation rings true: "The passage of time brings changes in viewpoints and standards of judgment. Chiefly for this reason the 'definitive' history so often acclaimed by the book reviewers can never, in fact, be written."

The Ancients

When mountains rise to entomb their treasures,
When continents quake and collide, I am there.
I am there when lava and ash sculpt calderas on the plain.

When wind, rain, ice defeat the caldera and scour the valleys clear,
I am there.
I am there when only the plain and oceans remain.

Yet Earth does not rest.

When calderas and mountains again burst skyward, I am there.
I am there when alpine lakes again break free.
When stealthy new glaciers cut paths to the sea,
I am there.

When sacred Uncompahgre sheds her mantel,
When she lays her treasure veins bare,
When the Two-Legged declare "last best chance"
With fatigue and failure beyond care,
I am **there**.

— Author —

Preface

The vanguard of dreamers wintering over in 1874-75 at the mouth of Henson Canyon was about to end the San Juans' fortress legacy. That was not why they were there, of course. That would be a consequence, not a goal. No, they were there to find treasure. The "San Juans excitement" had been ignited by the discovery of gold during construction of an Otto Mears toll road up the Lake Fork of the Gunnison river, and they were surely excited. More exciting still was what it took to get there. That decades-long journey, and the role the fortress played, is what *Fortress San Juans* is about.

The San Juan Range is one of the most rugged and difficult to reach mountain ranges in the American West, for centuries a veritable albeit natural fortress. Before it could be challenged, the western half of the North American continent had to be challenged and overcome. This story is about triumph of the human spirit in the face of suffering and death. It is a story about America's nineteenth-century transition from an anemic agrarian society east of the Mississippi and Missouri Rivers to a confident, industrial superpower spanning the North American continent.

Three nineteenth-century western mass migrations—the timing and nature of each determined by preconditions that had to be satisfied—populated the American West. At the same time, the San Juan Range of southwestern Colorado remained a pristine wilderness. Not even the fruitful gold rush to Colorado's Front Range and nearby High Country could muster the resources required to overcome its fortress-like features. That would require another decade and a half of satisfying additional preconditions. It also would require the perseverance and grit exhibited by the generation of emigrants that crossed the Great Plains and mountain west to Utah, Oregon and California, and a decade later mimicked their struggles crossing the prairie to Colorado.

America's mass migrations west were both precursors and products of a series of cascading, interrelated events beginning in 1821 with Mexico winning its independence from Spain. Had Mexico failed in its overthrow of Spanish colonialism, there would have been no Mexican republic. Absent a Mexican republic, there would not have been a Mexican-American war. Without a Mexican-American war, there would not have been an American California. Without the 1849 gold rush to American California, there would not have been a 1859 gold rush to Colorado. The devastating disruption of the American civil war delayed the fall of Fortress San Juans and development of San Juans silver and gold deposits another decade and a half, but that decade and a half also would produce essential capital and technology. Each sequential event was a necessary precedent to subsequent events leading to yet another bout of gold fever.

Where did these western pilgrims come from? What motivated their zeal to their dying breath? What can be gleaned from the character of ordinary men and women with backgrounds as diverse as society itself. Their path to southwestern Colorado was anything but straight or sure.

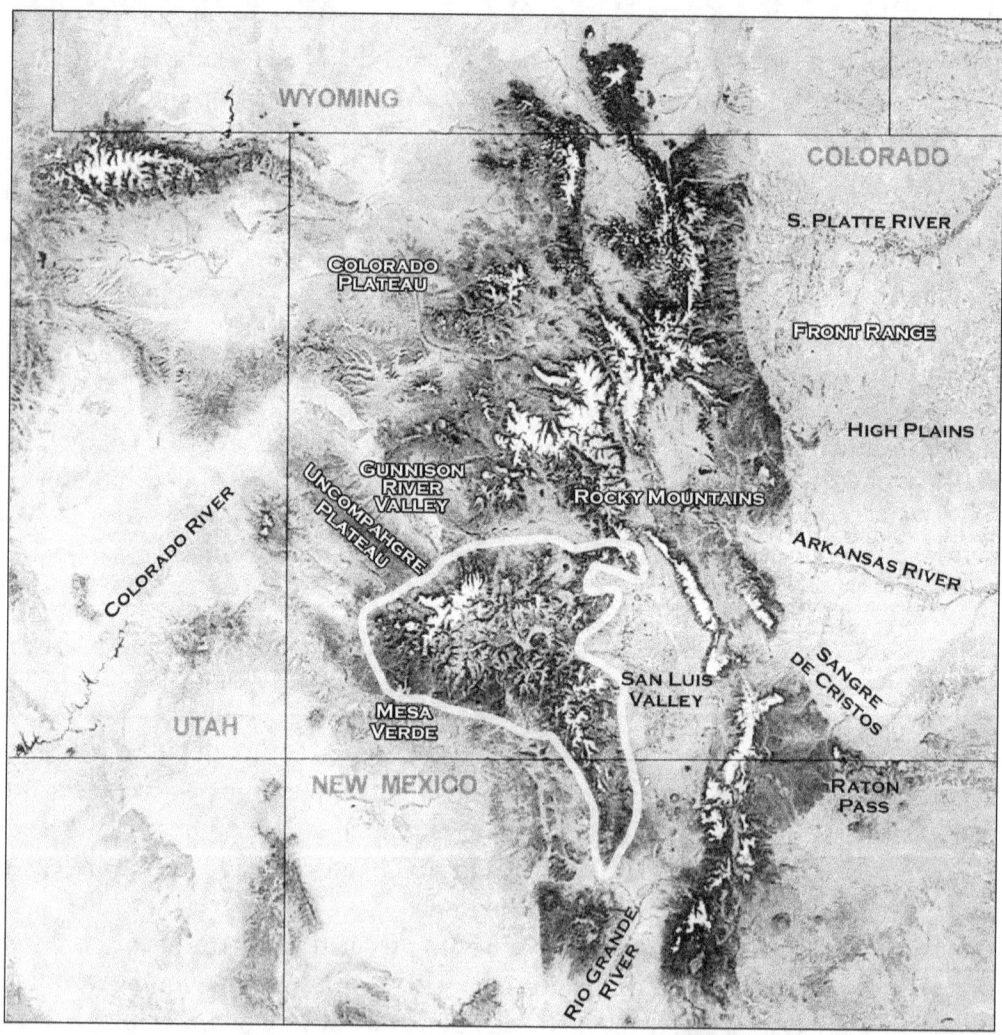

The San Juan Mountains. Adapted from NASA space photography, this map of the southwest quadrant of Colorado portrays the rugged and remote terrain between the Uncompahgre Plateau and the San Luis Valley. *(Courtesy of Western Reflections Publishing)*

The vanguard huddled at the mouth of Henson Canyon signaled the end of the San Juans fortress legacy. Soon their hardscrabble camp was Lake City. Within months it would be "Queen of the San Juans" bustling with prospectors and the mining class. Henson Canyon would reluctantly ease its grip on its gold and silver, as would the region as a whole. A few years more and the San Juans fortress legacy would be dead, its obituary written by a new generation of dreamers hard at work on a legacy of their own. But *Fortress San Juans* is not about the new generation of dreamers. It is about the generation that got them to the proverbial party, a party that began decades earlier in Spain's colonial Mexico and America's distant gold-fields. It is an account that weaves their quest for a better life into the colorful mosaic of the San Juan Range and the "new American West."

CHAPTER I

Ordinary Man

If you and I should chance to meet,
I guess you wouldn't care;
I'm sure you'd pass me in the street
As if I wasn't there;
You'd never look me in the face,
My modest mug to scan,
Because I'm just a commonplace
And Ordinary Man.

But then, it may be, you are too
A guy of every day,
Who does the job he's told to do
And takes the wife his pay;
Who makes a home and kids his care,
And works with pick or pen....
Why, Pal, I guess we're just a pair.

We plug away and make no fuss,
Our feats are never crowned;
And yet its common coves like us
Who make the world go round.
And as we steer a steady course
By God's predestined plan,
Hats off to that almighty Force. [1]

— Robert Service —

ollowing the Civil War, western entrepreneurs were plentiful and gold-seekers abounded. Bridging the mountain west and Great Plains with the transcontinental railroad system not only united the country, it supplied all manner of heavy equipment and household wares. It also facilitated the flood of both Union and Confederate veterans and immigrants seeking a fresh start. Those remembered today were ordinary people with exceptional courage. They were so unfulfilled by their daily lives and intrigued by promised treasures and opportunities in the West that they willingly embraced the hardships of trail and camp. Fearless or foolish, their adventures defined the human fabric of expansionist America. [2]

According to Will Bagley, "Western historians usually agree with Sylvia Sun Minnick: 'Beyond doubt, the California gold rush was the most momentous single episode in the development of the American West.' Bagley adds, "the explosive creation of the mining West was arguably second only to the Civil War in national significance during the nineteenth century." [3] Others would add that the Colorado gold rush, completion of a continental railroad system, and two world wars were rather momentous as well. Similarly, just as all frontier trails inevitably led west, we can see that some also eventually led to Colorado's San Juans Mountains and many a miner's last best chance to recover a fortune. With

Manifest Destiny. As mystical as real, the sense of purpose of young America was captured in this iconic illustration. It portrayed the individualism, independence, and initiative of two generations of emigrants that settled the West. *(Public Domain)*

eloquent insight, Bagley captures Elliott West's conclusion regarding young expansionist America's "manifest destiny," the product of countless "last best chances," this way:

> As "the republic changed in size, purpose, and values," Elliott West observed, gold reshaped how America saw itself. The great rushes "helped knit its parts into a newly imagined union—sure in its blessings, imperial in vision, blindly arrogant, naively confident of a future of untarnishable luster." [4]

The chroniclers in *Fortress San Juans* looked into the tired eyes of adventurers and emigrants that risked everything to pursue dreams and fantasies always west of wherever they were at the time. They populated social clans that represented generations and eras spanning several centuries and half a continent. Listening to their faint voices today helps personify the faceless crowds that transformed the continent. Of course their accounts are few among millions, and only skim the surface of volumes of first-hand observations and scholarly histories. Nevertheless, the experiences they documented ring common and true. Despite the passage of time, despite being lost in the flood of information deemed more encompassing, despite being forgotten in archives or boxes in attics inherited from kinfolk long ago dead, they still pulsate with life and meaning.

For context, remember the journey to Colorado benefited from journeys to Oregon and California, and consider the following dangers. Often accounts of the "American experience" began with trails, trails that led inland from Atlantic and Gulf Coast beaches, trails that led westward across the Great Plains. There were alternatives, of course, waterways with epic tales of their own. There was the open sea, or combination sea-land routes as distant as the Isthmus of Panama and Cape Horn, but cost and duration of travel was a deterrent. Still, with visions of San Francisco in mind, these routes were safer.

San Francisco, 1850. Rapidly populating San Francisco welcomed not only gold-seekers arriving by sea, but more importantly mail from the States and the world at large. *(George Henry Burgess)*

America's nineteenth century pilgrims were well acquainted with Biblical accounts of death angels, and most mid-century church-going immigrants rolling westward were acutely aware they too were subject to similar attacks. Deadly disease and plague shadowed every wagon train, a continuing reminder to every superstitious if not religious soul that there were more than hostile Native Americans lying in wait ahead. While this particular angst of westering was especially difficult to manage, more difficult in fact than agonizing over likely mischief, it added little to the already long list of reasons to stay home or go home. Oregon-bound missionary and Salt Lake Valley Mormon trains aside, the settlers and gold-seekers that followed them kept a watchful eye on Sabbath practices and the earthly consequences of falling into the hands of an angry God. Apprehensive but resolute, westward they rolled, but on Sunday, they rested.

Usually underestimated or taken for granted, the threats from weather and disease were ever-present. Both shadowed the earliest brave-hearts enroute to Santa Fe or Oregon. Of minor consequence when travel was light, both played devastating roles during the mass emigrations across the Great Plains. Prior to the California gold rush, the plains were in ecological balance. Climatic cycles, wet and dry seasons, abundant-grass and stressed-grass years, prairie fires and prairie floods—all home to immense buffalo herds and dozens of nomadic tribes—were in balance. Transitions from one extreme condition to the opposite extreme condition were certain and healthy, certain that is until mass migrations upset the balance.

Most affected were the northern routes. The Oregon, Mormon and California trails accommodated westward traffic during the 1840s, but only due to a decade blessed with abundant rain. Abundant rain accommodated abundant grasses, enough for both buffalo and livestock. By the end of the California gold rush, heavy traffic both east and west plus drought conditions were a dark harbinger for livestock and emigrant alike. With destruction of the balance, wildlife, livestock and pilgrims thirsted, starved and died. Ecological balance on the Great Plains was a precondition for heavy wagon usage. The inability of wagons to keep up with the demands of an exploding population was a precondition for the transcontinental railroad system.

Malnourishment and disease were no respecters of persons. President Polk was out of office less than a month when he died of cholera in the 1849 epidemic that swept through the Mississippi and Missouri valleys. The epidemic crossed the continent to the Pacific, decimating emigrant trains and imprinting horror scenes on the minds of survivors for decades to come. [In 1918, the Spanish flu pandemic accomplished the same. The "great influenza" reached even the remote San Juans and into isolated Henson Canyon, a powerful reminder that death has many servants.] The impact these invisible enemies exerted on the American character and spirit were unmistakable. According to Will Bagley:

The grim tales of death and dying on the overland trail in 1849 and 1850 were terrifying, but conditions in 1852 overshadowed all the previous horrors. The chief agent of death, cholera, had now spread north to the Council Bluffs Road and enlisted new allies. Gold seekers complained about and died of almost every ailment known to man – dehydration, diarrhea, dysentery, headache, smallpox, toothache, typhus, pleurisy, measles, sneezing, nasal convulsions, and constipation. A few mentioned yellow fever, but no one is known to have died of it. Their journals used traditional names for other diseases, including ague (malaria), whooping cough (diphtheria), mountain fever (probably Rocky Mountain spotted fever), consumption (tuberculosis), lung fever (pneumonia), the pox (syphilis), the clap (gonorrhea), melancholy gloom (depression), and irresipulus, irisopulus, and ursyphlus (erysipelas, an acute

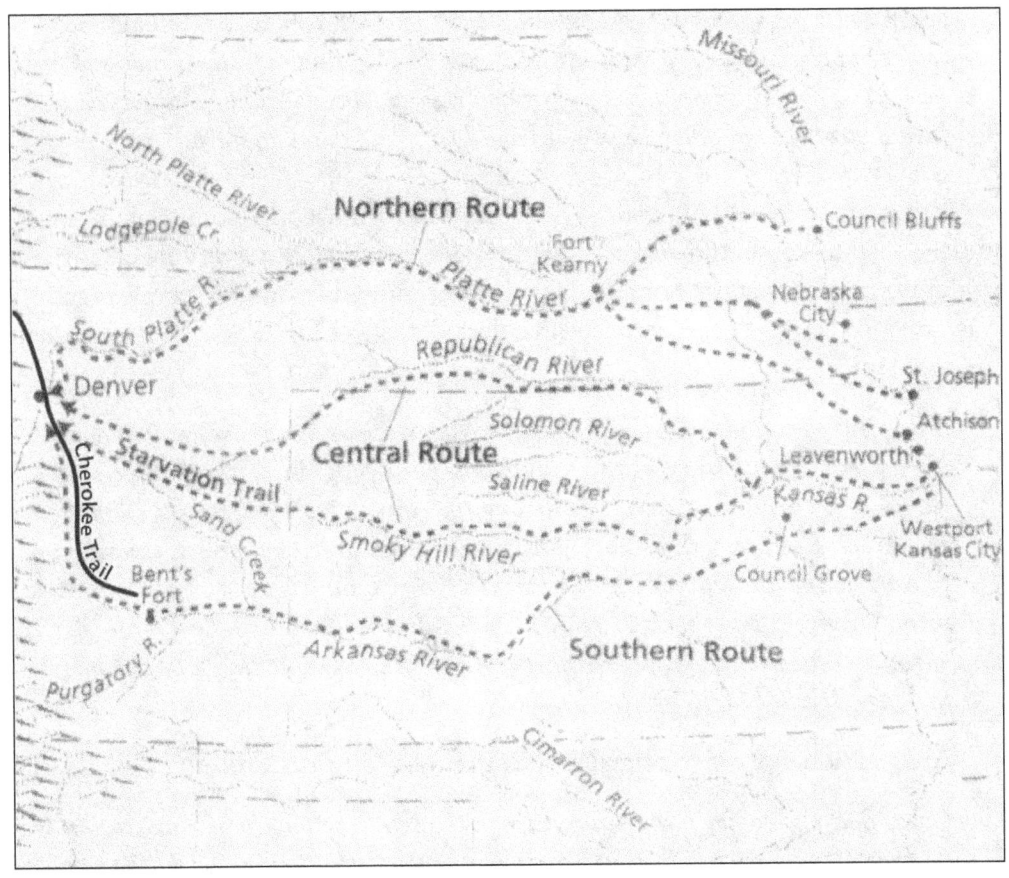

Trails West. North America was laced with ancestral trails worn by traders and wanderers for millennia. Mass migration of the White Man across the Great Plains in the mid-nineteenth century focused on the Oregon and California trails, and to a significant extent on the Santa Fe trail. Less well known trails like the Cherokee Trail also played a part in settling the mountain West beginning with the 1849 rush to California gold fields. *(Author)*

streptococcal bacterial infection). "Nervous affection" or prostration covered a variety of mental crises. The international cholera epidemic that coincided with the peak years of the California gold rush attacked the 1852 migration with a vengeance. [5]

Apparently, earlier travelers had outrun epidemics like cholera by the time they left the Platte Valley, but the press of emigrants caught up in the California gold rush was not that blessed.

Daniel Budd described how cholera morbus killed John Richardson seven miles east of South Pass. His friends had to go miles to find a spot where they could dig two feet into the rocky soil. "Buried him, without coffin, put his clothes into the grave. Buried him without a tear being shed, not a prayer offered, barely a general sigh as we took the last look of 1[sic] of our number who 9 hours before walked upright, & was a man of high Scotch spirit," Budd wrote. "When sickness gets a hold in camp all appears gloomy, he observed. "Had I known there would have been so much sickness I would not have dared to start." [6]

But start they did, upwards of a hundred-thousand—some claim many more—despite death and disease stalking all the trails. Not every facet of these epidemics was a mystery. Some believed water tainted by unwise camp practices was the root cause. Some observed reckless disregard for others that explained the problem.

A few travelers spread fatal afflictions such as smallpox with careless abandon. Nancy and Henry Bradley carefully tracked the progress of the "Small Pox team," who traveled "all the time among the emigration scattering the Small pox Broad Cast, they have no sighn [sic] out, they are very careless without, always taking the side of the road next to the wind, when any one passes them," Henry complained. "A man informed us that they had the Small pox aboard, & we passed on the side next [to] the wind, but had to drive out into the Sage Brush to do it." [7]

An occasional practice was quarantining those suspected of illness.

Great Salt Lake City had a quarantine ground at the mouth of Emigration Canyon, "and here is a hospital, or what pretends to be one, established by Governor Young, where all, both great and small, Jew or Gentile, are obliged to report," noted John Hawkins Clark. "Those who are well are privileged to continue their journey, but what they do with the sick or disabled I am unable to say." The hospital was barely large enough to hold the attending physician, a barrel of whiskey, and a few decanters. The infirmary contained no sick or disabled emigrants when Clark saw it. "The doctor was busily employed in dealing out whiskey and appeared to have a good run of custom in that way, but how many sick emigrants he attended to I did not stop to inquire." [8]

As if cholera was not scourge enough, other diseases were equally threatening, malaria and scurvy chief among them. Effective treatment of malaria was a half-century off, but scurvy was another matter.

British naval surgeon James Lind had demonstrated in 1747 that citrus juice could prevent or cure scurvy. Robert Gardner's experience a hundred years later at a Mormon refugee camp showed how poorly Lind's remedy was understood outside of elite medical and maritime circles. "Many of the older was taken with a disease called the black leg and was entirely helpless and many died with it," he recalled. "Their legs from their knees down would get as black as a coal," a symptom of scurvy, which burst blood vessels. [9]

Emigrants were not clueless concerning the shortcomings of their overland diets, diets of beans, bacon, and bread. This fare also was common in the gold fields and mines, and produced similar lethal results, but few seemed to care.

"Soup and fresh vegetables would prevent scurvy; there are many things they could name that are 'conspicuously absent from our daily fare,'" John Clark noted, but said the boys accepted the inevitable consequences of their diet. "We have good bacon, sugar, rice, dried fruit, etc. If we had as good feed for our animals as we have for ourselves, we should be content." [10]

Death on the Trail. Deadly disease, cholera the most dreaded, traveled with émigré trains. As many as five percent of Oregon-bound settlers died along the way. Death rates among the Forty-Niners and Fifty-Niners also were high. *(Public Domain)*

Sharpening the focus, Bagley presents yet another poignant account...

Government relief officers gave families stranded on the Lassen Trail in 1849 "pickles and sourkrout, as some of them had the scurvy." The last of those left in the snow were a "pitiable sight I had never before beheld. There were cripples from scurvy, and other diseases; women, prostrated by weakness, and children, who could not move a limb," Major Daniel Rucker reported. "In advance of the wagons were men mounted on mules, who had to be lifted on or off their animals, so entirely disabled had they become from the effect of scurvy."

... driven home by a lament if not mournful prayer...

"Death has been busy," John Hawkins Clark observed as he left the North Platte River. "There are graves at the crossing of every stream, graves at every good spring and under almost every green tree; there are graves on thy open and widespread plain and in the mountains that overlook thy swift rolling flood; in the quiet and secluded dell where the birds sing and make such beautiful music there are graves; young and old, innocent and wicked, all have found a resting place in thy lap; indeed, thou has been the 'valley and the shadow of death' to many."

... and capped with "excellent advice to all who set out to cross the plains:

Never get into trouble with the expectation of getting help; carry nothing but what is absolutely necessary, and mind your own business. There is but little sympathy for anyone on this road, no matter what may be his condition.... Everyone thinks he has trouble enough and conducts himself accordingly. [11]

By the time the Colorado gold rush began, the lessons learned from two previous decades of overland travel to Oregon and California were few. In their place were the familiar anxieties over Native American assaults, livestock provisions, and disease. Also familiar was the excitement that accompanied any great adventure. In defense of the Fifty-Niners, their journey to the Rocky Mountains was half the distance to California, but that was little consolation once civilization faded from view. Consistent with their typical stance regarding matters beyond their control or even understanding, for two decades more the "Overlanders" prayed, observed the Sabbath, birthed the next generation, and buried their dead in hard rocky ground barely off the trail and too shallow to discourage prairie scavengers from clawing them up in the night. Resolved to cope with the hand dealt them, while some turned back, tens of thousands went on. Their God-given destiny demanded it.

In keeping with all of the satisfied preconditions that had preceded it, the California gold rush set the stage for the Colorado gold rush a decade later. Both were of epic proportions. Bagley writes:

"The full and permanent effects of the California gold discovery cannot be estimated," Hubert Bancroft concluded long ago. *"All over the world impulse was given to industry, values changed and commerce, social economy, and finance were revolutionized."* The gold rush was *"a multiplier—an event that accelerated a chain of interrelated consequences, all of which accelerated economic growth,"* Gerald Nash observed. *The mineral wealth cascading from the Sierra galvanized the American economy. The nation had been starved for capital since its founding: in 1840 there was not more than fifty million dollars in hard cash in the entire Untied States. The enormous output of California's mines doubled the amount of money in circulation and pushed up prices. This massive infusion of capital "spurred the creation of thousands of new businesses, banks, and financial institutions. It stimulated rapid agricultural expansion, quickened the volume of trade and commerce, and created demands for new forms of transportation." California gold ignited a boom in shipbuilding, manufacturing, railroad building, and the trades. The surge in demand and golden capital from the West began a national economic expansion that lasted until 1857.*

The flood of capital created instant cities at San Francisco, Sacramento, Stockton, Portland, and Victoria. California mines poured capital into America's cash-strapped economy, fueling a boom that underwrote much of the industrial development of the North and widened its differences with the agrarian South. Western mines did not underwrite the triumph of the Union, as many gold rush veterans claimed, but the $197,961,875 in treasure California and Nevada shipped over the Isthmus between 1861 and 1865 helped Abraham Lincoln with the costly conflict. [12]

With modest adjustments, the assessment of the importance of the California gold discovery also could be applied to discovery of gold in Colorado. The abundance of California capital and the growth it spawned began drying up by 1857. The nationwide recession that followed incentivized the unemployed and underemployed masses to seek a new life on the far side of the Great Plains. Encouraging reports filtered back east from fertile Oregon and prosperous California. Underestimated as the risks and hardships were, still in 1858-60 the trails were more like roads, the guides and guidebooks were more helpful, and the distance from the better-provisioned Missouri frontier settlements to the Colorado Front Range was far less than the distance to California. It was only a matter of time, a short amount of time, that the trickle of reports of Colorado gold discoveries would unleash a flood of gold-seekers. Unknowable at the time, success or failure would depend on lessons-learned decades earlier and half a continent away in the Cherokee Nation eastern heartland.

Notes—Chapter One: Ordinary Man

[1] Service, Robert, "The Land of Beyond", *The Best of Robert Service*, pg. 152.

[2] The roots of the American industrial revolution reach back centuries before the war between the states, but the end of the war marked an explosion of investment and innovation that knit the nation together on many levels. Technologically, for example, it replaced wagons and the pony express with transcontinental railroads, telegraphs and telephones. It replaced iron with Bessemer steel strong enough and inexpensive enough to bridge the Mississippi River and support buildings that scraped the sky. It produced mining equipment, explosives, and ore processing techniques that underpinned the Rocky Mountain economy. It provided efficient alternatives like trucks and roadways to unprofitable railroads and even the faithful burro. The San Juans prospered from an age of incredible innovations—some so common yet profound as refined petroleum, steam power, electricity, and the internal combustion engine.

[3] Bagley, Will, *With Golden Visions Bright Before Them*, Vol. II, pg. 387. [See: Owens, Kenneth N., Ed., *Riches for All: The California Gold Rush and the World*, "Never Far from Home: Being Chinese in the California Gold Rush" by Sylvia Sun Minnick.]

[4] Ibid. [See: West, Elliot, "Golden Dreams: Colorado, California, and the Reimagining of America." pgs. 3-4, *Montana The Magazine of Western History*, Autumn, 1999.]

[5] Bagley, Vol. II, pgs. 343. [Numbers vary and are difficult to validate, but some report as many as 7,000 died of cholera on the plains in 1852, others estimate 1,500.]

[6] Ibid.

[7] Ibid.

[8] Ibid., pg. 344.

[9] Ibid.

[10] Ibid.

[11] Ibid., pg 346.

[12] Ibid., pgs. 388-389.

CHAPTER 2

Cherokee Gold

So it appears that what we long anticipated has come to pass at last, namely, that the gold region of North and South Carolina, would be found to extend into Georgia. [1]

The seeds of the 1859 Colorado gold rush first sprouted in Georgia in 1828 in the Cherokee Nation heartland. Twenty years later Cherokee gold mine experience was valued among California Forty-Niners nearly as much as gold itself. A decade later Cherokee prospectors had every right to claim they saved the 1859 rush to Pikes Peak from a greater humbug than it appeared to be at the time.

Granted to a select few is the gift of plenty. In the pursuit of gold, the gift of a "Midas touch" befell the man with an adventuress heart and a discerning eye. In the case of Georgia Cherokees, they literally tripped over their first gold find. Once alerted to the likelihood of more, they quickly mastered field geology. They learned when to pause and investigate and when not to waste their time. Acquired in Georgia, California honed and Colorado perfected this Cherokee skill.

Neither the breadth of a hostile continent nor the perils of a mountainous wilderness stayed the quest or long delayed the search for the prize for two Cherokee in particular. Lewis Ralston and Green Russell, savvy gold miner sons of Lumpkin County, Georgia, joined by John Beck in the "new" Oklahoma Cherokee Nation, surfaced at Sutter's Mill and in Colorado in critically important ways. The August 1, 1829 *Georgia Journal* marked the beginning of their journey.

> GOLD – *a gentleman of the first respectability in Habersham County, writes us thus under date of 22d (sic) July: "Two gold mines have just been discovered in this county, and preparations are making to bring these hidden treasures of the earth to use." [2]*

Within months thousands of gold seekers overran north Georgia, otherwise considered the Cherokee Nation. If the local *Niles Register* can be trusted,

4,000 staked claims along the Yahoola Creek drainage alone. [3] Sixty-four years later Benjamin Parks, believed to be the likely spark that ignited the hullabaloo, reported in the July 15th edition of the *Atlantic Constitution* his recollection of those days. His description could easily apply to Sutters Mill and Cherry Creek.

> *The news got abroad, and such excitement you never saw. It seemed within a few days as if the whole world must have heard of it, for men came from every state I had ever heard of. They came afoot, on horseback and in wagons, acting more like crazy men than anything else. All the way from where Dahlonega now stands to Nuckollsville (Auraria) there were men panning out of the branches and making holes in the hillsides.* [4]

One account of the Georgia gold discovery, incontestable on the face of it, credited Benjamin Parks and a friend out deer hunting on Cherokee lands. Benjamin "kicked a stone as he was walking…The stone's color caught Parks' attention, and he bent down to examine what would prove to be gold." [5] Thus began one of the nation's largest gold rushes, rightly or wrongly attributed to Benjamin. The friend along on the deer hunt, unnamed but quite likely, was friend and neighbor Lewis Ralston. Lewis Ralston is a name to remember.

Lewis and Benjamin were partners in a cattle and horse business. They lived outside of the vast Cherokee Nation, a semi-autonomous region spread across parts of Georgia, Tennessee, and North and South Carolina. Both Parks and Ralston grew up among the Cherokee, and had permission to graze their livestock "through the cool green forest" belonging to the Nation. In 1825, Ralston married Elizabeth Duncan Kell, the great-granddaughter of Cherokee Chief John Benge. Ralston, by virtue of marriage to a Cherokee woman, became an "Indian Countryman," an honor with considerable reward that was soon appreciated. [6]

In furtherance of their livestock business, the partners layed down a "lick-log" in a forest clearing, a hollowed-out log filled with salt that nourished their livestock. When the Cherokee were effectively relieved of their land in 1833, Lick-log grew from a "salt-lick" to a white settlement subsequently named Dahlonega. Dahlonega became the Lumpkin county seat, and in 1834 a courthouse was erected on the site of Ralston and Park's original lick-log. So how rich did the partners get in the midst of all this good fortune? They did not. But as so many treasure tales go, Ralston and Parks got another chance. Their mine was lost, but not their eye for gold.

A Baptist minister named Robert O'Bar leased from the Cherokee the forest where Parks found gold. O'Bar agreed to a forty-year sublease to Parks for a parcel of land along Yellow Creek. Parks found more gold-bearing rocks there, and with partner Ralston hired friends and built a sluice box. O'Bar, realizing his mistake, mustered church members and destroyed Ralston and Parks' mine. [7]

Offended but not defeated, Parks and Ralston began rebuilding their sluice, only to have a more powerful foe appear. South Carolina Senator John C. Calhoun, soon to be Andrew Jackson's Vice President, visited the site in 1828. He promptly bought the lease from O'Bar and with armed workers evicted Parks and Ralston. The Calhoun Mine became one of the region's major producers. Calhoun shipped $23,000 of gold to the U.S. mint in Philadelphia in the first month of operation. For good measure, the Senator named the settlement that quickly grew up around the mine "Auraria," Latin meaning "gold." As was so often the case, hometown names also accompanied hometown memories west to light anew on Colorado frontier camps. [8]

Outside local circles, Parks' contributions were a mystery, but Ralston's story was just beginning. In addition to losing the Calhoun Mine, he owned and lost through no fault of his own a number of other properties, some of which also produced gold. One property he retained was his home place near the confluence of a small stream (later named Ralston Branch) and the Chestatee River. His farm boasted a highly profitable peach orchard and corn to fatten his cattle. Cotton was not of interest to him, a road not taken that years later proved prophetic. In addition to building a substantial number of farm buildings, he also built a ferry landing managed by his slaves.

Along with the Georgia gold rush came the end of Cherokee national sovereignty. Little by little, Cherokee rights and Cherokee property were legislated away, and in most cases, the revised statutes did not spare Indian countryman

---

DAHLONEGA, CHEROKEE NATION

By 1832, what had been an unassuming watershed in the interior of the Cherokee Nation found itself worthy of more than a footnote in American history. The north Georgia gold region was a destination plotted on every contemporary treasure map of any worth. Auraria, Lumpkin County (named after the Governor), was the epicenter and a boomtown. The county seat long named Licklog, was now Dahlonega, ironically named for the Cherokee word "talonega" meaning "golden" or "yellow." In one sense, adopting the Cherokee word testified to the harmony among Cherokee and the "Whites," at the same time it belied the baser instincts of man that soon led to the winter 1838-39 forced migration of 20,000 Cherokee to present-day Oklahoma. No one could have imagined at the time that the new Cherokee reservation would become another prosperous Cherokee Nation homeland. It would soon serve as a way station and depot supplying services and provisions to the masses surging west.

rights and properties. Lewis fared better than most. Determined to save his farm and at least one of his gold mines, on October 7, 1830 he signed the "Oath of Allegiance to the United States of America." He retained his farm, most likely too marginal to be of much interest to others, but lost his last mine through a government lottery system designed to expropriate Cherokee lands and share gold mine opportunities with a larger number of Whites.

Over the course of the next few years the plight of the Cherokee Nation and the fortunes of Lewis Ralston sank. Noting the trend, many Cherokee took it upon themselves to abandon their homeland, some more cleverly than others. Two thousand Cherokee relocated to Tennessee. Another band known as the "Old Settlers Party" made their way to Oklahoma and served as the vanguard for later arrivals like the "Treaty Party," so named for ceding the Cherokee homeland to the Federal government. On December 29, 1835, perhaps lulled into a lingering false sense of Christmas goodwill, 100 unelected "representatives" of the Cherokee Nation signed the Treaty of New Echota between the United States of America and the Cherokee Nation. The treaty illegally "sold" the Cherokee Nation homelands for five million dollars and set the stage for the forced relocation of the Cherokee Nation to Oklahoma. October of 1839 marked the beginning of marches west on the "Trail of Tears." Among this first troop of Cherokee, most of the relatives of Elizabeth Ralston, including Cousin Jennie, slogged along in the cold. Retaining their last possession, the farm considered of little value, Lewis and Elizabeth Ralston stayed behind. [9]

Jennie Cloud married Peter Wimmer at the near-matronly age of sixteen. Bidding farewell to Georgia and Cousin Elizabeth, Jennie and Peter did not find Oklahoma to their liking. Instead, they braved the Oregon Trail until detouring to California, reasons unknown. There they entered the employ of Captain Johan Augustus Sutter, more commonly called "Captain John," who was building what he imagined to be a sovereign fiefdom deep in Mexican Territory near present-day Sacramento, California. Sutter possessed what amounted to a land grant from the Mexican government and was intent on securing what he considered autonomous rights by constructing a self-sufficient community, an empire by his way of thinking.

A sawmill was the latest improvement to his formidable complex of fort, castle and sundry facilities, that were much needed to supply his endless building program. To accomplish the task, John partnered with James Marshall, a master carpenter who had made his way to California from Oregon in 1844. Marshall employed Mormon Battalion veterans and Oregon emigrants including Georgia Cherokees, notably cousin Jennie as cook and husband Peter as a carpenter. Will Bagley writes:

On the morning of January 24, 1848, Marshall inspected the mill's tail race. That night, Henry W. Bigler wrote, "this day some kind of mettle was found in the tail race that looks like goald." He later inserted in darker ink, "first

America's Mass Migrations. Beginning in the 1840s, generally following what became commonly known as the Oregon, California and Santa Fe Trails, and continuing through the 1860s when railroads spanned the continent, wagon trains made mass migrations safer and feasible. *(Fossett, 1876)*

> *discovered by James Martial, the Boss of the Mill." Another worker, Azariah Smith, recorded that the metal was "found in the raceway in small pieces; some have been found that would weigh five dollars."*
>
> *"Boys," Marshall told his workers the next morning, "by G—d I believe I have found a gold mine." Marshall and Sutter tried to keep the discovery secret, but within four months gold fever had swept the region, and two thousand copies of the California Star were carrying the news to the East Coast.* [10]

Reactions back east were muted at first, and not much happened in California until May when Samuel Brannan, a San Francisco newspaper editor as well as "a retired Mormon preacher and partner at a trading post in the former bunkhouse at Sutter's Fort, bought up every pick, shovel, and Indian basket he could find." Bagley continues:

> *Brannan was nobody's fool, but until that point his business had to rely on gold from the pockets of travelers "wishing to cross the mountains with pack animals" and barter. "California banknotes" – cattle hides worth about a dollar – served as his primary medium of exchange.... No one in San Francisco had paid much attention to the stories, but when Brannan charged up Montgomery Street on 10 May 1848 waving a bottle of gold dust in one hand, swinging his hat with the other, and shouting, "Gold! Gold! Gold from the American River!" everything changed. By the middle of June "the abandonment of San Francisco was complete," Brannan's newspaper announced.* [11]

It took months longer for the second mass migration in the young nation's history to materialize, but by early 1849 materialize it did. Unbeknownst to either Sutter or Marshall, Cousin Jennie's letter bearing the news was also on its way to the new Cherokee Nation and relatives left behind in Lumpkin County, Georgia.

Cherokees who knew when glitter was indeed gold joined the rush. Ever vigilant, they discovered Colorado gold along the way, but in insufficient quantities to distract them from Sutter's mill. "Spanish California," now "Mexican California," to the extent it ever existed beyond the coastal network of old missions, would soon be a culture of the past. [12]

No one was more distressed with this development than John Sutter. Not the first to attempt to create a private empire, he was one of the most successful, and one of the most likely to succeed were it not for the bizarre irony of finding gold on his property. A blessing to anyone else, to Sutter it was a curse. Described "as a Swiss imposter with little more to rely on than charm, ambition, bluster, and Indian labor," Sutter was well on his way to establishing his fiefdom in the Sacramento Valley when emigrants began crowding in. Oregon may have been their dream, but Sutter's California became their destination. Despite his own immigrant journey, Sutter had little patience for fellow travelers, or family for that matter. In his early thirties, he had fled his creditors and his wife and children in Switzerland. In 1834, he arrived in the United States and made his way as a merchant, innkeeper, and Santa Fe trader on the Missouri frontier. No better a manager of money in America than in Switzerland, he was bankrupt by 1837. Bagley reports that according to the recollections of John C. McCoy,

> *it took him about eighteen months to gallop through his visible assets. Civil suits, attachments, and other legal contrivances made short work of his air castles. Sutter considered suicide, but in 1838, he again fled his creditors, who "could scarcely believe that such a noble foreigner would swindle them."* [13]

Sutter's Mill, 1850. Modest by any measure, the mill quickly became a beacon for the California gold rush and the demise of Johann Sutter's dream of his Helvetia empire. *(Wikipedia)*

Sutter slipped out of Westport with a band of fur traders, presumably worked his way to Fort Vancouver, shipped out to try his luck, presumably as a trader, in Hawaii, then Russian Alaska. He finally landed in California July 1, 1839. No doubt sensing new opportunities in a rich but lawless land, probably with someone else's money, he chartered four boats at Yerba Nueva, navigated the Sacramento River and founded the first white colony in California's Central Valley. Lacking neither spunk nor arrogance, Sutter later wrote:

> *I had the best chances to get some of the finest locations near the settlements; and even well stocked ranchos had been offered to me on the most reasonable conditions, but I refused all these good offers, and preferred to explore the wilderness, and select a territory on the banks of the Sacramento.* [14]

Sutter's first encounter with the locals was an encounter like so many other gold discovery encounters that had unintended consequences. His party of five white men and eight Kanacas he had recruited in Hawaii worked their way up river until confronted by two hundred Native Americans. Ten miles below the confluence of the American and Sacramento rivers, further advance did not seem like a good idea in the face of well-armed and painted warriors. Sutter was impressed with the gravity of the situation. So were his men who wanted to know how much longer he intended to travel with them in such a wilderness. He answered the next morning by pitching his tents on the left bank of the American River, what better a place to call home. Three of the five whites and the Kanacas agreed. Sheltered behind three cannons and a vicious bulldog, Sutter began building his dominion and an impressive adobe fort using Hawaiian workers and Indian labor acquired through intimidation and alliances with local leaders. Once again, his charming nature, trader instincts, and single-mindedness served him well. [15]

Johann August Sutter. Known in Spanish as "Don Juan," Sutter was a Swiss immigrant of Mexican and American citizenship known for his fortress in future Sacramento, capital of California, and his mill. While tens of thousands were lured to the region by gold, and many prospered greatly, Johann was not among the blessed. *(Wikipedia)*

INDIAN BUSINESS

According to historian Albert Hurtado, as many as fifty thousand Natives lived in the Sacramento valley, and during the early 1840s, Sutter "was primarily engaged *in the Indian business*." Hurtado reported, "he ruthlessly exploited the valley's Natives and instructed his overseer to keep his Miwok and Nisean labor force *strictly under fear*." Heinrich Lienhard recalled that when he first saw Sutter's fort in 1846, "a gruesome sight met my eyes: the long, black hair and skull of an Indian dangling from one of the gateposts." Sutter eventually kept between six hundred and eight hundred Indians "in a complete state of Slavery," James Clyman wrote in disgust, and fed them from wooden "troughs like so many pigs." [16]

Sutter's fiefdom and future sight of his famous mill were on 48,827 acres that he simply requested in accordance with Mexican custom at the time, or somehow persuaded Mexican Governor Juan Bautista Alvarado to grant him. This latter explanation would have been consistent with Sutter's shady style, and the need the good Governor felt to explain his actions supported this view. Regardless, by 1841, Sutter was a Mexican citizen, and Governor Alvarado was defending his generosity regarding Sutter by explaining it was "to prevent the robberies committed by adventurers from the United States, to stop the invasion of savage Indians, and the hunting and trading by companies from the Columbia." None of this would matter in the end. Neither Mexican citizenship nor Mexican sovereignty was sufficient to prevent complete loss of control of his property to the advancing hordes of gold-seekers. [17]

Sutter named his private empire *New Helvetia*. By 1843, a fortified adobe compound five hundred feet long and one hundred fifty feet wide guarded the mouth of the American River. Included within its high thick walls were a gristmill, distillery, tannery, blacksmith shop, and a large mansion. Nearby was an ideal site for a water-powered sawmill. While President Polk relieved Mexico of the Southwest and the British of their claim on the Pacific Northwest, Sutter's lead carpenter relieved any lingering doubt that braving the journey west was worth the risk. In a broader sense, John Marshal's gold find ensured the transformation of the entire western frontier. Far less appreciated, his journeyman's wife Jennie would contribute to the transformation a decade later of western Kansas Territory into the State of Colorado. [18]

Jennie Wimmer was a gossip. As was her custom, she wrote regularly to family in Oklahoma and in Georgia. Peter's first-hand account of gold was soon on its way east. She reported that some nuggets were "as large as a pea," and that prospectors were rushing to the area. When exactly she penned these words is not clear. What is clear is that the news reached Cousin Elizabeth in Dahlonega, Georgia, in January 1849, and her husband Lewis Ralston was quick to see opportunity calling. His neighbor and friend Green Russell was similarly disposed. Likewise, the men of Lumpkin County with two decades of prospecting and gold mining experience to their credit knew in the depths of their souls that Providence was giving them another chance. Their Georgia mines had played out, or others including Senator Calhoun had taken them, but by God's grace—by virtue of a cousin's letter entrusted to one traveler after another for delivery across the continent—they believed. The exciting news from California demanded action. [19]

How *did* Cousin Jennie's letter reach Georgia? Founding Father Ben Franklin did a fine job as America's first Postmaster General, but transcontinental service was a far cry from service between Philadelphia and Boston. Little did it matter. Prior to the California gold rush few considered the western half of the continent worthy of any form of services or practices taken for granted east of the Mississippi and Missouri Valleys. Prevailing upon or paying private travelers to

Contemporaneous Illustration of Sutter's Fort. Construction began in August 1839. Sutter represented himself as a Swiss guard officer displaced by the French Revolution, taking the title of "Captain". When completed in 1841, Mexican authorities granted him 48,827 acres. A few years later, Sutter supported the movement to declare California an independent republic. In response, John Fremont commanding U.S. troops seized control of Sutter's Fort. Outnumbered, Sutter conceded and Fremont withdrew. *(Wikipedia)*

deliver letters and small packages to the first public post office they encountered on their journey was the only option, albeit hardly a guarantee such exchanges would occur in a timely manner if at all. Will Bagley relies on an Oregon pioneer to help explain.

> *"There were no mail facilities whatever," Joseph Henry Brown complained after he reached Oregon in 1847. "We only received newspapers by the Missionary ships once a year, and letters from friends by emigrants across the plains, and the war with Mexico had been closed some six months before we heard of it." It required at least two years to send a letter home and receive an answer back from the United States. When mail service opened across Panama, Brown wrote, "we hailed it as one of the remarkable achievements of the day; we were then able to hear from our friends once every three months."* [20]

President Polk recognized this flaw in his vision for a transcontinental America early in his term. In August 1846, always on the lookout for ways to create or strengthen ties with western interests, he called on Congress to provide mail service west of the Rockies. The following March Congress enacted the "Post Route Bill" which set in motion sea-borne mail service from South Carolina to the east coast of Panama, overland across the Panamanian Isthmus, and back to sea along the Pacific coast to ports-of-call that included Monterey, San Francisco, and Columbia River settlements. The *USS California*, first contract vessel of the Pacific Mail Steamship Company, began scheduled voyages in October 1848. Vastly improved compared to alternative overland routes, and a clear blessing to both senders and receivers, the Washington government's new public service struggled to satisfy expectations. Sea routes were costly, and time-in-transit remained unacceptably high. From even the government's point of view, steamship companies were a losing proposition.

Not to be beholden to any power other than God, nor to patiently await the outcome of Washington political wrangling, Mormon settlers in the Salt Lake Valley organized their own mail service. Of course their vision did not include better unifying the country or even better communications with brothers in western outposts. Eastern interests were their focus. Early in 1848 the first commercial mail service was organized. Two years later Samuel H. Woodson inaugurated a "public mail" company with service to Missouri communities. In both cases, profit more than public service was the motive. By 1854, for a variety of reasons some of which were beyond human control, Woodson's company failed. But there were other entrepreneurs who recognized the need and were willing to risk fame and fortune to meet it.

Indeed, the need was growing with every passing season. In that day, emigrants relied on "go-backers," fur-traders, and Native Americans to carry parcels east to the first U.S. Post Office they encountered. Far from certain, for the most part these parcels eventually arrived at their intended destinations. With typical clarity of thought expected of eyewitnesses, James Field and Amasa Morgan give us a sense of pilgrim isolation and the "day and age" when written correspondence was cherished food for the soul. They also convey a sense of desperation given the lack of alternatives.

> *James Field: "Just as we camped, three gentlemen from Fort Laramie, returning to the States, came to camp, and spent the night with us. They told us they would take on all letters written, and next morning received a good-sized packet of them."*

> *Amasa Morgan: "I would give One Dollar for a newspaper, Five for a letter and Fifty to see our friends."* [21]

Little had changed by 1859. At the risk of oversimplifying a tumultuous decade, up to May of that year emigrants throughout the West depended on government post offices at Forts Laramie and Kearney for mail service to and from all points east. An occasional express coach traveled to and from Laramie bearing cargo more precious than gold. Ovando Hollister, an early mining engineer and sometimes philosopher observed that:

> *...the heart of the wanderer in the West goes ever back to the home of his childhood. Thence the winds bear him the perfume of the days that are no more—all*

Mail from Home. News from home was a precious commodity in Denver. The Leavenworth and Pike's Peak Express, the first passenger and mail service to reach Denver, arrived on May 7, 1859, with news that was only nineteen days old. *(Ludlow, 1876)*

the fond memories of young life. It is he who prizes letters from home. Often the want of them is the sole cause of his falling into bad habits. It leaves him sick at heart, and inclines him to recklessness. [22]

But on May 7, 1859, a remedy was at hand. The rush to the Colorado gold fields marked another monumental milestone when two *Leavenworth and Pike's Peak Express* coaches rolled into Denver after a nineteen-day journey from the States.

A construction [wagon] train accompanied these coaches, stations were established at intervals of twenty-five miles, and stock put on for a daily line. As run, the road was six hundred and eighty-seven miles long by odometer measurement. The company had fifty-two new Concord coaches, and made the first track on the route most of the way, under the supervision of B.D. Williams. A money, package, and letter express was added to the passenger business. [23]

By the end of the year so-called postmasters, routes, schedules, and the name of the company changed at least once. The *Leavenworth and Pike's Peak Express* became the *Central Overland California & Pike's Peak Express Company* and added a new service, the "pony express." For one dollar per letter, the pony express delivered mail between Leavenworth, Kansas and Placerville, California in ten days, half the length of time to travel twice the distance as the first "express" coach to Denver. Henceforth, matters only got better. On April 13, 1860, the first pony express delivery arrived in St. Joseph, Missouri from San Francisco in ten days. Glamorous as well as fast, the pony express was the rage of the West. Another pioneering rival, the *Butterfield Overland Stagecoach Line* from St. Louis through Texas and Arizona to California, could not compete. After a year of "firsts," their southern route fell out of favor and so did the *Butterfield*. Ironically, the life span of the pony express was not much longer, eighteen months from cradle to grave. [24]

So how did cousin Jennie's letter reach home a decade earlier—quite likely by a helpful soul returning to Westport or Fort Leavenworth, or even more likely by a Cherokee relative or neighbor returning to Tahlequah, Oklahoma or Dahlonega, Georgia. In any case, its impact in both places set in motion events that explain how the Cherokee Nation spared the 1859 Pike's Peak hullabaloo from degenerating into a Cherry Creek bust.

When Cousin Jennie's first-hand confirmation of rich California gold finds reached Dahlonega in January 1849, experienced and hungry miners were primed to hazard the journey west. Among those not persuaded was Dr. Matthew Stephenson, assayer at the Dahlonega Federal Mint. As more and more parties prepared to emigrate, Dr. Stephenson became more and more alarmed. Unable to remain silent, he organized a public meeting in the town square. Standing on the courthouse steps before 200 miners, the good Doctor "chastised them for allowing their heads to be turned by fantasies of gold in California." Gesturing toward the ridge above town, he continued, "Why go to California? In that ridge lies more gold than man ever dreamt of. There's millions in it." [25]

The men of Lumpkin County thought otherwise. Jennie Wimmer's letter struck them as a Godsend from the Almighty Himself. Written long before it arrived–possibly upwards of a year—its message still rang true and fresh. The

---

DAHLONEGA FEDERAL MINT

The 1828 Georgia gold rush had legs. There was indeed gold to be found, first in placers and then in lodes, enough gold to warrant the establishment of a federal mint. As prospectors and miners flooded into the region, so did tradesmen and merchants. With strangers came distrust. Currency, always in short supply and never held in high esteem, was accepted but not reassuring. As 1838 approached, local merchants increasingly insisted on payment on delivery, preferably in gold. To make matters worse, they were free to set their own rate of exchange. As for the local miners, they needed fair and consistent valuation of their gold. The solution for all parties was a local mint that could independently assay ore and exchange it for gold coins with face values no one would question. Congress

Dahlonega Federal Mint. The proven reserves of the 1828 Georgia gold rush justified establishing a branch mint in the heart of the Cherokee ancestral homeland. It also confirmed the Cherokee reputation for being savvy prospectors and skilled miners. Production of gold coins ceased with the outbreak of the Civil war. Cherokee contributions to Colorado's mining legacy fared well for nearly as long. *(Wikipedia)*

agreed and authorized the establishment of the *Federal Branch Mint at Dahlonega.* [Vice-President Calhoun's role in this matter, much less the increased value of his Lick-log Mine, is lost to history.] The Dahlonega Mint opened for business in 1838 and issued $100,000 worth of gold coins its first year. Despite Dahlonega's strong start, and the prestigious federal mint, by the early 1840s local gold mines faltered and fortunes began to turn. The Georgia placers yielded fewer returns and the lodes were deeper and more costly to work.

cousins in Tahlequah confirmed the news. Like Jennie, Elizabeth Ralston also was quite the gossip. Not only did she find time to raise thirteen children, tend to a farm, and manage Lewis' wanderlust, she also kept up with Sutter's Mill matters by way of her Oklahoma family, especially cousin Emily Duncan. Emily had married a Baptist minister by the name of John Beck, sometimes referred to as "Pastor John." Having Cherokee ancestors of his own, at times he was lovingly called "Beck the Cherokee." Nicknames aside, he also was known as a frontiersman accustomed to risky westward treks.

Letters home were the least of Johan Augustus Sutter's concerns. Even the dullest newspaper editor noted the excited claims of Sutter's laborers and tradesmen, and penned dispatches circulated and copied abroad. "Abroad" included the Cherokee Nation and its venerable newspaper, *The Cherokee Phoenix*. No one knows for sure, but Emily quite likely sent Elizabeth clippings from the *The Cherokee Phoenix* including a January 8, 1849 article on Sutter's Mill gold. First published decades earlier in Georgia, the *Phoenix* was a small but influential, typical booster of gold. A large and more influential booster was the *New York*

THE GRAND SALINE

For the vast majority of Forty-Niners who chose overland routes to the Pacific, they took on last-minute provisions and shoved off from Missouri River outposts, Independence and St. Joseph and Westport. Not the Lumpkin County Cherokees. They bid civilization farewell from their new Oklahoma homeland, from Tahlequah and the Grand Saline.

The Western Cherokee called Tahlequah home as early as 1832. In due course, they welcomed their displaced eastern relatives and merged their governments. In 1839, the newly constituted Cherokee Nation honored Tahlequah with the title "Capital of Ancestors." [26]

Nearby Grand Saline along with Tahlequah are located near the southwest foothills of the Missouri Ozarks. Later known as the "Old Salt Wells," later still organized as present-day Salina, Oklahoma, the Grand Saline supported indigenous peoples for thousands of years before Europeans discovered it. The Osage was the dominant culture when Hernando de Soto's expedition passed through the area in 1541. In 1721, Bernard de la Harpe's expedition did likewise. In 1796, Jean Pierre Chouteau, a French-Creole fur trader from St. Louis, raised the Spanish flag over his Osage trading post at the confluence of the Grand Neosho River and Saline Creek. At that moment, unbeknownst to him, he was standing in a remote corner of the Province of Louisiana.

In 1803, President Jefferson's Louisiana Purchase transferred title to the United States, and the United States in short order considered Chouteau's trading post a part of "Indian Territory" and ultimately Oklahoma. Chouteau and son August Pierre were

Herald. On August 19, 1848, The *Herald* reported Marshall's gold discovery. As usual, not even the mighty *Herald* was beyond scorn. Mockery abounded, that is until President Polk confirmed the find in a December 5, 1848 address to Congress. The rush was on. With confirmation from the Oklahoma cousins, count the Georgia Cherokees in. While not the first to fall under the influence of the siren's song, they were in the vanguard.

For Sutter, letter and newspaper accounts aside, within weeks of Marshall's January 1848 discovery, trespassers swarmed over his property. By March, the struggling village of San Francisco was ablaze with testimonies shouted in the streets. By Christmas, all of civilized America along with wide swaths of Europe and Asia had been smitten. By spring 1849, Dr. Stephenson's greatest fears would materialize–the cure for Cherokee gold fever was not to be found in the ridges above Dahlonega.

Nor was the cure in Oklahoma, but pausing at Oklahoma's Grand Saline on the way to California was wise. The Grand Saline was awash in provisions, information and trustworthy family. The Oklahoma cousins knew the ways of

indifferent as long as their trading arrangements with the Osage were secure. They were. By 1822, the Chouteau family outgrew the trading post and replaced it with a two-story log "palace" they named "La Grande Saline."

The lawn of this frontier palace was planted with flowers and shrubs, which included Paradise Trees imported from France. The home also became a center for social activities, with the family entertaining contemporary icons, Sam Houston, Nathaniel Pryor, Washington Irving and future notables like Jefferson Davis who was stationed at nearby Fort Gibson. [27]

For their part, the Osage adopted the practices of the indigenous cultures they displaced. They learned to distill salt from water surfacing through limestone rock a short distance from the trading post. The springs included a geyser that shot boiling water "8 to 10 feet in the air."

Chouteau obtained the springs in a treaty in 1825 and sold them to Sam Houston in 1830. A Cherokee Captain, John Rogers, began making salt from the springs and named them Grand Saline. Here is where salt was manufactured and sold to the Indians at fifty cents a bushel. Ox teams came from hundreds of miles and salt was hauled away by the wagon loads. The huge salt kettles used came from Pittsburgh, Pennsylvania, and were transported down the Ohio and Mississippi Rivers and up the Arkansas and Grand Rivers to a forge near where the Salina bridge is now located. Rogers built his home nearby. [28]

the Plains Indians and the latest intelligence on the California mines. For the more rambunctious, like Green Russell, a rendezvous with cousins or resupplying enroute was an unnecessary delay. He was a seasoned gold miner at age fifteen. His employer recognized a leader when he saw one and placed him in charge of one of his gold mines at age seventeen. Now, at age twenty-eight, he needed neither encouragement of man nor the company of cousins and neighbors to launch his journey west.

Lewis Ralston needed both. He listened carefully to his wife Elizabeth reading letters and clippings sent by the cousins. He, too, was a veteran of Dr. Stephenson's courthouse steps appeal. Quite likely, he was shoulder to shoulder with neighbor Green who no doubt had already decided to leave. But unlike

THE CHEROKEE TRAIL

In the pre-dawn of the California gold rush, two major trail systems led west from the Missouri frontier, the Santa Fe to the south and the Oregon to the north. Decades of trade and an occasional military expedition accounted for the popularity of the Santa Fe route. The Mormon exodus to Utah, Oregon homesteaders, and military forts accounted for the popularity of the northern route. Culled from both southern and northern trails was an advantageous shortcut largely overlooked through ignorance and haste. In the shadow of Colorado's Front Range, the Cherokee Trail was a rough and little known trace that bridged the two.

Fully extended, the Cherokee Trail connected Fort Smith, Arkansas on the lower Arkansas River with Fort Bridger, Wyoming, located west of the Continental Divide. Fort Bridger was the last major way station and trading post enroute to Mormon settlements in the Salt Lake basin and Oregon Territory. The segment between Bents Fort on the Arkansas River near present-day Pueblo, Colorado, and the lower South Platte near present-day Denver was part of the old Trappers Trail. The Trappers Trail connected Taos and Fort Laramie, Wyoming, located east of the Continental Divide. The Trappers Trail saw little use until the Cherokee, heeding the advice of earlier hunting parties, followed it north. Their subsequent use and prospecting along the way in the late 1840s and 1850s displaced its early fur-trader legacy and earned a name change. The Colorado "Cherokee Trail" should not be confused with the "Trail of Tears."

neighbor Green, Lewis returned home. The cares of his world gave him pause, or more likely Elizabeth gave him pause. His rendezvous with cousins at the Grand Saline and reunion with the Wimmers at Sutter's Mill also would have to await another day. [29]

The Grand Saline was well known and well situated to benefit from the Santa Fe Trail. The western Cherokee had their salt, and benefited from wagon roads and navigable rivers leading to distant markets around the Gulf of Mexico, northern Mexican routes across the southwest, and the upper reaches of the Missouri, Mississippi and Ohio Rivers. The eastern Cherokee had their gold mines, that is until the 1835 Treaty of Echota and the 1838 Indian Removal Act forced all but a small remnant out of Georgia and Tennessee. Destitute when they arrived

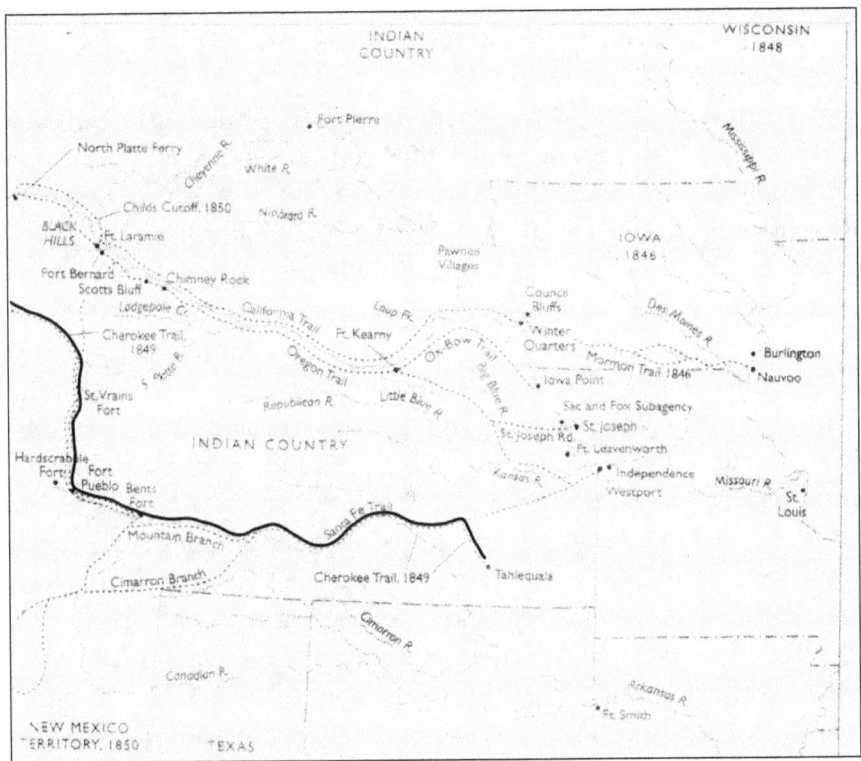

Cherokee Trail. Formerly known as the Trapper's Trail in the shadows of Colorado's Front Range, Cherokee prospectors enroute to 1849 California goldfields pioneered a shortcut between Arkansas River (southern route) and Platte River (northern route) trails. Beginning in their new Oklahoma homeland, what became known as the Cherokee Trail followed the Santa Fe Trail to present-day Pueblo, Colorado, then swung north on the old trapper's trace to the Platte watershed before turning west through the Front Range into southern Wyoming. *(Author)*

at the Grand Saline and Tahlequah, they were readily absorbed into a red-hot economy stoked by salt. Not yet appreciated, their contribution would be gold mining experience and their willingness to demonstrate it in fields faraway.

By 1839, Captain Rogers operated 115 salt kettles. In 1844, a new Federal law forced transfer of the salt works to the Cherokee Nation. While a setback for Captain Rogers, the new arrangement was a windfall for the Nation and for Lewis Ross. His brother, John Ross, was chief of the Nation and blessed Lewis with a lease on the business, far from the first instance of political patronage. Lewis built a house and operated the salt works using African-American slave labor. In 1849, drilling for salt water, Ross instead discovered the first of many oil deposits in Indian Territory. First salt, then oil, soon rewards from western gold fields, prospered the trading post and the town. Already wealthy by any frontier measure, straddling southern routes collectively considered the Santa Fe Trail further enhanced the Grand Saline's value as a forward base for an 1850 assault on the Rocky Mountains and the new California gold fields beyond. The Cherokee pump was primed.

By the spring of 1850, Lewis Ralston also was primed. He and Elizabeth were satisfied his sons John age twenty-four and Lewis Jr. age seventeen no longer needed his help working their farm. Times were tough and reports from California offered solutions to many problems. The family agreed his gold prospecting and mining expertise was more useful in gold fields than in farm fields. Moreover, cousin Jennie at Sutter's Mill and cousin Emily in Tahlequah bolstered their confidence. Emily Beck did more. She reminded Lewis that her husband was not just Pastor John but also trail savvy. She advised that he and fellow countryman Captain Clement Van McNair were organizing two Cherokee expeditions departing the Grand Saline in April. She urged Lewis to join. John Beck and Clement Van McNair would lead separate trains but travel together for safety. Both needed to be well-enough armed to deter Plains Indian attacks, and the more experienced gold-seekers among the armed party the better would be their prospects in California. They welcomed Ralston with open arms.

John Beck was a veteran of earlier ventures to the Colorado Mountains and California. As recently as the previous year, Captain Louis L. Evans quite likely with Beck as a scout successfully led forty wagons and 130 prospectors to the "California diggings," pioneering in the process a route that became known as the Cherokee Trail. Captain Evans widely shared a detailed account of his travels with other wagon-masters and no doubt with the cousins around and about the Grand Saline. His writings relieved much fear of the unknown and stoked John Beck's spirit of adventure.

In 1848, as many as ten troops of Cherokee, John Beck among them, departed from the Grand Saline enroute to California. They followed the Cherokee Trail, and "discovered gold in a stream bed [later known as Cherry Creek] in the South Platte basin." [30] Understandably eager to get to their destination, they did not stop to work their find. Who would? They did trumpet their good fortune with fellow tribesmen probably while in California, certainly back home in Oklahoma, and by means of letters to family in Georgia.

Significant in this regard, one of the largest Cherokee trains reached Fort Bridger at the end of July 1849. Three months earlier, something on the order of 130 Arkansans and Cherokees equipped with forty wagons and organized as the *Washington County Gold Mining Company* left the Grand Saline salt works. A number of its members, our Dahlonega town square veterans, Green Russell chief among them, were about to add another campaign to their pedigrees.

From the Grand Saline, the company broke a short trail north across present-day Oklahoma to the well-worn Santa Fe Trail, then followed the Arkansas River to Bents Fort near present-day Pueblo. Leaving the Santa Fe Trail, they picked up a rough track referred to by some as the old trappers or traders trail. The party threaded its way along the base of the Front Range and across the Continental Divide on a course far more wagon-friendly than South Pass, the customary route to the Pacific, further embellishing their trail naming claim. [31]

Not all Grand Saline gold-seekers were Cherokee, but the wiser among them valued the frontier experience of a tribesman. Some even valued the divine comfort afforded by clergymen like John Beck. The Spanish conquistador rarely ventured far from his mission without the spiritual covering of a Father. Pastor Beck, Beck the Cherokee when it suited circumstances, similarly served double-duty as scout and padre. For trains less fortunate, covering their venture with a mantle of prayer and in some cases mandatory Sabbath rest was a tolerable albeit less-comforting alternative. [32]

Captain Clement Van McNair led the Beck and Ralston party. Van McNair was the son of another Indian Countryman. He was well educated and a delegate in the failed 1846 Cherokee Nation mission to Washington D. C. to preserve eastern Cherokee property rights. His family lost everything in the western relocation. Like Beck, he was a kind and gentle soul who also kept the Sabbath, a practice that caused great angst among those under his command who could not get to California quickly enough. Certainly a fine pedigree for gentry, Van McNair's background did not serve him well on the frontier as a wagon-master. No matter. More important is the role of his scribe in documenting the activities of Lewis Ralston.

The Captain's party included "Anglo-Saxons" and a young Cherokee boy named John Lowery Brown. Not surprisingly, John Lowery was kin to Ralston and Beck. Family ties were strong in the Cherokee Nation. Brown's mother, Elizabeth Ralston, and Emily Beck shared common ancestry. Like his "aunts," young Brown was a gifted writer and soon earned the title and duties of "camp scribe." In some circles, the "Brown wagon train" instead of the "Captain Van McNair" wagon train was the unintended consequence of his poignant journaling.

That aside, his attention to detail sheds much light on the California migration. Brown wrote in his journal for May 5, 1850, "105 men, 15 negroes and 12 females all under the command of Clem McNair." While his May 5 entry was insightful, his June 22, 1850 journal entry was historic. It earned Lewis Ralston a prominent seat in Colorado's "gold rush hall of fame." [33]

On June 22, 1850, according to young Brown's trail journal, the McNair Party completed a difficult crossing of the flooded South Platte River and struggled six miles farther to a creek where they camped for the night. Brown wrote, "We called this Ralston's Creek because a man [in our party] of that name found gold here." [34]

No doubt honored but generally unimpressed, neither Lewis Ralston nor the majority of his companions was tempted to linger along newly named Ralston Creek, patience generally lacking during a gold rush. Nevertheless, some of the party voted to interrupt their journey. To avoid dividing his forces, the Captain ordered a brief stand-down. Those who were inclined to pan for gold were free to do so for one day. Some including Ralston scraped up small quantities of gold, but not enough to derail their California plans. With the morning dawn they rolled north to the Oregon Trail and on to Sutter's Mill. Ralston had five dollars of Colorado gold in his pocket. Slim pickings even in that day, it was enough to become an enduring memory that would not be lost in the passage of time. John Lowery Brown's journal entry dating Ralston Creek gold secured Ralston's place in Colorado gold rush history. Perhaps also secured in Ralston's mind was the thought of returning one day to pursue his find.

Captain McNair's wagon train departed Ralston Creek with no record of whining over leaving behind a gold mine. Accounts of Sutter's Mill prospects were too strong an intoxicant and promised more certain rewards for anyone with pluck enough to get there. In any case, their return trip home, each man no doubt rich beyond belief, would afford plenty of opportunity to exploit Ralston's find if it even mattered then. As for those who only heard camp chatter about Ralston's good fortune, it sounded like just another unpersuasive tale among many unpersuasive tales. After all, reports of Rocky Mountain gold dating from centuries-old Spanish expeditions and decades-old U.S. Army survey teams never led to rushes. Still, one had to wonder if this time would be different.

Notes—Chapter Two: Cherokee Gold

[1] "Gold Rush," *New Georgia Encyclopedia (NGE)* .

[2] Ibid., [In 1799, a farmer's son in Cabarrus County, N.C. found a 17 lb. gold nugget in a creek. Three years later the farmer discovered it was gold. Other farmers also found gold, and by 1804 commercial mining was underway. However, word of this never spread and thus unlike Georgia, no "rush" occurred. Cited in "This Day in Georgia History," GeorgiaINFO, an online Georgia Almanac.]

[3] "Gold Rush," *NGE*.

[4] "Gold Rush," *NGE*.

5   "Gold Discovered in Georgia," *This Day in Georgia History*, October 27, 1828.

6   Linstrom, Lois C., *Ralston's Gold*, unpublished manuscript, 1986, pgs. 9-12.

7   Ibid.

8   Ibid.

9   Ibid., pgs. 15-18.

10 Bagley, Will, *Overland West*, Vol. I, pg. 373. [Also see Paul, Rodman W., ed., *The California Gold Discovery*, pg. 62; Smith, Azariah, *The Gold Discovery Journal*, pg. 108; and Bigler, Henry W., *Bigler's Chronicle of the West*, pg. 89.]

11 Bagley, *With Golden Visions Bright Before Them*, Vol. II. pg. 11.

12 [California in the 1840s was a lawless wilderness full of boundless treasures promised to any power that could defend it. Nominally Mexican territory, Mexico would soon find that it was not up to staunching American expansionism. To the north, Britain's tentative hold on the Pacific Northwest would not survive the decade, best negotiated away rather than lost to one of its truculent cubs in a painful third war. Indigenous peoples would suffer the same fate indigenous peoples across the continent had suffered, either decimated by disease or battle, or assimilated into a relatively benevolent if intolerant white culture.]

13 Bagley, Vol. I, pg. 206.

14 Ibid.

15 Bagley, Vol. I, pg. 207. [Hawaiians were known as "Wyhees" in Sutter's day. They were occasionally referred to as "Blue Men" allegedly because their skin took on a bluish hue during the winter. They were almost universally known as "Kanakas," a term apparently derived from "kanaka maoli," Hawaiian for "true human being."] [Also see Owens, Kenneth N., ed., *John Sutter and a Wider West*, and Albert L. Hurtado's *John Sutter: A Life on the North American Frontier* (Bagley, Vol. I, pg. 332).]

16 Ibid. [Frontier cultural norms were defined largely by local circumstances and the force of arms. Sutter's conduct beginning with his arrival in America, but especially in California, exemplifies this dimension of Manifest Destiny.]

17 Ibid. [The Governor's statement is an excellent summary of the geopolitics at play that would soon result in President Polk's dream of the United States stretching from Atlantic to Pacific.]

18 *"Helvetia"* is derived from the Celtic Helvetii people who first entered Switzerland around 100 B.C. Helvetia was the Roman name for the region that is now western Switzerland. John Sutter was of Swiss decent.

19 [Forty-Niners Chronology:
   • Jan. 24, 1848 – James W. Marshall finds gold, Sutter's Mill, Coloma, CA.
   • Mar. 1848 – Samuel Brannan, San Francisco newspaper publisher and merchant.
   • Aug. 19, 1848 – *New York Herald* report.
   • Dec. 5, 1848 – Polk address to Congress.
   • Jan. 8, 1849 – *Cherokee Phoenix* article.
   • Apr. – May 1849 – Capt. Louis L. Evans leads 40 wagons, 130 prospectors to CA.
   • Apr. 1849 – Jennie Wimmer letter arrives in GA.
   • Apr.-May 1849 – Dr. Stephenson's courthouse steps plea.
   • May 1849 — Green Russell leaves GA.
   • Jan.-Mar. 1850 – Beck in Oklahoma organizes prospecting party; Emily Beck advises Elizabeth Ralston in GA.
   • Apr. 1850 – Ralston joins Van McNair year after Jennie letter arrives.
   • Apr. 20 1850 – Reverend Samuel Houston Mayes/McNair/Ralston/Brown Party leave OK.
   • May 5, 1850 – Beck Party catches up on trial, Brown records: "105 men, 15 negroes (sic) and 12 females all under the command of Clem McNair." [pg. 29 Linstrom]
   • Jun 22, 1850 – Ralston pans $5 from Ralston Creek, tributary of Clear Creek, future site of Arvada. John Lowery Brown diary entry: "Lay Bye. Gold found."]

[20] Bagley, Vol. I, pg. 275.

[21] Ibid., pgs. 275-277. [Bagley: emigrants employed clever techniques to communicate during their journeys. They wrote messages on buffalo skulls, small strips of smooth planks, and on paper strips stuck in a split at the top of a stake driven into the ground. "Animal skulls became renowned as the 'post office of the plains'".... also known as the "bone express."]

[22] Hollister, Ovando James, *The Mines of Colorado*, pg. 99.

[23] Ibid.

[24] Ibid., pg. 101.

[25] "Gold Rush," NGE. [The phrase "there's millions in it" was popularized by Mark Twain in his *Gilded Age*. It was corrupted even in north Georgia into "thar's gold in them thar hills." See "Rush to the Rockies, 1859," Agnes Wright Spring, *Colorado Magazine*, April, 1959.]

[26] "Tahlequah, Oklahoma," www.en.m.wikipedia.org.

[27] "History of Salina, OK," https://www.salinaok.org/history.

[28] "History of Salina, OK," https://www.salinaok.org/history. [On balance, the social and economic fabric that enveloped Tahlequah and the Grand Saline was complex. It was not a dusty oasis along the Santa Fe Trail, or a lone trading post manned by white interlopers in an otherwise disadvantaged indigenous culture. The indigenous culture was neither homogenous nor peaceful. First the Osage, then the Cherokee, dominated the region. The Cherokee were territorial, entrepreneurial, and fully capable of absorbing their eastern cousins.]

[29] Linstrom, pgs. 17-18.

[30] "The Colorado Gold Rush," *Western Mining History* Online: https://westernmininghistory.com/articles.

[31] Bagley, Vol. II, pgs. 186-87.

[32] Linstrom, pgs. 26-27.

[33] Ibid., pgs. 29-30.

[34] Ibid., pg. 34.

CHAPTER 3

Polk's Prize

Once more on Hangtown's hills we delve,
On Murderer's Bar we mine,
At Niger's Tent and Boston Jim's,
You Bet, Red Dog, Port Wine.
On Poker Flat and Poor Man's Shack,
Once more our luck we try,
Where nuggets once were found as thick,
As planets in the sky. [1]

— Anon —

The nineteenth century witnessed America swelling with emigrants, and swelling with politicians prepared to dislodge foreign powers from western lands they coveted. Many barriers stood between the States and the Pacific Ocean, some foreign and some natural. The 1840s American frontier during the era of mass migrations stretched from the Mississippi and Missouri river valleys westward to the Pacific Ocean. Polk's prize—President Polk's prize—was the American West. In 1840, it belonged to foreign powers. A decade later, it belonged to the United States of America.

The future of that frontier was determined in large measure by the collective outcome of five factors. First, would Mexico and European powers cede territory through negotiation, sale, or as a consequence of war. Second, thanks to the proliferation of horses, how would increasingly mobile indigenous peoples with expansionist notions of their own interact with adjoining tribes and accommodate the flood of immigrants? Third, could overland wagon transport keep up with the staggering volume of provisions and merchandise settlers required? Fourth, would the availability of grass, determined by range fires (some caused by lightening strikes and some caused by man) and the abundance or lack of rain and snow, recover year upon year from the added burden of mass migration and associated livestock? Generally taken for granted, in reality weather, climate and grass played a critical role at all levels of prairie life. Fifth, what would be the long-term

President James K. Polk. President Polk's vision for America was a two-ocean continental republic which was immortalized in the term "Manifest Destiny." His vision did not include sharing North America with Mexico or European powers. *(Wikipedia)*

impact of the West on the state of the Nation at large? Unimaginable to most, three waves of mass emigration over two decades would lay the foundation for America's rise to continental superpower status.

Characteristic of historian Will Bagley's style, he describes the context, then explains sea-state changes through accounts of those close to them. In the case of America's march westward, the central theme made crystal clear is that the Great Plains ecological balance that was maintained even in the face of horse-mounted Native Americans and prolific herds of bison came to an end under the added impact of émigré wagons, livestock, and diminished rain and grass. [Ironically, the proliferation of horses among the plains tribes also facilitated enhanced harvesting of the bison herds.] Decimation of the Platte watershed, effectively the northern-most and preferred route to Oregon, California and the Colorado Front Range, was typical of most westering trails. The most telling consequences would be relentless hardship and death on the trail.

Will Bagley sums up the matter this way:

> *The Wild West in 1840 was not wild: it was a controlled natural system.*
> *When Colonel Henry Dodge [soon to become the first Territorial Governor of Wisconsin] marched his dragoons to the South Platte in 1835, they found sufficient wood for fuel below the forks, "and occasionally a solitary tree standing in bold relief against a clear blue sky."*
> *Ten years later James Field found that the North Fork of the Platte below Fort Laramie appeared "to have been lately quite well timbered, but it is now nearly all destroyed by fire, the dead and dry wood strewing the bottom." By 1849 the trees had either vanished entirely or were quickly disappearing.*
> *When Pierre-Jean De Smet came to the "noble highway" along the North Platte in 1851, it was "as smooth as a barn floor swept by the winds:" not a blade of grass could sprout on it due to the continual passing of wagons and livestock.*

"Grass is not as good this season as it commonly is," William Porter wrote while waiting to cross the North Platte in 1848. A party returning from Oregon warned that "grass is very scarce on the route from this [point] on, and it will be very difficult getting there." [2]

The scale of the degradation was obscured by the scale of the Great Plains, and the incremental pace of change naturally interrupted by the seasons. Indigenous peoples were quick to see their world changing for the worse, but who could fault the transients. Most estimates of their scale number in the thousands, even tens of thousands between 1840 and 1861, and with them came their thousands of wagons and carts, and their tens of thousands of livestock. Their eyes were fixed on the western horizon, paying attention to their immediate circumstances only to the extent their immediate survival depended on it. Distant homesteads and goldfields—of course there were risks and costs—were motivations sufficient to any sacrifice. This sentiment prevailed at least as long as their Missouri jumping-off settlements remained in view behind them.

The condition of the prairie environment that greeted the Forty-Niners was not their concern. Rightly or wrongly, they chose to rush along the northerly Oregon Trail to the California gold fields. Once committed, they had to make the best of their circumstances. One factor in their favor, they were fewer in number and traveled lighter than the homesteaders a decade earlier. If they did not

Horse-Aided Bison Hunt. More horse-mounted Plains indigenous peoples meant fewer bison. Any benefit this provided regarding the health of the prairie grasslands was offset by declining rainfall and the effects of droughts. *(Alfred Jacob Miller)*

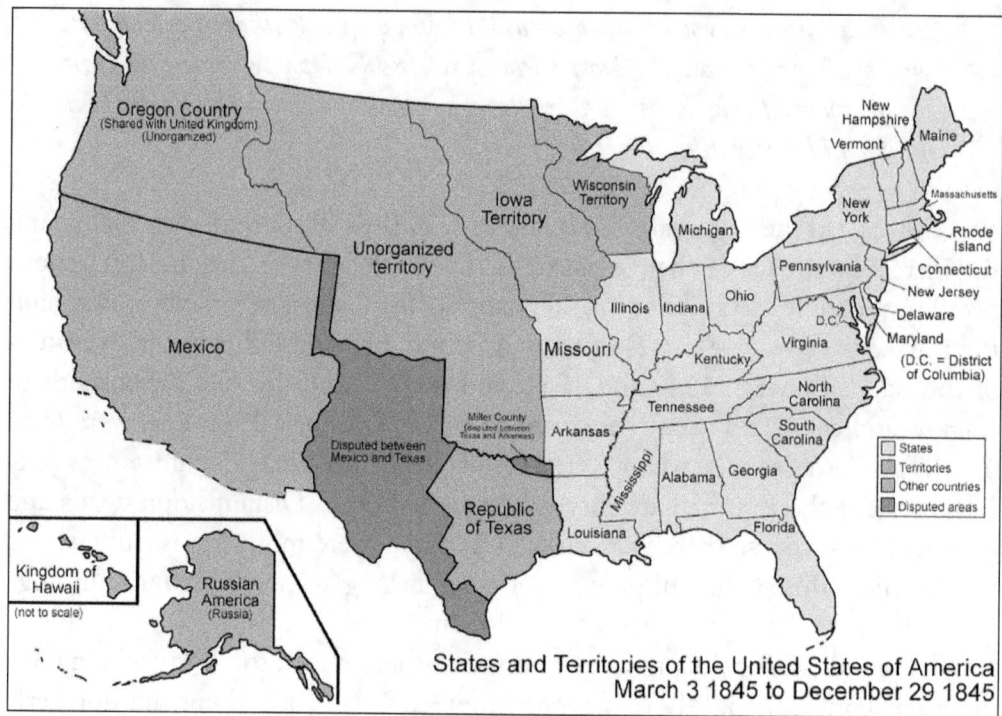

1. Expansionist America – 1845. During President Polk's single term in office, he presided over the fulfilment of his vision of a continental nation. *(Wikipedia)*

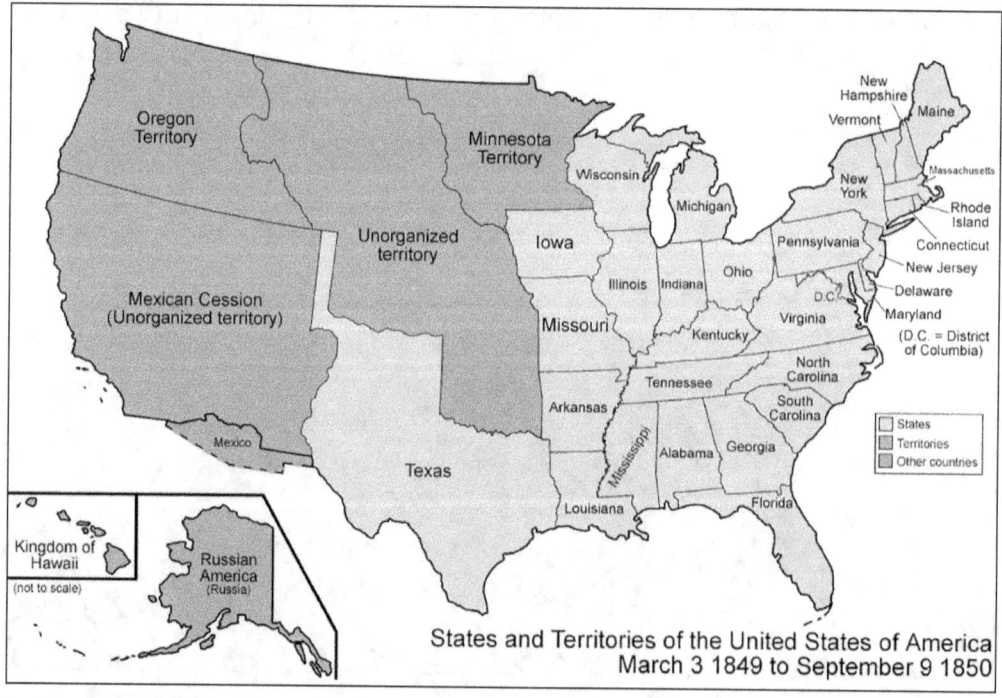

2. Expansionist America – 1850. By 1850, aided by victories in two southwestern wars, two waves of western mass emigration, and gold discoveries in California, President Polk's vision was secure. *(Wikipedia)*

travel lightly upon departure, they did soon thereafter as their teams wearied and their wagons collapsed under the weight of excess baggage. Abandoning "essential gear" was heartbreaking, but their only option.

The lull between the surge of homesteaders enroute to Oregon and the surge of gold-seekers headed to California was anything but calm. High stakes geopolitics filled the void. Unappreciated at the time, Independence Day 1845 was a watershed for the destiny of three countries. It marked the day the "Lone Star State" of Texas accepted President Polk's invitation to join the Union, and it was the day it dawned on the Mexican government that its remaining northern regions were next. Mexico recalled its Minister to Washington to protest the Texas annexation and braced for the worst. To the political savants, the question before the house was "would the remaining Mexican territories north of the Rio Grande be lost to war or through negotiations?" Even more consequential, "were all of Mexico and even the northern hemisphere the ultimate prize?" While the jury deliberated, American adventurers reached their own verdict. The "Lone Star" would not be the last star added to the American flag. The British Parliament formally wigged in their London chamber arrived at the same conclusion.

The signs were unmistakable, really. President Polk, ever wary of Russian northwest ambitions, had grown increasingly aggressive with the British over the "Oregon Question," and British diplomats in Washington had not been remiss in noting his frustration. Polk wanted definitive resolution lest the Czar and the Crown miscalculate American resolve. British mastery of global strategy, save for loss of the American colonies of course, was a hallmark feature of the British Empire. Even so, that steamy 1845 July witnessed the emergence of two unfamiliar terms—"brinkmanship" and "manifest destiny"—that summed up all the conniving underway on both sides of the Atlantic. The President, by forethought if not by nature, was adept at reminding the British that the Pacific Northwest was a long and costly way from Europe and the heart of British strategic interests. [European Russia also was a long and costly way from Alaska and the Pacific northwest.] By contrast, contested territories were rapidly filling up with American settlers willing to fight for their new homes. Conversations of this nature, just short of threatening hostilities, were the handmaidens of Polk's "brinkmanship." Less apparent, they also were the handmaidens of "manifest destiny."

In New York that July of 1845, an editorial in John L. O'Sullivan's *United States Magazine and Democratic Review* declared that it was America's "*manifest destiny* to overspread the continent allotted by Providence." The term "manifest destiny" resonated with a country of opportunists full of themselves. Accustomed to having their way, and undaunted by the unknowns of western lands obviously theirs for the taking, the term stuck. It more than stuck. It became a mindset and a mantra for any politician bright enough to appreciate its popular appeal. America by virtue of divine appointment was not simply empowered to populate the continent, it was obliged to do so.

Much intrigue along with Presidential initiatives ensued. Polk and his supporters worked on plans to acquire the Pacific region by any means possible. Entrepreneurs and Mormon leadership did their part to increase emigration to Utah, California and Oregon Territory and to foment the belief that the region was ripe for acquisition. Numerous claims circulated that the settlers already there had concluded long ago that their future did not rest with Mexico or British Canada, but instead with a government of their own, as "one Free Republic." This was music to the ears of those plying the corridors of Washington's power. Entrepreneurs, lobbyists and want-a-be outfitters piled on, all advancing similar sentiments:

> ... *the Republic of California should arise... From ten to twenty thousand emigrants will enter California next summer [1846]. There will then be population enough to authorize the step; and we shall have force for any contingency.* [3]

USS Congress. At the end of October 1845, the USS Congress set sail from its Hampton Roads homeport for California with "sealed orders" for Commodore "Fighting Bob" Robert F. Stockton. The Commodore, new commander of America's Pacific Fleet, was assigned the task of securing California for expansionist America. *(Wikipedia)*

By winter of 1845 American homesteaders demonstrated that wagons with full loads could reach Oregon and California in five months, and their government was poised to support their sovereign claims. President Polk informed his Cabinet on September 16, 1845, that he envisioned a continental nation, meaning the acquisition of California. Left unsaid for the moment, no doubt the Oregon Territory was also in mind. The President sent a letter to this effect to the State Department in October. At the end of October, the *U.S.S. Congress* set sail from its Hampton Roads homeport for California with Commodore Robert F. Stockton in command. An ardent expansionist known to his sailors as "Fighting Bob," the Commodore was the new commander of America's Pacific Fleet. During his prior command of the *U.S.S. Princeton* stationed in the Gulf of Mexico, reportedly the Commodore encouraged the Republic of Texas to "manufacture a war" with Mexico, which he assured the Texans the U.S. government supported. Declining the honor, nevertheless the Texans remained in good graces by sending Stockton back to Washington with "the glad tidings of annexation." [4]

The significance and implications of these matters did not escape the notice of the Mexican government, nor the British for that matter. Alarmed as they may have been, the Republic of Mexico was impoverished and the Oregon Territory was indeed a long way from London. Between 1846 and 1848, American military might and settlers filled the vacuum. They not only wore and widened western trails into roads, they also upset the Western Hemisphere's balance of power.

Tensions in the American west, tensions that reached as far afield as Mexico City and London, appeared to be reaching unmanageable levels by the mid-1840s. Probably to the credit of both parties, Washington and London settled their northwest America claims without a shot being fired. Not so regarding the southwest. Mexican and American forces exchanged gunfire for the better part of two years before U.S. troops under the command of General Winfield Scott landed in Veracruz and in September 1847 laid siege to Mexico City's Chapultepec Castle. The Treaty of Guadalupe Hidalgo signed on February 2, 1848 ended any doubt concerning Polk's southwest vision of manifest destiny. Noted historian H. H. Bancroft was quick to appreciate the larger meaning of these matters. So too Will Bagley:

> *By 1845, California chronicler H. H. Bancroft observed, the road to Fort Hall [southeastern corner of Oregon Territory, present-day Idaho] was a great national highway, "without hardships or dangers so excessive as to prevent the travelers from being born and married and buried on the way." Over the next three years the United States established its sovereignty over Oregon and the Southwest, the Latter-day Saints established the first major settlement along the trail, and the tenacity, suffering, and endurance of ordinary American families captured half a continent, finished forging the road across the plains, and opened all the primary routes of the Oregon-California Trail.* [5]

From Mexico's perspective, eliminating any doubts concerning the sanctity of their border with the United States was a primary directive. Exactly where that border layed depended on who answered the question. After all, the origin of their troubles was an example how the consequences of misjudgments could get out of control. In late April 1846, U.S. Army Captain Seth Thornton and his sixty-three dragoons, patrolling the northern bank of the Rio Grande in Cameron County, Texas in search of Mexican intruders, was ambushed and defeated by 1,600 Mexican cavalry and infantry in a brief skirmish at Rancho Carricitos. Fourteen Americans died and Thornton and forty-nine others were imprisoned. Thornton and his troopers did not reach the high station earned by the defenders of the Alamo, but their fate served the same purpose. It was the primary justification for President Polk's demand that Congress declare war. Congress did so and April 25, 1846, marked its beginning. With the loss of thousands of soldiers and a third of their republic, Mexico learned a hard lesson. [6]

The Treaty of Guadalupe Hidalgo brought peace to America and Mexico and launched California on its way to statehood, *a fait accompli* if not for that annoying "free state-slave state" matter plaguing the U.S. Congress. In little more than a decade this political infighting would escalate into a civil war, but satisfying a few more preconditions had to come first. The reality of a national consciousness—a sense of national purpose and destiny—exhibited by America's Founding Fathers was largely absent among most early nineteenth century politicians. Not so James Polk. Polk envisioned a republic destined to stretch from "sea to shining sea." Securing territory from foreign powers was necessary, but insufficient. Fulfilling his vision required the introduction of safe and seaworthy steamboats, long-distance railroads and bridges capable of carrying them over wide rivers, first and foremost the Mississippi and Missouri, and the telegraph. Fulfilling the vision, strategically speaking, also would require two mid-century gold rushes, a civil war, and an industrial revolution.

Long before James Polk took office, he was a firm believer along with many restless Americans that the United States had a God-given right, even duty, to acquire the Pacific coastal lands and everything between there and the Mississippi. In particular, he wanted the Mexican Republic out of the southwest and "Alta California," and the British out of the Pacific Northwest. In 1846, the British, still smarting over two lost American wars in a single generation and far from eager to risk a third, abandoned its claims below the 49th parallel. Mexico, from the 42nd parallel to the Rio Grande and the Sea of Cortes, exerted tenuous influence over local affairs until the 1848 Treaty of Guadalupe Hidalgo relieved them entirely of that responsibility. American successes on the battlefield, softened by the payment of fifteen million dollars to the Mexican Republic, resulted in the transfer of a half-million square miles of western lands. America's Southwest was birthed. So was North America's two-ocean superpower.

Polk ended his Presidency struggling with Congress to seat a government in "Alta California" before Alta California declared independence and seated one of their own. Will Bagley summarizes the gravity of the matter:

> California's mineral wealth "and other advantages" would attract a large population, but Polk feared that "among the emigrants would be men of enterprise and adventure" who would "probably organize an independent Government, calling it California or the Pacific Republic, and might induce Oregon to join them." Sectional politics complicated the issue, since the fate of slavery was inextricably bound up in the future of this newly conquered province, but Congress took no action to prevent losing California to a band of reckless and ambitious opportunists. [7]

Matters worsened. Polk's successor, General Zachery Taylor, during their carriage ride to his inauguration at the U.S. Capitol, informed Polk that he considered California and Oregon remote, probably ungovernable as a consequence. Better they govern themselves. Polk was horrified. His decade-long work to create a continental nation was more than at risk, it was at death's door. The General's confession was worse than Polk's worst nightmare, but he did not lose sleep for long. The outgoing President was dead of cholera three months later. Nor was there much to worry about—actions he took while a lame duck, and his legacy on the frontier, were certain to outlive any mortal man. Now engrained in the fabric and consciousness of the nation, no longer a lofty philosophy or undefined bravado, "Manifest Destiny" was a governing principle every aspiring politician had to embrace. Moreover, President Taylor did not govern long. In little more than a year he too died, according to his physicians also from cholera. [8]

As for California gold, James Polk had played another lame-duck presidential card. In his last message to Congress on December 5, 1848, in which he confirmed reports of Sutters Mill gold, he in effect layed down unmistakable markers assuring a continental America by declaring the Mississippi Valley no longer the country' frontier, but its center. Indeed, the acquisition of a half-million square miles of territory afforded by the Treaty of Guadalupe Hidalgo changed not only the definition of the frontier—acquisition of territory on the scale of all of Europe was irrefutable testimoney to manifest destiny.

President Polk's confirmation of California gold was persuasive.

The day would come when scorn accompanied Presidential declarations, but not in 1848. James Polk's confirmation of the truthfulness of California gold strikes first reported in August by the *New York Herald* was the final blow to skeptics. Fall trickles of westbound gold seekers grew into spring torrents. The rush to California was on. By early June 1849, a Fort Laramie trader reported that 11,000 wagons and forty-four thousand emigrants were on their way west. As for President Polk's fear that Californians would declare their independence, indeed emigrants put that notion to an early vote. Probably surprising to many of its organizers, on October 13, 1849, a Monterey convention comprised of first-generation settlers voted to join the Union. Oregon trail veteran Peter Burnett was elected governor of the provisional state of California. A year later he was Governor of California, besting John Sutter among others for the crown.

Easterners were not the only ones that overran California. Homesteaders scarcely settled on their Oregon Territory farms and other lightly settled outposts west of the Colorado Rockies converged on Sutters Mill. Compatriots from as far away as South America, Asia and Europe outpaced the measured exploration and settlement of earlier decades. Overland trails to California, almost all of which hosted a few pilgrims and traders in centuries past, took on characteristics of commercial thoroughfares networking cities and villages east of the Mississippi. Guidebooks, maps, trading posts, and isolated farms and ranches

PETER HARDEMAN BURNETT

Elected Governor of California while California was still a territory, his countenance befitted his disposition. Born into a slave-owning Missouri family, with his business interests in disrepair, he hazarded the Oregon Trail and found his future in law. He served the Provisional Government of Oregon as Supreme Judge. He also advocated banning African Americans from Oregon. In 1848 he moved to California. Despite arriving with the vanguard of the gold-seeker class, he again pursued politics and the law. While serving on the California Supreme Court, he again distinguished himself by his racist beliefs and actions. Curiously, he opposed California entering the Union as a slave state, but he did lobby for the total exclusion of African-Americans. He was even less tolerant of Native Americans and foreign laborers, notably the Chinese. Little of a positive nature can be said of the public man other than the fact that be survived the Oregon Trail and was the first elected governor of California.

Peter Hardeman Burnett (1807-1895). First Governor of California, Burnett not only was an early pilgrim on the Oregon Trail, he also pioneered the principal wagon road from Oregon settlements to California goldfields. *(Wikipedia Commons)*

encouraged perseverance. Trails broadened and deepened into wagon roads, into military highways, and often into not-to-distant railroad right-of-ways.

Most accounts of California's 49ers and Colorado's 59ers depict the shock of jumping off from commodious settlements along the Missouri River and blindly wending ones way across a trackless prairie if not desert only to confront the nearly insurmountable Rocky Mountains. If California or Oregon was the goal, congratulations were in order upon reaching this halfway mark, but more of the same and worse layed ahead. Actually, the "Great American Desert" and beyond were not trackless wildernesses. Dry prairies laced with dry mountains checkered with dry gulches sparsely settled by white men would be a fairer description.

By 1849, "tracks and traces" passing for wagon roads provided general direction for anyone with determination and grit to bear up under all manner of privations and routine Native American confrontations. At some river crossings, it was possible to come upon a crude ferry built and operated by an earlier pilgrim who had concluded providing ferry service was reward enough. By 1849, U.S. Army forts commanded strategic locations. Native American traders had built their mercantiles, and oases like the Grand Saline and the Mormon settlements in the Great Salt Lake basin were thriving. No, "trackless wilderness" was not the case— sparsely settled and largely devoid of white men was a fairer description.

Will Bagley's description of the matter is the "gold standard." "When the gold rush began, it was possible to count the number of trading posts between the Missouri and the Pacific on two hands." [9] Finding even one trading post worthy of the name between the Missouri and the Rocky Mountain Front Range was unlikely, dependent for sure on the year and the season. Under the pressure of homesteaders and gold-seekers, prairie culture and the balance of power among indigenous peoples and Europeans changed forever. By 1852, the infrequent wagons jostling toward Santa Fe markets or Salt Lake Valley and Oregon settlements yielded to tens of thousands of gold seekers and emigrants that transformed these rough wagon traces into

Around Cape Horn. President Polk favored overland routes to California believing that they would help populate the interior of the country and knit the east and the west into a single culture. Sea routes to California by way of Panama or around Cape Horn appealed to those who could afford the time and expense. "Swift" Clipper ships provided a viable compromise. *(Wikipedia)*

national wagon roads. The "hand-full" of trading posts blossomed into hundreds of "posts" and scores of villages soon boasting churches and angling for railroad depots. Sometimes they took root where weary travelers or exhausted livestock were unable to go farther. Sometimes they took root where there was water, seasonal as it may have been. Sometimes they took root for no good reason, but usually they took root where needs and wants presented opportunities that looked brighter than the lure of gold mines beyond the horizon.

> *The westering impulse infected its victims both with a burning desire to seek out new routes and to devise new ways to profit from them. One stalwart reportedly drove a flock of two thousand turkeys from Missouri to California, while an entrepreneur named Patterson invested his profits from a Salt Lake freighting operation in chickens, loaded them onto seven wagons with custom -built decks, and sold the fowls at an enormous profit in the gold-fields.* [10]

Mid-decade the flow of travelers both east and west ebbed and so did prairie investments. Fledgling villages surrendered to the elements. Trading posts retreated to strategic commercial locations, notably the nascent Salt Lake basin and points west. The prairie facing the Fifty-Niners, save for the Platte River wagon roads, looked as ominous to this new wave of gold-seekers as it looked to the Forty-Niners a decade earlier. Still, both mass movements served a larger purpose, a nation-building purpose. Overland routes west, settlers with heavy wagons grading and widening rough Mormon and Oregon trails, were preconditions

TERRITORIAL NOMADS [11]

Territorial warfare among indigenous peoples, routinely flaring up century upon century, was certain to embrace the new Americans as well. Nomads were no more apt to welcome intruders to their hunting and grazing grounds than they were apt to survey and plat the land.

In 1834, Congress created "Indian Country" west of the Missouri frontier, but the affected Nations would have none of it. Shoshone leader Washakie said as much to the governor of Wyoming Territory: "You know as well as we, that every foot of what you proudly call American, not very long ago belonged to the red man." [12] In fact all lands between the Missouri and the Pacific Ocean was the domain of the "red man." That did not mean all was peaceful. Chief Washakie spoke of his race, not his tribe. Before 1700, before European pressure from the Atlantic seaboard, the Absaroka, Lakota, Pawnee, Cheyenne, and Arapaho hunted and farmed amidst the Great Lakes and along the Missouri and Mississippi Rivers before emigrating westward ahead of more easterly tribes themselves pressured westward by the white man.

The Great Plains and the mountains and basins beyond were a complex society comprised of customs and expectations born out of impressive travel, trade, and communications among starkly different language groups. Goods from as far away as the Gulf Coast found their way to the Pacific Northwest and vice-versa. Similarly, Native Americans of the West knew of the whites long before they encountered any of them.

Word of the arrival of hairy white-skinned men raced across the continent. Many Indians could greet the first white men in their land as the Comanche Ten Bears welcomed an emissary from Washington: "I heard of your coming when you were many sleeps away." Spreading from one people to another over ancient trade routes, European technologies, goods, animals, and deadly diseases reached the tribes well in advance of the mercenaries, merchants, and missionaries who brought these wonders to the New World. [13]

for trails to California. The California gold rush was a precondition for expending the effort to grade and widen California trails into wagon roads. Wagon roads to California and Oregon were preconditions for wagon roads into the Colorado Rockies and the ultimate success of the Colorado gold rush.

The mass migrations westward to the California and Colorado gold regions also were preconditions for the transformation of a transcontinental wilderness into a hardrock mining and hardscrabble agricultural region with growth potential not even the wildest dreamer could fathom. In the half-dozen decades required for the American experiment to vanquish the foreign powers that resisted America's westward expansion—Spanish, French, Mexican, and British chief among them—the spoils were incalculable. President Polk envisioned it, but another quarter-century was required to reap it. While foreign threats had been blunted, the Nation's resources would have to turn next to domestic challengers still prepared to defend their centuries-long way of life. In the east, predominantly, the slave states would take up arms. In the west, indigenous peoples, the Plains Indians and the mountain Ute in particular, would do likewise.

The pre-gold-rush American West, home to a complex indigenous society of dozens of sometimes warring, sometimes allied, mostly nomadic Indian tribes, greeted the early Europeans with disdain. At first, the introduction of a handful of white men beginning with the Spanish, French and British did little to upset cultural norms. That would reach a boiling point after the American Civil War. Prior to that, aside from occasional atrocities and targets of opportunity, Europeans were considered oddities that provided useful trade goods. First encounters generated bewilderment and humor more so than angst, often reflected in the need to develop new vocabulary to capture the experience.

Will Bagley cites Sarah Winnemucca of Paiute lineage to illustrate the point. Early on, wagon trains were a novelty among her people. Sarah remembered one season when her tribe "talked of nothing but their white brothers." The following year they learned from their scouts that the white men were on their way with something all ablaze. It looked like a man with legs, hands, and a head. The head no longer burned, but was black. "There was the greatest excitement among my people everywhere about the men in a blazing fire." Sarah continued. The burning men, they discovered, were "two negroes wearing red shirts." [14]

Introduction of the horse further unsettled the precarious balance among indigenous societies. In Bagley's judgment, no single factor impacted Native American cultures and the West more than the horse. The horse was "a living engine that could transform the most immense resource on the Great Plains—grass—into a power Indians could harness to travel, hunt, trade, and make war.... The horse made a man more than a match for the fiercest bison—and for traditional adversaries who had not yet acquired the new technology." [15]

Proliferation of the horse upset geopolitics and social order from the Missouri and Mississippi Valleys to the Pacific coast more than proliferation of the White

Man. The horse was the currency and measure of wealth among tribes and tribes-men. It also was another reason to war. Not only did the horse provide strategic advantages, it also required more territory. The more horses a tribe owned the more conflict over acquiring additional territory to graze. Acquiring more territory meant taking it from a nearby albeit nomadic neighbor, often upsetting traditional alliances and aggravating previous rivalries. [16]

Into this dynamic realm entered the emigrant, and increasingly since President Jefferson's 1803 Louisiana Purchase, "new Americans." By the beginning of the 1850s, these new Americans had settled the troublesome matter of distant foreign government claims on North American territory. Dazed by disease and warfare among themselves, the equally troublesome matter of displacing indigenous peoples simmered but did not boil over for another generation. That season came upon the heels of a decade of drought and the extinction of buffalo and grass. It came with the discovery first of western gold and then silver, and the mass migrations they spawned.

Westward wandering is a recurrent theme in the American experience. Among the literate class, "westering" was coined to describe a journey without a destination. In America's earlier decades migrating west meant claiming fertile flood plains west of the Appalachians. In short order, the Ohio and Mississippi River Valleys struggled to accommodate the young Republic's swelling population. For those bored with genteel lifestyles, pushing beyond the settled frontier

"Out to See the Elephant" was a popular quip of the times. Loosely defined, during gold rushes it usually meant that a person was in search of elusive treasure. When associated with outfitting for such a quest, "Elephant Corral" was applied to mercantiles and livery stables. Established supply depots like Denver and boom-towns like Lake City all had their elephant corrals where all manner of provisions, livestock, entertainment, and often lodging awaited the newcomer. (*J. Harrison Mills*, Harper's Weekly)

usually meant hazarding Spanish or Mexican territory to foster trade in Santa Fe
or settlements in Texas. The Rocky Mountains and the northern plains, mapped
to the extent that they were mostly through rumor and myth, awaited their turn.
With the Louisiana Purchase came opportunity and legal status, begrudgingly
to be sure.

In every wave of "westering" there was an elephant. "Out to see the elephant"
was a popular westering phrase. Anyone brave enough to leave home understood
it described why curiosity eventually trumped fear, especially if the elephant was
gold and silver. For President Polk the elephant was a continent united under the
American flag. For the emigrant it was opportunity to pursue one's dreams of free-
dom and a means of being self-reliant. For the homesteader it was boundless fertile
fields, enough for everyone to own a fair share. For the Mormon it was religious
liberty. For the Forty-Niners and Fifty-Niners, it was gold, but silver would do.

Of course, there were no back-flow valves governing the direction of migration. Ironic as it seemed, gold was not magnetic, yet it attracted adventurers
worldwide. Nor was its attraction irreversible. Forty-Niners who found treasure often returned home to comfortable eastern lives. Those who failed often
resorted to businesses and services new settlements craved, but most dragged
themselves back home. However, there was always a cadre of die-hards that
scurried off to the next rumored gold find. This latter group of discontents,
Rodman W. Paul concluded, was sizeable. Their "westering" days were over, but
not their search for the elephant. That impulse survived even though the compass point changed. From California, they made their way back east into the
Rocky Mountain interior, an "interior" ranging from Mexico to the Yukon. Paul
defines "interior" this way:

> *At the eastern edge of the Rockies begins what geographers call "the cordilleran*
> *portion of North America," by which formidable term is meant the vast ele-*
> *vated region that includes everything from the Eastern Rockies to the western*
> *foothills of the Sierra Nevada and Cascade ranges. Between those two massive*
> *mountain systems lie the dry Columbia and Snake River plains in the north,*
> *the desert Great Basin of Utah and Nevada in the center, and in the south*
> *the high Colorado Plateau that straddles southern Utah, and Colorado and*
> *northern Arizona and New Mexico. South of the Colorado Plateau, deserts*
> *and mountains extend endlessly into Old Mexico.* [17]

In Paul's opinion, one could not imagine a less promising region for rapid
development. Yet, tens of thousands of expectant treasure seekers and camp followers both reputable and otherwise flooded the region beginning in 1859.

> *Almost simultaneously, gold was discovered in Colorado, on the eastern edge of*
> *the cordilleran region, and silver was found on the Comstock Lode of Nevada,*

near the western edge. The one was the beginning of an abrupt advance of placer miners and gold-quartz operators into the Rocky Mountains, along a thousand-mile front that extended from southern British Columbia to southern Colorado; the other was the introduction to a new type of precious-metal mining — silver — that lured men into the Great Basin, the Rockies, and the southwest. [18]

Fair enough, but in continuing Paul brushes aside conventional westering wisdom as mere "notions:"

Despite traditional notions of the frontier as a "westward movement," the mining advance was a series of thrusts from both east and west into the cordilleran middle. Men from California, Oregon, and Washington, calling themselves "Yon-siders" (yonder siders) crossed the Sierras or Cascades to meet "pilgrims" (greenhorns, tenderfeet) coming from the settled lands east of the Great Plains. Out of their joint efforts grew a succession of mining districts and supply centers that, however transitory some proved to be, forever altered the hitherto little-settled interior. [19]

As usual, there is merit in both explanations. There also is more to the story. Without exaggerating, the mass migrations to Oregon settlements, California placers, and Colorado goldfields between 1840 and 1860 are rich with insightful contrasts and comparisons. Underpinning both decades, the social and economic engine for the exploration and settlement of the "interior," was a stubborn national economic depression. Debts accruing from the Mexican-American War prolonged the "panic of 1837" currency crisis. The seeming shortage of fertile farmlands and high unemployment was further heightened by surging immigration largely from agrarian Europe, but also from around a hungry world as well. Having little incentive to remain in the States, and every fanciful reason to make their fortunes in the bounteous West, emigrants by the tens of thousands accepted the challenges of getting there. Virtuous settlers first set their sights on fertile Oregon bottomland. Frenzied fortune-seekers, farmers especially, soon followed with sights set on California gold. Once again, Will Bagley captures the emotions of the day.

"The gold excitement spread like wildfire, even out to our log cabin in the prairie, and as we had almost nothing to lose, and we might gain a fortune, we early caught the fever," recalled Luzena Wilson. "It sounded like such a small task to go out to California, and once there fortune, of course, would come to us."

The hysteria became a worldwide phenomenon, attracting thousands from Central America and Polynesia, spreading to South America, crossing the Pacific to Australia and China, and finally infecting Europe. "Many die unheeded, many come off rich," wrote California's military governor, "but there are ten arriving from each quarter of the globe to replace everyone who goes—Chinese, French, Sandwich Islanders, Chileans, Peruvians, Prussians, Mexicans, English, Irish, outnumber as yet the Americans, but the latter will soon have their share."

As Malcolm Rohrbough observed, "When California discovered gold, the world discovered California."

[Reports of California gold powerfully appealed to Americans and foreigners for a variety of personal reasons. Some even claimed unselfish motives.]

Our object is to endeavor to make something in California so as to support them in their old days as well as to enable us to remove them from unpleasant recollections," wrote Alexander Graham, seeking to justify abandoning his aging family.

Francis A. Hardy said he was leaving all that was dear to him on earth "to procure the means (if possible by industry, honesty and persevereance [sic]) to render my family (a wife and infant son) comfortable and happy."

[Francis, in light of his "if possible" phrase did not seem to rule out slothfulness and chicanery if that would serve him well.]

"It was a period of National hard times and we being financially involved in our business interests near Clinton, Iowa, longed to go to the new El Dorado and 'pick up' gold enough with which to return and pay off our debts," recalled Catherine Haun, rather delicately obscuring the mountain of unpaid bills she and her new husband left behind.

James A. Tate set out for "the much famed Land of Gold in California, to repair a ruined fortune. [He died shortly after arrival.]

Dr. Charles E. Boyle felt "determined to make one mighty effort to disenthrall myself from the slavery of the detested sin of being poor, and here I am on my way to California." [20]

Not only was "westering" a journey without a destination, it was a journey without direction. Oh, there were traces and trails aplenty scaring the plains and mountainsides, like spider webs spread in all directions, but the challenge was which one led where. Hiring a scout, red or white, who had solved the riddle, was one solution. Ideally, that "someone" was disposed to shepherd "lay-abouts" wholly unprepared for the hardships ahead. A frugal solution was investing a dollar or so in a guidebook prominently displayed at frontier outposts and local mercantiles, and, if possible, sign on with the next available wagon train. Hopefully, its boastful Captain had actually crossed the plains before. The first mass migration to Oregon, including the Pacific coast south into California, required the greatest vision and courage. [The second mass migration to the California gold placers benefited from the first, and the third to Colorado's Front Range was less fearsome still, but each of them was daunting.]

Experienced Captain or not, ever-resourceful entrepreneurs were eager to help. Guidebooks that proved valuable and others worthless quickly appeared. Philip Leget Edwards's *Sketch of the Oregon Territory: or, Emigrants' Guide*, hit the streets in 1842. Bidwell's letter-journal found its way into print between 1843 and 1845. The Reverend Joseph Williams's 1843 *Narrative of a Tour from*

WESTERN EMIGRATION SOCIETY [21]

Westport in the spring of 1841 was no place for the faint of heart, certainly not Bidwell and Bartleson. Pressed together on the banks of the Missouri River, they pondered their next move west. Will Bagley explains the Western Emigration Society's failure to meet the challenge, and why it did not matter.

> The odd gathering of missionaries, sportsmen, veteran and would-be mountaineers, and families now known as the Bidwell-Bartleson party marked "the inception of the emigration across the plains," Josiah Belden proudly remembered. "This party opened the road, so to speak, [this] was the beginning." The venture started "as an exploring expedition to find their own way out there, and see what the country was," he continued. "This expedition should have the credit of starting the emigration to California. Those who joined it were really pioneers, for there was no emigration before; there was nothing known of the road, or how to get there." It was, as Belden observed, "something of a perilous undertaking, and it was the beginning of the whole settlement of the country."

So, by one account at least the Bidwell-Bartleson Party won the 1841 "Westering Prize" for being first off the mark. Arguable no doubt, but typical of what many pathfinders experienced. Bidwell and Bartleson faced a fearsome unknown. Nothing west of the Continental Divide was American territory, and disputes lingered over much of what was east of the Divide. The most reliable reporting on the northern region was in Lewis and Clark's journals published in 1814. On occasion letters and personal accounts of traders and mountaineers found their way into eastern newspapers, but how factual were these? What better way to slake the thirst of a Nation accustomed to new vistas than organizing a "fraternity of the curious."

On February 1, 1841, the *Western Emigration Society* was born. Within a month, five hundred bored souls signed up to see the elephant. Pledging to assemble everything

the State of Indiana to the Oregon Territory in the Years 1841–2 depicted his adventures with the epic *Western Emigration Society's* Bidwell-Bartleson Party. Sadly, it neglected to detail preparations, distances, campsites, and the availability of wood and water that the best trail guides included, and that spelled the difference between life and death. Sadly for pilgrims who put their trust in it, shortcomings of this nature often dawned on them too late to make a difference.

Perhaps the most popular book on overland travel appeared in 1843 in the form of a government document based on John C. Fremont's *Report of the Exploring Expedition to the Rocky Mountains.* It only mapped his first expedition

required for the journey, they agreed to meet in May "armed and equipped to cross the Rocky Mountains to California." When the appointed day arrived, only John Bidwell reported for duty. Undeterred, he quickly revised his plan by joining like-minded Bartleson in command of a small band of other visionaries. Reflecting on those days, John recalled, "Our ignorance of the route is complete. We know that California lay west, and that is the extent of our knowledge."

Departing Westport, the Bidwell-Bartleson party took a soon to become well-worn path along the Kansas, Big Blue, and Little Blue rivers to the Platte River Valley. This classic route first crossed rolling prairie described by Nicholas Point as "endless undulations which bear a perfect resemblance to those of the sea when it is agitated by a storm." The Platte Valley flood plain put an end to any thought of an agitated sea. The valley was broad and flat, and the river was "a thousand miles long and six inches deep," except during spring runoff from the distant mountains when shallow-draft boats could still cope with currents. Moreover, while occasional cottonwood groves once lined its banks, wood was nearly nonexistent by the mid-1840s. News of the party's experiences eventually trickled back to the Missouri frontier with the net effect that the Platte served nobly as a guide to the Rocky Mountains due to its reliable source of water. No one yet imagined what the impact of tens of thousands of followers would be.

By the end of 1848, perhaps twenty thousand Americans turned their backs on civilization in search of their elephant. Not only did they leave the comforts of home under a cloud of uncertainty, in most cases they left under a barrage of scorn. From New York to New Orleans newspapers "ridiculed those who chose to undertake the 'madness and folly' of a journey to the pacific. Leaving behind fertile lands and a stable government to strike out across the wilderness had "an aspect of insanity," Horace Greeley wrote in New York….Tempting women and children to cross "this thousand miles of precipice and volcanic sterility to Oregon was "palpable homicide," he charged." Greeley may have later advised, "Go west, young man, go west," but in 1843 he strongly encouraged everyone to stay home.

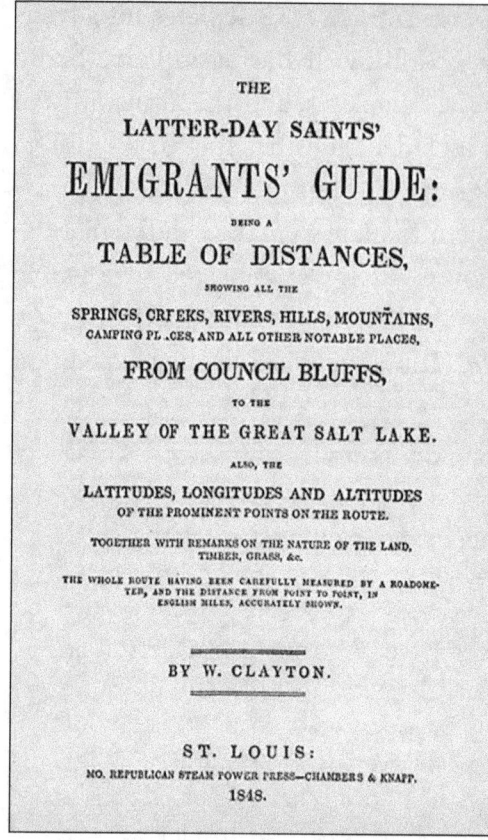

THE

LATTER-DAY SAINTS'

EMIGRANTS' GUIDE:

BEING A

TABLE OF DISTANCES,

SHOWING ALL THE

SPRINGS, CREEKS, RIVERS, HILLS, MOUNTAINS,
CAMPING PLACES, AND ALL OTHER NOTABLE PLACES,

FROM COUNCIL BLUFFS,

TO THE

VALLEY OF THE GREAT SALT LAKE.

ALSO, THE

LATITUDES, LONGITUDES AND ALTITUDES
OF THE PROMINENT POINTS ON THE ROUTE.

TOGETHER WITH REMARKS ON THE NATURE OF THE LAND,
TIMBER, GRASS, &c.

THE WHOLE ROUTE HAVING BEEN CAREFULLY MEASURED BY A ROADOME-
TER, AND THE DISTANCE FROM POINT TO POINT, IN
ENGLISH MILES, ACCURATELY SHOWN.

BY W. CLAYTON.

ST. LOUIS:

MO. REPUBLICAN STEAM POWER PRESS—CHAMBERS & KNAPP.
1848.

The Latter-Day Saints' Emigrants' Guide. Considered the best guidebook of its time, Clayton's guide included mileage between way-points utilizing his invention of a wagon "roadometer" (odometer.) and other detailed information. It was written in 1848 based on Clayton's experiences and observations following the Mormon Trail to Salt Lake City. *(Courtesy, Perry Special Collections, Brigham Young University)*

to Wyoming's South Pass. An 1845 revision included his second expedition to Oregon and California in 1843-44. Reportedly of little value as guidebooks, nevertheless the Fremont name sold tens of thousands of copies and inspired many Americans to head west. Perhaps the worst guidebook authored by Lansford Hastings also began circulating in 1845. *The Emigrants' Guide to Oregon and California* made claims about trails that did not exist much less that he had traversed. It did contain helpful information on equipment, supplies and teams, and for some reason reprints appeared under varying titles as late as 1857.

Overland guidebooks hitting the market in 1846 were much improved. Overton Johnson and William Winter's *Route Across the Rocky Mountains*, John Shively's *The Road to Oregon and California*, and Joel Palmer's *Journal of Travels over the Rocky Mountains to the Mouth of the Columbia River* described what to expect of the trails. The 1846 emigration also produced T. H. Jefferson's *Map of the Emigrant Road from Independence, Mo., to San Francisco, California*. Published in New York in 1849, it provided a mile-by-mile description of the California Trail and Hastings cutoff.

Best of all, according to Historian Bagley, the most helpful westering guidebooks included a "waybill" listing "campsites, trading posts, landmarks, river crossings, and the distances between them." They also offered advice on provisions, routes, and importantly "how to deal with Native Americans." William Clayton's *The Latter-Day Saints' Emigrants' Guide* made the grade. Available in St. Louis in 1848, it relied on an odometer invented by a member of "Brigham Young's 1847 pioneer company." It ended at Salt Lake City, but provided the first reliable measure of distances. [22]

The physical and psychological barriers presented by the Great Plains and the mountains beyond should not be underestimated. The array of life-threatening risks was limited only by one's imagination. Not even the legacies of the two previous mass migrations had much of a helpful effect on the mass migration to Colorado. On balance, spotty accounts of Oregon settlers and guidebooks had been poor traveling companions for Forty-Niners and would be no different for Fifty-Niners. Even the best remained inadequate to the task, and in any case were discounted, ignored, or overshadowed by the zeal of men and women eager to start a new life on the far side of the prairie. With the added lure of untold prosperity at the end of the western rainbow, the rush for California gold had not seemed risky until circumstances proved otherwise. With the passing of another decade, the absence of practical guidebooks, or guides for that matter, also was of little concern. The Colorado Fifty-Niners, often veterans of California and often still stinging from having arrived there too late to share in the bonanza, were not about to make that same mistake. Prepared or not, certain of their path or not, to Pike's Peak and Cherry Creek they would go. How hard could that be? After all, Colorado gold fields were half the distance to the Pacific.

A year later, 1860, sanity reigned.

Partly due to outposts, notably present-day Denver that barely survived its own first Rocky Mountain Front Range winter, the wave of migration in 1860 was kinder to pilgrims for several reasons. An abundance of seasoned "go-backers" willing to try again, and the loving if strident admonition of women with children outnumbering the men, resulted in provisions and equipment better suited for the months ahead of them. Armchair entrepreneurs produced more guidebooks, but like their predecessors, books served alongside family Bibles more as a comfort when all else failed. More importantly, those who heeded advice wisely stocked their wagons. They would fare well on the 1860 trail.

However, not just any wagon would do. "Better-prepared" also meant better wagons designed for heavy loads transported long distances over rugged roads. Unlike early Santa Fe traders able to profit from a few hundred pounds of manufactured goods, emigrants required enormous quantities of staples and the means of reproducing a semblance of the civilization they were leaving behind. In the case of Oregon and California, sea transport was an option for personnel and light cargo, but it was slow and could not keep up with demand when it came to the daily needs of tens of thousands of settlers, miners, manufacturers, and farmers. Railroads would help, but they had to wait their turn behind an impending civil war. Heavy-duty wagons specifically designed for their transcontinental task was the only near-term solution, but they were not a quick solution. They too required a war effort that demanded mass production of equipment capable of heavy loads. The Fifty-Niners were all about "quick," and consequently paid a heavy price.

"Quick" meant "farm wagons." Farm wagons were available to anyone who had the patience to deal with them. They were plentiful—if well constructed and lightly loaded they accommodated the rigors of road-less if not trackless open ground. Easily modified with a cover, pulled by a double team or more, they carried upwards of a ton of cargo. Waiting beside the barn, the farm wagon also offered more than transport. It was living quarters and mobile general store, and a source of milled lumber for floorboards, doors and shutters at journey's end. Nevertheless, a one-ton wagon was still too small to handle the absolute essentials for a new life in a commercial wasteland half a continent away. Their owners, all but the frailest or youngest, often walked alongside, not to lighten the load but to make room for more "essentials."

From pioneer Jesse Looney's perspective, the fuss over wagons was misguided. To begin with, early emigrants rarely used Conestoga wagons. Given the options for most, the common farm wagon was their only real choice. Small, light, nimble enough to accommodate rough trails, it also was affordable. But for Looney, a successful settler and seasoned connoisseur of prairie schooners, the debate should not overlook the choice of the draft animals. Brushing aside the pros and cons of various wagons, he did not mince words.

Emigrant Wagons came in many styles and sizes. Farm wagons were lighter and more common, thus more affordable and available. They were capable of carrying one ton, but quite often overloaded and likely to breakdown on the trail. Seasoned prairie wagoneers nevertheless preferred them, disdaining the more stylish Conestoga they considered too unwieldy for road-less terrain. *(Ingersoll, 1883)*

The large one, two horse Yankee wagons are the most suitable wagons I have seen for the trip. You should have nothing but your clothing, bedding and provisions—flour and bacon. Goods are cheaper here than in the states. Put as much loading as one yoke of cattle can draw handily, and then put on three good yoke of cattle and take an extra yoke for a change in case of lameness or sore necks, and you can come through without difficulty. [23]

Few heeded advice on cargo, especially laborers and craftsmen traveling with tools as well as households. Better received was advice on wagons. When it came to reliable freighting, simplicity and quality of construction were more important than elegance, size, or popularity. Use of seasoned as opposed to green wood was an absolute essential given the low-humidity environment that layed ahead. "Buy a light strong wagon, made of the best seasoned materials", advised J. M. Shively, "for, if the timbers be not well seasoned, your wagon will fall to pieces when you get to the dry, arid plains of the mountains." [24]

While there were some that believed big was best, most wagoneers disagreed. A small, well-designed and assembled wagon best performed the range of duties required of it. It should have a waterproofed cover to protect its contents (and sleeping quarters) from storms and the blistering sun. The ability to separate a well-constructed box from its running gear in order to haul it over obstacles was handy. So was a tailgate to serve as a dining table. A caulked box doubled as a small barge able to float across rivers. And of course, trail veterans consistently warned not to overload the wagons. Weight was the silent foe. Bagley makes this point crystal clear. [25]

"An ordinary two-horse wagon, with eighteen-hundred weight, good double cover, and three yoke of light, active cattle are the best outfit a man can have," Captain Medorem Crawford advised twenty-one years after his first trip to Oregon: wagons should only be loaded to half their capacity, and each person should take at least 250 pounds of provisions, consisting of flour, bacon, sugar, coffee, teas, rice, and dried fruit. "Each man should be armed, and keep his gun convenient," but not capped....

Trail veterans consistently warned not to overload the wagons. "No useless trumpery should be taken," wrote Joel Palmer. "You should not start with a pound of any thing that can be done without," Samuel Crockett advised in 1845, "for it is much better to throw away an unnecessary article than to haul it." Few emigrants were able to estimate their practical requirements accurately, but if family treasures were not left behind at the beginning of the journey, almost inevitably they joined the piles of abandoned furniture, tools, stoves, tinware, crockery, clothing, saddles, carpets, and even firearms that lined the trail from its start to its end. The "roads about the mountains are literally covered with such articles," Peter Lassen reported from South Pass in

1848: he cautioned there was "no danger in the world to be feared from any cause but overloading."

Painful were the lessons learned during this first era of transitioning from pilgrims and gold-seekers to settlers and miners. While these lessons were not unknown, early surges of Overlanders largely ignored them—the sense of urgency demanded otherwise. Ironically, in the case of many Forty-Niners and the first rush of Fifty-Niners, their oversight was the opposite of "too much." Lack of adequate provisions was their undoing. Difficult to understand, apparently concern for winter weather, food, and shelter was nowhere in their thinking. "Going out to see the elephant" was sport for the nimble and "reason-enough" for the fool.

When President Polk validated the reports of gold in California, America east of the Mississippi and Missouri rivers was primed for another surge westward. The hardships of the mass exodus to Utah and Oregon were a vague memory if remembered at all. A second emigrant surge was not to be denied. This time, the pilgrims had advantages afforded by Mormon nation-builder and Oregon homesteader experiences, and a decade of prairie developments, if only they had taken time to profit from them. For the most part, they did not, the improved trail system being a notable exception. Comparing westering at the beginning of the 1840s, the end of the 1840s, and the start of the Fifty-Niners rush to Colorado proves the point.

A Great Babel. At times considered the best "jumping off" point for the major trails west, languages from around the world could be heard in the streets and shops of Independence, Missouri. Similar scenes were common in Westport and St. Joseph, strong competitors for emigrant and frontier business. *(Wikipedia)*

Stretching northward from Westport and Independence two hundred miles to St. Joseph and Council Bluffs, these early 1840s Missouri riverfront settlements nurtured and bid farewell to westbound caravans for two decades—the farther northwest the "jumping-off point," the longer one enjoyed the relative safety and comforts afforded by the States. In 1849, Westport was the preferred outpost for Overlanders convinced traveling due west was the shortest and therefore quickest route across the prairie. Those who understood the importance of better roads leading to the Platte River Valley and abundant water all the way to the mountains preferred Council Bluffs. Both Westport and Council Bluffs owed their popularity to Independence. [26]

As far as westering was concerned, in 1837 Independence was the end of civilized America. Its reason for existing was to serve Santa Fe and Rocky Mountain traders. Well-stocked general stores, stables, and skilled blacksmith shops nimbly adapted to the growing needs of wave upon wave of elephant seekers. Bagley portrays these "jumping-off points" in human terms requiring little imagination. [27]

"Parties of emigrants, with their tents and wagons, would be encamped on open spots near the bank, on their way to the common rendezvous at Independence," Francis Parkman wrote as he traveled up the Missouri River. Every store was adapted to furnish outfits, and "the public houses were full of Santa Fe men and emigrants. Mules, horses, and waggons at every corner." Hardy, good-looking emigrants; "piratical-looking Mexicans" in broad, peaked hats; black slaves; and Delaware, Wyandotte, Osage, Sac and Fox, Shawnee, and Kanza tribesmen crowded the busy streets.

J. Quinn Thornton called Independence "a great Babel upon the border of the wilderness." It's population of about one thousand in 1846 lived around the courthouse on the public square, but solid frame and brick homes were replacing log cabins....The town site was more than three miles from the Missouri River, which proved to be a disadvantage, and many Overlanders preferred to land a dozen miles upriver at Westport, a village that Parkman thought bore all the characteristics of the extreme frontier. The thirty or forty houses that made up this "border village" stood only a mile from the Missouri state line, and Westport was called "the usual rendezvous" for travelers bound for the Rocky Mountains as early as 1839.

Thirty miles upriver from Westport stood the army's great citadel of the West—Fort Leavenworth, established in 1827. Four miles above the fort and across the river, former dragoon Joseph Moore founded Weston, Missouri, in 1837, and both sites became starting points for overland emigration after a wagon train first set out from the fort in 1844. Weston was a much better place to start the journey, wrote James Carleton, who accompanied the military expedition that improved the wagon road from Forth Leavenworth to the Oregon Trail in 1845. As he pointed out, the road began at the extreme

AMERICAN MELTING POT

Nationalism and the lure of gold aside, the twin promises of opportunity and free-dom to pursue it created population pressures that only pushing beyond the cur-rent American frontier could relieve. Actually, a westering impulse influenced the American psyche long before patriots chartered the Thirteen Colonies, certainly before firing shots at Lexington and Concord. The 1840s experienced a notable resurgence with signs everywhere that interest in Polk's transcontinental country was popular. Once again, Will Bagley makes a complex subject clear with insightful citations. [28]

As Francis Parkman approached the Missouri frontier in 1846, he saw "signs of the great western movement that was then taking place": he felt the parties of emigrants he met represented "that race of restless and intrepid pioneers whose axes and rifles have opened a path from the Alleghenies to the western prairies." As a Boston patrician and an unabashed chauvinist, he also saw "some thirty or forty dark slavish-looking Spaniards, gazing stupidly out from beneath their broad hats," a band of Indians "belonging to a remote Mexican tribe," and French hunters from the mountains with their long hair and buckskin dresses."

Parkman later saw Pierre D. Papin's boats stranded on the Platte River—the prominent French-American trader was reclining on a pack of furs—and the young writer thought he was a "rough-looking fellow." But the appearance of the multinational workers manning the flatboats was equally singular: "The crews were a wild looking set," Parkman wrote, referring to the buckskin-clad French and American traders who had their "hair glued up" in Indian fashion, while "the oarsmen were Spaniards."

A stroller on the [Independence] courthouse square on any spring eve-ning in the 1840s might encounter silver-adorned Mexican traders in spurs and sombreros, English nobles bound for a safari on the Great Plains, black stevedores, Indians from tribes as far away as Mexico or Oregon, Protestant and Catholic clerics, fur-trade magnates from old French-American families, and mountaineers on a spree. Five years later, westbound emigrants from virtually every state in the Union and most of the countries of Europe joined the crowd.

western bend of the Missouri and avoided the Kansas River and several other bad crossings and "those notoriously adroit and impudent thieves, the Kanzas Indians" on the Independence Road.

In 1843, Joseph Robidoux, then an old man but still "a very energetic, enterprising, shrewd manager," founded Saint Joseph near his sixteen-year old trading post in the Blacksnake Hills. Within a year of its birth, the boomtown began displacing Independence as the most popular outfitting depot. When John Minto passed through on his way to join the 1844 emigration, he found a mere village of two or three stores and a single hotel, but by early 1846 the town's boosters were promoting it as the most "favorable point at which to rendezvous, and where all their necessary outfits can be procured, at the least possible expense." By then the town had about a thousand inhabitants and thirteen large stores that could furnish "every article in the Grocery and Dry Good line that may be required for an outfit, at prices as cheap as the emigrant can bring in from St. Louis." Plenty of steamboats offered a passage to Saint Joseph for the same price as a ticket to Independence.

Whatever its benefits may have truthfully been, St Joseph thrived. Population doubled between 1846 and the beginning of the California gold rush. It doubled again before the frenzy ended a couple of years later. However, by then the "Independence Road" and the "St. Joseph Road" were major "highways" to the Platte River Valley and points west. According to Will Bagley, the "most popular jumping-off point shifted almost annually, but for three decades overland emigration was big business in the frontier towns along the Missouri." Not until post-Civil War reconstruction and completion of the transcontinental railroad system did

Horace Greeley. Fabled editor of the *New York Tribune*, Horace was not desk-bound despite his New York City attire. Upon visiting the Colorado goldfields, he became one of its most influential boosters. *(Mathew Benjamin Brady, Library of Congress)*

this change. Still, there were preconditions yet to be satisfied. Gold discovered in California was one; gold in the Colorado Rockies was another. These elephants aroused far more curiosity and fever than homesteads in Oregon or Mormon sovereignty in the Great Salt Lake basin.

Once on the Platte River trail, most emigrants encountered "French Indians." The French were predominant as western pathfinders. Descended from French, French-Canadian and Spanish families who were the earliest Mississippi watershed settlers, most were American citizens by 1840. Nevertheless, they lived so long among the tribes that they were as much Indian as not. Out of necessity or convenience, it mattered little. These men adopted indigenous customs as well as wives. By some estimates there were upwards of five thousand men west of the Mississippi, four thousand of French origin. Any doubt concerning their influence and contributions to "westering" should vanish in the face of the multitude of French names for towns, lakes, and waterways across the region. Influence, however, did not equate to admiration. Quite the opposite, non-French emigrants disdained the French-Indian and more often distrusted them intensely. They thought, and with some justice, that these men bore them no goodwill. Many believed the French encouraged the Native Americans to attack and cut them off. Such beliefs persisted for years. In 1851, Amelia Hadley complained, "the Indians are every day committing some depredation or other, they steal and rob from every train and those dirty french put them up to it." [29]

That said, there was some acknowledgement that the ability of these men to live peacefully among the tribes, facilitated by marriage, naturally entailed becoming as much like their hosts as possible. Moreover, as the need for waystations and ferries or bridges increased dramatically throughout the decade, often the French-Indians stepped forward to provide these services. Logistically, the only places emigrants could hope to resupply in 1840 were at three ramshackle outposts on the Laramie and Snake Rivers. Outposts increased with the continued flow of travelers, but never caught up. As the surge subsided, the number of outposts declined. By the time the Forty-Niners massed for their assault, resources along the way were not much better than the Mormons and Oregon homesteaders encountered a decade earlier.

To be fair, newcomers to the frontier did not regard Anglo-mountaineers much differently than the French-Indians. Bagley writes that Edwin Bryant estimated the "white" population of the Rocky Mountains in 1846 was five hundred to one-thousand, "scattered among the Indians or living like nomads around the trading posts." His opinion of white men with Native American wives was commonplace.

"Adventure, romance, avarice, misanthropy, and sometimes social outlawry, have their influence in enticing or driving these persons into this savage

wilderness," he concluded. They rarely returned to civilization except to visit. Many of them have Indian wives and large families. Polygamy is not uncommon. They conform to savage customs, and from their superior intelligence have much influence over the Indians, and frequently direct their movements and policy in war and peace." [30]

Mormon and Oregon homesteaders had much in common—Forty-Niners and Fifty-Niners marched to a different drummer. They fitted no common mold, but they sang common songs. Quite telling songs, at that—songs that in a few short lyrics captured both hope and despair.

> *On Poker Flat and Poor Man's Shack,*
> *Once more our luck we try,*
> *Where nuggets once were found as thick,*
> *As planets in the sky.*[31]

The gold-seekers represented a wide range of economic classes, races, ages, and nationalities. They also represented an astonishing quality of optimism. If fortune did not pan out in California, it would pan out elsewhere. Surprisingly perhaps, as common an attitude as this was, there were other motivations in play. To a person, testimonies boil down to "opportunity." Will Bagley's cast of eyewitnesses explain the matter well. [32]

> *Americans chose to abandon their homes in the East and brave the ordeals of the overland trails for reasons as varied as the "honest looking open harted (sic) people" themselves. One 1846 traveler noted that his companions all "agreed in the one general object—that of bettering their condition," but their individual hopes and dreams "were as various as can well be imagined."*
>
> *So were the emigrants themselves. Americans of all sorts crossed the plains—rich and poor, black and white, young and old. "Our party consisted of thirty wagons, 300 head of cattle and a lot of hands made up from Mexico, Ireland, England, Wales, France and Germany," wrote Joseph P. Hamelin, Jr., in 1857. "I took three ladies, purely out of charity." Before its story ended, the most famous of all California wagon trains, the Donner party, included Mexican and French frontiersmen; Miwok Indians; Irish, English, Belgian, and German emigrants; infants and elders; and Catholics, Protestants, Mormons, and perhaps an Austrian Jew.*
>
> *"Like a great many boys who have picked [up] novels I have read of the life of mountaineers. I was very conscious to make a trip across the plains so that I could Kill (sic) buffalo, etc., deer etc., and have a good time," recalled*

Antonio B. Rabbeson. "That was about all of my motive—a young fellows idea of adventure."

    Some wanted to see what had seldom been seen before. "My greatest pleasure in travelling through the country is derived from the knowledge that it has seldom been traversed, or at least never been described by any hackneyed tourist, that everything I see or look upon has been seen my me before it has become common by the vulgar gaze of description of others," Dr. Joseph Middleton observed....Some travelers left home seeking pleasure or profit, missionary Nicholas Point concluded, but "still others, of the age of the prodigal son, only to relieve their families of their unfortunate presence."

    Patriotism became increasing prominent as a motive in recollections. "My husband [was] fired with patriotism to help keep the country from British rule, and I was possessed with a spirit of adventure and a desire to see what was new and strange," Miriam Thompson Tuller recalled.

    Observers came to similarly diverse conclusions about why people exchanged settle life for such an unknown future. "Many were in pursuit of health. Some were actuated by a mere love of change; many more by a spirit of enterprise and adventure; and a few, I believe, knew not why they were on the road," Jessy Quinn Thornton recalled. He also noted that many were looking for a better climate or fleeing "pecuniary embarrassments"—and even as prominent a figure as Peter Burnett [first California governor] went to Oregon hoping to pay off his debts.

    Gabriel Brown took his six daughters—the "Belles of Oregon"—west in 1842 seeking better prospects for finding a husband.

    James Clyman concluded that such irrational risk taking [what drew Americans west] was simply part of American culture: "It is remarkable... and strange that so many of all kinds and classes of People should sell out comfortable homes in Missouri and Elsewhere pack up and start across such an emmence Barren waste to settle in some new Place of which they have at most so uncertain information but this is the character of my countrymen."

Courage alongside ignorance surely underpinned every traveler. Often unaware of their responsibility for basic provisions and self-sufficiency, they were also woefully shortsighted when it came to what a thousand miles of prairie entailed. Resupply depended on encountering Indian hunting parties, or more worrisome war parties, more in the mood to trade buffalo meat for manufactured goods than to take scalps. Forgetting essentials altogether was common but unforgivable. Only on the rarest of occasions would a fellow traveler share provisions more often than not inadequate for their own needs.

Finally, among the tens of thousands of emigres that crossed the Plains and another thousand miles of mountain and desert were the "unwashed" class of that day. Unwelcome in most circles, rightfully untrustworthy in many cases, nevertheless they too dreamed of a better life, and they too possessed redeeming qualities. When Commodore Robert Stockton called for volunteers to fight the Mexican War in California, some of these "rough-hewn emigrants" impressed Seaman Joseph T. Downey of the *U.S.S. Portsmouth* to write:

"Ragtag and Bobtail Class." Emigres from all stations in life melded into a hardy and resilient gold rush class that helped define "young America." Seemingly instant American patriots, they were quick to answer Commodore Stockton's call for volunteers. *(Wikipedia)*

Such a mass was never seen before by mortal man. They were literally the ragtag and bobtail of all Creation. Here they came, some with coats and some no coats—some with deer skin trowsers (sic) and some with awful looking things in the shape of trowsers, some with moccasins, some with Boots, some with shoes, and a great majority with no covering to their feet. In one thing they were uniform: they had good rifles and shocking Bad Hats. [33]

This "ragtag and bobtail" class melded effortlessly with every other class of émigré, apparently even society's elites, that survived the trek west. Surviving the journey created its own unique "melting pot." Honorary membership in the "Overlander Club" was assured even if material rewards were not. After all, there was no guarantee in life, no respect of persons among frontier hardships—all were simply ordinary men. Fortunately for young America, there were millions more just like them eager to come alongside. Will Bagley has done us all a great service by providing a just sample.

Notes—Chapter Three: Polk's Prize

[1] Everhart, *The Mining Frontier*, Forward.

[2] Bagley, *Overland West*, Vol. I, pgs. 387-389.

[3] Ibid., pg. 253.

[4] Ibid., pgs. 254-255.

[5] Ibid., pg. 287.

[6] Captain Thornton has the honor of commanding U.S. forces both in the first and last battles of the war. During the first engagement, the reason for declaring war on Mexico, survivors of his troop are imprisoned. Thornton's release led soon thereafter to loss of his life in the last engagement of the war. [Accounts vary concerning many details. For example, one history begins the war in late April 1846; Thornton was in command of seventy dragoons. The Mexican force was 2,000. Eleven dragoons died and fifty-two were imprisoned.]

[7] Bagley, *With Golden Visions Bright Before Them*, Vol. II, pg. 13. [Polk was not paranoid — he was well informed of much intrigue underway to organize an independent California.]

[8] Ibid., pgs. 13-14. [President Polk died in Nashville in the 1849 cholera epidemic that swept up the Mississippi and Missouri valleys and across the plains. Thousands upon thousands died—especially hard hit were the Plains Indians who added this blow to their existence to the growing list of other grievances that would eventually flash into open warfare.].

[9] Ibid., pg. 350. [Bagley's trading post count included "the fur company forts of Laramie, Hall, and Boise; and a few scattered independent operators such as Joseph E. Robidoux at Scotts Bluff, Bridger and Vasquez on Blacks Fork, and Pegleg Smith on Bear River. Four years later small trading stations were scattered from the Platte to the Pacific offering everything from Indian goods, to blacksmith services, to what Abigail Scott called 'a bottle of oh, be joyful.' Edmund Cavileer Hinde found trading stations 'started all along the road' over the Sierra; Daniel Budd described 'near a hundred trading posts' in Carson Valley alone. The prospect of profiting from the overland trade made parts of the road west look like a canvas strip mall. Frontier entrepreneurs lined the trail with huts, tents, hotels, groggeries, ferries, bridges, and gambling hells (sic) from beginning to end."] Hawgood, *First and Last Consul*, *"Hastings to Marsh Letter,"* 26 March 1846; *"Farnham to Marsh Letter,"* 6 July 1845, pgs. 23-24, 52. Cited by Bagley, Vol. I, pg. 253.

[10] Ibid., pg. 336.

[11] Native peoples were fond of "calling it the way they saw it". At first sight, "horses" were "four-foots." Spanish "conquistadors" probing the San Juan Mountains were "two-legged." Hawaiians among the first emigrants to the Pacific coastal region were "Blue Men."

[12] Bagley, Vol I., pg. 18.

[13] Ibid.

[14] Ibid., pg. 334.

[15] Ibid., pgs. 21-22.

[16] Ibid., pg. 22.

[17] Paul, Rodman W., *The Far West and the Great Plains in Transition 1859-1900*, pg. 24.

[18] Ibid., pg. 25.

[19] Ibid.

[20] Bagley, Vol. II, pgs. 16-17.

[21] Bagley, Vol. I, pgs. 85-90, 121.

[22] Ibid., pgs. 132-134.

[23] Ibid., pg. 135.

[24] Ibid.

[25] Ibid, pg. 135.

[26] [Council Bluffs, the region thereabouts having a military and trade history dating back to

Lewis and Clark, gained prominence during the Mormon and Oregon Trail emigrations. It served as an important outfitting site for travelers coming from northern locations.]

27 Bagley, Vol. I, pgs. 172-173.
28 Ibid., pgs. 70-71.
29 Ibid., pg. 74.
30 Ibid., pg. 75.
31 Everhart, Forward.
32 Bagley, Vol. I, pgs. 122-123, 125.
33 Ibid., pg. 128.

CHAPTER 4

Young America

Oh the Gold! The Gold!—they say
'Tis brighter than the day,
And now "tis mine, I'm bound to shine,
And drive dull care away." [1]

The westering impulse of young America had never before showed signs of weakness. With the benefit of well-worn wagon-roads to the Pacific, even the rumor of Colorado gold half as far from the States should have been a powerful incentive to hazard crossing the Great Plains. But it was not. The launch of the third and last mass migration in American history first required a prolonged nationwide economic depression, a decade more of Colorado placer finds, and a six-month long crescendo of gold quartz vein announcements. In the end, the irresponsible exuberance of the newspaper class was required to keep open the floodgates of humanity known as the Colorado gold rush. That would have to do—there would be no Presidential endorsements delivered to a fawning U.S. Congress. Nor would there be thousands of jubilant prospectors boasting of their finds. Instead, in contrast to the rush to California, of the tens of thousands who descended on Colorado's Front Range, less than a score of these pilgrims with no forethought to speak of would turn "Pikes Peak or Bust" on its proverbial head and redefine the nature of western mining prospects in the process. [2]

At the risk of making too much of the differences between the 1859 and 1860 "pilgrims" collectively referred to as the Fifty-Niners [America's third mass migration], the clearest example of the nation-building effects of America's manifest destiny is viewing the 1840 to 1860 period of westering as a twenty-year migration albeit executed in four distinct phases comprised of two general classes of society. Phase One was defined largely by families motivated by opportunities to establish prosperous new farms and communities in fertile Oregon Territory valleys. Their journey labored under the burden of wagons overloaded with all manner of provisions and materiel for homesteading. Phase Two and Phase Three were defined largely by single men traveling lightly by the quickest means affordable, sometimes even on foot. Reading the personal accounts of these men, the Forty-Niners and Fifty-Niners, it is easy to lose track of whether they are destined for California or Colorado. This is not surprising given that their journeys were barely a decade apart and the circumstances that account for their behavior were little changed over that span of time. Phase Four, beginning in 1860, looked a great deal like Phase One. By the spring of 1860 the 1858-59 Colorado gold rush had evolved into a more tempered occupation. Heavy wagons lumbered along in the place of carts and wheelbarrows and men on foot. Women and children accompanied the men. They still might have prospector dreams, but they were destined to become miners and settlers. Like their Oregon-bound soul mates, they also were destined to secure a place for their new homes in the American dream.

The Oregon-bound vanguard of farm families set in motion the transformation of the entire nation. In so doing, their sacrifices and accomplishments revealed a depth of character and commitment to a vision that came to be known as the "American Experience." More cryptic, the phrase "young America" also would gain traction. The discovery of California gold at Sutter's mill drew a second wave of adventurers with similar grit that further established a sense of national purpose. The collapse of Augustus Sutter's New Helvetia at the hands of hordes of treasure-seeking trespassers and the vast quantities of placer gold they found ensured American control of the far west.

As important as the sheer magnitude of the gold was to the national economy, the sheer audacity of the emigrants was more profound. Tens of thousands of ordinary, often quaint, albeit ill-prepared adventurers somehow persevered and transformed the landscape and culture surrounding transcontinental travel from the Missouri River valley to the Pacific Ocean. Will Bagley summarizes this epic change this way. [3]

> *In the American West, the California gold rush changed everything. More than any other single event, it permanently transformed the nature of transcontinental wagon travel. Unlike the handful of land-hungry pioneers who had opened the trails, these thousands of gold-seekers "came not to settle or build but to plunder." The Oregon Trail became the California Road. In addition to its enormous numbers, the great rush from 1849 to 1852 had characteristics that distinguished those who made the trek during those years from those who traveled the trails to the Pacific before and after. Previous migrations consisted mostly of farming families in which women and children often outnumbered the men, but the Forty-niners proved to be largely young males.*
>
> *Alongside a leavening of gamblers and criminals, they included a surprising number of educated professional men from respectable families—men who were bedazzled by the prospect of instant wealth, especially when contrasted with the limited opportunities available in the cash strapped economies of the South and Midwest.*

Commenting on the California emigrants in January 1849, the New York Herald *found them to be "remarkably orderly, respectable, and intelligent" and mourned the loss of "the finest portion of our youth."*

"It is surprising to see how many doctors are going to California," wrote William Rothwell. "Every train has 2 or 3. About every tenth man is a 'professional character.'"

Thirty wagons and 127 men formed Hagan Z. Ludington's Star Brilliant Company No. I, including "2 Physicians and Chemists; Blacksmiths, Carpenters, Wagon-makers, and tradesmen of every kind with tools of every description..."

Every age group joined the rush west. They came from virtually every state in the Union, and diarists reported Meeting Mexican, English, Irish, Norwegian, Continental French, and Italian emigrants, along with entire parties of "Dutch-men"— meaning anyone from Northern Europe.

Ordinary American men and women had accomplished all this pretty much on their own hook.... The United States government, [Edwin] Bryant observed, had long wanted to open the best possible routes to the Pacific and had even appropriated large sums of money for the task, but whatever had been accomplished in the way of exploration was due to the "indomitable energy, the bold daring, and the unconquerable enterprise, in opposition to every discouragement, privation, and danger, of our hardy frontier men and pioneers, unaided directly or remotely by the patronage or even the approving smiles and commendations of the government."

THE INDEPENDENT GOLD HUNTER ON HIS WAY TO CALIFORNIA.

Educated Professional Men. Among the "ragtag and bobtail class" were "the finest portion of our youth." Caricatures illustrating this also appear a decade later, adding colorful insight to the Fifty-Niners as well. *(Kellogg and Comstock, Buffalo Ensign & Thayer, c. 1850)*

Colorado's gold rush was populated in much the same way with pilgrims of similar background and bearing. The Forty-Niners exemplified what ordinary man could achieve. The Fifty-Niners demonstrated that Forty-Niner traits transcended time and place. Equally significant, critical to the success of the rush to Colorado was the direct contribution of a handful of individuals, California veterans among them, who demonstrated skills as well as character. Notable were our gold-savvy Cherokees who had pioneered a shortcut to California, sharp eyed enough to have spotted placer gold along the Front Range on their way, and who less than a decade later would snatch "Pikes Peak or Bust" from the "bust bin." They and a cohort of pathfinders like them rooted a frontier culture that enabled other ordinary pilgrims to establish permanent settlements including present-day Denver six hundred miles west of civilized Missouri.

These characteristics of nineteenth-century Americans were typical of an age during which self-reliance and independence were taken for granted. In fact, these characteristics were even more pronounced among immigrants from around the world. Imagine the courage and determination required to abandon every familiar aspect of life, board a ship of questionable seaworthiness, and disembark in a strange land crowded with people speaking foreign languages. Then, scarcely getting ones bearings, venturing farther afield, to the western frontier and beyond. Ordinary men and women in many respects, extraordinary to be sure.

How extraordinary did they have to be? Ovando James Hollister, miner and historian, as close to an eyewitness as one could hope to find, described the challenges they eagerly embraced in searching for their "elephant:"

> *At the time of which we are speaking—September 1858—there was little of that semblance of Tartaric civilization on the Plains which now [1867] characterizes them. Forts Riley and Santa Fe, Forts Kearney and Laramie, Salt Lake City and Camp Floyd, were about the only inhabited points. The first hunters for told (sic) at Pike's Peak had no smooth, hard road, with occasional stations occupied by the white man, to follow; no accompanying endless train of white-topped emigrant wagons and fleets loaded with merchandise. The Salt Lake mail passed them regularly until they struck the California crossing of the Platte [currently Julesburg, Colorado]. They met a small party from Cherry Creek once in a while, all of them with goose-quills or little vials of gold dust, which some of them called "the elephant," and were carrying home to show their friends, hoping thereby to save them a pilgrimage to the mountains to see it; others were going to use "the elephant" to obtain reinforcements.* [4]

Rodman W. Paul, far from being mistaken for an eyewitness, describes a far more hospitable environment confronting the Fifty-Niners. Clearly, both trails and destinations were much improved. However, Ovando Hollister's descriptions of everything else seem more consistent with the vast majority of first-hand accounts of those who survived the journey. Still, it is worth considering what Paul no doubt gets right.

By now travel across the plains was by well-worn trails. There had been an enormous change since the beginning of the California gold rush in 1849. From 1849 to 1860 some two hundred thousand westward-bound individuals had taken the trail to California, fifty-three thousand to Oregon, and nearly forty-three thousand to Utah. Trading posts or way stations had sprung up to serve them. Usually known as "ranches," these roadside places provided meals, liquor, supplies, wagon repairs, blacksmithing, fresh draft animals, and ferry or toll-bridge service across the rivers. "In 1859 and 1860 there were, literally, hundreds of supportive facilities en route," usually spaced twenty-five to thirty miles apart. Of course from Denver there was still a hard climb into the Rockies, and from Salt Lake City a four-hundred-mile haul north to Montana. New Mexico and Tucson drew their supplies by a different route, the famous old Santa Fe Trail. [5]

Whatever local discouragements there might be, in Colorado as in Montana and Idaho prospectors soon moved deeper into the mountains. Although even the passes in the Colorado Rockies were at altitudes of eleven thousand feet or more, both prospectors and the miners who followed them crossed the Continental Divide in 1859 and opened diggings on both slopes. Especially notable was California Gulch, on the headwaters of the Arkansas River, where some of the best diggings in Colorado developed at an altitude of ten thousand feet, despite the fierce winter storms and short working season that that altitude implied. Although thousands tried their luck along the ten-mile length of California Gulch in 1860 and 1861, and some succeeded handsomely, thereafter the fickle crowd abandoned California Gulch as decisively as they left comparable diggings in Idaho and Montana. [6]

So, how *was* the Pike's Peak gold rush birthed? Exactly how did it begin, and what accounted for the outbreak of gold fever that affected adventurers worldwide? Well, not exactly "worldwide." Ironically, another fifteen years was required before the fever swept through the San Juans a mere 250 miles away.

Not only did the rush to Colorado's Front Range benefit from Oregon settlers and the rush to California, not only did it benefit from being half the distance to the Pacific coast, it also benefited from the knowhow of a loose fraternity of former trappers and a small cadre of returning Forty-Niners. Whereas the Forty-Niners had a bitter and unhelpful John Sutter awaiting them, a few resourceful veteran mountain men and fledgling Denver entrepreneurs greeted the Fifty-Niners with prospecting and survival skills, and without exception a hot meal.

The Colorado rush also benefited from the early placer finds of our family of Georgia Cherokees, and the soon realization that the placer sources were mother-lodes of untold wealth. To say that these gold finds were the sparks that ignited the third mass migration westward is no exaggeration. But early discoveries would not be sufficient — they were simply the life-blood of rumors. No, at minimum, a tightly knit series of paying quantities of gold discoveries were required, followed in short order by persistent clarion calls. In the case of "Pikes Peak or Bust," also required was a mountain man turned Denver entrepreneur, and a failed Lawrence, Kansas expedition that managed in the nick of time to demonstrate redemptive qualities. First the clarions.

The most influential of a long list of clarions was John Cantrell. Flawed in many ways, his first failure as a clarion was geography. He persuaded many that a gold field surely existed, but he failed to mention it was nowhere near Pikes Peak. Locating gold discoveries at Pikes Peak, western Kansas Territory at the time, was the creation of eastern newspaper editors who never witnessed a western sunset much less a Colorado mountain. Another quarter century would pass before anyone found Pikes Peak gold. Instead, paying quantities of gold were located in tributaries of present day Denver's South Platte River including Cherry Creek, Clear Creek flowing through Clear Creek Canyon west of Golden, and Ralston Creek. The surge of prospectors, traders, merchants and flim-flam artists eventually drawn to these sites quickly led to organizing the cities of Denver and Golden, the Colorado Territory in 1861, and the State of Colorado in 1876. Those drawn to prospects near Pikes Peak, and who predictably remained empty-handed through autumn, joined the "go-backers" and "hum-bug" choir angrily trying to explain away their western foolishness.

As misguided as it was to promote Pikes Peak sixty miles south of Cantrell's boast, doing so was understandable. "Cherry Creek or Bust" was never going to

Pike's Peak Bust. Pike's Peak was a bust, but Cherry Creek was not. The Colorado gold rush was real and soon was renamed to reflect where gold was being discovered. The better prepared, or better endowed, gold-seeker enjoyed the relative comforts afforded by "covered wagons" and companionship. *(Miners' Hand-Book, 1859)*

catch on regardless of the fact that Cherry Creek sported the gold. In defense of Pikes Peak, its notoriety at 14,110 feet above sea level and location midway between the Arkansas and South Platte River routes to the Rockies, served as a reassuring harbinger of a hard prairie journey nearly done. On a clear day, its snowcap was a visible beacon reflecting sunlight a hundred miles across the prairie. The nation also firmly and widely enshrined it in Rocky Mountain lore dating back nearly a half-century to Lieutenant Zebulon Montgomery Pike's Colorado expedition. Oft challenged—Zebulon never set foot on the mountain—"Pike" stuck, reinforced periodically by officialdom, poetry and prose. "Pike" had gravitas, so did "Pikes Peak or Bust."

"Ralston Creek" also stuck, as did the 1850 accounts of gold Lewis Ralston discovered there. What did not stick were the 1848 Cherokee discoveries in the south Platte basin. Doing so would have helped put Pikes Peak into perspective, but little did it matter in the end. With the benefit of hindsight, Ovando Hollister picked up the story in early 1859 and explained the preponderance of evidence emerging in support of a Front Range gold field worth risking life and limb to exploit. The deciding factor was uncovering the sources of the placer gold, crumbs swept from the King's table. Gold-bearing quartz was the main course, the proverbial mother lode, proof that the region was a treasure trove. George Jackson, John Gregory and Green Russell would earn the bragging rights in this regard. Hollister explains:

> On Ralston Creek, a small tributary of Clear Creek, diggings were opened and worked with considerable success [by Green Russell]. The creek bars were a mass of boulders of all sizes, and it was soon observed that the gold always occurred in scales, like flattened shot. From this it was inferred that it and the boulders came from a long distance in the Mountains, and from the same place.
>
> Gold had already been struck in the mountains, too, at that time. It was about the end of January that B.F. Langley lighted upon some placer or bar-diggings in a gulch on South Boulder Creek, which was full of fallen timber. Hence the name "Deadwood Diggings." By the end of March, quite a number of men were engaged at Deadwood, and considerable gold was being taken out.
>
> About the first of April, George Jackson, with a party of men from Chicago, struck gold at the mouth of a branch of South Clear Creek, near what is now Idaho [Springs], which branch they named "Chicago Creek," after their home. The diggings were called "Jackson Diggings."
>
> And now we have arrived at the discovery which at once settled the fortunes of the Pike's Peak community in the minds of everybody in it capable of reasoning from facts. The discovery of the lode called after himself, by John H. Gregory, would seem to rank among those great events whereby the race at large has profited. [7]

What Hollister went on to explain was not only one of those "great events of the race," as he put it, it also was an account of divine appointments far more gratifying than thinking of them as coincidences. John Gregory's blessing was just such an example and astounded even Hollister.

That in a section of broken mountains, extending the whole length and one-third the width of the United States, a man, enroute *for a distant country [Frazier River, British Columbia], should have been diverted in the midst of his journey two hundred miles to the south, should have proceeded directly to the spot—a ravine two or three miles in length—and in it and on its bordering hills have struck the heart of as rich and extensive gold, silver, and copper mines as are known in the world, is indeed marvelous.* [8]

Nearly a decade had slipped away between Lewis Ralston's Front Range placer find and John Gregory's mother lode Hollister described. Between these bookend-events rests the story of how Colorado's gold rush was birthed. Had Ralston not been lured back to his namesake Creek by continued rumors of gold in the Colorado Rockies and encouragement from needy family and friends, chances were that his five dollars of 1848 gold would never have risen above just another rumor. Ralston Creek would have taken on someone else's name. Like Ralston, others located gold and proved it when trading for provisions at frontier outposts, but even when able to describe where they panned it [often not the case], curiosity and interest in joining the hunt was not aroused. That required gold-bearing quartz.

It was only natural and nearly a Cherokee family duty that Lewis Ralston, Green Russell, and Pastor John Beck returned to the Front Range together. Unlike Ralston and Green, Beck was not a prospector. He was an adventurer who became a scout when he was not a Pastor. He learned the ways of the Plains Indians and how to pass through their lands unharmed. He also learned humility and was

William Greenberry Russell. Given name aside, "Green" was what he answered to. His July 1858 placer gold find marked a pivotal moment in the ultimate success of the Colorado gold rush. His expertise was honed in California gold fields, but had its birth in Georgia in 1829 in the heart of the Cherokee homeland, thus explaining why the Cherokee were well-equipped to play key roles in both western gold rushes. *(Harper's New Monthly Magazine, June to November 1879)*

never heard complaining about the blessings of others. A party to many gold strikes, John Beck was claimant of none.

Indian countryman by marriage ideally seated Beck in the midst of communications among "Sutters Mill Jennie," "Lick-Log Elizabeth," and Tahlequah wife Emily. In 1848, he was indispensable to Captain Evans. In 1850, Captain Clement Van McNair valued his prairie savvy and Cherokee Trail experience. In 1850, Beck witnessed Lewis' epic Ralston Creek find. In 1858, Green Russell and

GREEN RUSSELL

William Greenberry Russell was his given name. Too awkward for even his family, he responded better to "Green." Green spent his childhood more in Lumpkin County forests and gold mines than in schools. His father James was a gold miner and so were all his brothers. Green was the oldest of four boys, all of them miners from an early age. He was a young teenager when his father died and left the family "without means." According to Cousin J. H. Pierce, who joined him on Rocky Mountain hunting trips and prospecting adventures in California and later in Colorado,

> He and the other boys worked in the mines in Lumpkin County, Georgia, and made the support for the family. He married when about 28 years old. He left his wife and children in Georgia when he went to California. He did well there, and bought a good farm when he came back, and also (sic) some Negroes. His family still owns part of the place and lives there. [9]

W. L. Steele, another one of Russell's prospecting companions, recalled his pluck.

> I was well acquainted with Green Russell and I have always regarded him as an able, trustworthy and honorable man. He has often conversed with me about his early days; he told me once that he went to the Georgia mines when only a child. Mining always had a fascination for him, and his skill and ability in this line can be inferred from the fact that he was placed in charge of a mine in Dahlonega when but 17 years of age and retained the positon until he resigned to join the California rush in 1849. His mother was a poor widow with several children and Green Russell's labors supported the family.
>
> In 1849, he was infected by the California fever, and made the journey overland, accompanied by his brother John. He followed the Santa Fe Trail, along the Arkansas, until it turned south; he then cut across to the northwest for the Platte and struck Cherry Creek at about the point where Denver is now located. He prospected Cherry Creek and several other streams in that vicinity. In due course of time he arrived in California, where his knowledge of mining enabled him to accumulate several thousand dollars in a few months. [10]

Ralston again relied upon him to get them back to the "Cherry Creek Region," Ralston Creek and soon named Russell Gulch.

In the fall of 1858, in Dry Creek Gulch a short distance from Ralston Creek, with Pastor Beck and Lewis Ralston nearby, Green Russell discovered gold. In fact, his discovery was better than gold, it was gold-bearing quartz. It was the mother lode of the Ralston and Dry Creek gold float. Dry Creek Gulch was renamed Russell Gulch and gave camp followers reason to claim his lode was Colorado's first. Green Russell was no egotist and cared less. Likewise, Lewis Ralston never claimed his 1850 gold find was first—much later others would make that claim on his behalf. Instead, throughout the winter both men were focused on survival and selling their "mines" to the highest bidders.

Organizing an expedition in 1858 was dangerously close to being late to the treasure hunt. True, rumors were unmotivating, but enough of them eventually were self-fulfilling. Early 1858 marked that tipping point. Green Russell's Party found gold quartz and John Cantrell sounded the trumpet call. By September, amazingly within just a few short weeks, the region was crowded with newcomers. They staked their claims with stone monuments as prolific as "prairie dog mounds." [11]

Green was undisputed Captain of the team, but John Beck and Lewis Ralston did their part. They guided the party to Ralston Creek without incident. Now it was up to Green Russell to make something out of nothing. He was not shy about tackling challenges. A Georgia gold miner at age fifteen, he hunted in the Rocky Mountains with his Oklahoma cousins years before crossing the prairie was commonplace. Nor did he hesitate leaving home for California in 1849 with the first wagon train out of Lumpkin County, Georgia.

Green returned to his home in Georgia by steamship from San Francisco around Cape Horn to the States in 1850. One can only imagine the impressions of such an adventure he carried with him the balance of his life. He bought two farms on the Ettowah River, one for his mother and one for his family. Still restless and certainly ill disposed to farm life, he soon gathered his brothers together and departed on a second trip to California. They returned to Georgia after this second expedition with $8,000 to $10,000 each for their troubles.

Back in Lumpkin County, Russell, like Ralston, returned not to gold mining but to farming. The era of Georgia gold mining was all but gone. Along with his Cherokee neighbors long since relocated to Oklahoma, and despite being white, his ownership of land also was all but gone. Somehow, he retained the title to his farm that supported his Cherokee wife and thirteen children. Green Russell never owned any of the gold mines he worked, but he learned what gold-bearing minerals looked like and how to retrieve them. His Georgia experience paid dividends in the California gold fields, enough to become a Lumpkin County squire. Prospering with the landed gentry of his county filled his larder, but did nothing to fill a longing for adventure in his heart. According to friend Steele,

Green had a restless, roving disposition, and farming was distasteful to him. Immediately upon returning to his home after this second journey to California, he purchased a wagon and a span of mules and soon converted the wagon into an ideal camping outfit. He then proceeded to gather up the boys from neighboring farms and took them up to the mountains on hunting and fishing excursions. When his companions had to return to their farming duties he would drive them home and immediately proceed to get together another party for another outing. He excused this seeming indolence by affirming that he was not a farmer, that when he was away from home his wife and the Negroes attended to things intelligently, but when he was around they looked to him for advice and directions upon matters foreign to his tastes and training.

On one of these hunting excursions he excited the sporting blood in his companions' veins by relating his knowledge of and experiences with big game east of the Rockies and incidentally suggested that gold diggings might be found in the mountains. The party agreed to start on the trip across the plains the following spring (1858) for the purpose of having one season's good sport and to test their luck at mining. [12]

William Steele's portrayal of Green is revealing. As a young man in the 1840s, Green was comfortable crossing the prairie simply to catch trout and hunt big game in the mountains. Imagine how the prospect of gold motivated him in 1849. He was quick to find his way to California in search of it. Soon after returning to Georgia, he resumed visiting Colorado on hunting and prospecting adventures. In February 1858, he organized his last expedition hoping, as was his nature, that it would be epic in its consequences. His Lumpkin County party consisted of eight other Georgians, his three brothers — John R., J. O., and Dr. T. J. — and six companions including neighbor Lewis Ralston. He enlisted cousin Pierce and of course John Beck along the way. Like Brown on Ralston's 1850 expedition, Pierce also turned out to be a scribe. Shortly after departure, Luke Tierney joined the party. He, too, was a scribe, and wrote a decent "guidebook" to prove it. Both eyewitnesses offered a rare opportunity to draw close to one of the first Fifty-Niners and the times in which he lived. [13]

Pierce was family. Luke Tierney was a stranger but bonded with Green Russell on the Santa Fe Trail. He joined the Russell/Ralston Party at Rock Creek, Kansas Territory, on May 16, 1858. Tierney with two others were warmly welcomed into the group. Three additional pilgrims brought the total armed contingent to "20 men, 4 wagons, 10 yoke of cattle and 3 horses." [14]

On June 3, 1858, the Russell/Ralston/Tierney Party rendezvoused on the Santa Fe Trail with John Beck's Tahlequah troop, bringing the expedition to "70 men, 14 wagons, 33 yoke of cattle, 2 horse teams and about 20 ponies." [15] On June 22, the party reached the headwaters of present-day Cherry Creek. After a one-day lay-bye and another difficult day crossing the flood-swollen Platte River, they camped on Ralston Creek. On June 25, Tierney recorded in his journal that the group now consisted of "104 men from different sections, Georgia 10, Missouri 27, Cherokee Nation 58." [16] The numbers did not add up to 104, but Tierney did not claim to be a mathematician. Neither did anyone seem to mind that competing strangers banded together. Strength in numbers was more important than competitors crowding the creek banks. Competition notwithstanding, the talk about camp was always about gold, or the lack thereof. Up Ralston and Clear Creek Gulches, they scratched away at the banks and bars and panned the gravel, returning at dusk with little to show for their efforts.

Unknown to the Russell party, Green's reputation for a nose for gold preceded him. How this could happen on a sparsely populated 1850s frontier remains a mystery. What was clear, town folks noticed the comings and goings of strangers stocking up in Missouri frontier settlements, especially if they were already burdened with livestock, wagons and provisions for prospecting. According to historian Frank Hall, when Green accompanied by his Cherokee brothers departed Independence, Missouri, his purpose and general destination was an open secret.

Soon after they had passed through Missouri and Kansas, companies were formed in those States to follow the trail of the Georgians, whose purpose in the expedition had become known, and if possible head them off before they should have staked out and occupied all the richer gold mines. The first company of Kansans left Lawrence in May, 1858, and having reached the Arkansas River where Pueblo now stands, celebrated the Fourth of July, the first observed as a great national anniversary on that remote frontier. [17]

First out of the gold rush chute, the Lawrence Party deserved credit for their foresight and intelligence gathering. Beating Green to the gold was not one of their accomplishments. Not only was present-day Pueblo far from Ralston Creek and Russell's gold-quartz lode, navigating the final leg of their journey was nothing any gold rush expedition should have had to endure. [Their notoriety did reach a level that secured them a place in "Fifty-Niners history."] At the same time, Green Russell and company continued to experience their own setbacks as more adventurers mobilized in their wake. Luke Tierney, Green Russell and Jim Pierce prospected up Clear Creek gulch. Others in their bloated party struggled up Ralston Creek, explored lesser gulches, or trudged much farther afield and panned the banks of the Boulder, Big Thompson and Bear Creeks, all to little avail. Many were slow to realize that there was no easy fortune in placers, but there was always reason to be hopeful. If there was "fine sifted gold" in the watershed, surely there was a mother lode somewhere upstream.

While the Lawrence Party celebrated the Nation's birth near present-day Pueblo, Tierney's journal entries for July 3 and July 4 were far from celebratory.

On the evening of the third of July ... the company all assembled together for consultation... all were silent... considering whether to return home without

*further search or remain and risk further disappointment…. Sunday, July 4,
the greater part of our company …. was making active preparations to return
to their homes.* [18]

Sure enough, according to Tierney, the next morning a large part of the
Cherokee and Missouri contingents "took their departure" for the Platte River. They
had all they could stand of weeks of backbreaking work in frigid water with little to

LEWIS RALSTON

Abandoning his second attempt to find gold in the Rocky Mountains on July 5,
1858, Lewis Ralston found circumstances awaiting him in Lumpkin County no more
encouraging. Happy to be home with Elizabeth and the children, he was not happy
to see the plantation lifestyle he grew up with threatened by northern abolitionist
politics and literature. The election of Abraham Lincoln in November 1860 without
a single Electoral College vote from eleven southern states signaled that civil war
was imminent. Three months before the inauguration of the President-elect, South
Carolina declared it was seceding from the Union. On January 19, 1861, Georgia,
Florida, Mississippi and Alabama did likewise. A month later, the Confederate States
of America elected Jefferson Davis President. On April 14, 1861, Fort Sumter built
on an artificial island in Charleston harbor, following a brief bombardment surrendered to Confederate forces.

    On August 1, 1863, at age fifty-nine, Lewis Ralston enlisted in the Confederate
Army as a Private. He had responded to local calls for volunteers to counter the
threat of General Sherman's advancing Union forces. On September 19-20, 1863,
Lewis' 11th Battalion of Georgia State Militia fought in the Battle of Chickamauga,
the first Civil War battle on Georgia soil. As was the case with many families on
both sides of the conflict, Ralston's oldest son, Lewis Jr., was a Union soldier. Having
married and moved to Mount Vernon, Missouri shortly after Lewis Sr. returned
from the Front Range, he had joined the Union Army three months after his father's
enlistment in the 11th Battalion. Whether either father or son knew of each other's
allegiances is unknown. Also unknown is whether either saw combat during the
Battle of Chickamauga, much less faced one another.

    Private Ralston remained in the Confederate Army until war's end. He returned
to a farm and home in shambles He worked to restore what he could, but gave
up and in 1870 moved sixty miles away to Whitfield County. No official records
exist, but family lore is Lewis and Elizabeth were buried in Whitfield County in
1875 and 1898 respectively. Lewis Jr. mustered out of the Union Army July 1, 1865.
Recognizing the benefits of his Cherokee heritage, he and wife Eliza relocated to the
new Cherokee Nation in Oklahoma. On January 8, 1880, at age forty-three, Lewis
Jr. declared his allegiance to the Cherokee Nation and received an allotment of land
on which he lived the remainder of his life. [19]

show for their labors. Nearly losing all of their supplies trying to re-cross swollen Clear Creek, they regrouped and continued home on the northern route. According to J. H. Pierce writing some years later, Green was not having any of that.

> *Green Russell, though a man of iron nerves, was shocked to see his cherished scheme about to become a failure… he said, "Gentlemen you can all go but I will stay if but two men will stay with me." Only 12 men stepped forward, including his brothers and cousins, and all the balance went home.* [20]

Missing among the thirteen lion-hearts was Pastor Beck. His duties fulfilled—organizing a formidable Tahlequah force, scouting Green's Party through Indian Territory to the Front Range, presiding over Sabbath rest—he too was over the thrill of it all. Beck returned to his family and flock in Tahlequah. Also missing was Lewis Ralston. Worn out trying to recover enough float to justify the effort, and frustrated trying to locate the quartz veins from which it came, and what he knew from experience was the real prize, Lewis joined Beck.

Green had every reason to join his home-bound friends save for his indomitable spirit, a spirit that no doubt explained his reputation for finding gold whenever he chose to look for it. The twelve who stood with him, largely family and scribe Tierney, believed in him. They bid adios to their compatriots and pushed farther up Clear Creek. [21] As was so often the case, what a difference a day could make. Tierney journaled:

> *Marched up the Platte (west) in the direction of the mountains.….on the very day the last party deserted us… we found the first cheering prospect of gold – the diggings yielding about $10 a day for each hand.* [22]

Cousin Pierce also remembered that day. With highly discouraged fellow Georgians, some four miles up the Platte Canyon, they unearthed about ten cents worth of gold, but that was all the encouragement they needed. From that spot, and two miles farther up Dry Creek, Green and company recovered about $300 worth of gold. According to Pierce, writing in 1905, forty-five years after the fact, "those discoveries on the Platte and Dry Creek were all that we made, of any note, in 1858." [23]

Twenty-five years after the fact, Pierce was more talkative when he reported his recollections to the *Rocky Mountain News*. Green Russell had started up the Platte toward the mountains, prospecting along the way. Most of the company had passed ahead of their wagons—Russell was behind them.

> *When about four miles up the river I saw a bank which looked as if it might contain gold. I stopped, got a pan of the dirt and gravel and began panning it out. I was about half through when Green Russell came up, took the pan and*

Dreaming of Home. Prospecting was hard work with little or no reward. Most "go-backers" did so within weeks of reaching Colorado's Front Range, certainly when their provisions ran out. The few who remained, and many who came the following season, found less taxing ways to profit, often by dishonest means. *(Thayer, 1887)*

finished it. It contained ten cents. "Run ahead, boy," he said, "and call the others back, our fortune is made." Being only twenty-one years old, I was the kid of the party, so I went and brought back the others, when we went into camp. We made a rocker out of a cottonwood log, and the first day obtained about six dollars in gold dust. These diggings were not very rich, however, but in prospecting around we discovered some dirt on Dry Creek, some three or four miles from the Platte, from which we took three ounces the first day. These diggings paid very well, and from all of them we secured some $600 to $700 during the summer. [24]

Once again, Green Russell had lived up to his gold-finding reputation. Not only the dollar value, but also the nature of the gold cheered them. The "drifted gold," not as promising as a gold quartz lode, nevertheless signaled that a quartz lode was the likely nearby source of their good fortune. Ten days later, another pocket panned twelve dollars to eighteen dollars per man, and a third pocket worked ten days yielded similar values. Clearly, persistence was a virtue. Historian LeRoy Hafen named this third site "Placer Camp," later known as Montana City. Today, all that remains of Montana City is an historical plaque on Dry Gulch/Little Dry Creek in present-day Englewood, Colorado. Englewood abuts present-day Denver. [25]

Ovando Hollister embellished the account, writing that a small dry creek that put into the Platte seven miles south of the mouth of Cherry Creek attracted Russell's attention. It was a decent "prospect" that

*one evening rewarded their labors and enlivened their hopes. They dug large
holes in the wet sand, put their "rockers" down in them, and dipping in water
with cups washed out in a few days several hundred dollars' worth of gold. As
soon as they got to work, some of the party returned to Kansas with the news.
Pike's Peak was the nearest notable natural object, and so the new gold field –
the "Dorado" of many feverish dreams – took its name from that.* [26]

But "enlivened hopes" were fleeting. Fairly well left to their own devices
would not last long. What remained of the Russell Party enjoyed the seclusion of
the mountain frontier until the last day of July when horsemen rode into camp.
Accounts vary, but common to them all was John Cantrell from Westport. Cantrell
was an Indian trader and Army supplier. While at Fort Laramie, Wyoming, he
had learned that white men were prospecting on the Platte River. Always alert to
opportunity, he and his companions rode south, no short distance, to investigate
and locate what turned out to be Green's camp. Imagine the tense atmosphere
surrounding that first conversation between Russell and Cantrell. Russell was
curt but respectful. Cantrell was condescending but inquisitive. Wise to the ways
of prospectors, rather than rely on the testimony of his newfound "friends," John
Cantrell settled in for a stay. In the end, with Russell's blessings or otherwise,
Cantrell took the liberty of carrying off a sack of pay dirt when he broke camp.
Pierce remembered Cantrell this way:

> *While we were working on Dry Creek, a man named Cantrell, who had
> made a trip from the Missouri river to Fort Laramie alone, came along on his
> way home and camped with us. He saw our dust and asked for a bushel or so of
> the dirt. We gave it to him, and when he reached home at Westport, he panned
> it out and published the results, with an affidavit setting forth the facts just
> recounted. This was late in the fall of 1858, and is what started the gold hunt-
> ers in such crowds across the plains.* [27]

Expected or not, the bonafide results of the assay of Front Range samples
was the critical difference between just another rumor and good reason to rush
there. Cantrell's gift of gab also helped fuel the boom.

Russell, too, was wise to the ways of prospectors, and of frontier traders. Men
like Cantrell were not lily-livered main street shopkeepers, they were hardened
adventurers accustomed to having matters go their way. Even if Cantrell did not
return, treasure-seekers like him would. It was only a matter of time before his
solitude would end. His good fortune shared "in confidence" would spread like
wildfire. With little discussion necessary among Russell's party, plans changed.
Rather than rest on their laurels, the thirteen die-hards divided into small groups
and set out to locate the motherlode or at least richer placers. Sure enough, when
the thirteen rendezvoused at their Platte River and Cherry Creek basecamp on

September 20, 1858, they found company had arrived in time for dinner. John Cantrell's assay had pleased Westport adventurers, now Green Russell neighbors.

Exhausted, short on provisions, and no doubt discouraged by how quickly company had arrived, now even Russell was ready to return home. With $500 to $700 [accounts vary] of gold among them, Green's partners divided into three groups and broke camp for the winter. Green, brother Oliver and cousin Jim Pierce rode back to Georgia. If their original intent was returning to Georgia farm life, the long ride provided time for reflection. Most likely, they only contemplated a short visit. By Christmas, they were all about re-provisioning and recruiting more men for a return trip.

The second party included Levi Russell, Tierney the scribe, William McFadding and William McKimmons. They rode south to Fort Garland to buy supplies, reportedly paying with Levi's gold watch. The five remaining men, along with some of their newfound friends—the customs of the day did not consider them trespassers—built a double log cabin at the confluence of Cherry Creek and the Platte River. By the time Levi and company returned with supplies to the only structure on the site, plans for a town already danced through their heads. Named for gold and their Lumpkin County home, they birthed Auraria. As also was the custom of the day, it only took a few discontents to organize competing town companies, St Charles being one of them. Why not—did not they pioneer their way across the prairie, too? November 22, 1858 witnessed renaming St. Charles as Denver City in honor of Kansas Governor Denver, a politically wise gesture. In the foothills, Arapahoe City morphed into Golden. Idaho Springs, Black Hawk, Central City, Breckinridge and points west soon followed. To the north, still others incorporated Boulder. In just three short months, from John Cantrell's unwelcome arrival in Russell's camp to town building on the Front Range, the exploitation of the Rocky Mountain "Mineral Belt"[28] was underway. Still missing were other essential preconditions required for sustained life such as location of the mother lodes, settlers, machinery, roads and railroads. More critical still, missing was a reliable supply of everyday provisions. Also missing was the often comical, nearly tragic Lawrence party.

The Lawrence party, delayed by one misjudgment after another, misguided from the outset, fairly represented another major class of Fifty-Niner. Admirable and at the same time odd was their demeanor and resilience in the face of failure and fraud. Equally noteworthy was their finesse at wheedling their way into competing companies racing to the goldfields. Perhaps most important of all, accounts of their journey provided westering insight into three emerging and divisive national social movements. Feminism that doubled the voter pool, environmentalism that put conservation of natural resources in conflict with exploiting them, and abolition of slavery that would require a civil war to resolve were on the verge of transforming the frontier West along with the entire nation. These movements also transformed the Lawrence party from just another crazed bunch of gold-seekers into a dynamic microcosm of mid-nineteenth century society. In the backwaters of all this, collectively, they also earned a place in Fifty-Niner history. At the end of their chaotic journey to the Cherry Creek diggings, they contributed greatly to the remnant that saved Denver.

Described by ignorant souls as "a group of promoters," considered colorful characters if not misfits by those who knew them best, the Lawrence party initially numbered forty-eight men, two women and a child. Not blessed with a leader of stature or bravado, there was no one worthy of the title "Captain." Absent a respected "Captain," the train took the name of its origin. "Lawrence," a fledging Kansas territorial outpost striving to become the preeminent gateway to the west, would have to do.

Failing to recruit a Captain, a scout was more important than ever. Fall Leaf was that man. Blessed with the services of a seasoned Indian scout, or so they thought, the Lawrence Party finalized plans to head west. Fall Leaf's tepee was across the Kansas River from Lawrence on the new Delaware Indian Reservation. Lawrence also was the home of the U.S. Army's First Cavalry. The First Cavalry patrolled the Rocky Mountain Front Range from Fort Laramie to the Arkansas River valley. Fall Leaf was their lead scout when he felt up to the task. He knew the Front Range well, or said he did.

In 1858, the citizens of Lawrence finally mastered their skepticism over one Rocky Mountain gold rumor after another when Fall Leaf returned from a patrol with a handkerchief full of gold nuggets. He testified he found them near Pike's Peak. He tickled the fancy of all willing to hear him out with the announcement that he was prepared to guide wagon trains to the mother lode. The Lawrence party took him up on his offer.

By May of 1858, thirty-five men had signed up for just such a Front Range treasure hunt. The enlistees included an attorney, two merchants, a typesetter, a telegrapher, and a civil engineer who insisted on bringing his surveying instruments. Intending to rely on pack mules, Fall Leaf demonstrated some wisdom and salesmanship by persuading the wannabe prospectors that they needed wagons to transport not just all the provisions they would require, but all the gold they would find. In possession of a "certificate of honesty,"—a document common for the day signed by a military officer stating the bearer was trustworthy—Fall Leaf claimed that the Pike's Peak region was a "veritable open-pit mine." Fall Leaf assured all who would listen, "not the sands only, but the rocks and earth for miles around are studded—nay filled—with particles, nuggets, even boulders of purest gold." [29]

The Lawrence party accepted Fall Leaf's advice, purchased eleven wagons with oxen and mule teams, and filled them with six months of provisions, revolvers, Bowie knives and Sharp rifles. Initially the party included veteran Forty-Niner John Tierney and his brother Luke who soon secured his place in history as Green Russell's scribe. Some evidence suggested that John Tierney was "Captain

Harbinger of Civil War, May 1856. Founded by abolitionists associated with the New England Emigrant Aid Company, Lawrence was the center of pro- and anti-slavery violence from its beginning until the 1863 Lawrence massacre by Quantrill's Confederate raiders. The Lawrence Party departed for Colorado gold fields late May 1858, no doubt manned with both factions more interested in prospecting than settling the slavery issue that would soon destroy their home town. However, abolitionist Julia and "Little Hornet" Holmes did fit in well given their aggressive attitudes and low if any priority given to gold prospecting. *(State Historical Society of Missouri)*

of the train," but if that was ever the case, the honor was short-lived. Tierney did not serve long, if at all, no one more thankful for that than John. A more reliable account is Brother Luke's trail journal in which he recorded that the Tierneys joined Green Russell at Rock Creek, Kansas on May 16, 1858.

Tierney's departure did not distress the Lawrence party for long. They still had Fall Leaf. The cohort was small and lacked cohesiveness, but Fall Leaf exuded confidence and his advice rang true. Finally, all was ready the third week of May, except for Fall Leaf. On the appointed morning of departure, he was a no-show. Eventually located, and after enduring many excuses, the search team lost patience. Reportedly, he was too drunk, too battered from a brawl, too fearful of Plains Indians, or all three, to travel. Regrouping, the party hastily selected George Smith to lead them southwest to the Santa Fe Trail without the Tierneys or an Indian scout. Only the Tierneys and Fall Leaf were wise enough to care. The balance of the train was just happy to be underway. After all, what more could go wrong? More to the point, they would never catch up with this Green Russell fellow with the Midas touch and his Cherokees if they delayed much longer.

Camped west of Lawrence in various states of disarray were a growing number of pilgrims and vagabonds looking for compatible mates willing to form up a train. If unable to join a train coming down the trail, eventually they would amass enough other "rejects" and courage to form their own party. Several weeks had slipped away since Green Russell's party passed them by. He did not appeal to any of them—they may not have appreciated who he was—but none of them appealed to Green. Most likely, Green was satisfied with those already in his care. In any event, he knew where he was going and how to get there, and they did not.

Nearly a month later, the Lawrence party was finally underway. Now impatient to a fault, these "rejected roadside pilgrims" liked the looks of any troop that would have them and the Lawrence party would certainly do. Leader Smith thought likewise of the roadside pilgrims. Anyone with a lick of sense would have valued strength in numbers at least until they crouched shoulder-to-shoulder panning for treasure along some mountain stream. Among the waiting wagons were the Middletons with a three-month old baby and four milk cows. Practical people, they were prepared not only for their journey but for immediate departure. They too were heartily welcomed to the Lawrence party train. Especially welcome were the four milk cows.

As these matters went, farther down the trail James and Julia Holmes, along with Julia's eighteen-year old brother Albert Archibald directly off the family farm, camped at Cottonwood Creek. Alone, somehow they had found the trail and were looking to join with others. They had no way of knowing that they too had missed an opportunity to join the Russell party, neither did they have reason to be concerned. The trail west was fresh and there were other westbound trains on the horizon. When the Lawrence crowd arrived, James, Julia and Albert signed on.

In fact, James and Julia Holmes were not concerned about much of anything. At this point in their adventure, it is doubtful they appreciated the rigors of prairie travel or the danger Plains Indians posed. Camping alone along the trail indicated they scarcely appreciated the benefits of large, well-armed trains. Cottonwood Creek was not far from civilization, but it was far enough away to be a convenient target for Native American attack. That James, Julia and Albert marched to a different drummer soon became apparent. This frame of mind also clouded their judgment. For them, the months-long prairie crossing was a lark. Opportunity to experience firsthand the unknown environment they loved was motivation enough. The joy of the untainted prairie, of meeting its noble inhabitants, of one morning awakening to behold the regal Front Range, easily masked any thought of danger or hardship.

In all likelihood, neither was searching for gold anywhere in their thinking. They were simply along for the thrill of it all. If prospecting ever crossed their minds, surely panning placers in a pristine mountain stream posed no threat to nature. Hardrock mining was another matter, but that circumstance was foreign to all but the most seasoned Fifty-Niners. They traveled with pans, not picks, shovels and powder. Nor did the possibility of troubles with interesting new "people groups" encountered along the way—in particular those organized into war parties—seem to raise much concern. In short, the Holmes trio was far from stereotypical gold-seekers. They represented a segment of the westering public, small to be sure, overlooked nearly always when explaining why Colorado's mass migration occurred in the first place. Leader Smith and the balance of the Lawrence party soon saw the light.

First signs of trouble surfaced early. Husband James proudly demonstrated a cantankerous attitude and his proclaimed nickname—"Little Hornet"—characterized it well. Imagine a man of slight stature with an aggressive attitude strutting about like a Banty rooster. In circumstances beyond his comfort zone, he was aggressive in his defensiveness. Unhelpful in the extreme, crossing through what was unmistakably a hostile wasteland already had everyone on edge. In fact, the hostile wasteland was not the source of either his demeanor or his nickname. "Little Hornet" was proudly earned during violent exploits as an Abolitionist. He belonged to the notorious Free State Raiders, joined the John Brown faction, and

BLOOMERS

Julia Holmes wore Bloomers and gave the Lawrence Party more to worry about than hostile Plains Indians and the follies of seeking gold. "Bloomers" were an "in your face" challenge to the social norms of the day that demonstrated the pervasive influence of the growing feminist movement even in the midst of westering.

"Bloomers," introduced to society in 1851 by three leading women's rights activists, one of whom was Amelia Jenks Bloomer, were ensembles consisting of knee-length dresses over full trousers. In 19th century America, trousers were for men only. A woman wearing trousers in public was a spectacle. "Freedom dresses" are another term for "bloomers." A woman wearing bloomers was more than a fashion statement. She was a political statement, a frontal assault on social norms. In typical fashion, Will Bagley summarizes the matter, a phenomenon really, this way: [30]

> *How quickly could women's fashion, a phenomenon seemingly remote from the frontier, affect western migration? Almost immediately. Soon after the national press first mentioned a new form of female attire, "bloomer girls" dressed in the bloomer style" started appearing on the road west.*
>
> *"There is a many ladys going through this Spring; many of them are dressed in the bloomer stile (sic)," Solomon Kingery wrote as the 1852 emigration began. "They wore Short dresses & pantaloons & Coets & hats. They look quite handsome."*

fought against a proslavery colony of Georgia settlers at Osawatomie, Kansas. Osawatomie was an intentional but unwise choice for a proslavery colony that abolitionists as far afield as the *New England Emigrant Aid Company* challenged. Little wonder Green Russell's Georgia Cherokees and the Holmes were not traveling companions. For quite different reasons, neither would Green and the Holmes prospect Cherry Creek together.

As for wife Julia, she too was scrappy. Gorgeous to a fault though offended should anyone suggest it, she was the daughter of an abolitionist father and a feminist mother whose Kansas home had long been a station on the "underground railroad." Feminist in her own right, Julia wore "the bloomer costume, in her case 'a calico dress reaching a little below the knees, pants of the same...'" [31]

The "bloomer revolution" not only became a symbol of emerging liberal feminism but also had a profound effect on emigrants, male and female, setting out across the plains. Acceptance did not come quickly or easily, but the practical nature of the fashion was undeniable. According to Will Bagley,

> *Daniel H. Budd camped with an Illinois train in April 1852 with a lady dressed "in bloomer costume. Have seen a number of the bloomers for a week past," he wrote. "Nothing new the balance of the evening."*
>
> *Bloomers were more than an innovative fashion—they represented a revolution in how women dressed. The style quickly found supporters among independent women who felt that the conditions women encountered in the West compelled them to replace their cumbersome traditional apparel with something more sensible. The notion that women going west should wear serviceable clothing was not entirely new.*
>
> *"Side-saddles should be discarded—women should wear hunting-frocks, loose pantaloons, men's hats and shoes, and ride the same as the men," was T. H. Jefferson's "Brief Practical Advice" in 1849.*
>
> *Not long after Eliza Farnham arrived in California that year, she began building a boarding house. The "extreme inconvenience" of wearing a long dress while doing carpentry induced this resolute and resourceful widow "to try the suit I had worn at home in gymnastic exercises." Her outfit matched what soon became "famous as the Bloomer," she recalled—and once she put it on, "I could never get back into skirts during working hours."*
>
> *Actress Fanny Kemble was simultaneously scandalizing Bostonians with "a loose flowing dress falling a little below the knee, and loose pantallettes or drawers," which the press thought looked suspiciously masculine. In December 1849 woman's rights advocate Amelia Bloomer defended Kemble, who had been "ridiculed, laughed at, and condemned for being so 'masculine'" as to put on pantaloons."*

On the road to Pikes Peak in 1858, the comments and curiosity about Julia Anna Archibald's "American costume" inspired a virtual feminist manifesto: "I wore a calico dress, reaching a little below the knee, pants of the same, Indian moccasins for my feet, and on my head a hat. However much it lacked in taste I found it to be beyond value in comfort and convenience, as it gave me freedom to roam at pleasure in search of flowers and other curiosities." [32]

Julia's spunky nature unhinged the Lawrence Party for other reasons. She cooked camp dinners on a heavy iron stove, surely a weighty burden, in her bloomers of course. And she insisted on standing guard at night like every other able-bodied waggoneer was expected to do.

That first night on Cottonwood Creek, as Julia cooked dinner on her large black stove, the Lawrence men crowded around to gaze in wonder at her singular outfit. Soon there was talk in camp of "weak-minded men [that would be James] and strong-minded women [that would be Julia]." Matters were not helped when Julia approached George Smith, requesting that she be allowed

Julia and Bloomers. Julia was the first white woman, no doubt attired in "Bloomers", to ascend Pikes Peak just prior to abandoning the 1858 Lawrence Party. She epitomized a growing segment of American society that would fuel unrest and violence for decades to come. Nevertheless, there was a place for virtually anyone among emigrant trains. In the case of Julia and husband, they would settle in Santa Fe. *(Wikipedia Commons)*

to stand guard duty alongside her husband.... At length, Mrs. Middleton
[mother with child and four milk cows] felt compelled to give Julia some ma-
tronly advice: "If you have a long dress with you, do put it on for the rest of the
trip, the men talk so much about you." [33]

Mrs. Middleton did not impress Julia, but a passing Santa Fe mail driver did.
He warned every train he passed that Plains Indians ahead would attack the train
for its women. Not relishing thoughts of becoming an Indian squaw despite the
obvious opportunity to better experience their culture, Julia kept a low profile
during the day and at night left guard duty to the men. There is no record of how
she filled her spare time, but it is clear her pluck remained. One month later, in
the shadow of the Front Range, on a cold, snowy August 5, 1858, Julia Holmes
with husband James and two others in tow, was the first white woman (maybe
first woman, period) to climb to the summit of Pike's Peak. Julia lingered there
long enough in the numbing cold to write letters to her mother and some friends.
Letting the emotions of the day overwhelm her environmentalist leanings, Julia
also took time to cut her name into a large boulder with her bowie knife where
presumably it remains.

The Lawrence crowd had scarcely dipped a pan when time after time they
listened to accounts of the "go-backers." Each time, the Lawrence party despaired
on the brink of joining the retreat. To go on searching for gold or to go home
was the never-ending discussion around the evening campfire. Already, for every
wagon train headed west, one retreated east. The following account epitomized
the frustrations typical of all-too-frequent "lay-byes." Ironically, this particular
Lawrence party lay-bye to celebrate the Fourth of July involved "go-backers"
from the very same Green Russell party they were hoping to overtake. On the
morning of July 5, 1858, the groggy revelers had barely broken camp when they
were surprised to see two covered wagons lurching down the trail towards them.
Though aware of the companies in advance of them for nearly three weeks, this
was their first encounter with any of their fellow Argonauts. They were not prepared for what they heard. The two wagons were filled with homeward-bound
Cherokees angry with "Captain Beck because they could not make twenty dollars
per day, as [they alleged] he had told them..." Moreover, they said,

that they thought he would be killed; that they "had worked hard prospecting
the Platte and Cherry creek FIVE WHOLE DAYS (sic)"; that they could not
make more than "two bits" per day; that they "had farms and niggers at home,
and home they were going." [34]

The Lawrence party was a menagerie of innocents. Weary of travel, discouraged by go-backers—especially Russell's Cherokees—failing to find gold near
Pike's Peak or anywhere else for that matter, the party lost what little cohesion it

ever had. Absent loyalty or leadership, the party dwindled little by little with each passing troop headed home. On July 12, 1858, just as another Lawrence contingent was about to wheel east, not one but two supposed godsends gave them pause.

On that July morning, with fourteen wagons remaining, the Lawrence party met head-on twelve wagons with fifty-six more disgruntled Georgia and Cherokee Nation gold seekers returning home. The fact that they were not more Russell party defectors, instead traveling under the banner of a "Captain Doke," did not comfort them. Discerning that they nonetheless were knowledgeable men worth hearing out, they were further troubled. Although deflated by their testimonies, the Lawrence remnant was not quite ready to accept defeat. Increasingly concerned over their own loss of firepower, they invited Captain Doke's party into their ranks. To a man, the fifty-six declined another chance to get rich on Cherry Creek gold, but the two parties did agree to circle their wagons at Camp Creek in present-day Garden of the Gods and send a small scouting party westward into South Park. Most likely part of their reasoning was that weather and fishing in July should be excellent. Factual or not, there was plenty of time before winter to find out, and the prospect of gold was an ever-present temptation made even more alluring by what many considered a lucky coincidence and others a divine appointment.

> *As luck would have it, a Mexican named Nicholas Archuleta happened by soon after. Archuleta had been packing flour and whiskey over the old Ute Trail, when he noticed the white-topped wagons and stopped by to see what the men were doing. On learning that they were searching for gold, he claimed that he could lead them to mountains of the yellow stuff, enough to fill many wagons. Accordingly, Archuleta was hired as guide.* [35]

Archuleta was Fall Leaf by another name, a pied piper to be sure. Ten Lawrence men with more courage than discernment volunteered to follow him westward up the Ute Trail, an ancestral route ascending the Front Range still heavily traveled by Ute hunting parties. Heavily traveled as it may have been, Archuleta promptly lost his way. In the words of Jason Younker, one of the adventurers:

> *Suffice to say we followed the Mexican for eight days when he finally brought us out of the mountains at South Platte canon, and insisted that we were then on the western slope! We had suspected for several days that our guide was lost; now we knew it. We made our way along the foothills across the Divide back to camp in the Garden of the Gods.* [36]

Not easily dismissed, Archuleta persuaded those in camp that he had made an honest mistake by starting the journey on a trail farther north than intended.

Our Kansans, having already demonstrated their gullibility by succumbing to Pike's Peak gold fever in the first place, invited further chastening. They gave the Mexican another chance. With three Lawrence brave-hearts, Archuleta headed back into the mountains. Captain Doke's discontents and the balance of the Lawrence party, wiser in their ways, were content to stay in camp and see.

For the Georgia-Cherokees, contentment was always short-lived. Idleness was not their nature. Two weeks after joining the Lawrence Party, just a day or two after Archuleta resumed his quest, ten of their twelve wagons pulled out for the States. Unimpressed, the Lawrence Party bid them farewell and God's speed. Sixteen days after Archuleta and his three volunteers left camp, they returned "half-starved and wholly disgusted." [37] They sent Archuleta packing, albeit more enriched for the outing. Only discouragement enriched the Lawrence men. Better had discouragement also dampened their zeal for gold and their gullibility when it came to finding it. Instead, they had another hard lesson to learn. Enter yet another Mexican vagabond reporting that gold seekers to the south were hard at work on the Sangre de Cristo Pass, pocketing at least ten dollars a day to the man. How predictable was that evening's campfire chatter given this news?

> *A general meeting was called on Camp Creek to decide what course of action to take. Six of the gold seekers elected to call it quits and take the Santa Fe Trail back to the settlements. Two more decided to journey east by way of the Republican River. A few others opted to head north and join up with what was left of the Russell Party on the South Platte. The majority, however, voted to once again follow a Mexican rumor—this time south towards the Sangre de Cristo range—in hopes of finally locating some gold.* [38]

On August 10, 1858, while Green Russell, Lewis Ralston and recently arrived George Jackson were closing in on South Platte gold, our gullible Kansans folded tents in preparation for another Mexican jaunt in the opposite direction. The Holmes wagon was among them. Broaching the rutted Taos-Fort Laramie Trail, they all soldiered south over Sangre de Cristo Pass to within six miles of old Fort Massachusetts, later relocated farther west and renamed "Fort Garland." Alas, there were no miners in sight, no ten dollar's worth of gold per man.

It was in light of this latest foolishness that sassy Julia, with husband and brother onboard, gave up looking for their elephant. The only sensible thing for the rest of the party to do, so stated Julia, was to "go fishing." For "her party," given the choice of returning to Kansas or continuing on to Taos, they turned their wagon south towards Taos. Never smitten by gold, but apparently not enamored with Kansas farm life or the prospect of an approaching civil war either, their decision probably was not a difficult one. They bid what remained of the Lawrence party fare thee well. Taos would be their new home. The "Little

Hornet" and his brother-in-law were lost to history. Julia taught school. Any accounts of further activism on any of their parts were also lost to history.

Back at Fort Garland, amazing what a night's sleep and another rumor could do for the spirit. The day after the Holmes and brother depart, a Utah dispatch courier enroute to Fort Garland with news of the Russell party sent the boys back to the campfire with newfound optimism. The courier reported that Russell's faithful thirteen found a bed of alluvial gravel bearing seven cents worth of "nice scale gold" per pan. They then fashioned a hand rocker and washed out $200 in thin scale gold. By the time the courier happened by, each of the thirteen Argonauts sported $400 of Front Range gold. That was all the Lawrence remnant needed to know—Dry Creek, Clear Creek and the South Platte or bust. No less skeptical than before, nevertheless they took the bait.

The Lawrence remnant, lingering at Fort Garland no longer than it took to replenish supplies, reached the South Platte on September 6, 1858. Had they not cycled like a yoyo at every rumored bonanza or humbug, adopting the disillusionment of go-backers in the process, their journey from Kansas would have been months shorter. In their defense, they were among the earliest vanguard of the rush to Colorado. And they were not unique. Their ignorant lack of preparation and flawed expectations, overshadowed by their naive enthusiasm, was common even among those who followed them a year later. In the midst of one misstep after another, they nevertheless would contribute to shaping the course and pace of the Fifty-Niner rush.

Fort Garland – San Luis Valley. Fort Garland was a classical frontier garrison that provided some protection to early settlers and provisions for the first wave of Fifty-Niners. It remained a reassuring if not especially threatening symbol of American governmental authority throughout the Civil War and development of the San Luis Valley. (*Crofutt's Grip-Sack Guide*)

Upon arrival at Clear Creek, the Lawrence remnant found the Russell diggings abandoned and learned that the Russell party was off on a prospecting trip farther into the mountains. In their place were newly arrived "mountain men" with their Native American families and pathfinders like themselves from the States. More arrived daily. The Colorado gold rush was about to erupt. So too was winter.

Snow came early in the Colorado Rockies in 1858 and it dawned even on the Lawrence crowd that preparing winter shelter would be wise. On the right bank of the Platte, five and a half miles from the mouth of Cherry Creek, they began work on a permanent settlement. Not well versed in the ways of the frontier, a number of them were well versed at profiting from chartering town sites and selling lots. Within days, they organized a town company and a surveyor among them staked off lots, birthing flash-in-the-pan Montana City. Oddly enough, despite so many previous setbacks that could have destroyed their sense of purpose, it was establishing Montana City that delivered a near-fatal blow. Where to locate the town site amidst anxiety over an early winter was the issue. Never of one mind nor led by strong leaders, conflict was inevitable. One faction settled on an inviting site far from the junction of the Cherokee Trail and the South Platte River crossing, Montana City. Another faction disputed this decision, ultimately locating St. Charles at the Cherokee crossing. Still others had their fill of both sites and frontier life altogether. By early October, eighteen of them were wheeling east along the Platte with more to follow. More town sites also followed, the handiwork of entrepreneurs more adept at staking and bartering lots than panning sand and gravel. [39]

By the onset of 1858 winter, all but a few of the Lawrence party along with most others returned to Kansas. There, inexplicably given their utter failure as gold-seekers, they joined John Cantrell in boosting the "Pike's Peak" gold fields through interviews, letters, newspaper articles and hastily written guidebooks. They added credibility to Cantrell's bluster. Like Fall Leaf, Archuleta, and the Utah courier misinformation, in failure they too contributed in their own small way to transitioning Colorado from frontier furrier to mining empire. Montana City became Denver City, and Denver City enabled a mass emigration. Pike's Peak, far from the gold, nevertheless symbolized the hullabaloo long after the world knew better. In the end, it did not matter. The Front Range treasure was not so much its gold but its agriculture and infrastructure. Denver soon took its rightful place as guidepost, provisioner, and guardian. Lawrence party gravitas helped tip the scale.

The colorful Lawrence party exemplified young America's resiliance and vision. Just as unlikely, so did the contributions of the last of the 1840s mountain men, chief among them Uncle Dick Wootton. By any measure, what became Denver owed its survival that first winter to an unintended consequence of Uncle Dick's mountain savvy and his aborted return home.

Notes—Chapter Four: Young America

[1] *Lawrence Republican*, September 2, 1858. Cited by LeRoy R. Hafen, Colorado Gold Rush, pg. 39.

[2] Smith, Duane A., *The Trail of Gold and Silver*, pg. 9. [See P. David Smith's manuscript on pre-1858 gold finds in the San Juans.]

[3] Bagley, *With Golden Visions Bright Before Them*, Vol. II, pgs. 17-19; *So Rugged and Mountainous*, Vol. I, pg. 400.

[4] Hollister, Ovando James, *The Mines of Colorado*, pgs. 11-12.

[5] Paul, Rodman W., *The Far West and the Great Plains in Transition, 1859-1900*, pg. 47. [The ranches and outposts Rodman notes may have had a better survival rate west of the Rocky Mountain Front Range. Based on first-hand accounts, way-stations that sprang up to serve the Forty-Niners across the prairie between the Missouri Valley and Colorado seem to have been abandoned in keeping with greatly diminished traffic by the early to mid-1850s.]

[6] Ibid, pg. 31.

[7] Hollister, pgs. 59-60.

[8] Ibid., pgs. 60-61.

[9] "Green Russell, Colonizer," *Herald Democrat*, January 1, 1906, Leadville, Colorado. [J. H. Pierce letter to Mr. Fen G. Barker, Society of Leadville Pioneers]

[10] Ibid.

[11] "Green Russell, Colonizer," *Herald Democrat*, January 1, 1906.

[12] "Green Russell, Colonizer."

[13] Ibid.

[14] Linstrom, Lois C., *Ralston's Gold*, pg. 52.

[15] Ibid.

[16] Ibid., pg. 54.

[17] Hall, Frank, *History of Colorado*, Vol II, pg. 227.

[18] Linstrom, pg. 55.

[19] Ibid., pgs. 78-80.

[20] Ibid., pg. 56.

[21] Frank Hall documents another version of Cousin Pierce's role in Green Russell's fame, reported thirty years after the fact and published in the *Rocky Mountain News* dated August 13, 1888. "…Russell started up the Platte toward the mountains, prospecting along that stream (Platte). Most of the company passed ahead of the wagons, while Green Russell was somewhat behind them. 'When about four miles up the river,' says Pierce, 'I saw a bank which looked as if it might contain gold. I stopped, got a pan of the dirt and gravel and began panning it out. I was about half through when Green Russell came up, took the pan and finished it. It contained ten cents. 'Run ahead, boy,' he said, 'and call the others back, our fortune is made.' Being only twenty-one years old, I was the kid of the party, so I went and brought back the others, when we went into camp. We made a rocker out of a cottonwood log, and the first day obtained about six dollars in gold dust. These diggings were not very rich, however, but in prospecting around we discovered some dirt on Dry Creek, some three or four miles from the Platte, from which we took three ounces the first day. These diggings paid very well, and from all of them we secured some $600 to $700 during the summer." [*History of the State of Colorado*, Frank Hall, Vol. IV, pg. 19.] [Also see: "The Colorado Gold Rush," *Western Mining History* Online: https://westernmining his-tory.com/articles/11/page 1.] [Linstrom, *Ralston's Gold*, pgs. 78-80.]

[22] Linstrom, pg. 56.

[23] "Green Russell, Colonizer."

[24] Hall, *History of the State of Colorado*, Vol. IV, pg. 19; *Rocky Mountain News*, August 13, 1888.

[25] Linstrom, pg. 56.

[26] Hollister, pgs. 8-9.

27 Hall, Vol. IV, pg. 19.
28 The Rocky Mountain "Mineral Belt" is a geological ban of metal-bearing ores that cover an area stretching from Montana south into Mexico. The portion in Colorado trends northeast from the San Juan Mountains in the southwest to the Front Range near Jamestown.
29 Gehling, "C–The Argonauts," pgs. 2-4.
30 Bagley, Vol. II, pgs. 338-341.
31 "C-The Argonauts," pgs. 4-5.
32 Bagley, Vol. II., pg. 340.
33 Gehling, "C–The Argonauts," pg. 5.
34 Ibid., pgs. 8-9.
35 Ibid., pg. 11.
36 Ibid.
37 Ibid., pg. 13.
38 Ibid., pg. 14.
39 Ibid., pgs. 18-19.

CHAPTER 5

Close Calls

"While I was never particularly in love
with hard work, I wasn't afraid of it." [1]
— Uncle Dick Wootton —

The 1858 winter along Colorado's Front Range was early but mild. Still, any Rocky Mountain winter was capable of killing the ill prepared. The vanguard of the mass migration to Colorado had thinned considerably within a month or two of reaching the Front Range. A month or two later the troop was perhaps less than a few hundred. Not only had prospecting proved harder and less rewarding than expected, this remnant was starving. To save "Pikes Peak or Bust" from busting, two preconditions had to be met. The first, immediate precondition was adequate provisions and equipment akin to what could be found in Missouri frontier outposts. The second precondition was demonstrating that the source of Front Range placer gold was not fleeting, but rather erosion from "inexhaustible" mountain gold-bearing quartz veins. Two mountain men, Uncle Dick Wootton and John Simpson Smith, satisfied the prime directive. Green Russell, John Gregory, and George Jackson, another mountain man, would satisfy the second. Both were close calls.

Unbeknownst to Uncle Dick, his November arrival in fledgling Denver with two wagons loaded with staples intended for trade with the Arapahoe and Cheyenne was in the nick of time. The camp was occupied by what was left of the Lawrence party and stalwarts like them were cold and hungry. Failure to survive the winter could well have stunted or thwarted the growth of Denver into the pre-eminent supply depot for quartz mining in the Colorado Rockies. Transcontinental railroad management lost no sleep over their decision to bypass Denver in favor of Cheyenne and South Pass. Imagine what else would have bypassed Denver had it remained a destitute camp instead of a thriving regional metropolis.

Wootton saw no need to claim any role in this matter. Secure in his strength of character, his demeanor and accomplishments spoke for themselves. The closest he came to braggadocios was his recollections in later life on his western legacy. Historian Frank Hall described Uncle Dick this way:

One of the very earliest of our pioneers, contemporary with the Bents, St. Vrain, Kit Carson and the original guild of hunters and trappers, and one of the most magnificent figures that ever tailed an Indian, or trapped a beaver.... [2]

More than an interesting character, Wootton's westering provided valuable context and perspective concerning the final chapter of the mountain man era and a segment of society that was seldom addressed in Colorado gold rush accounts. His eyewitness recollections of personalities and circumstances provided rare insight into the early development of the Colorado mining industry. He also stood out for his turn of phrases and raw characterizations of frontier peoples and practices. His unfiltered perspective may explain why few will ever know of him.

Unlike many others in his generation struggling to find their way, young Wootton had vision as well

Uncle Dick Wootton. After outliving the fur trade in the Colorado Rockies, mountain-man Wootton became a freighter, rancher and merchant. On what he thought was his final trade with Arapahoe and Cheyenne villages located at present-day Denver before retiring back to the States, instead he found the starving vanguard of the Colorado gold rush. Saving them from almost certain death, he abandoned plans to retire. *(Wikipedia Commons)*

as courage. He also manifested early makings for success that he did not expect to fulfill anywhere near home. In plain language,

I shall just begin at the beginning and tell you in an off-hand way, which will sound natural to those who know me—and I reckon you will find a good many such people in one place and another—what my experience has been in the mountain region. I shall not try to make it appear that the mountaineers were a lot of highly educated, polished gentlemen, nor shall I make them talk like a pack of savages, as they generally do in frontier stories, because that would be doing all of them a rank injustice.

When I left Independence in the summer of 1836 I was a little under nineteen years of age, but I was pretty near full-grown and had been away from home long enough to know how to take care of myself. I could use a gun as well as anybody, knew how to handle a team, and while I was never

particularly in love with hard work I wasn't afraid of it, and when there
was anything to be done I was always ready to do my share. That was all
that was required of me as a wagon man, and I got along first-rate from
the start. [3]

UNCLE DICK WOOTTON [4]

Born May 6, 1816 in Mecklenberg County, Virginia, his cumbersome name was given
by his father, a fourth generation Scotsman with titled gentry roots. His American
ancestors were among the earliest Virginia settlors. According to Howard Louis
Conard, the historian to whom Wootton dictated his memoirs, "Richens Wootton"
changed to "Dick Wootton,"

> *or rather to Dick Hootton, the surname not even being quite satisfactory in its*
> *original form, and Dick he was always called by the old timers, ["Uncle" was*
> *annexed decades later in Denver as a result of his kindnesses extended to all*
> *who needed a helping hand.] while to all the boys and girls who have grown up*
> *around him of late years, he is Uncle Dick."*

At age seven his family moved to their tobacco farm in Christian County,
Kentucky, where "he secured what in those days was considered a fair business edu-
cation." At the age of seventeen, we find him on his uncle's Mississippi cotton plantation, and two years later in Independence, Missouri where in 1836 he signed onto
a wagon train destined for Santa Fe. What his home life amounted to is anyone's
guess, but like so many adventuresome young men and even boys of that era, leaving
home was common practice. And like Wootton, never returning was common, too.

In 1836 the Missouri-Kansas border was not just the end of civilization. For
all practical purposes, the river to the northwest led nowhere any normal person
would want to go. The Arkansas River to the southwest was even less inviting. From
Independence, the sun set on 800 miles of plains and mountains before reaching
the centuries old Spanish outpost of Santa Fe. In 1822, the only opportunity to
find provision on the way was Bent's Fort on the north bank of the Arkansas River
near present-day La Junta, Colorado. The trail between the two was simply a track
stomped into hard-pack by mules and occasional livestock herded by drovers. By
1836, it was somewhat "improved" by small wagon trains transporting states-side
food and trade goods westward. Returning trains labored under the weight of beaver and buffalo pelts. Much later, the bulk of cargo was human, gold seekers and
all the provisions and gear that a mass migration required. In young Wootton's first
adventure, none of this was imaginable. His job was provisioning Bent's Fort. Fending
off hostile Indians along the way was a collateral duty, an unspoken part of the deal.

Wootton departed Independence, Missouri in the service of William Bent and the St. Vrain brothers. The St. Vrains handled the wagon trains supplying Bent's Fort. Apparently, Wootton never said, his first prairie crossing was all the prairie adventure he could stand. He left St. Vrain's employ at the fort, more or less stranded in the "middle of nowhere." By any account, Bent's Fort was one of the earliest and loneliest American outposts between the Missouri River frontier and Santa Fe. Prior to the Mexican revolution, neither the Spanish nor the Plains Indians welcomed travelers. At Bent's Fort, unemployed but unfazed, Wootton's natural giftings quickly led to hiring-on to lead a party of thirteen men and ten wagons to trade for furs among the Sioux of northern Colorado and Wyoming. His party returned several months later ladened with valuable furs, an immense reward for his employers.

Not resting on his laurels, Wootton undertook numerous trapping and trading journeys into the mountains where hostile Native American encounters were common. That autumn he joined a party of nineteen for an unprecedented two-year, 5,000-mile expedition from Bent's Fort northwest to the Columbia River valley and Vancouver, British Columbia. From there, the party turned south into California, then governed by Mexico, eventually swinging east through Arizona, Utah, and back to Bent's Fort. Wootton's biographer captured the magnitude of the accomplishment:

> *It was an astonishing enterprise, undertaken years in advance of the explorations which brought subsequent fame and fortune to John C. Fremont. Although Wootton does not claim to have been its leader, he made himself its only chronicler. Five of the original nineteen members of the party died violent deaths in the course of the expedition. The survivors returned to Fort Bent to learn that the price of beaver skins had taken a sudden and appalling fall.* [5]

Wootton was not only fearless—he was an opportunist. Quickly recognizing that the prevailing price for beaver pelts, one dollar per pound compared to eight dollars per pound previously, barely covered the costs of trapping. Along with Kit Carson, Wootton again signed on with Bent and St. Vrain, this time to provide buffalo meat to the fort. At some point he tired of the hunt and pivoted to rearing buffalo calves on a ranch he acquired on the site of present-day Pueblo. When the first wave of gold seekers encountered him on their way to California, he was operating a stagecoach and freight business. By the time the second wave of gold seekers arrived in 1858-1859, his Pueblo ranch was also an irrigated farm prepared to sell much needed produce. Many mountain men were of similar mind, but most lacked his entrepreneurial flair. Most also lacked his flair for storytelling, tales that go a long way in explaining why seeking gold in the Rocky Mountains was a dangerous pursuit. An excellent example was his lengthy description of local frontier customs and prairie welcoming committees awaiting the Forty-Niners and Fifty-Niners along their way. Despite his harsh tone, there was not a bone of hatred in his body. If anything, frustration and animosity regarding those who romanticized what he knew to be nonsense was never far below his skin. The man is best understood through his own words quoted extensively on the following four pages. [6]

[Wootton:] *I suppose I ought to tell you something about the Indian tribes of the far West, to give you a correct idea of where they were located when they were at home. That is, where you might expect to find them when they were not on the warpath or away on some kind of stealing expedition.*

To begin then at the western border line of Missouri, coming west we traveled through the territory claimed by the Sacs and Foxes, or if we kept farther south, through the country claimed by the Cherokees, Choctaws, Creeks, Senecas, and other bands of what is now the Indian Territory proper. [Tribes relocated from eastern regions.]

The Pawnees and one or two other tribes who spoke the same language were in the country at the mouth of the Platte, on the Missouri River, although they wandered pretty much all over Kansas.

The Comanches were scattered all over central and western Kansas and along the upper Arkansas River. North of them were the Cheyennes and Arapahoes, and then came the Sioux, who roamed over Nebraska, northern Colorado, and Wyoming, and were considered home anywhere along the upper Platte River. There were more of the Sioux in the country when I first came west than there were of any other Indians. I think I must have known as many as thirty different bands of them, and possibly more.

In the country northwest and west of the Sioux were the Blackfoot and Monarch Indians, who lived together, the Nez Perces, the Crows, and the Flatheads, spreading over Montana, Idaho, Oregon, and Washington Territory. The Blackfoot Indians could always be found along the upper Missouri River and in the Yellowstone Park.

In the Salt Lake region and other portions of Utah were the Utes and Pah-Utes. There were Utes farther south and east too, in New Mexico and Colorado, and they frequently got a long way east and north on their marauding excursions. The Snakes and Shoshones, who spoke the same language, had about the same customs and traditions, and belonged to the same family, were scattered over a great deal of the country between the Rocky Mountains and the Sierra Nevadas, and could be found almost any place in that region. The Apaches belonged in lower New Mexico and Arizona, and the Navahoes [sic] in northern New Mexico.

Wootton did not shy away from challenging the views of Easterners he considered ill informed at best. In fact, like most westerners of his day who pioneered crossing the plains and interior Rockies, he was unimpressed with anyone who idealized indigenous societies and lamented their corruption by white men. There is no known record of Uncle Dick and Julia Holmes meeting. The "Holmes trio" parted company with the remnant of the Lawrence Party before it reached present-day Denver, but had they met, exchanging viewpoints concerning the "noble savage" rather than "bloomers" would have been more likely and would have yielded more heat than light. On this matter, Uncle Dick brooked no dissent.

> [Wootton:] *Now I am going to tell you what kind of terms they were on with each other, and farther along what kind of Indians they were.*
>
> *Some of those people who have never seen an Indian more hostile than those with Buffalo Bill's Wild West Show, or more dangerous than the wooden Indian in front of a cigar store, are always talking about the extermination of the unfortunate natives of this country, by the Whites. I want to tell these soft-hearted, well-meaning, but not well-informed people that if there are fewer Indians in America to-day than there were when the Continent was discovered, the white man is not to blame for it. All the Indians who have ever been killed by white settlers, traders, trappers, hunters, and soldiers between the Atlantic and Pacific Oceans within the past two hundred years would not be a corporal's guard in comparison with the army of red skins slaughtered in wars, quarrels, and brawls of various kinds which they have had among themselves.*
>
> *It is not true either, as some people seem to think, that their treachery, cruelty, and vindictiveness have been the result of the treatment which they have received from the Whites. Long before a White man had found his way into this country the tribes which had never seen a White man, and possibly never heard of one, had the same distinguishing characteristics which they have had ever since the Whites came in contact with them. Before there were Whites to rob and plunder and steal from, they robbed and stole from each other. Before there were white men in the country to kill, they killed each other. Before there were white women and children to scalp and mutilate and torture, the Indians scalped and mutilated and tortured the women and children of their enemies of their own race. They made slaves of each other when there were no pale faces to be captured and sold or held for ransom, and before they commenced lying in ambush along the trails of the white man to murder unwary travelers the Indians of one tribe would set the same sort of death traps for the Indians of another tribe.*

Uncle Dick did have kind words for some tribes, but not many. In his opinion, the Creek, Cherokee, Choctaw, Delaware, and Shawnee got along with each other and with Whites, but most other tribes were constantly at war with one another.

> [Wootton:] *The other tribes however, were always fighting with each other, and I have personal knowledge of thousands of them having been*

killed in these wars. The Arapahoes and the Cheyennes were closely related to each other and were always allies. Among their inveterate enemies were the Kiowas, a tribe which used to make its headquarters about where Pueblo now is. They kept up a war with the Arapahoes and Cheyennes until there was but a remnant of their tribe left, and then they joined the Comanche band and, I think, have remained with them ever since.

The Arapahoes and Comanches, and the Arapahoes and Utes, were always at war. When they fought the Comanches on their own ground, that is in the mountain region, the Arapahoes were generally the victors, but on the Kansas prairies, where the Comanches were at home, the Arapahoes were badly worsted in several encounters. There were bloody battles within my recollection between the allied Arapahoes and Cheyennes and the Utes on Apishapa Creek above Trinidad, on the Sugarite in New Mexico, and at one or two other places. Both bands were good fighters and neither seemed to gain much advantage in either of these battles. The Utes and mountain Apaches were never on good terms. They quarreled on all occasions and killed each other whenever opportunity offered.

The Comanches and Utes were always hostile to each other and had a great many fights at one time and another. The Utes and prairie Apaches— not the mountain Apaches—were allies once in fighting the Comanches and Kiowas. They met at Cimarron City, and left about as many dead Indians on the field as were ever left on a western battlefield.

The Crows and the Cheyennes were the best warriors of all the Indian tribes of the West. The Comanches and Pawnees always sought to have the odds largely in their favor, and would sometimes hoover for days around an enemy waiting for an opportunity to kill without taking any chances of being killed.

Nothing better illustrates the Comanche character than his queer notion about killing rattlesnakes. The only time they kill the rattlesnake is when they find him in that sluggish condition in which he fails to rattle when approached. Judging the snake instinct by his own, the Comanche says, when the snake fails to warn the Indian of his presence, "he is on the warpath," that is, he is lying in ambush for an enemy and wants to bite him. There was never any such thing as honor among the Comanches, and it was on account of their stealing that they were in trouble so much of the time with other Indians.

The Apaches were always just what they are now; a dirty, thieving lot of cut-throats, who would rather steal than live by any other means. They lived on horses and mules stolen from the Mexicans and other Indians because they were too lazy to hunt game, although there were always plenty of deer in their country.

Naturally, Uncle Dick and mountain men like him were best acquainted with the Ute and most comfortable among them. Early prospectors, generally regarded as trespassers, were more leery and more often attacked. With the mass influx of prospectors and settlers crowding ancestral Ute hunting grounds, Ute tempers worsened.

> [Wootton:] *The Utes were more honest than the Apaches, but they were sometimes bad tempered, quarrelsome, and vindictive to a remarkable degree, even for Indians. You could never tell when they would take offense at some trivial thing and go on the warpath. As a rule, however, they killed to satisfy revenge rather than for the purpose of plunder.*

As stewards of the land went, the Ute were more congenial than most, but they too had their limits. Wootton understood their limits well, witnessed by his ability to prosper in their sacred homeland as well at mountain trapping and trading as on the plains trading and farming among the Arapahoe and Cheyenne. Less astute, the prospectors, hardrock miners, and settlers that followed often learned the hard way and as a consequence intimidated those who followed.

Wootton also was quick to respond to changing times. When trapping ran its course, then buffalo hunting, ranching, scouting, farming, freighting, trading, hotel keeping, store keeping, and saloon-keeping took their turn. "Jack-of-all-trades, master-of-none" described him well. Threaded throughout it all was marriage and child rearing. Also memorable, Dick Wootton brought to every endeavor a positive attitude and heart-felt fairness. All this notwithstanding, after twenty-five years away from home, twenty-two years of scrapping together a living on the frontier, he was done. He explained his urge to return to the States:

> *The yearning to revisit the scenes of my childhood and meet again my friends and old time associates was stronger than it had been at any time in the twenty-five years which had elapsed since I said good-bye to the old folks at home and started out on my adventurous career.*
>
> *With this object in view I settled up all my business at Fort Union and got ready to start back to the States. On my way I intended to make one more trade with the Indians and that was to wind-up my affairs in the Rocky Mountain region. I loaded several wagons with goods, pocketed the drafts on St. Louis in which the bulk of my fortune had been invested, and early in October found myself again on the road, but with a different object in view from what I had had when setting out on my former trips.* [7]

Little did Dick Wootton know his destiny did not include his childhood home. It did include Denver, non-existent at the time. The combined, pathetic camps of Auraria and future-Denver were only able to boast of a single well-built log cabin. Nearby, what was left of the Lawrence Party and Green Russell's

Larimer Street, Denver, 1859. (Richardson, 1867.)

Queen City of the Plains. Uncle Dick Wootton, enroute to his last trade with Cherokee and Arapahoe villages on Cherry Creek, trades instead with half-starved Fifty-Niners in the process of turning Denver camp into a "Queen." *(Richardson, 1867)*

winter crew were barely surviving. Still, civic-minded visionaries, probably totally ignorant of the peril they were in continued to plan a settlement and a state. Heavy snow fell on October 31, 1858, and grounded the restless pilgrims. Ovando Hollister captured the moment:

> *Next day the adventurers were confined to their camps, and true to their instincts began to talk politics and town-sites. By the 4th of November a town-plat had been surveyed on the west side of the Platte opposite the mouth of Cherry Creek by William Foster, and christened "Auraria" by Dr. Russell [one of Green Russell's brothers] whose party had come from a town of that name in Georgia. This region was then within the bounds of Kansas, and a county was defined and called "Arapahoe," after the neighboring tribe of Indians. An election was held on the 6th of November, there being about two hundred inhabitants in the new place, "six hundred miles from nowhere," as they designated it. H.J. Graham was elected without opposition, Delegate to Congress, and instructed to get the Pike's Peak gold mines set apart from Kansas as a new Territory. A. J. Smith was elected Representative from Arapahoe County to the Kansas Legislature.* [8]

Hollister concluded that this frontier proceeding was a wonderful illustration of the "organizing, assimilating character which our countrymen bear in common with the old Romans." Quoting William M. Slaughter, one of the earliest pilgrims and later Mayor of Central City, Hollister completed his profound observation:

*Just to think that within two weeks of the arrival of a few dozen Americans in
a wilderness, they set to work to elect a Delegate to the United States Congress,
and ask to be set apart as a new Territory! But we are of a fast race and in a
fast age and must prod (sic) along.* [9]

Dick Wootton was many things but he was never a politician or a bureaucrat,
and he would never be caught "prodding along." Unfazed by those interested in
territorial status or statehood, upon arriving in future-Denver in November his
attention turned immediately to problems of survival. Chief among them was
the care and feeding of the destitute pilgrims. He had expected to find Arapahoe
and Cheyenne winter encampments, instead Wootton found half-starved Cherry
Creek gold-seekers huddled around fires in front of crude shelters. Once again, a
change of plans was called for. In his own words, "There I came to a stop, and all
my plans and I suppose the whole course of my after life was changed." [10]

By "after life," he surely meant his imagined new life back in the States, back
on a comfortable Kentucky farm, but maybe not. He had long demonstrated a
heart for the souls of his fellow man. As for his plan, what probably seemed like
a minor deviation from Indian trading to sharing provisions with "wretches-in-
need" was in for a major upgrade. Again, in his own words:

*I should have very much preferred to carry out my original plan of trading
with the Indians, because in the first place I should have made a better profit
on the goods traded, and in the second place I should have been able to go East
with several loads of peltry, which would have sold at a handsome profit in
Kansas City. I found it impossible, however, to resist the importunities of the
pioneer settlers of Denver, and I finally agreed to unload my goods and remain
there until I traded out what merchandise I had in stock.* [11]

Somewhat leery of the "penniless mob," Wootton unloaded his wagonloads
of merchandise and whisky by the barrel. To his great delight, these struggling
immigrants, scores more by the day, were desperate for his goods and able to pay
for them. How could they not be desperate? Whatever they expected to find
on the far side of the prairie, gold in the streams and goods in the stores, they
found not. Instead, having arrived at the Front Range with scarcely more than
the clothes on their backs, with provisions for a few weeks if that, they were
quickly destitute. There was little gold in the streams and no stores much less
goods. There was no hotel district with restaurants awaiting them, no shelter
from the howling winter weather save for what they themselves hastily constructed. Motivated partly by commercialism, partly by compassion, Uncle Dick
Wootton saw needs he believed he had a duty to satisfy. His journey home would
have to wait. Finding the beginnings of a decent log cabin in which to set up
shop, Wootton reported, "there wasn't much more style about my first store-room

than there was about the average Indian lodge....I had several barrels with me which I rolled alongside of each other and used as a counter." [12]

Wootton sold out quickly, and once again, he saw his life at a crossroads. Apparently not as motivated to return east as he had thought just a month or so earlier, he decided he would linger on the frontier just awhile longer. Out of merchandise but as full of pluck as usual, he determined to take his chances with the weather and return to the Arkansas to resupply. Left unsaid in his account of early Denver, or perhaps simply forgotten, Uncle Dick was not the only budding mercantilist that set up shop that first winter, but his timing and resupply was critical and reassuring.

Frank Hall described his understanding of the state of affairs as the Front Range pilgrims coped with their first Rocky Mountain winter:

> On the 29th of October, during a severe snowstorm, Blake and Williams train of wagons laden with groceries and provisions, arrived from Iowa, and the owners built the fourth cabin in the west side settlement which had been named "Auraria," where they opened a store and thereby gave that side of the creek its first important commercial enterprise.... A few days later, Messrs. Kinna and Nye arrived from Nebraska, located in Auraria and opened the first tinware and stove store. The next train of goods, flour and groceries, and the first assortment of dry goods was brought in by Uncle Dick Wootten from New Mexico, arriving on Christmas day. Wooten's storeroom twenty by thirty, with clapboard roof and a four light glass window was then the largest building in the country. [13]

By Wootton's estimation, there were a few hundred treasure hunters, nearly all men, hunkered down on Cherry Creek and off in the foothills chasing after the mother lodes.

There also were enterprising "City Fathers" who claimed title to the land upon which they all stood. Wootton may not have needed further inducement to stay on, but they offered them and he accepted. In exchange for opening and operating a general store, he received 160 acres in what became the heart of the "Queen City of the Plains." In December 1858, the Queen City was in dire straits and a daunting challenge for even Uncle Dick—what a difference a year would make. According to Hall,

> Up to this time there were only three white women in this cheerless country, namely, Mrs. Henry Murat, from Kansas, who arrived at the Montana settlement November 2nd, 1858, and was sheltered in the only cabin then completed at that point; Mrs. S. M. Rooker from Utah, who reached Auraria August 30th, and Mrs. Dick Wootten, from New Mexico, who arrived in Auraria on Christmas day. Everything here was uncertain and unstable with

a long winter ahead, and, with plenty of nothing but poverty and priva-
tion, the pioneers had to make hope the main anchor of their souls. Without
sawmills, not even a whip-saw to cut lumber, with neither nails nor glass,
destitute of tools for constructing the conveniences of life, these early settlers
suffered countless hardships during the first year of their sojourn in this desert.
The prices of staples were enormous. Lumber was worth one hundred dollars a
thousand feet in 1859, and extremely scarce at that; shingle nails cost a dollar
a pound; flour ranged from twenty to forty dollars per hundred, while sugar,
coffee, tobacco and whisky were at times worth their weight in gold. [14]

Discouragement was not a Wootton trait. The plight of his Auraria brethren appeared much like he could have imagined confronted the Plymouth Rock
pilgrims, but resupplying them was far easier. Once committed to permanent
Denver residency in what promoters and flim-flam artists passed off as a city,
Uncle Dick busied himself with building a two-story log building "in which to
carry on my business and commence merchandising on a larger scale. This was
the first business block put up in the city, and in fact the first building constructed
of material so expensive as hewn logs." [15]

According to historian Hall, "the first frame house erected in Auraria was
built by Dick Wootten at a point near Sigi's brewery, in June, 1859." [16] Always the
entrepreneur, the Wootton general store soon included a pawnshop and bank. If
a patron had assets or could otherwise demonstrate financial integrity, the bank
was there to serve. If not, the pawnshop might do.

There was not much money in the town, or the camp, as we called it, but
I got the most of what there was and when the miners didn't have money they
generally had something to barter, and so we managed to keep business moving.

New men kept coming into the camp very rapidly that winter, and it
seemed that about nine-tenths of all those who came were gamblers. They
would reach Denver broke, and the first thing to do, of course, was to make
a raise. They nearly all came through with ox-teams and they would come to
me and leave a good yoke of cattle as security for a loan of twenty-five dollars.
On the day following they would bring back thirty dollars or forfeit the cattle.
This was a matter of such frequent occurrence that loaning money in this way
became a part of my business. [17]

Flush with cash and all other forms of local barter, Wootton built a frame
house for his family. He also housed on the second floor of his "log business
block" his new friend's newspaper, the *Rocky Mountain News*. Editor Byers had
much to overcome in 1859 in order to get out his "sheet." Printers' supplies, quite
likely procured by friend Wootton, were hard to come by. Sometimes wrapping
paper had to suffice. Uncle Dick recalled more serious challenges, as well.

I remember one time, when [Byers] had been carrying on something of a war-fare against the lawless element in the town, that two desperate characters made their appearance in the neighborhood of the building one morning and shot all the windows out of the printing office. The fire was returned from the inside and before the shooting ceased one of the desperadoes was killed. About the first question Byers asked of an employee in those days was whether he could handle a gun to good advantage, and a printer who was handy in this respect stood well with the proprietors of the paper, even though he had a mul-titude of shortcomings as a compositor. [18]

William N. Byers. Plain talking, gun-toting editor of the iconic *Rocky Mountain News*, Byers was probably best known for his shameless "Boosterism" regarding regional mining interests. *(Frank Hall)*

Wootton also operated a saloon and built a hotel. The hotel failed, according to accounts, due to Wootton's willingness to provide free room and board to every "down-an-out" soul who asked, and there were many who asked. His compassion earned him his endearing name, "Uncle Dick."

There were hundreds of bitterly disappointed men who seemed to have come to Colorado thinking they could pick up gold nuggets almost anywhere, who found it difficult to pick up a square meal once a week. I fed a great many of them and did that much, at least, towards building up the city. One of the first, if not the first hotel started in the town was one in which I was interested. That hotel enterprise failed financially for the reason that neither the manager nor myself could understand that only men who had money had a right to eat. Whenever a man came to me and said he was hungry and had no money I used to send him around to the hotel for a meal, and the manager made it a point never to turn away a man who made the same sort of appeal. Our house was well patronized, but in view of the fact that the most of our patrons were free boarders I suppose it is not surprising that we did not make a success of the hotel business. [19]

Uncle Dick's pivotal role in the establishment of fledgling Denver also earned him "City Father status," but his mountain man pedigree earned him the rank of

Brigadier General of the Colorado Militia. Faced with both Cheyenne and civil disorders, emigrants accustomed to authority recognized the value of some form of authoritative government. Representatives of the local settlements assembled on April 11, 1859, in *Wootton Hall*, the only place large enough to accommodate the crowd. Uncle Dick, with a touch of irony and tongue in cheek, explained the honor of it all.

> *So many people came into the country in the winter of 1858–59 that a strong agitation sprang up in favor of cutting loose from Kansas and organizing a new Territory. In the spring of 1859 the friends of this project got together and took steps to bring about the organization of a new Territory.... The effort to secure the organization of Jefferson Territory was not successful, and it was not until 1861, when Kansas was admitted into the Union as a state, that we got a territorial form of government, the new Territory formed taking the name of Colorado.*
>
> *While we were endeavoring to secure recognition as a new Territory we organized a provisional government with R. W. Steele as Governor. One of the first things which we undertook to do under the provisional government was to organize a territorial militia for protection against the Indians. I had the honor of being appointed a brigadier general of the militia under this arrangement, but as the resources of our government were very limited I never had any militia to command and consequently had no opportunity to distinguish myself as a general.* [20]

Uncle Dick shared his largesse in other ways. He celebrated Christmas 1859 in Denver with a party for all who wanted to come. Historians estimate that more than a hundred-thousand pilgrims passed through Denver in 1859, but only a small fraction of that number stayed on. At the end of the year, there still was not much to Denver—perhaps a couple hundred frustrated gold-seekers too weak or too fearful to hazard retreat back to the States. Waylaid by the pleas of penniless, half-starved Denverites, Uncle Dick continued to part company with his trade goods to meet needs as best he knew how. What started out as a final trade stop on a long journey east by way of the Platte turned out to be a four year stay. As Uncle Dick shared, he prospered, and so did Denver. Always fragile, its shallow roots gradually became sufficient to support expeditions into the foothills. Uncle Dick's log business-block and William Byers' boosterism laid the groundwork to salvage the hardiest of the 1859 fool-hearts and prepared a palatable oasis for the flood of 1860 settlers.

By 1862, Uncle Dick had fulfilled his Denver mission and his longing for mountain living returned. Disgusted by the disruptions accompanying the outbreak of Civil War, bored with city life, his only option was retreating into his past.

The breaking out of the war in 1861 kept back immigration, and that and the following year were comparatively dull years in the mountains generally and particularly dull in Denver. I sold out my business there, and concluding to try ranch life again, I started in on the Fountain River nine miles above Pueblo. That was where my farm was located, but I built a house first on the site of Pueblo near the old fort which gave the place its name. [21]

Uncle Dick also bought acreage on Raton Pass, built a ranch there, hired a tribe of Utes led by Chief Conniache [22] to grade a toll road, and eventually sold the right-of-way to the Atchison, Topeka and Santa Fe Railroad. Flexibility and courage, hand in hand, led to a full and productive life quite typical of the times. He died in his house on Raton Pass in 1893 having outlived five wives and seventeen of his twenty children. Ironically, "1893 is the same year the U.S. Census Bureau declared an end to the 'American Frontier'." [23]

GEORGE ANDREW JACKSON

George was born July 25, 1836 in Glasgow, Howard County, Missouri. At age sixteen, according to his daughter, he left home in 1853 for a five-month journey across the plains to the California gold fields in the company of his famous cousin, Kit Carson, and mined there until the spring of 1857. Late to the "mountain man" club and a short-lived member at that, Jackson was just the sort of man that was able to earn his way into that elite brotherhood. According to an interview printed December 14, 1859 in Golden, Colorado's *Western Mountaineer*, "he is in robust health, in stature near six feet, a genial companion, generous and free-hearted." The fact that he merited an interview in the first place was testimony to character traits that would serve him well throughout his frontier life. [24]

Departing Sacramento for Glasgow in May 1857, George re-crossed the plains with seven others, a dangerously small company in light of the hostile wilderness and its native stewards along the way. Apparently still less than enamored with home, he wintered over, then in the summer of 1858, he made his way to Fort Laramie. Learning of gold finds on Cherry Creek from mountaineers with whom he easily identified, Jackson along with a small party of white men duly impressed with Jackson's mettle, and twenty Sioux, began a methodical trek south into Colorado. Prospecting unsuccessfully along the way, and with harsh weather increasing, they decided to build cabins at the mouth of Thompson's Fork, a tributary of the Big Thompson River in Larimer County, Colorado, and hunker down for winter. Present-day Fort Collins, the present-day Larimer County seat, is nearby. Ever restless, Jackson earned his place in Colorado mining history a few months later near present-day Idaho Springs. His gold quartz find fired the starting pistol for advances from the Front Range into Colorado's "High Country" where motherlodes that had shed their gold flakes for eons waited. [25]

If a single class of individuals could somehow capture the heart and soul of the American frontier, the mountain men would be a good choice. Over the course of a decade or two preceding the Colorado gold rush and after the market for beaver-pelt haberdashery no longer supported a trapper's needs, perhaps as many as 300 men like Uncle Dick and John Simpson Smith needed to find a new livelihood. Elite graduates of renowned academies they were not–the wilderness and each other were their mentors. Those with pluck, those who were teachable, struggled to adapt their frontier lifestyle to their changing environment. The arrogant and foolhardy, regularly imperiled by Ute war parties, wild beasts, encroaching civilization, and weather, perished. Among this formidable army, a score or so appeared in "dime-novels," circuses, and wild-west shows. Even fewer, Uncle Dick Wootton, John Simpson Smith, George Andrew Jackson, and John Gregory appeared in the "Colorado Gold Rush Hall of Fame."

Wootton and Smith served the Denver camp. Wootton sheltered the vagrants and prepared the way for the next season of immigrants. Smith brokered prairie into Denver real estate and piloted city government through Indian and pre-Civil War perils. Jackson and Gregory were instrumental in proving to the satisfaction of the Nation that rushing to the Front Range was worth the risks. Success in this matter was sweet. There was indeed Front Range gold. Jackson, ever the loner who was more content in the wilderness than in a cabin much less a city, demonstrated that the transition from short-lived "hit and miss" placer mining to a long-term hardrock mining industry was no pipe dream. Gregory did the same.

While Wootton and Smith fulfilled their destiny in Denver, Jackson and Gregory fulfilled their destiny locating gold-quartz veins in the foothills.

Like John Lowery Brown's trail journal that documented Lewis Ralston's contribution to the Fifty-Niners, George Jackson kept a similar journal that served the same purpose. He abandoned the relative security of placer mining amidst other fearless pathfinders and pushed into the wintry Ute homeland in search of less crowded quarters and hopefully quartz motherlodes. The timing of his quartz lode discovery, complimented in short order by John Gregory's better publicized good fortune, could not have come at a more opportune time. Deadly winter conditions and Ute defenders be damned, Jackson's grit and discovery encouraged a surge of others to hazard the Rocky Mountain High Country, a precondition to hardrock mining of silver as well as gold.

George was teachable and respected his elders. In California, he learned about gold mining and with cousin Carson and friends, Uncle Dick included, he learned mountaineering. The "brotherhood of mountain men" was an exclusive one and entry requirements were stiff. Somewhat contradictory, congenial humility and ruthless survival skills were the price of admission. The winter of 1858 required both traits. Fabled Horace Greeley, thankfully also a brave-heart willing to get out from behind his city desk, sat around George Jackson's campfire and discerned much. Months later, on June 21, 1859, Greeley's *New York Tribune* published his thoughts:

The old mountaineers form a caste by themselves, and they prize the distinction. Some of them are Frenchmen or Franco-Americans, who have been trapping or trading in and around these mountains for a quarter of a century, have wives and children here, and here expect to live and die...Others came years ago from the states, some of them on account of a 'difficulty,' wherein they severely killed or savagely maimed their respective antagonists...This class is not numerous, but is more influential than it should be in giving tone to the society of which the members form a part. Prone to deep drinking, soured in temper, always armed, bristling at a word, ready with rifle, revolver or bowie knife, they give law and set fashion which, in a country where the regular administration of justice is yet a matter of prophecy, it seems difficult to overrule or disregard. [26]

JOHN SIMPSON SMITH

Often overlooked, the 1850s frontier of interior America, in particular the Colorado Rockies, was not devoid of white men and their homesteads. Spanish expeditions aside, traders and trappers along with American army fort builders and surveyors wore paths between the States, Santa Fe and points south and west. Trappers and traders morphed into settlers, scouts, Indian agents, translators, and gold seekers. John Simpson Smith's mountain lifestyle morphed into that of a Denver real estate speculator and high mucky-muck.

John was thirty years into his mountain escape from Frankfort, Kentucky and St. Louis when he dismounted in Denver camp. Three decades earlier, in 1810, he was an apprenticed tailor, but St. Louis haberdasheries were not his dream. Like so many teenagers of that era, Smith ran away to the mountain frontier with a party of beaver trappers. By 1840 the beaver were too scarce, the pelt market too depressed, and his legs too weary to go on. Instead, with Cherokee wife Wapola he settled in at Bents Old Fort on the Arkansas River, the Santa Fe Trail, and became an Indian trader and Cheyenne interpreter, "White Blanket" by name.

As far from a tailor shop as imaginable, his destiny was that of a mountain man who survived to play a supporting role in the birth of Denver and the gold rush it hosted. The Russell Party profited from him lingering three weeks to share prospecting advice. Belatedly, the Lawrence remnant benefited from his experience, and his contributions to the founding politics of Denver were legion. He traded mountaineering for city building by becoming a charter member of the few crude structures and twenty-five dollar lots that blossomed into present-day Denver. Prospecting was hard, frustrating work. The rewards of real estate were more certain albeit far less exhilarating. [27]

George Jackson was neither a subscriber to New York newspapers nor a follower of Horace Greeley. Sitting on his rough cabin doorstep on the banks of Thompson's Fork, he instead pondered the risks of winter and their disruptive effects on his search for gold. Out of boredom or need, we have no record, but this we know. Jackson "the placer prospector" yielded to Jackson "the mountain man." Requiring little preparation, he left camp and headed west into the snow-covered mountains to hunt elk. Instead of elk, he found sheep and Careajou, translated "wolverine" but used by French-Canadians for "mountain lion." Prospecting was not a priority—he did not even take a shovel—but he could not help himself.

We pick up his trail on Clear Creek on his way to the soda springs, present-day Idaho Springs. Accompanied by his dogs Drum and Kit, by the time he reached West Chicago Creek his mood had improved. The winter of 1858-59 would usher in a good new year, that was his resolution. He described this sentiment in his trail journal.

Survivalists. While beaver pelts were popular and beavers were plentiful, a small cadre of courageous, self-sufficient men trapped them throughout the western frontier. By the time the Colorado gold rush gained traction in 1858, the few remaining mountain men turned their attention to prospecting and to helping the newcomers survive their hostile surroundings. *(Frederic Remington, 1888)*

Jan. 1: Clear day. My supply of States grub short; 2 lbs. bread, ½ lb. coffee, ½ lb. salt. Plenty of meat for myself and dogs, so here goes for head of the creek. Told Tom [Golden] I would be back in a week to our old camp above Table Mountain [future site of Golden, Colorado, named after Tom]. Off; good traveling most of the way; killed mountain lion today; made about 8 miles and camped at Mineral Springs [Soda Springs] near the mouth of small creek coming in from south. Snow all gone around the spring. Killed fat sheep, and camped under three cottonwood trees. 1,000 sheep in sight tonight. No scarcity of meat in future for myself or dogs.

Jan. 2: Drum and Kit woke me by low growls at daylight. Sheep all gone. Mt. lion within twenty steps. Pulled my gun from under the blanket and shot too quick, broke his shoulder, but followed up and killed him. Clear, high wind and very cold. In camp all day. Built boughhouse, and eat fat sheep all day. Bread all gone: plenty fat meat: "no wantum bread."

Jan. 3: Still clear and very cold. Sun dogs. Sheep came down again; are very tame; walk up to within one hundred yards of camp and stand and stamp at me and the dogs. Mt. lion killed one within three hundred yards of camp today, and scattered the whole band again. Went up the main creek to another tributary [Chicago Creek], coming in from the south, a little larger than this one.

Jan. 4: Pleasant day. Made a long tramp today, followed up the Main Fork five miles. Here the main creek forks; each one about the same width; followed up the North Fork about three miles; canons and plenty of snow. Got back to camp after dark. Mountain lion stole all my meat today in camp; no supper tonight; D—n him.

CAREAJOU

In the earliest days of the misnamed Pike's Peak gold rush, wildlife including mountain lions heavily populated the region. "Careajou" is French-Canadian for mountain lion—corruption of Indian name for wolverine—commonly used among the mountain men. The Ute and mountain men routinely encountered them, but reportedly, the big cats were a novelty to 1858-1859 emigrants. Hollister, with uncharacteristic humor, explained.

> *For a few days parties were constantly arriving and prospecting and hunting were carried on with vigor. There does not seem to have been much success in the former line, only the Dry Creek before mentioned yielding an encouraging prospect. But the latter paid better. Antelope, deer, elk, bear and sheep were plentiful, and it was not unusual for the mountain lion to present his countenance in camp, once going so far as to peer into a tent where a man had died of fever. In the dusk they were at first taken for the large gray wolf of the prairie; but soon one of them was shot, when they were found to be a species of panther, standing two feet high and with a body four feet long—a new and formidable kind of wild foul. But who ever knew the Western pioneer to quail before anything with his trusty rifle?* [28]

In fact, for much of the preceding decade veterans of earlier "westering" ventures characterized big game hunting as prospecting expeditions. The potential rewards of finding gold probably received a warmer reception around the farm dinner table than a hunting lark. In any case, hunting was universally understood to be a great deal more rewarding and a great deal less work than prospecting irrespective of the cost and risk of doing so.

Jan. 5: Up before day. Killed a fat sheep and wounded a Mtn. lion before sunrise. Eat ribs for breakfast, drank last of my coffee. After breakfast moved up half mile to next creek on south side; made new camp under big fir tree. Good gravel here, looks like it carries gold. Wind has blown snow off the rim but gravel is hard frozen. Panned out two cups; no gold in either.

Jan. 6: Pleasant day. Built big fire on rim rock to thaw the gravel; kept it up all day. Careajou came into camp while I was at fire. Dogs killed him after I broke his back with belt axe; H—l of a fight.

Jan. 7: Clear day. Removed fire embers and dug into rim of bed rock; panned out eight treaty cups of dirt, and found nothing but fine colors; ninth cup I got one nugget of coarse gold. Feel good tonight. Dogs don't. Drum is lame all over; sewed up gash in his leg tonight – Careajou no good for dog.

Jan. 8: Pleasant day – well, Tom, old boy, I've got the diggings at last, but can't be back in a week. Dogs can't travel. D—n a carcajou. Dug and panned today until my belt knife was worn out, so I will have to quit or use my skinning knife. I have about a half ounce of gold; so will quit and try and get back in the spring.

Jan. 9: Filled up the hole with charcoal from the big fire, and built a fire over it. Marked the big fir tree with belt-axe and knife thus; [here occurs a map of the camp, tree and prospect hole.] Cut the top off a small lodge pole pine on a line from fir tree in a westerly direction. All fixed now; will be off down the creek tomorrow.

[Five days later, nearly barefoot George A. Jackson entered basecamp and the history books. His journal entry for January 14 read:]

Got out at mouth of canon just at dark, and got down to the old camp and had a good supper of States grub. Tom was getting uneasy – a little. After supper I told him what I had found, and showed him the gold, and we talked, smoked and ate the balance of the night. I could hardly realize I had been away nineteen days. [29]

Jackson had staked his claim according to the customs of the day. Notwithstanding his forced winter march, slightly more than his fair share of Carcajou and sheep hides, and a half ounce of hard-won gold to show for his ordeal, he counted it an even trade. In retrospect, it was more than an even trade. George had successfully traced gold float to its source, a quartz motherlode. Back in base camp with time again on his hands, Jackson laid plans for spring. He knew he needed help, partners and funds. Thomas Golden was both a friend and a partner he could trust, but he was no better off financially than George. A group of recent arrivals, the "Chicago Company," had the fullest larder and finest tools. They also had cash. Recognizing George's mountain skills, nose for gold, and most importantly staked claim, a betrothal soon followed. [30]

In May, George Jackson returned to his diggings on West Chicago Creek, now named after his Chicago benefactors, where he worked hard to promote his find. After mining "Jackson Diggings" for some weeks and taking out four to five thousand dollars' worth of gold, he skillfully portrayed his claim as a bonanza. [31] Where George acquired his business savvy is a mystery, but it is clear he preferred marketing to mining. Word of Jackson's bonanza spread quickly and the gulches began filling with fellow travelers. At risk of naive speculators outbidding them, the Chicago Company bought out Jackson's share and George retreated with his profits to the comforts of Arapahoe City, soon to be renamed Golden. [32]

Survivalist Turned Mine Entrepreneur. George Jackson earned his place in Colorado gold mine history the hard way. Surviving winter conditions that could easily have killed him, his quartz lode discovery and handy sale to Chicago investors provided a handsome grubstake for other pursuits. Other pursuits included a stint in the Confederate army and a ranch near Ouray on the western slope where he died of a self-inflicted gunshot wound. *(Frank Hall)*

Destiny fulfilled. George's contribution to Colorado gold rush history was complete. The fruit of his perseverance in conjunction with the discoveries of Russell and Gregory set the stage for 1860 developments that would assure Colorado's emergence as a mining mecca. With three quartz strikes in quick succession, the evidence was nearly undeniable. The roots of Front Range placer-gold were indeed gold-bearing quartz lodes in the foothills, and by extension in the High Country. In other words, gold-bearing ore along with other valuable metals, in contrast to water-borne flakes and nuggets, filled quartz veins too prolific to calculate. From the perspective of the national economy, an infusion of new wealth on the scale of California gold could not come soon enough. From Jackson's perspective, he was grateful he could cash out with little more invested than his mountain skills and a few months of hard labor. He seemed satisfied with his fair share.

To no ones surprise, he was not satisfied with city life. The mountain man in him did not rest. Spring 1860 found him back in the hunt for gold in California Gulch. Near present-day Leadville, 1860 California Gulch was the tip of the spear jabbing farther and farther into the foreboding Rockies. Neither did his adventurous spirit and southern loyalties rest. A year later found

Lieutenant-Colonel Jackson leading Confederate forces in the Civil War. The Colonel survived four years of war and returned to Colorado mining. In 1888, he settled in Ouray County where he promoted and owned a number of mines. On March 13, 1897, George Andrew Jackson died from a self-inflicted gunshot wound—as close to dying in bed as this risk-taker could manage—pulling his rifle from a sled.

John Gregory was not as long-lived, but his contribution to pulling the Colorado gold rush back from the brink of failure was no less impactful. Included in the 1858-59 cadre of remaining mountain men, he did not survive Civil War service. Yet, like Jackson and Russell, his motherlode discovery fulfilled his destiny. Nearly within sight of one another, Green Russell located gold quartz up Clear Creek. George Jackson located gold quartz on the southern branch of Clear Creek, and John Gregory located gold quartz on the northern branch of Clear Creek. If Jackson's quartz mine was not assurance enough, Gregory's find established beyond doubt, "thar is gold in them thar hills!" With the help of John Cantrell and boosters like him plying the Missouri frontier with glowing reports, the Pikes Peak gold rush was an unstoppable "go" even if it was poorly named.

On no less authority than acclaimed Colorado historian Frank Hall, John Gregory ranked alongside Green Russell as "the two great pioneers of discovery, from whose trails such mighty consequences have been wrought in the years that have elapsed since their names and deeds thrilled the continent." [33] Hall was referring to Gregory's Central City/Black Hawk lode. He did not put much stock in George Jackson's earlier and harder-won discovery of gold quartz in present-day Idaho Springs. Nor did he explain his reasoning. Perhaps it was simply that Gregory's claim was easier to get to. Journalists of that day seemed to think so. Hall continued, "in May 1859, John Gregory had solved the problem of Colorado's future, which instantly dispelled the winter of our discontent and made glorious summer for the disheartened..." [34]

What was Hall saying? A tipping point had been reached, that's what. From his perspective, gold discoveries up until Gregory's were insufficient to support further investigation much less a mad rush across the plains. More threatening, fledgling Denver and surrounding settlements struggling through their first winter were surely destined for ghost town status absent Gregory's find. As evidence, Hall cited A. D. Richardson, acclaimed editor of the *New York Tribune*, who in 1859 visited the region to see for himself and truthfully report on "the extent and value of the golden magnet that is impelling thousands across the great American Sahara...." The most excitable adventurers did not need more first-hand accounts to fire them into action. The tens of thousands who did quickly fell in behind the vanguard. Richardson was not finished.

It was an uncontrollable eruption, a great river of human life rolling toward the setting sun, at once a triumph and a prophecy. Denver was a most forlorn

*and desolate looking metropolis. There were only five women in the entire gold
region. The men who gathered about our coach on its arrival were attired in
slouched hats, tattered woolen shirts, buckskin pantaloons and moccasins, and
had knives and revolvers suspended from their belts.* [35]

Unwilling to leave 1859 Denver at that, Hall took more umbrage with the
struggling outpost:

*The roof of the cabin he (Editor Richardson) occupied, an example of a major-
ity, was of baked mud upon a layer of split logs and grass; the floor of hard
smooth earth; no window invited adventurous burglars, and the solitary door
that swung upon wooden hinges, opened to the touch of no key but a pen-knife
or a string. The chief articles of diet were salt bacon, dried apples, beans and
coffee; flour when to be had, fresh meat when game abounded. The social fabric
was a singular medley, Americans, Mexicans, Indians, half-breeds, trappers,*

JOHN H. GREGORY

Not to quibble over who was first or foremost, Jackson or Gregory, both deserve credit
for giving legs to the 1859 rush to the Front Range sparked by Lewis Ralston and Green
Russell. Regarding the fundamental differences between a short-lived mining camp and
an enduring settlement, both helped Uncle Dick Wootton save Denver. Locating gold
nuggets and the nearby quartz lodes they came from, compared to gold beaten into
flakes by lengthy journeys downstream, were game-changers. The first practical effect
of their good fortune, and the crowd pressure from wave after wave of gold-seekers
panning every Front Range watershed and gulch, pushed men and beasts farther and
farther into the foreboding mountains. John Gregory landed in present-day Central
City-Blackhawk. Blackhawk quickly grew into Colorado's first home of its gold and silver
ore processing industry.

　　According to Ovando Hollister, who did not have the benefit of Frank Hall's hindsight, Gregory was another Georgia "cracker," or Indian countryman depending on who
was doing the introductions. His family moved from South Carolina in the early 1830s
to take advantage of the 1832 *Gold Lottery* in which Lewis Ralston and most Cherokee
landowners lost their gold-rich properties. John's father was a gold miner, and so was
John. John also was well versed in mining law and contracts. According to local sources,
he was an outgoing individual albeit discreet about his business affairs, a trait that
seemed contrary to his Gregory Gulch dealings several decades hence. By 1850, John
owned a 1,000-acre plantation. After several local moves, in 1860 he relocated with
his family to Marshall County, Alabama. At no time during these years was there any
indication Gregory knew Lewis Ralston or Green Russell, suggesting that he was not
a countryman. Maybe his family's involvement in the *Gold Lottery* was known and too

speculators, gamblers, desperadoes, broken-down politicians, ruined bankers, real estate speculators, and now and then an honest man.

One lady, by sewing together gunny sacks for a carpet and covering her log walls with sheets and table cloths, gave to her mansion an appearance of almost aristocratic refinement and comfort. Stools, tables, and pole-bedsteads were the staple furniture, while rough pine boxes did duty as bureaus and sideboards. The vacant places in the lower part of the embryonic city were occupied by Indian lodges, enlivened by squaws dressing the skins of wild animals, or cooking dogs for dinner; naked children playing in the sand, and braves lounging on the ground, wearing no clothing except a narrow strip of cloth about the hips.

Such was the picture in 1859. It was not materially changed in the spring of 1860, except that more and better buildings had arisen and the population amazingly augmented. All roads leading to the mountains were lined with ox or mule trains with white sheeted wagons winding their way slowly to the newly discovered and exceedingly prosperous gold mines. [36]

---

bitter a pill to swallow. Various accounts indicate that Gregory learned of their Cherry Creek discoveries in 1859 while wintering at Fort Laramie.

John was thirty-seven years old and married with children when he left home in 1857. His motivation was unstated, but logically it had to do with the nation-wide depression and the fact that his gold mining skills might be more useful in the West. The Fraser River gold rush in British Columbia seemed like a good idea at the time. John worked his passage as a deck hand on steamboats to Fort Leavenworth. From there he drove a government team to Fort Laramie where winter caught up with him. While at Fort Laramie, his British Columbia gold fever broke. In its place, rumors of gold discoveries south on the Platte River captured his fancy. Arriving in Green Russell and George Jackson's backyards, probably late February or early March, John set to work. At the mouth of what soon became "Gregory Gulch," he panned colors that he suspected "had not traveled far in its transit." [37]

Gregory traced the gold float to its source. With generous support from an Indiana benefactor, he developed his find into a valuable mine that he then sold to speculators.

According to family records, John Gregory left Denver in 1862 a very wealthy man. With considerable difficulty, he managed to get back to Alabama despite Union forces blockading the customary routes to the South. On September 26, 1863, he enlisted in the Confederate Army as a private in Company H, 65th Georgia Infantry. Captured at Marietta, Georgia on July 3, 1864, he died from chronic diarrhea in Camp Morton Prison at Indianapolis, Indiana on January 22, 1865. Had it not been for the Civil War, John Gregory could have lived a comfortable life anywhere he chose. He left the Colorado gold fields a financial success and with a legacy in Colorado history. [38] Ironically, he died in the state from which his benevolent partner David Wall and prospecting companion Wilkes Defrees hailed. [39]

John Gregory was not new to gold mining, but his journey to Colorado did not demonstrate a sense of urgency or a firm grasp of Front Range prospects. According to Ovando Hollister,

[John Gregory] drove a Government team from Leavenworth to Fort Laramie in 1858, where, by a succession of accidents, he was detained until the Spring of 1859. Meanwhile he heard of the discoveries of gold on the South Platte, and started on a prospecting tour along the base of the mountains, south, early in January. He found nothing satisfactory until he arrived at the Vasquez Fork [Clear Creek] of the South Platte, which he follows up alone, his plan being to prospect thoroughly wherever the creek forked, and to follow the branch which gave most promise. In this way he toiled up the Kanyon (sic), perhaps the first white man who had ever invaded its solitude, to the main forks of the creek, fourteen miles above Golden City; then up the north branch to the gulch that bears his name, seven miles, beyond which he could obtain nothing of consequence. Here he left the creek, and took up the gulch.

Where the little ravine, immediately south-east of [what became] the Gregory Lode, comes in, he again prospected, and finding it the richest of the two, he turned aside into it; but as he approached its head the "color" grew less, and finally entirely failed. Gregory now felt certain that he had found the gold; but before he could satisfy himself a heavy snow-storm occurred, during which he nearly perished. Upon its clearing up, he was obliged to return to the valley for provisions, and leave his discovery unperfected. [40]

Gregory knew from Georgia and California experience that he needed to thoroughly examine and stake his gulch, but heavy snow cover made that impossible for the time being. Gregory also knew that the area swarmed with other gold-seekers, some who traveled south with him, most who organized their own parties. George Jackson was included in this latter category. Interestingly, Jackson, Gregory and others—all competitors, and all driven by the press of time and weather—agreed to rendezvous at Arapahoe City [Golden] in a few days and share information. At this meeting, Gregory, if it was possible, was both exuberant and despondent at the same time. He had located what he considered a motherlode, but he was destitute. Whether at this meeting, by happenstance or by divine appointment, John met a new arrival by the name of David K. Wall from South Bend, Indiana. He and the affable Hoosier consummated a history-making deal, much along the lines of Jackson and the Chicago Company—"lack of money problem" solved.

David Wall did not risk his life crossing the Great Plains in 1859 to prospect for gold. He crossed to plant a garden. Knowing something about irrigation, and apparently about soil conditions along the Front Range, he brought with him farming implements and enough seeds to grow produce in quantities that would "make his living." The irrigation laterals he dug from Clear Creek to his homestead just east of Golden brought water in abundance, and in abundance his seeds would provide vegetables prized by his fellow emigrants and income for himself.

At least that was his vision.

Wall was of modest means, but like so many pioneers of his day, he nevertheless was generous and willing to help a fellow pilgrim in need. John Gregory was just such a pilgrim, and for his part also was a likeable sort. Moreover, he was a mature family man in contrast to the typical frontier "runaway." A partnership soon evolved. With David's "grubstake," only late winter storms now stood between Gregory and his motherlode. [41]

On May 6, 1859, accompanied by another "David Wall Hoosier" by the name of Wilkes Defrees, John Gregory returned to his claim and properly staked it.

John Gregory. Gregory is credited with one of the first discoveries of gold quartz which confirmed there was a fortune to be uncovered in the Rocky Mountain Front Range. Unlike many of his contemporaries, he sold his claims to investors and returned east to fight and die in the Civil War. *(Courtesy of the Gilpin Historical Society)*

[Gregory] ascended the hill between Bobtail and Gregory Gulch and in the midst of a grove of young pines and aspen, found the blossom rock of a gold-bearing lead cropping out of the hill; he scraped away the leaves and filled his pan with dirt and fragments of quartz that had been rendered friable by the action of the weather, carried it down the gulch, and upon panning it down his greatest expectations were more than realized. There in the bottom of his pan was a quarter of an ounce, or something over four dollars' worth of bright yellow gold. [42] [Often reported, that night Gregory could not sleep. "My wife shall be a lady," he said over and over to himself, "and my children will be educated." [43]]

Ovando Hollister has Gregory and Defrees reaching this site in a tedious journey of three days over the hills and ridges. This little party is hardly less an object of interest than Magellan seeking with a will of iron, with an intelligence in advance of his age, and with faith "as a grain of mustard-seed," to circumnavigate the globe; or than Columbus, after eighteen years of painful effort, sailing from the Roads of Saltez through unknown seas to discover a new world. His attention turned thither by flying reports, Gregory had sought the unbroken wilderness on the heads of the South Platte; alone and penniless but with a ripe intelligence, the fruit of years of experience, he had commenced operations and now, through the assistance of a stranger, is about to realize the bright dreams that have haunted him for months.

That night he did not close his eyes. Defrees dropped asleep about three o'clock in the morning, and left him talking; Defrees awoke at daybreak, and he was still talking. They washed out forty pans of dirt, and obtained forty dollars. Then they returned to the valley to get their friends. [44]

Another late winter snowstorm held John and Defrees at bay until May 16, 1859. From the 16th to the 22nd, they worked five hands and sluiced out nearly a thousand dollars of gold from what became "Claim #5." Not great production, apparently its promise was convincing enough. John sold "Claims #5 and #6" shortly thereafter for $21,000 and became a consultant. For the generous sum of $200 per day he spent his remaining days in the mountains prospecting for others. Clearly gifted, and apparently not greedy, Gregory departed Denver for home with $30,000 to show for his efforts. [45]

Like Frank Hall, Duane Smith credits John Gregory's gold discovery with being "the prime factor in saving the Pike's Peak rush." He cites Editor Byers and his belief that Gregory "almost single-handedly saved the day and hailed him:"

"No one had labored harder to develop our resources than he nor with better success." He took with him the "good wishes of the whole country" and, probably more importantly, carried "$25,000 in gold dust" back to his home in Georgia, after previously forwarding "some $5,000 to his family." Byers hoped to see him again in "the coming spring with machinery and facilities such as we know he will operate as it should be done." When the spring of 1860 came, Gregory arrived with his quartz mill, which he soon sold. [46]

Byers should have said that Gregory's discovery was "icing on Jackson, Russell and Ralston cakes," or highlighted "machinery and facilities." As distinguished from "pan," a quartz mill signaled a profound change. Colorado Rockies' mineral reserves justified [and required] great investment. There was no doubt Gregory played a pivotal role in demonstrating that gold lodes were prizes available to anyone willing to challenge the mountains above Cherry Creek, but his singular accomplishment was elevating Colorado prospecting from "flash in the pan" to hardrock mining. Ironically, that accomplishment did not include more quartz mills.

John Gregory's mine confirmed already mounting evidence that Colorado gold was no joke. His discovery of another Front Range mother lode added critical mass, hard evidence–the proverbial last straw–that increased the volume and believability of the boosters. His equipment marked the start of a new era uncovering treasure. The cumulative effect of Gregory's quartz vein located in close proximity in space and time with Jackson, Russell, and Ralston claims provided more than enough fuel to reignite the rush.

The 1859 emigrants had gotten the message. So would the next wave. All signs pointed to 1860 being another raucous year. Even many thousands of "go-backers" would take on a more hopeful tone–maybe Colorado gold was not a "humbug" after all.

Too Crowded for Comfort. Early Colorado Front Range gold placer discoveries that quickly lead to quartz lodes ensured a flood of newcomers. Unwilling to deal with the crush of activities, movement into the foothills and High Country soon led to additional mother-lodes. *(Richardson, 1867)*

News of Gregory's strike had reached Denver within a week and by June "Gregory Gulch" teemed with 4,000 prospectors. The rapidity and magnitude of this invasion far exceeded anything Ralston, Russell or Jackson could have imagined, further indication that the tide had turned. As was generally the case in these matters, the 4,000 swelled to 20,000 by late summer, other settlements sprang up, but with the approach of winter and the reality that there was never going to be thousands more "John Gregory finds," the surge of Argonauts ran its course. Nevertheless, Gregory Gulch produced $1.5 million dollars' of gold in 1859, and the Clear Creek Mining District organized around it became known as the "richest square mile on earth." [47] "Easy gold"–near-surface deposits accessible with pick and shovel—accounted for the good fortune. "Hard gold" would require heavy mining equipment, engineering, and spring weather. Until that was at hand, most gold-seekers concluded it was wise to winter at home. Many joined the "go-backers," but many with new field experience and equipment in tow would return. The impending Civil War and resurgence of Indian troubles sorely stressed the newfound excitement 1860 traveling weather brought with it, but close calls with Denver's ghost-town status and a Front Range humbug were already a faint memory. So, too, were the hardships the first wave of Fifty-Niners had endured crossing the Great Plains. [48]

Notes—Chapter Five: Close Calls

[1] Wootton, Richens Lacy, *Uncle Dick Wootton*, pg. 20. [*Also* profiled in Hall, *History of Colorado*, Vol II, pgs. 233-241.

[2] Hall, Vol. II., p. 233.

[3] Wootton, pg. 21.

[4] Ibid., pgs. 17-18. [Bent's Fort, originally named Fort William in honor of William Bent, was designed to survive Indian attack. Its adobe walls were 2-4 ft. thick and 15 ft. high, enclosed a 135 ft. by 180 ft. area with towers at two opposing diagonal corners. Within the enclosure were low earth-roofed rooms and a corral. "Fort Bent became the outstanding trading post of the Southwest, sharing both the mountain trade and the overland trade to Santa Fe."]

[5] Ibid., pg. 2.

[6] Ibid., pgs. 72-78.

[7] Ibid., pg. 240.

[8] Hollister, *The Mines of Colorado*, pgs. 17-18.

[9] Ibid., pg. 18.

[10] Wootton, pg. 241.

[11] Ibid., pg. 243.

[12] Ibid.

[13] Hall, Vol. II., pg. 229.

[14] Ibid., pgs., 232-233.

[15] Wootton, pg. 244.

[16] Hall, Vol. II., pg. 233.

[17] Wootton, pg. 244.

[18] Ibid., pg. 245. [The first issue of the *Rocky Mountain News* was published April 23, 1859. Footnote 102 on page 246 reads: "While the *News* was being printed in the night of April 22 the roof of Wootton's emporium leaked so badly that a tent cover had to be placed over the press to keep it dry. It continued publication throughout the summer with 'tolerable regularity,' although isolation from the East and paucity of printers' supplies rendered its publication highly uncertain. Laramie, Wyoming, over 200 miles distant, was the nearest post office, and even their arrival of the mails was irregular."

Neither paucity of printing supplies or of news, however, served to daunt the resourceful editor, who devoted much space to boosting the country, reporting new mining strikes, and depicting the brilliant future in store for Colorado, thereby earning, at the hands of disgruntled immigrants, the reputation of being one of the most capable and dangerous liars in the country.

A.D. Richardson, a contemporary eastern reporter and traveler, who visited Denver in 1859, wrote: "The establishment was always in a state of armed neutrality. Printers and editors were moving arsenals, with revolvers at their belts and shotguns standing beside their cases and desks." [p. 246 FN.]

[19] Ibid., pg. 250.

[20] Ibid., pgs. 248-249.

[21] Ibid., pgs. 251-252.

[22] Typically, historians spell the Chief's name "Kaniache."

[23] Richens Lacy "Uncle Dick Wootton," http://www.sangres.com/history/uncledick.htm, pg. 2.

[24] "Western Mountaineer," Golden, Colorado, *The Colorado Magazine* December 14, 1859. Cited in "George A. Jackson's Diary, 1858-1859," edited by LeRoy R. Hafen, Denver, Colorado, Vol. XII, No. 6, November 1935, pg. 201. [Jackson is credited with redirecting gold-seeker attention away from placers to quartz lodes, away from Front Range streams to High-Country hardrock mines. His prospecting/mining pursuits lasted a life-time, but shortly after his initial successes they took a backseat to family and farming. He spent his later years comfortably surrounded by Ouray, Colorado neighbors.]

[25] Fort Laramie served many critical functions throughout its frontier history. It was a vital way-station on the Oregon, California and Mormon trails, a rendezvous site for trappers and traders, a staging point for numerous military expeditions and treaty signings, an 1860 pony express

station, and the closest post office for fledgling Denver 200 miles to the southwest.

26 Gehling, "F–The Mountaineers," pg. 16. [Greeley's assessment, Gehling suggests, "may have been somewhat severe." More representative was Uncle Dick Wootton, William McGaa and the like who settled into communal life and played key roles in the establishment and growth of Denver and lesser towns throughout the Front Range. McGaa, less generous than Wootton, settled in to shop-keeping, real estate, and Denver civil service. "Of all the mountaineers, McGaa seemed to best realize that the profits to be made from the Indian trade were fast coming to an end. The day of catering to the needs of the gold seeker was at hand." [pg. 17] McGaa stayed on in Denver, becoming a city father. Uncle Dick in due course retreated to Raton Pass separating Colorado and New Mexico where he ranched, improved a section of the Santa Fe trail into a toll road, and sold its right-of-way to the advancing Santa Fe railroad system.]

27 Ibid., pgs. 2-3.

28 Hollister, pg. 17.

29 *Western Mountaineer*, pg. 206.

30 Gehling, "F–The Mountaineers," pg. 10.

31 "Gregory's Discovery of Gold Opened New Era In Colorado," *Steamboat Pilot*, February 11, 1943, pg. 8.

32 Gehling, "F–The Mountaineers," pg. 16.

33 Hall, Vol. IV., pg. 26.

34 Ibid.

35 Ibid.

36 Ibid., pgs. 26-27.

37 Spring, Agnes Wright, "Rush to the Rockies, 1859," pg. 105.

38 "Gregory's Discovery of Gold Opened New Era In Colorado," pgs. 1-8.

39 North, Pam, "Glimpses of Past & Present: John H. Gregory, Man Behind the Mystery," pgs. 1-3.

40 Hollister, pgs. 61-62.

41 "Gregory's Discovery of Gold Opened New Era in Colorado," pgs. 5-6.

42 Spring, pg. 107.

43 "Gregory's Discovery of Gold Opened New Era in Colorado," pg. 6.

44 Hollister, pgs. 62-63.

45 Spring, pg. 107 FN; Hollister, pg. 63.

46 Smith, Duane A., *Trail of Gold and Silver*, pg. 42.

47 "Central City, Colorado – Boom & Bust," *Legends of America*, pg. 1.

48 "Central City–Black Hawk Historic District," *Colorado Encyclopedia*, pg 2. [1860 witnessed the arrival of equipment. In the spring of 1860 the Black Hawk Quartz Mill Company installed stamping equipment to separate quartz from gold. Black Hawk became the hub for processing and transporting ores from the areas hardrock mines. Black Hawk, more precisely the "Gregory Diggings," proved the principle that hardrock quartz lodes, the source of placer gold, could be found throughout the Front Range and in the land beyond. Also, in February 1860 the first steam engine was assembled to produce shingles and could be used to power stamping mills. The engine cost $1,500 when sold in late 1859 by the Chicago foundry that built it. In March 1860 it sold for $15,000. "Central City, Colorado – Boom & Bust," *Legends of America*, pg. 2, https://www.legendsofamerica.com/co-centralcity/ .] [Word spread quickly, along the Front Range and back to the States. The largest mass migration in American history was about to launch. "Pikes Peak or Bust! said all that needed to be said. Ironically, Cherry Creek and the South Platte always disappointed, but as we shall soon learn, Idaho Springs, Central City and Blackhawk sang a different song. By 1860, for example, Central City had a population of over 10,000 people. Denver and Golden witnessed a surge estimated at 100,000 to 150,000 (most of whom went home). "The Colorado Gold Rush," *Western Mining History* Online: https:// westernmining history.com/articles/11/page 1.]

CHAPTER 6

Rapscallions, Nincompoops and Ninnies

I am not one of those who in expressing
opinions confine themselves to facts. [1]
— Mark Twain —

Oregon Trail homesteaders had little in common with the rush of California-bound Forty-Niners and Colorado's Fifty-Niners, but the Forty-Niners and Fifty-Niners were nearly indistinguishable. In many cases, they were one and the same. Just as the gold-savvy Georgia Cherokees enriched the Forty-Niners, so too they and many Forty-Niners enriched those who shrugged off the ridicule of naysayers and responded to Colorado's siren song. The 1858-59 vanguard of what grew into a mass emigration, outfitted with little more than great expectations, dwindled to a remnant when faced with natural hardships and human disappointments. Nevertheless, the timely discovery of gold-bearing quartz veins and the passions aroused by rapscallions, nincompoops, and ninnies, as well as honest brokers, energized another surge of pilgrims yet another year.

Lewis Ralston, Green Russell, George Jackson and John Gregory had been the tip of the spear. They did the field work and replaced rumored gold with the real McCoy. Uncle Dick Wootton had done his part. He pulled fledgling Denver back from the brink of starvation. During those earliest of hard times, John Simpson Smith also gave up mountaineering to organize the Denver camp into a city. But without the "boosters" small and great—John Cantrell, William Byers, A.D. Richardson, Horace Greeley, Andrew McGrew and scores of ordinary scribes far and wide–the flood of emigrants they encouraged would have been a trickle.

In 1859, the Plains Indians commanded the prairie and the Ute commanded the mountains. Neither were fond of intruders, white or red. As explained by Wootton, mountain men were somewhat tolerated, prospectors to a lesser extent, miners and settlers not at all. The United States Army resolved this problem in due course and not to the satisfaction of any, but during the Colorado gold rush there was no compromise in sight. At best, white intruders remained wary and the Indian nations remained threatening. Along the Front Range, essentially "no man's land," the Arapahoe and Sioux claimed sovereignty northward, Cheyenne and Arapahoe southward, Ute the High Country. Inter-tribal trade across unmarked ancestral boundaries was common. So was war.

Long before even Spanish Conquistadores arrived, tribal alliances jelled and dissolved depending on leadership and resources. Forays into neighboring territory were routine. Usually Ute raiders suffered defeat on the plains, plains raiders suffered defeat in the mountains. As for the Cherokee, they played the dandy, ever respectful and leery of all their neighbors. Likewise, the tribes alien to the region, those relocated from their eastern tribal lands in order to make room for more immigrants, avoided their hostile brothers as best they could. No surprise that Fall Leaf, the Lawrence party's Delaware scout, and gentrified Tahlequah Cherokee pathfinders guiding Ralston and Russell, preached safety in large numbers. They also made it a habit to honor local customs and to turn for home at the slightest hint of offense.

Most Likely from New York. No one was immune to gold fever, not even the gentry-class who already were well-to-do. Subject to ridicule, they also were individuals who the ruffian-class sought out when in need of a grubstake or a partner. *(Frank Leslie's Illustrated Newspaper, June 7, 1879)*

Between 1840 and 1860, several positive developments fostered a more welcoming frontier. The 1821 Mexican independence ushered in an interest in trade that replaced Spanish paranoia concerning American southwestern expansion that would threaten New Spain. Republic of Mexico traders rolled both east and west along the Santa Fe Trail. Of course, the Spanish, wise in the ways of the world, had been prophetic. The American defeat of Mexico in 1848 eliminated any semblance of foreign jurisdiction and law. Spanish and Mexican culture survived, albeit overshadowed with President Polk's doctrine of Manifest Destiny. If further evidence was required, the U.S. Army replaced private trading posts with new forts strategically sited throughout former Native

Can't Wait for Spring. Prospecting along the Front Range frustrated most newcomers, but reports from Gregory's Gulch and other quartz lodes encouraged herculean efforts to get there regardless of the season. (*Crofutt's Grip-Sack Guide*)

American and Spanish territories. Almost overnight encroaching civilization appeared in the form of settlements, farms and ranches. Along the Front Range, the end of the fur trade forced mountain men into other pursuits, and gold-seekers unable or unwilling to retreat to family farms and ranches in the States, instead scratched them out anew. Crude irrigation ditches also were scratched out to bring adequate water from nearby streams to gardens worked into fields. On the prairie, checkerboard style, settlers willing to pull up short of their distant dreams, anchored themselves instead to shabby outposts that would grow into villages and towns. [2]

Those caught up in this transition could not grasp the profound nature of all the change. The 1859 rush to Colorado's Front Range, just a part of the larger transformation of the region, was different only with respect to its speed and its chaos. The following year would be much the same. Ovando Hollister, writing from first-hand experience, reported that "never did spring open on a more hopeful people" than during the rush of 1860. "The richness and great extent of the new gold fields were considered proven. Immigrants were arriving from the States at the rate of a hundred a day." Duane Smith explains Hollister's optimism this way:

What made Hollister's outlook so sanguine? Among other things, the mining experience that had been gained, the mining machinery that had arrived, the laws and regulations that had been established, the roads that had been built and bettered, and the support industries and agriculture that had been developed. Finally, he noted a "great influx of people, many of them women, many of them bringing more or less capital, and coming at least prepared for the emergencies of the season." [3]

Rodman W. Paul writing in *The Far West and the Great Plains in Transition* adds:

The Colorado rush, although started largely by false reports, seems to have attracted more participants than any of the other rushes [throughout the northern Rocky Mountains from British Columbia through Idaho and Montana] save the great original one to California in 1849. Although the Federal census credited Colorado with only 34,277 in 1860 and 39,864 in 1870, a well-informed contemporary estimated that more than 50,000 took part in the rush of 1859, and that 100,000 people were in Colorado for varying periods between 1858 and 1870, with no more than a third of that total present in the territory at any one time.

In other words, as in Montana and Idaho, there was constant coming and going by the unstable gold-rush crowd, but the turnover seems to have been unusually large in the case of Colorado, probably because Colorado was closer to the 'States' than were the camps of the northern Rockies. Dangerous though it might be to travel six hundred to seven hundred miles across the plains, nevertheless the journey between Colorado and the Missouri River towns was entirely possible. After all, as Editor Greeley's trip demonstrated, stagecoach service between Denver and the Missouri frontier was available even in 1859. [4]

Food was also available, albeit at first in unpredictable quantities in keeping with the unpredictable splurges of pathfinders and mountain men. Demand might outstrip local sources of supply, but entrepreneurs usually were quick to respond, Uncle Dick Wootton a case in point. Robert Brown's *Empire of Silver* describes a much improved but still fragile supply chain a decade later in the San Juans, an even more remote region of the Colorado Rockies.

[Brown:] A number of people in the San Juan district soon discovered that there were means other than with gold and silver by which a fortune could be made. Farming and stock raising became very profitable businesses. The greater portion of the cattle brought to the San Juans was driven in from eastern and northern Colorado, with some herds from New Mexico and Texas. One livestock supplier who took animals into the San Juans recalls a time when he used a total of sixteen wagons, some two- and some four-horse teams. An ox-team ordinarily consisted of five yoke of oxen. Coming over the range they were able to make only two or three miles a day. It was necessary to take one wagon a mile or two and then come back for another, keeping the whole group together. They had a large bunch of cattle and also hauled both hogs and chickens. They often carried enough supplies from Denver to last for a year. The miners bought sheep from them occasionally along the road for seventy-five cents per head.

Where the hillsides were steep, they took out a plow from their stock and plowed a furrow for one wheel and lashed poles to the wagon. Then a bunch of the men rode the end of the pole to keep the wagon from tipping. Progress at this rate was extremely slow. Such pack-trains rarely made more than ten miles a day.

At various times there was said to have been over twenty thousand head of livestock in the San Juan country, exclusive of horses and mules. All had free access to the open ranges. Although beef on the hoof was always low in price, it could be made to pay under the circumstances. The Grimes brothers drove in seven hundred head of cattle one fall from Texas. When the spring roundup came around, only two hundred of them could be found. Flour sold at fourteen dollars per hundred pounds, coffee at forty cents per pound, sugar three pounds for a dollar, and dried fruits at twenty-five cents per pound. Some women in the San Juan country parched chicory and barley to make a cereal drink which served as a coffee substitute. Before the winter was out, some men expressed a feeling that it was better than coffee.

The vegetable situation was not quite as favorable, although a fairly good assortment of canned items such as corn, peas, and tomatoes could be purchased. Dried fruits were available with monotonous frequency and most miners came to dread their appearance on the table. For some unknown reason there were few jellies on San Juan menus. Naturally, there were no fresh vegetables available during the long winters. Parsnips were often buried in snowbanks and some said that the longer they were frozen, the sweeter they tasted.

Along about February the farmers in the San Juan country had begun to cut the eyes out of potatoes. They were saved for seed because potatoes were so hard to

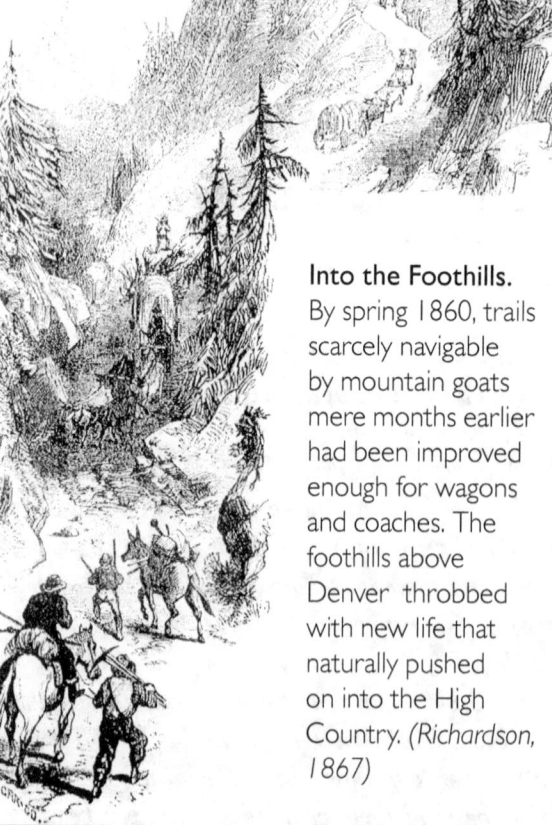

Into the Foothills.
By spring 1860, trails scarcely navigable by mountain goats mere months earlier had been improved enough for wagons and coaches. The foothills above Denver throbbed with new life that naturally pushed on into the High Country. (Richardson, 1867)

get. Some soaked them in the community water dish for a couple of days before planting because they had, of course, dried out. In March shipments of lettuce and radishes began arriving from Grand Junction. From truck farms to the north of Ouray came fresh vegetables of all kinds as the growing season progressed. Each fall brought wagonloads of fresh fruits from Paonia. Four horses were required to get each load over the passes to Silverton.

[Brown logically concluded that the dietary situation among the San Juan miners was healthier than often reported. They had choices that were reasonably varied and generally wholesome. Since labor shortages were a constant concern, men often left their place of employment to seek work elsewhere simply because the food was better elsewhere. As such, cooks were in high demand.]

[Brown:] Biscuits, hot cakes, pies, potatoes, and roasts were common. Steaks were somewhat scarce. Cereals of several varieties were plentiful, and milk was almost always abundant. When fresh milk was not available, canned or condensed milk was mixed at the ratio of two cans to a large pitcher of water.

Food in the San Juans, unless one happened to be an intimate of Alfred Packer, did not differ materially from that consumed in other mining districts. Meat and potatoes made up the staple backbone of most diets. When not baked or boiled, they were fried in lard. A variety of homemade breads and pastries were available to the married men, while bachelors purchased such 'goodies' from the limited number of women who reaped small fortunes operating bakeries and eating houses. Bacon, eggs, 'salt side' (pork), and chickens were readily available. Ham brought sixteen cents a pound while a hindquarter of beef, which would keep through the cold of winter without refrigeration, could be purchased for only eight cents a pound. Some chose to vary the fare with a hind quarter of pork. Many of the permanent settlers kept cows, hogs, and chickens for their own convenience. [5]

Clearly, Brown is skimming the surface, a surface spanning decades at that, but still most emigrants were not in danger of starvation. As for wholesome nutrition, young A. D. Richardson confidently reported:

The experience of every mining region demonstrates that pork is the most nutritive and stimulating diet for miners.... As agriculture was not begun, vegetables were unattainable for love or money. Late in the season however, a few enormous watermelons appeared in market, selling at two or three dollars apiece. The chief meat was antelope, always abundant at fifty cents per pound. Though more tasteless than the flesh of the deer, it is pleasant and nutritive. [6]

All that said, deciding to leave the comforts of the "States" for the frontier was no small matter and no small risk. Contributing to the decision-making process in 1860 was the nation-wide economic depression, the impending Civil War, the propensity of Americans young and old to go out to see the elephant, and a resurgence of gold-fever despite a growing appreciation of the darker side of "boosterism." John Cantrell, our inquisitive and conniving frontier whiskey peddler last seen scurrying out of Green Russell's camp with a sack of sand and gravel, epitomized this class of promoter.

When it came to trumpeting the richness of the Colorado gold fields, many considered John Cantrell a rapscallion of the first order. To be fair, he had a great deal of company. He certainly was a gossip with ulterior motives, but account-able for spreading gold-fever throughout the States was an exaggeration. The proverbial straw that broke the camels back would have been a more appropriate characterization of his role. For a decade or more, credible reports of gold in the Colorado Rockies made their way back to civilization. Cantrell just happened to be in the right place to grab a gold sample that the right people needed to see. Voices that were more respectable also would soon sing the Siren's song, but it was not music to everyone's ear.

Ridicule most often greeted the cacophony of "Pikes Peak or Bust" clarion calls. Evaluating which Front Range accounts heralded truth and which heralded fraud and avarice salted conversations from barrooms to barbershops throughout the States. Newspapers nationwide documented the evidence supporting either perspective or both perspectives. Humbug and boosterism, opportunity and bounty, Cantrell had followers and detractors of all persuasions.

Drama aside, Cantrell made his living on the frontier. The more frontier souls in need of his advice and merchandise, his trades dominated by whiskey and guns, all the better for John. Whatever his other qualities or foibles might be, he was courageous. When it came to relating his time spent with Green Russell, his stories were not always consistent. Which version should one believe, if any? Consider the differences in the two John Cantrell "interviews" obtained just a few days apart, and the Green Russell daily journal entries often quoted long after. The most reliable account should be Green Russell's version preserved for us in a letter written years later by Cousin Pierce, but this assumption also is suspect.

If John Cantrell's character was not concern enough already, the next most reliable account should have been his interview shortly after returning from "the mines." Here also were exaggerations if not outright lies. Printed in the August 28, 1858, *Kansas City Journal of Commerce*, Cantrell shared his fresh experience with the *Journal's* subscribers eager for goldfield news:

> *Mr. John Cantrell, of Westport, arrived home on Thursday, from the gold mines at Cherry creek (sic) and Pike's Peak. Mr. Cantrell is well known to the people of this region of country, and his statements are of great interest. He left*

the mines on the 20th of July, at which time there were from thirty to thirty-five people at work, digging and prospecting.

Mr. Cantrell and party prospected all the small streams in the vicinity of the first discovery, and found gold upon all of them. They also found it from two to eight feet below the surface. This corresponds exactly with the first discoveries of gold in California.

Mr. Cantrell has with him samples of the gold, washed, in the sand, and in the quartz. The washed gold is the regular placer gold, in fine scales of extraordinary purity and richness. This was scraped up at various points during his prospecting tour.

He has also samples of the gold mixed with black sand, taken from the banks of the streams and from the bedrock. To an old miner this black sand settles the question, even without the gold itself, as it is infallible index to rich diggings. Mr. Cantrell also has a few specimens of quartz picked up away from the streams which contain gold, but from the want of proper tools and other facilities, no examination could satisfactorily be made in this respect. A portion of Mr. C's party remained at the mines, and will continue their prospecting operations until the return of the remainder and Mr. C. with tools and outfit… [7]

Within a week, the *Journal of Commerce* wrote what seemed more likely Green Russell's version of Cantrell's visit with the certain exception that Cantrell's "dirt is not discovered" by Cantrell, but instead by Green who offered it to him.

We had a call from Mr. Cantrell, on yesterday, with whom we had a lengthy and satisfactory conversation about the new mines of Pike's Peak.

Mr. Cantrell is an old California miner himself, and has had much experience in gold digging. He went out last spring with a lot of goods to trade with the army and emigration crossing the plains. After closing out his stock, and hearing that several parties had been prospecting on the headwaters of the Platte, he determined to visit the country and see for himself.

He first arrived at Cherry creek (sic), and there learned that a party of about one hundred men, a portion from Arkansas and Missouri, and a portion of Cherokee Indians, had been in the country for several weeks during the spring, but from the unusually high waters, the country being flooded beyond what had ever been known, they became discouraged, and many of them returned home. He learned, however, that a party of fifteen [actually only thirteen] men, under Green Russell of Georgia, had remained and were up nearer the mountains. He set out to find this party, which he succeeded in doing. They had been at work for ten or twelve days and had taken out about $1,000, a portion only being at work, and with no mining tools.

Mr. Cantrell traversed about seventy miles of the country, and in every stream he prospected he found gold. In one place where he prospected, three pans of dirt paid 66 cents, weighed with apothecary's scales. Mr. Cantrell brought about three bushels of dirt in his wagon, which was tested in Westport yesterday morning, by Edward Payton and other experienced miners, and which yielded about fifteen cents to each two quarts of dirt, and Mr. C. informs that he prospected bars that would yield from 20 to 25 cts. to the pan." [8]

John Cantrell, courtesy of the *Journal of Commerce*, threw kerosene on long-smoldering accounts of Front Range gold discoveries appearing from time to time on editorial pages across the country. Fanning nationwide gold fever back to life, first-hand accounts of gold discoveries sold newspapers and among Missouri River frontier towns all manner of gold-seeker paraphernalia as well. To be sure, there were ample accounts—accounts dating back to the rush to California—and even physical evidence to collaborate Cantrell's claims of gold recovered by his very own hands. For a population accustomed to adventure, how could the young or the desperate resist the Pike's Peak excitement, the Siren calls parroted from what seemed like every trusted sheet in the nation. Oh, there was an abundance of warnings to the contrary, but discouraging words from "go-backers" and naysayers—on occasion, like the Lawrence party, later contradicting themselves with good reports—did little to stem the enthusiasm of the hopeful.

With the fickle benefit of a decade of reflection, one *New York Tribune* journalist in particular portrayed with unrivaled authenticity the national mood and the darker side of those frontier days. Albert Deane Richardson, better known as A.D.R., captured first-hand realism in *Beyond the Mississippi*. Personally enmeshed in the 1859-60 rush, his recollection of those waves of mass humanity is invaluable. In 1867, close enough to the subject to be contemporary, he recalled early 1859 when even investment in public transportation, available to any emigrant able to scrounge up the fare, rose to meet the occasion.

[Richardson:] Thus far, there were no trustworthy reports of gold in paying quantities among the Rocky Mountains. But every newspaper on the Missouri River expressed absolute confidence that rich mines existed; and demonstrated irresistibly that the town wherein said newspaper was published was nearer the mines than any other, and therefore <u>the</u> place for emigrants to purchase cattle, wagons, provisions and mining tools.

In the early spring of 1859, there was a grand stampede for the mountains. The hitherto solitary plains suddenly became densely peopled. A line of daily coaches was put on from Leavenworth to Denver, via the new Republican route, costing three hundred thousand dollars before the first vehicle started, and involving a running expense of eight hundred dollars per day. Stations from "one" upward were established from ten to twenty-five miles apart, over prairie and desert. A thousand mules and a hundred stages were scattered along the route. The fare from Leavenworth to the mountains was one hundred dollars; way tariff twenty-five cents per mile.

[Most emigrants caught up in the rush preferred their own means of travel fraught with added dangers.]

[Richardson:] Every great thoroughfare was white with wagons, and by night the smoke of ten thousand camp-fires curled to the astonished clouds. Some emigrants drew their entire supplies in handcarts, to which they had harnessed themselves; others bore them packed upon their backs – each a domestic Atlas, with his little world upon his shoulders.

Some who started too early had hands and feet frozen. Others consumed all their provisions before one-third of the journey was accomplished, and were fed for weeks by those more bountifully supplied. Thousands took an unexplored route, up the Smoky Hill River, where grass and water proved woefully scarce and fearful suffering prevailed. The road was lined with cooking-stoves, clothing and mining tools, thrown away to lighten the loads. [9]

A.D.R. was a member of the "booster class." He also wrote of a countervailing rush, one back to safe havens among the Missouri settlements. On this topic, his sentiments hardly mattered. Many expected retreat would occur with the onset of cold weather or the realization that finding gold required hard work, or that the hardships of getting to the mountains or the fact that what gold existed actually originated elsewhere was disheartening enough.

The rush to the mines was now succeeded by a panic quite as contagious. Reports that the exhibited gold had

Albert Deane Richardson. Better known simply by his initials, "ADR" like his mentor Horace Greeley did his best reporting in the midst of his subject matter. The developments he noted in Denver and along the Front Range in just a few years impressed him greatly. *(Richardson, 1867)*

come from California and not from the mountains, turned back thousands of emigrants — some before they had gone fifty miles from the river and others when they were within twenty-five of the alleged gold region.

Still many pressed forward, and large parties of undismayed adventurers continued to start daily. The country had known nothing like it since the great California excitement ten years before, when thirty thousand emigrants crossed the plains. It was an uncontrollable eruption — a great river of human life rolling toward the setting sun — at once a triumph and a prophesy. [10]

Authenticity notwithstanding, A.D.R.'s accounts were swamped by "booster accounts". Agnes Wright Spring summarizes the matter in the following series of dispatches. [11]

[New York Tribune, *January 29, 1859.*] *Ho for Pike's Peak! There is soon to be an immense migration, especially from our western states, to the new El Dorado....There is scarcely a village west of Ohio in which some are not fitting for and impatiently waiting the day when a start may be prudently made for the neighborhood of Pike's Peak. We shall be disappointed if less than 50,000 persons start for the new gold diggings within the current year. Many go to dig, perhaps quite as many to speculate on the presumed necessities, or fancies, or vices, of the diggers.*

[Chicago Press-Tribune, *February 19, 1859.*] *Dear Parents: We have a fine place here, situated on the Cherry Creek and Platte River. There are 200 houses and about 2,000 men here, six white women and plenty of red ones. Everybody has a little gold dust and the miners are making, when they work, from three to ten dollars a day. Our place is on the South Platte, at the outlet of Cherry Creek. I have got a little gold dust myself of which I send you a sample. It is hard to dig it, but that I am used to...Our cattle are doing very well here on grass, as we are having very fine weather this winter; we can work in our shirt sleeves. As for game and wild meat we have plenty; such as bear, buffalo, black and white tailed deer, antelope, turkeys, etc. Your affectionate son, Folsom Dorsett, Jr., Chicago, Ill, 1859.*

[Missouri Republican, *March 10, 1859.*] *Pike's Peak is in everybody's mouth and thoughts, and Pike's Peak figures in a million dreams. Every clothing store is a depot for outfits for Pike's Peak. There are Pike's Peak hats, and Pike's Peak guns, Pike's Peak boots, Pike's Peak shovels, and Pike's Peak goodness-knows-what-all, designed expressly for the use of emigrants and miners...We presume there are, or will be, Pike's Peak pills, manufactured with exclusive reference to the diseases of Cherry valley, and sold in conjunction with Pike's Peak guide books; or Pike's Peak schnapps to give tone to the stomachs of overtasked gold diggers; or Pike's Peak goggles to keep the gold dust out of the eyes of the fortune hunters; or Pike's Peak steelyards (drawing fifty pounds) with which to weigh the massive chunks of gold quarried out of Mother Earth's prolific bowels…At this moment there are hundreds of professional pickpockets, pigeon droppers and 'confidence men' here, ready to take all the cash and valuables brought by the strangers visiting the place. The levee is thronged, and the Missouri river boats particularly are beset by them from morning till night…*

[St. Louis Evening News, *March 17, 1859.*] *You see nothing but Pike's Peak flauntingly blazoned on every fabric of iron, wood, wool or cotton, that a mortal is presumed… to stand in need of.*

[Kansas City Journal of Commerce, *March 25, 1859.*] *Here on this spot, where now you see a flourishing and enterprising town of nearly one thousand inhabitants, with dry goods stores, tin shops, real estate agencies, blacksmith shops, law offices and doctor shops, four months ago was a beautiful valley filled with game of every description.…The people here are expecting a heavy emigration next spring. H. L. Bolton, Denver City, February 12, 1859.*

[Kansas City Correspondent, *March 21st.*] *Here they come by every steamboat, hundreds of them, hundreds after hundreds from every place—Hoosiers, Suckers, Corn crackers, Buckeyes, Red-horses, Arabs and Egyptians—some with ox wagons, some with mules, but the greatest number on foot, with their knap-sacks and old–fashioned rifles and shot-guns; some with their long-tailed blues, others in jeans and bob-tailed jockeys; in their roundabouts, slouched hats, caps and sacks. There are a few handcarts in the crowd. They form themselves into companies of ten, twenty, and as high as forty-five men have marched out, two-and-two, with a captain and clerk, eight men to a hand-cart, divided into four reliefs, two at a time pulling the cart…Onward they move, in solemn order, day after day, old and young, tall and slender, short and fat, handsome and ugly, the strong and the weak…*

A. D. R. recalled the electricity in the Leavenworth air when on May 21,1859 the first coach returned from the mountains. Onboard was gold dust worth $3,500, how many labor-hours by how many laborers no one knew or cared. Rather, the "richly decorated" coach and its banner, "The gold mountains of Kansas send greetings to her commercial metropolis," drew all the attention, as if the emigrants filling the streets needed more reason to board the next outbound.

Two coaches, each drawn by four mules, leave Leavenworth daily and make the entire trip together, for protection in case of danger from Indians. A crowd gathered in front of the Planters' House to see our equipages start. Amid confused ejaculations of "Good-by, old boy." "Write as soon as you get there." Better have your hair cut, so that the Arapahoes can't scalp you." "Tell John to send me an ounce of dust." "Be sure and give Smith that letter from his wife." "Do write the facts about the gold."

The whips cracked and the two stages rolled merrily away. [12]

If any doubt remained that the Colorado goldfields were not worth the trip, the *Hannibal Messenger* did its best to drive that point home. To the contrary, the *Boston Evening Transcript* published encouraging word of John Gregory's landmark good fortune. The June 9, 1859 *Messenger* reported that "the spectacle of 100,000 people…coming back, begging, starving, cursing, and many of them hopelessly ruined, is one never before witnessed." Better received, the June 11 *Evening Transcript* "electrified the country with the story of Gregory's lode discovery on May 6th, near present day Central City." [13]

Then there were the guidebooks, many of them written by reputable pathfinders, but generally shameless just the same. Like newspapers across the country but especially from towns along the Missouri River, they carried a preponderance of glowing accounts. Most of the guidebooks, eventually over twenty written out of conscience or greed, mimicked the overall tone of the newspaper editors.

LEWIS H. GARRARD

Hector Lewis Garrard, otherwise known as Lewis H., ventured west during the war with Mexico. A Cincinnati youth of seventeen, he departed home for St. Louis and western regions beyond in poor health. From St. Louis, he made his way to Westport, now a part of present-day Kansas City, and joined one of the caravans destined for Taos and Santa Fe. His caravan leader was the experienced and well-known Ceran St. Vrain, who partnered with William Bent to build and operate Bent's Fort. Lewis lived at the Fort several months and accompanied venturesome traders to Cheyenne lodges where he was introduced to Cheyenne customs, some reportedly enjoyable, some appalling. In response to the 1847 Mexican revolt in Taos in which a number of Americans including Charles Bent, New Mexico governor and William's brother, were murdered, William organized a troop of volunteers to retaliate. Lewis enlisted and set out with the troop to "kill and scalp every Mexican to be found…" Delayed by weather and difficult trails, hostilities were resolved before the troop reached Taos. They lingered long enough to witness the frontier court proceedings and hanging of the rebels.

Back at Bent's Fort the following spring, Garrard concluded he had experienced enough frontier hardship. He joined a military train returning east. At Fort Mann, located west of present-day Dodge City, Kansas, he changed his mind again. The newly established garrison, lightly defended, faced Indian attack. Lewis had never been in an Indian fight. He signed on for a one-month tour of duty. One dangerous month later, he

Lining the pockets of hometown outfitters was the goal of some. Some were largely extracts from newspapers and quotations from seasoned miners. Some were based on information from men who had no personal knowledge of anything the guidebooks contained.

Of the seventeen guidebooks to the Pike's Peak region issued in 1859, five hailed from New York City, three from Chicago, two from Cincinnati, and one each from Boston, Pittsburgh, Pacific City (Iowa), Washington (Kansas), Leavenworth, and St. Louis. One did not indicate a publisher. No one attempted to count the number of guidebooks sold, but sales must have been significant. In any case, of particular interest was friend Luke Tierney's *History of the Gold Discoveries on the South Platte River*. Tierney based much of his advice on his prospecting with Green Russell. Written in the third-person, a common practice in his day more than an act of humility, he nevertheless introduced his "guide of the route" with heart-felt sincerity.

Accompanying the first company in their search for gold on the South Platte, and remaining with them in all their vicissitudes, keeping a faithful record of

resumed his trip east to Fort Leavenworth, arriving a few weeks afterward.

In the midst of worsening health, Garrard wrote *Wah-to-yah and the Taos Trail* about his ten months in the West. Published in 1850 and well received, its popularity faded quickly. Nevertheless, it served as sound advice for naïve Argonauts. Its value was its unpolished descriptions that prepared travelers for prairie realities. He admired the rude and unforgiving life of the frontier including his companions, the traders, mountain men, "bucks and squaws and papooses." He deplored the barbarity and ignorance of the Indian, but no sooner had he expressed such sentiments "than he hurried on to report good hours with the Cheyennes, good tales from the mountain men, good times all around while the cup or the pipe passed and a stew fretted over the fire."

Garrard returned to Cincinnati, studied medicine and maybe law, relocated into the interior Northwest, and was an early settler of Minnesota. At one time or another, he was a "county supervisor, township chairman, state representative, bank founder, and mayor. He moved back to Cincinnati. At fifty-eight he is dead."

Lewis wisely anticipated the revulsion spawned in polite society by *Wah-to-yah and the Taos Trail*. His unapologetic defense, one applicable to any contemporary writer that is true to the language and attitudes of the dark times in the past, ended his introduction to his experiences with the following defense:

An accusation of grossness may be raised, and that the characters use seemingly uncalled-for expressions. I have naught set down in malice, and it is no more my prerogative to exclude than to add. [14]

their transactions from day to day, his [Tierney's] opportunities for giving a reliable and truthful statement are unparalleled. Falling in with the various companies which followed, and becoming disheartened, returned home without making any important discoveries, he can easily account for the unfavorable accounts which have reached the States. Having spent several months in prospecting, with varied success, he has endeavored to point out with accuracy where the precious metal may be found, and where it is useless to search for it. [15]

A key section in many guides and central to Tierney's advice are accounts of navigating the Native American nations, much in keeping with the contemporary advice of Dick Wootton and decade-old admonitions of Lewis Garrard.

As an example of what set Tierney's guide apart from most others, Luke wrote,

About four o'clock we were hailed by the Cheyennes, at Pawnee Fork, where several hundred of these warlike Indians lay encamped....The Indians manifesting no hostile intentions, we exchanged some provisions, powder, and lead for some ponies, and taking a friendly leave of them marched six miles, where we partook of supper." [16]

LeRoy Hafen provides us with the rest of the story quoted from an account written by one of the party.

The first Indians we saw were at Pawnee Fork, and there was a large camp of them: Arapahoes, Cheyennes, Kiowas, and Comanches who, we were told, were holding a council of war to decide whether or not they should go to the mountains to fight the Utes, as they had the year previous and in which battle it was reported they got the worst of it. At the same time these Indians of the plains were friendly with the whites. Some of the chiefs had small passbooks or papers that had been given them by the soldiers or freighters, reading "These Indians are friendly. You had better make a treaty with them by giving them such supplies as you can afford." This we did by giving them a little flour, sugar, coffee, and tobacco and passed on. [17]

"Indian passbooks" were a cultural commodity of the time that defused the urge on the part of both Indian and emigrant to shoot first and talk later. Tierney also advised staying out of the way of Native American wars—the white man's turn would come soon enough. In this regard, his recommendations sounded like wisdom from a man that knew of what he spoke.

The tribes of Indians likely to be met on this route are: the Pawnees, the Sioux, the Cheyennes and the Arapahoes. These tribes are at present on friendly terms

with the whites, and if properly treated will probably remain so. The less emigrants have to say to Indians the better. If they are met, and manifest a friendly spirit, extend to them the usual salutation and pass on, manifesting no fear, and as little emotion of any kind as possible. If you make a trade with an Indian, and he is not satisfied, trade back without hesitation.

The principal danger of collision arises from meeting a WAR PARTY. In a war party, there are no squaws, and the braves usually are on horseback. In approaching an emigrant train they frequently ride as though they were about to make a CHARGE, when in reality, they are only excited by curiosity. If they should stop a train, and demand presents, they will usually leave after receiving a little tobacco or flour, or something of that kind. Should this fail, and there is danger of collision, the best weapon that can be used is an ox-goad or whip. Let some stout man, without paying any attention to their weapons, seize his whip and thrash away at them, and they will run much sooner and faster than if a dozen were killed. The proper plan for each emigrant train is to select one of their number to act as captain, and let it be his duty to do all the talking with the Indians—the others having little or nothing to say to them. If these rules are observed, there need be no apprehension of difficulty with any of the Indians. [18]

The final blessing guidebooks offered to the novice frontiersman was lists of suggested provisions and the costs of each. Tierney assumed the minimum party would be four men. Provisions for four men for six months should cost about $146. Add the costs of teams, implements, weapons and camp equipment and for $517 or thereabouts the troop would be good to go. Go they did, albeit in 1859 rarely prepared for six months. Unappreciated at the outset, for most that hardly mattered. For most, they were homeward bound long before six months.

Not all gold-seekers were hardy, foolish, and flush with enough cash to outfit their own transit across the Great Plains. Some relished the relative ease and security of "public transportation." Accustomed in the East to rail and coach service, and freighters as numerous as Amish buggies, by spring of 1859 these amenities of city life began appearing in Missouri frontier towns. Within a few short years, the extension of railroads westward from Council Bluffs, Iowa and eastward from the Oakland Long Wharf on San Francisco Bay arrived. Not even the nation's Civil War could do more than slow the advance of the gandy-dancers. Entrepreneurs closed the gap between the Missouri frontier and distant California with the Colorado Front Range halfway between. [19]

In the spring of 1859, William Russell and John S. Jones launched the *Leavenworth and Pike's Peak Express*. The first coach reached Denver on May 7. Henceforth, news from the Front Range made its way to the States daily. Unlike the year-long transit to Georgia for cousin Jennie's Sutters Mill letter, word of Jackson's and Gregory's diggings bolstering the significance of Green Russell's find, and Horace Greeley's critical assessment shortly thereafter, arrived in days. Of the three, Greeley's dispatch had the biggest impact. [20]

Horace Greeley was no copy room or barber shop pundit despite appearing unfit to grace a saddle. When a preponderance of evidence supporting Colorado goldfields reached his New York City desk, he was soon on his way to the frontier to see for himself. His eastern readership could not get enough western reporting, and Horace was up to the task. Duane A. Smith explains:

> *For his Victorian stay-at-home readers, fascinated by the goings-on in the West, Greeley recounted his adventures in a report from "Gregory's Diggings, June 9, 1859." They learned that six weeks earlier, the "ravine was a solitude, the favorite haunt of the elk, the deer, and other shy denizens of the profoundest wildernesses." By the time of publication, though, "probably" one hundred log cabins were being constructed, "while three or four hundred more are in immediate contemplation." [21]*
>
> *As yet, the entire population of the valley—which cannot number less than four thousand including five white women and seven squaws living with*

Fast But No Match for the Telegraph. In 1859 the delivery of mail between St. Joseph, Missouri and Sacramento, California was in great demand and commanded a high price. The Pony Express served that purpose well, but was short-lived. It could not compete with the telegraph, nor could it keep up with the exploding volume of mail. That would require coaches, and eventually railroads. *(Harper's Weekly)*

white men—sleep in tents or under booths of pine boughs, cooking and eating in the open air. I doubt that there is as yet a table or chair in these diggings, eating being done around cloth spread on the ground, while each one sits or reclines on mother earth. The food, like that of the Plains, is restricted to a few staples—pork, hot bread, beans and coffee. [22]

Greeley did not stop there. Maybe from a vision, maybe just a visionary, Duane Smith shares his prophecy.

Mining quickens almost every department of useful industry. A blacksmith was on the scene, sharpening picks "at fifty cents each," a "volunteer post office [had been] established." Looking into the near future, he foresaw that a provisions store would soon be needed, "then groceries, then dry goods, then a hotel, etc., until within ten years the tourist of the continent will be whirled up these diggings" over easier roads. This visitor "will sip his chocolate and read his New York Paper—not yet five days old—at the Gregory House, in utter unconsciousness that this region was wrested from the elk and the mountain sheep so recently as 1859." [23]

In June 1860, the *Western Stage Company* began daily stagecoaches from Denver to the mountain settlements. The trip to Central City took 7-8 hours compared to 3-4 days a year earlier. [24] In April 1860, the famed Pony Express began mail and newspaper deliveries between St. Joseph and Sacramento, making the 2,000 mile trip in ten days. Operated by the *Central Overland California and Pike's Peak Express Company*, the *Pony Express* only survived eighteen months due to the expense of its service, affordable only to the wealthy and useful only to convey messages. With the completion of a transcontinental telegraph network in October 1861, its principle advantage was lost. Completion of a transcontinental railroad nearly produced a similar outcome for freighters and coach lines.

So it was, and so it had to be. The gold excitement that surfaced in the winter of 1858-59, ebbed by summer and flowed again by fall, cycles driven by seasonal weather, mood swings and the general tenor of the latest persuasive report from the frontier. Excerpts of boosterism and humbug filled books, all helpful insight into the human condition of that era. In total, the point they made was that the mass migration they stirred, dampened, and stirred repeatedly was not without reason, not without purpose, and not without preconditions. Those lost identities known simply as the "Pikes Peak or Bust mass migration," or simply the "Fifty-Niners," knowingly or not stood on the shoulders of Spanish expeditions and Anglo-mountain men that had broken their trails.

Ordinary men accomplishing extraordinary feats explained why so many others risked so much and most often gained so little. By most accounts, the 1859 mass migration numbered 100,000, some estimates are as high as 140,000, others as low as 50,000, but upwards of 90% returned eastward by the outbreak of the Civil War. What kind of people were they? How can we understand their influence on their generation? Those that are most flamboyant often offer amazing insights about the common mob. Joining this class alongside the mountain men and abolitionists were the colorful and more desperate wheelbarrow men, Andrew O. McGrew, chief among them.

McGrew was not the only wheelbarrow man headed to the Colorado gold fields. Nor was he the first to attempt this incredible feat, that could have been Forty-Niner James Gordon Brookmire wheeling "his all" to California a decade earlier. Like his kindred spirit Andrew, James epitomized a class of vagrants willing to risk everything they held dear, which of course was virtually nothing. Curiously, both Andrew and James were Pennsylvanians. Both lived lives that tell us much about family expectations and the young nation they navigated.

JAMES GORDON BROOKMIRE

James Gordon Brookmire was a stereotypical wheelbarrow man. He was an Ulster Scot who landed in America in 1831 just in time to orient himself in a strange land before suffering the nationwide effects of the economic panic of 1837. Still, with hard work and frugal behavior he managed to acquire a farm. In 1850 at age forty, most likely at ropes end, he sold fifty acres of his farm to finance his journey to the Pacific and support his family while gone. He left six children and a wife behind, reportedly "in very indigent circumstances." Unlike many Eastern gold-seekers eyeing California, Brookmire did not set out by sea, perhaps because it took months longer or was unaffordable. Instead, he traveled down the Allegheny and Ohio Rivers to the Mississippi, then upriver to the Missouri River and frontier settlement of Leavenworth. Many who followed a decade later, inspired by his tale if not his charmed life, chose the same route. Historian Will Bagley explains:

> Brookmire "started out with a band of Kentuckians but switched to a wheelbarrow at Fort Kearny [Leavenworth, Kansas]." He and his faithful dog survived being struck by Rocky Mountain lightning. He lost his wheelbarrow and almost drowned in Utah's Weber River but Brookmire reached Hangtown that fall. Many gold rushers died broke, but early in 1852 he "returned with about fifteen thousand dollars of the 'dust', all of which he has dug up and washed with his own hands. And as it is very apt to pour when it rains, his wife received legacies during his absence to the amount of ten thousand dollars, falling to her upon the death of some relations in Scotland." Back home, Brookmire invested his fortune, educated his children, and lived "in more than comfortable circumstances, which he and his wife are worthy to enjoy." The wheelbarrow man died at age ninety, still hearty. [25]

Brookmire's triumph over daunting circumstances with little more than determination and his wheelbarrow was not lost on the likes of others like him, no less courageous in 1859-60 than a decade earlier.

Will Bagley writes: "Some towns in Missouri are nearly depopulated by the 'yellow fever.' Many who are not able to purchase animals are starting on foot, packing their provisions on their backs," Adam Brown wrote at Saint Joseph. "one stout-hearted Missourian started, several days since, with a *wheelbarrow*." [26]

Humor was often the case when Scots were involved. At Fort Laramie a company of Mormons encountered such a wheelbarrow man. Invited to join several companies willing to haul his belongings, Bagley reports:

> *The hard-charging Scot "thanked them kindly, but wished to be excused, as he could not wait on the tardy movements of a camp. He never was afraid of the Indians stealing his horses, and he never lost any rest dreading a stampede."* [27]

Bagley also cites the following accounts as further insightful examples of humor, mockery, and irony in this matter. [28]

[William Temple] described the astonishing parade as tens of thousands of crazed Argonauts swept west using "all kinds of ways of going, some in carts, some a foot." Perhaps the oddest sight was "three large stout men with a wheelbarrow, no joke."

[Orin O. Wright, St. Joseph, Missouri] "There are a great many emigrants at this place, men from every State and Nation under the sun – old men young men one-legged men and some that don't happen to be men. They were going with horses, cattle, mules and jack-asses, and twenty-five men had "started afoot and to bring up the rear one fellow has started with a wheelbarrow."

[William Rothwell) "An Irishman passed on a few days since actually carrying his

Wheelbarrow Men. Both the rush to California and to Colorado goldfields had their share of wheelbarrow men. Most abandoned the effort, but some persevered, two of the most notable being James Gordon Brookmire and Andrew O. McGrew. (*Leslie's, April 30, 1859*)

clothing provisions &c on a Wheel barrow with nobody in company but himself. He is now going he said to the 'Gould (sic) diggings.' It is reported that the Indians were so kind as to relieve him of his loading about 40 miles out."

[Finley McDiarmid.] "While taking our dinner a man with his outfit in a wheelbarrow rolled up big as life. We asked this gallant son of Massachusetts if he wanted any supplies. 'Sugar' he said was all he wanted . . . Mr. Truitt gave him half a loaf, for which he returned many thanks [and] placed it in his wheelbarrow, bid us a friendly good bye and rolled on." The next day his train passed "our wheelbarrow man."

[John Gunnison] believed it was a sturdy German who almost achieved immortality as the "wheelbarrow man," but reports mentioned sojourners from Ireland, Scotland, Missouri, and Massachusetts pushing carts. The German "trundled his wheelbarrow along as rapidly as the teams advanced, and had the prospect of reaching the end of his two thousand miles in safety," but he made the mistake of ferrying the swollen Weber River. "The raft floundered in the swift current, and the wheelbarrow, with 'his all,' was swept down into the boiling kanyon (sic) below, and lost beyond redemption," Gunnison wrote.

[Observer, Fort Kearney] Perhaps the most intriguing of the wheelbarrow men was a hard-charging "Scotchman," who made other travelers eat his dust. Well-armed and about thirty-five years old, he passed Fort Kearny on 29 April 1850 "with a wheelbarrow, refusing to join any company, saying in his own particular dialect, "Na, na, mun, I ken ye'll all break doon in the mountains, an I'll gang along mysel'." He appeared not to be the least fatigued. Two weeks later, he might have reached Fort Laramie—at least "the most distinguished character" who appeared at the fort was identified as the "wheelbarrow man." He had left Saint Joseph about twenty-five days previously and was "carrying his all in a light wheel barrow" that had "out-stripped almost everything on the road." He was in high spirits and confident he would be the first man in the diggings. "He enquired how the grass was ahead, but reckoned his animals wouldn't want much. He pushed on to the tune of Yankee Doodle towards the setting sun – such a man must succeed."

[Robert James, Fort Laramie] "One man is going through with a wheel barrow, who out travels our mule teams." (A preacher, James had left his young sons named Frank and Jesse behind in Missouri). [Remember Jesse James, and his partner in crime brother Frank?]

[D. A. Millington] said a man had rolled his wheelbarrow all the way to Yellow creek on today's Utah-Wyoming border. "Here he had broken it and left it having got in with a wagon and we sacrilegiously made fire of the wheelbarrow to cook our supper."

Will Bagley uncovered no one reporting on wheelbarrow men in 1851, much less noting that frugal Scotsmen dominated that class of traveler. Wheelbarrows returned "in force" in 1852, but afterwards were unreported until the next great westward emigration [Colorado] began in 1858-59. Despite somewhat improved conditions and more choices available to the Fifty-Niners, wheelbarrows remained an option for desperate and determined men like Andrew McGrew. Unlike McGrew—gold drove the others—an inquisitive nature and a desire to be a journalist drove McGrew. He also possessed an entrepreneurial spirit that would serve him well in frontier Denver.

In 1858-59, frontier society held neither entrepreneurs nor journalists in high esteem. Neither could be trusted to tell the truth despite occasionally being caught doing so. California gold created tremendous wealth and an equal increase in schemes and ventures designed to empty the pockets of the gullible. The fledgling journalist class was often complicit. Long on curiosity and short on knowledge, this cohort was apt to run with any information realistic or otherwise if it pertained to Colorado gold mines or likely to sell another paper.

McGrew was unfazed by the low public esteem for journalism. He had a gift for writing and more than a fair share of idealism. He also was innocent to a comical extent, all of which worked out to his benefit. At home in Pennsylvania, he was "Andy" to friends and family. In 1858 frontier Denver, he was *the* "Wheelbarrow Man." Decades later he was City Editor of the *New York Evening News*.

Patience was not an Andrew O. McGrew gift. He was a scholarly man, a printer by trade and rightly honored as Denver's first street reporter, but patient he was not. "A self-appointed correspondent, he set out from his native Pittsburgh with five cents in his pocket determined to cover the Pikes Peak gold rush." [29] His plan was to catch up with a group of hometown gold-seekers and cross the Plains in their company. Somewhere enroute to Westport, it occurred to him that surely newspapers he encountered along the way would be interested in first-hand accounts of "western Kansas" gold. This was not an original idea, but seldom embraced by tight-fisted Editors. He arrived in Westport ahead of his erstwhile companions without a newspaper assignment.

McGrew was prudent enough to dally a short while in Westport waiting for his friends. After several days wait, he could wait no longer. Making his way to Leavenworth, he loaded his scant supplies—blankets, pick and shovel, a gun and ammunition—into a wheelbarrow provided by a benefactor and set a course westward, alone and on foot. Intriguing about Alexander's journey to Denver was not simply the rigor of his trek, but the acclaim his wheelbarrow afforded him once he got there. Neither the first nor the last to cross the Great Plains, child-like charm and enthusiasm earned McGrew, the wheelbarrow man, folk-hero status that would become another symbol of the new American experience.

Andy often covered as many as thirty miles a day. Such energy and spirit was not lost on those he encountered on the trail. Invited to join a wagon train several hundred miles into his journey, "too slow for me," he reportedly replied. [30] A few hundred miles farther along he was prepared to change his mind. Halfway to

Denver, weary and footsore, he traded his wheelbarrow, henceforth used to gather buffalo chips to fuel evening campfires, for a ride into camp.

McGrew's first work was not digging for gold along the tributaries of the South Platte. He most likely bartered his tools for food and shelter shortly after arrival. No, his first work was his dream job, writing a freelance article about Christmas in frontier Denver. He reported by letter to the *Omaha Times*, also with broad distribution to eastern newspapers in mind. He described the harsh conditions of the shabby collection of treasure-seekers and their shelters about to enter their first Rocky Mountain winter. Not exactly an account of baby Jesus, it did have the flavor of Spartan quarters akin to stable and manger. As devoid of gold news as it could be, it still fed the insatiable appetite of eastern readers starved for any news from the goldfields.

Perhaps most revealing in McGrew's 1858 Christmas letter was the sentiment one might expect in a letter home. Having described the community dinner scrapped together by the frontier pilgrims, sumptuous by any standard, he ended with an account of a late night street dance he literally stumbled upon.

> *Adjourning to Auraria, we found the town alive with an influx of miners, some of whom were dressed in the most fantastic and grotesque manner that an active imagination, and the application of the skins of wild beasts could possibly devise. In a short time an immense fire was blazing in the public square, and Terpsichore answered to the voice of Orpheus. Light hearts, merry countenances, and active feet were soon in motion, and the dance continued until midnight. Beneath many a rough exterior, were hearts that throbbed with pleasant thoughts of home. Groups of Indians, with their squaws and papooses, filled-up the background. It was a picture that Rembrandt would have contemplated with delight. On Monday the Masons held their annual celebration in honor of St. John's Day; and in the evening had a fine supper as I am not so fortunate as to belong to the fraternity, I was not present.*
>
> *You may doubtless hear many reports in the States; some of which are doubtless true, while others are false. Many come here who, because they cannot make independent fortunes in a day, leave, and curse the country. Let them go; we have no use for them here; they are much better at home, where they can have someone to wash their faces every morning, and see that they do not stray too far from home. We are satisfied with our prospects here, and intend to stay here until the whole country is explored.* [31]

The lad could write. He could work up a mighty thirst, too. With little more to celebrate than his own arrival, he celebrated hardily which on that bitter winter night was too much for him to manage. Moreover, it was impossible to neglect Uncle Dick Wootton's first Christmas Party, open to all who cared to attend. Recall Wootton's unplanned trades with the ragtag pioneer Denverites instead of the Arapahoes. His barrels of whiskey served more than tabletops displaying his other goods. Andy drank more than his fair share. Unable to reach his cabin, he crawled into the back of a wagon to rest. The following morning his frozen feet, "deformed and punctured with holes," would challenge him the remainder of his life. So too would his fondness for strong drink. But like his wheelbarrow days, neither alcohol nor punctured feet harnessed his drive. When word of the outbreak of hostilities between the States reached Denver, yet another reason to abandon the treasure hunt moved McGrew to enlist in the Union Army. Remembered throughout his days in Denver as the "wheelbarrow man," throughout the Civil War he was remembered as a brave and spirited Yankee who served his country with honor.

The wheelbarrow men represented the tattered edge of the 1859-1860, third and final mass migration to the American West. Less appreciated but more eye-catching, there also were wheelbarrow women. Women in bloomers aroused the interest of more than one journalist marveling over the westward migration, or perhaps the changing fashion trend.

ANDREW O. MCGREW

Denver's wheelbarrow man and first street reporter survived the Civil War and returned to journalism. With gifted writing his only compass, with crippled feet no hindrance to his zeal, he capped his career as City Editor of the *New York Evening News*. Boosterism and humbug aside, McGrew's contributions to his day were grounded in grit and pluck, ordinary characteristics of his generation taken to higher ground. More insightful, he and wheelbarrow men like him more than any other class of Fifty-Niner, demonstrated that in their folly the angst of a young Nation about to rip itself apart could be overcome for a time. The year 1860 was a final year of grace, another year of mass migration to help forestall the inevitable collision of two irreconcilable societies. [32]

Make no mistake, the overwhelming majority of the "Fifty-Niners" and the more prepared second wave of 1860 emigrants bore much resemblance in life-style or character to the pathfinders who preceded them. The Fifty-Niners profited some from lessons-learned by the mountain men and the Forty-Niners who returned to the hunt, but paid dearly despite available advice. Nevertheless, a year did make a difference – 1859 boosterism, naysaying, and thoughtlessness aside, the prairie was tamer and Colorado's Front Range was closer. The second wave in 1860 fared better still.

To be sure, there were loners that did not choose wheelbarrows. Wheelbarrows were affordable and a better choice than backpacks or satchels, but less manageable than carts. While some loners had pack animals of every sort, many did not. Gehling calls them "walkers–the 'footing gentry' of song and legend, who elect to set out for the mountains 'without anything but a blanket and a brazen face.'" [33] The poorest of "the footing gentry" could not even afford wheelbarrows.

A correspondent for the Missouri Republican *wrote from Leavenworth that he could discern three distinct classes of Fifty-Niners leaving for the gold fields: the poorest of all, departing on foot; the more fortunate, with their handcarts and wheelbarrows; and those he called 'flush,' those who had the money to 'purchase cattle, mules and wagons, and go well provided with all that is necessary to make a trip on the prairies with comfort and pleasure.'* [34]

So what did the main stream of the migration actually look like? To say it looked like a cross-section of the country at large was probably as fair an observation as any other. In the minds of those who observed the phenomenon, they too struggled for words to describe what they saw. What they saw seemed determined largely by which side of the prairie viewed them. "Still they come!" was not a welcoming cheer when voiced by trail veterans struggling with their own inadequate circumstances. The phrase expressed "bewilderment nearly beyond belief"

"Footing Gentry." The poorest among the gold rush crowd, unable to afford even a wheelbarrow or perhaps too hurried to find one for sale, joined wagon trains and attempted to walk to the Front Range. Quite a few succeeded, but usually in the company of wagons filled with pilgrims willing to help out. *(Harper's Weekly, 1859)*

when uttered by the "Magpie class," frontier journalists comfortably perched in their "city rooms." Richard Gehling captures the mood of the moment in a series of accounts on the following three pages. [35]

[*St. Louis* Missouri Republican, *March 25, 1859*] *"Still they come! Who come? The Pike's Peakers and gold seekers–fortune hunters. Every boat from the Ohio is crowded with them, and every boat for the Missouri goes up jammed with people. Boats now loading for this port and the Missouri River, at Pittsburg and Cincinnati are thronged with emigrants. Those on their way here are in the same condition. They are coming down the Mississippi and Illinois, too–the Pike's Peakers. They are flocking overland across the country– the Pike's Peakers."*

[*Boston* Daily Journal] *Two weeks later, correspondent A.D. Richardson wrote back to the Boston Daily Journal that the roads leading west from the Missouri River were "white with the wagons of the Pike's Peak emigrants." He estimated that there were as many as fifteen thousand camped in large parties along the waters of almost every Kansas stream, waiting for the grass to green before proceeding.*

[*Brownsville* Nebraska Advertiser] *"The travel from this point to the gold mines is still on the increase; it may safely be said not to be scarcely begun yet. The bottom of the Missouri side opposite us looks like any army encampment, so many trains are there encamped waiting for grass."*

[*Council Bluffs* Bugle] *Babbett and Carpenter... kept a record of the number of emigrant teams passing their office during the third week of May. "Sunday 40 teams; Monday 66 teams; Tuesday 90 teams; Wednesday 108 teams; Thursday 111 teams; Friday 94 teams; Saturday 75 teams; A total of 584 teams."*

[*Kansas City* Journal of Commerce] *A similar report was filed...: 1,351 teams recently counted on the Santa Fe Trail between Council Grove and the Arkansas Crossing, with as many more on the way.*

[*St. Joseph* Gazette] *Commenting on the traffic from that city to Fort Kearny, reported that the road was "lined almost the entire distance with trains of emigrants, For several seeks past, one hundred trains on an average, have crossed the Big Blue per day."*

[*Westport* Border Star] *H.M. McCarty... noted not only the number of Fifty-Niners, but also their physical make-up. "They continue to come—all sorts, sizes and descriptions. The world seems all a moving. They are passing our office every hour of the day.*

There is a fellow from 'Illinoy,' (sic) who wants to know which is the shortest cut to the Peak, and whether he can get there by Sunday next.

Then comes one all the way from the Green mountains, with a stump-tail mule and a keow (sic) with crumpled horns...

*Then follows a Tennessee rip-snorter (sic), who started to go, and he's
gwyne tost and up to the rack, fodder or no fodder...*

There goes a motley crew of six b'hoys (sic) from St. Louis...

Next follows a tidy little red wagon, drawn by four sleek, well-fed oxen...

*They are scarcely out of sight when slowly creeps along a sort of Jersey cart,
drawn by a jaded mule, driven (the driver as usual on foot) by a travel-soiled,
care-worn old man...*

*Right behind this group—now alongside of them—now ahead—is a wheel-
barrow or hand-cart chap–going on his own hook, and as independent as a
wood-sawyer...*

*Now comes two seedy, half-starved, suspicious looking fellows, with noth-
ing but carpet-sacks."*

[Far from a scientific sampling, still, Richard Gehling's colorful stereotypes
fairly contribute to understanding the nature of the migration.]

*Hoosiers there were, Buckeyes, Hawkeyes, Badgers, Pennsylvania Dutch and
Georgia Crackers. There were farmers in their faded jeans and slouched hats,
clerks in their long-tailed blues, scolding mothers and their squalling babies,
merchants, doctors, lawyers, millers, politicians, printers, bankers, and even a
newspaper editor or two. Some among them were old, some young, and some
just approaching middle age. A few were hometown heroes. A few more were
on the run from the law. "The observant editor was correct in assuming that
there was not a typical Fifty-Niner in the crowd."*

*[Nebraska City News.] And even though the great majority could
rightfully be called "honest, industrious poor men," there were enough misfits
among them to induce the editor of the* Nebraska City News *to later charac-
terize the whole emigration as "a shiftless, lazy, lousy, scurvy, profane, insane
and idiotic herd of rapscallions, nincompoops and ninnies."*

[Just the same, wheelbarrows and carts were not simply low-budget and
comical, they also had advantages.]

*"Editor McCarty was also correct in his observation that prairie travel had
taken on an entirely new dimension." The familiar canvas-topped wagon,
so long thought indispensable for any successful emigration to Oregon or
California, was not a necessity for these Pike's Peakers setting out on a much
shorter trip to the Rocky Mountains. After all, the Rockies were only six or
seven hundred miles from the Missouri River, little more than one fourth the
distance to the West Coast. The trip required only three to five weeks of provisions instead of the usual six months' supply. With this fact in mind, many
were taking to the trails unencumbered by wagon or team. They were hauling
whatever they needed in two-wheeled carts, on pack mules, or on their backs.*

[Contrary to popular opinion, rather than ridicule handcart crews, some extolled their virtues. Foregoing the use of wagons was not only more efficient, it was more "manly." Gehling explains:]

A good number of these Fifty-Niners chose the handcart. It was lightweight, easy to pull, and—if constructed of properly seasoned lumber—extremely durable. Moreover, it had been tested for several years by the Mormon emigration to Utah, members of which had reduced this mode of travel to a science.

[Omaha Times.] The advantages of the cart were advertised early on in the gold rush by an article in the Omaha Times. *This article an-*

One Way or Another. Affordable and nimble, Mormon pilgrims demonstrated the benefits of handcarts years earlier and Fifty-Niners followed their example. Often ridiculed, they could outpace heavy wagons and transport far more provisions than wheelbarrows. Capable of carrying as much as four hundred pounds, they were maneuverable on rough terrain and did not require expensive draft animals to feed and care for along the way. (*Leslie's, April 30, 1859*)

nounced the formation of a company composed of one hundred men, who proposed "starting to the mines with hand carts–a la Mormon…Each hand cart will be manned by from three to four men, and be freighted with one hundred pounds to the man. The whole cost of their outfit–carts, clothing and provisions–at the Omaha market, will be about twenty dollars per man. This train will go through quicker than mules. One hundred pounds each, will enable them to take provisions enough to last them through, with two week's supply after they get there; three month's clothing; and all the necessary cooking and mining utensils. The labor of pushing their carts through will be nothing; those who go out with teams have to walk, the hand cart men are even with them there; those who take teams have to herd their cattle and mules nights, and charge around for an hour every morning hitching up, the cart men can lay down to sleep and in the morning take the road without delay; teamsters have to depend on grass, cart men can camp any place; teamsters have their teams and provisions to take care of when they get to the mines, carts will be worth ten times their original cost; wagons will be useless, carts a convenience. We feel proud of our hand cart boys, and every person who becomes one of their number and goes through shows himself a man."

Occasionally other newspapers were moved to write similar editorials, conveying some degree of respectability and making handcarts somewhat popular. Pulled by teams of men taking turns between the shafts two by two, pulled by all manner of animals including dogs, even pulled through St. Louis by "bloomer girls." [36]

Mocked as they were, these Fifty-Niners, "nincompoops" and "ninnies" overall, "rapscallions" among them by God, still they served a higher purpose. They opened a hurting nation's back door, temporary relief to be sure. The hardships of their passage and new life paled in comparison to the hemorrhaging of the Civil War and the destruction of the southern economy and culture. Yes, they learned hard lessons and failed at their dreams most often, but in so doing they served those who followed. There were lessons learned. With the onset of 1860, a another wave of emigrants as determined as the Fifty-Niners

A.D.R.

Like so many other teenagers of his day, seventeen-year old Albert left the comforts (and no doubt hard work) of the family's Franklin, Massachusetts farm to find his fortune in the West. In 1851, the "West" was the Missouri River frontier and beyond. We find him first in Pittsburgh, Pennsylvania, where he spent about a year trying his hand at various pursuits including reporting for the *Pittsburgh Journal*. Finding himself well suited for journalism, he determined to pursue it as his life's work. Gifted with a writer's ability to capture the heart and soul of a matter, he also saw the value of learning shorthand to absorb more quickly the totality of the emotions he experienced.

In the fall of 1852, Albert moved to Cincinnati. Apparently unmoved by the stampede of gold-seekers passing through the city enroute to California, he devoted his attention to local affairs. He joined the *Cincinnati Sun* as an Editor. In subsequent years, he worked for several other Cincinnati publications before his earlier interest in the West returned. In late 1857, with a young wife and son in tow, he relocated to Kansas Territory where the Free State movement quickly caught up with him. Operating more or less as an independent correspondent, he wrote persuasively in the fight against slavery for the *Boston Daily Journal*, the *Cincinnati Times*, and other eastern papers. Albert demonstrated yet another gift – he knew the value of casting his net widely to serve as many "sheets" as would have him. His abolitionist convictions also sidetracked him into Kansas politics.

Mid-July 1857 found Albert serving as Secretary of the Free-State convention at Topeka. In March 1858, he settled in the Missouri River town of Sumner, Atchison County, where he took on the duties of a general land agent. He ran, unsuccessfully,

would set their sights on the Rocky Mountain Front Range. Generally lumped in with the 1858-59 rush, this troop was different. It was more in keeping with the Oregon homesteaders two decades earlier. Most came prepared to stay, partly due in small measure to better guidebooks, partly due to advice from a small cadre of frontline journalists like McGrew, A. D. Richardson, and iconic Horace Greeley. Of course there were others, notably William Byers at the *Rocky Mountain News,* and mining camp editors from any camp with promise of surviving at least a season. But they were seen for what they were, unvarnished boosters. Their accounts did not ring with the same degree of authenticity as Easterners with first-hand experience.

Albert Deane Richardson enjoyed the rare journalistic privilege of simply signing his frontier dispatches with his initials. When newspapers were "sheets," dispatches were "letters," and publishers were "editors," honor beyond

for Atchison County Representative to the territorial legislature. Not unappreciated, he went on to serve in the January-February 1859 Kansas Territory legislative session as Clerk of the House.

Also not unappreciated, Albert concluded politics was not his calling. He needed to return to his first love. Early in 1859, he and family returned to Franklin to prepare for travel to the "far West," to the new gold discoveries of the Pike's Peak region. On May 25, he boarded one of the first *Leavenworth and Pike's Peak Express* stage coaches to Denver. Unbeknownst to Albert, his divine appointment awaited him at Manhattan, Kansas Territory, a short distance down the road. At Manhattan that pleasant spring day, Horace Greeley, famed publisher of the *New York Tribune,* and journalist Henry Villard, boarded Albert's coach for the twelve-day journey to Denver. With a great deal in common, and a great deal of time on their hands, the three writers bonded for life. Within a year, A.D.R. was the Western Correspondent for Greeley's *Tribune.* He traveled back to the Front Range in 1860 and wrote extensively of his experiences and observations.

Albert returned to New England in November 1860 to write and lecture. Early in 1861 he went on a secret mission (details unknown) into the South for the *Tribune.* When the Civil War erupted, he went into the field as a war correspondent. In May, 1863, along with other correspondents he was captured behind Confederate lines and imprisoned. In December 1864 he escaped. Returning home in poor health, he discovered that his wife and infant daughter had both died during the year. In the spring of 1865 in the company of friends he traveled by stagecoach to California. Returning much improved in health, he wrote and published *Beyond the Mississippi.* He returned to California by train in the spring of 1869, then to Kansas in the fall and on to New York. On November 25, 1869, he was shot in his office by the recently divorced husband of his wife to be. Married to Abby Sage McFarland, Albert died of his wounds on December 2nd at the age of thirty-six. [37]

his years befell young A.D.R. Running with the likes of Horace Greeley also helped. His readers and therefore his editors craved both his humor and his raw honesty. He wrote what he felt based on what he saw. In the face of the "political correctness" of his day, like Lewis Garrard, he was courageous and brazen enough to ignore it.

A.D.R. kept good company among a rare breed of writers who were as interesting as their writings. His road to fame began with his divine appointment with Horace Greeley. Meeting Greeley, not a god but widely considered "other worldly" at least among the journalist-class of his day, was life-changing. According to Rodman W. Paul who wrote with the familiarity of a brother, Greeley was "one of the striking figures of his generation."

> *His very appearance and manner were so bizarre as to be unforgettable: a pink baby face fringed with throat whiskers, a squeaky voice, acute absent-mindedness, illegible handwriting, and the careless costume that became his trademark—white overcoat and socks, shapeless trousers and crooked cravat, a broad-brimmed hat.*
>
> *Yet the readers of the highly influential newspaper that he created, the* New York Tribune, *followed his crusades and his sometimes eccentric enthusiasms with intense interest. The* Tribune *circulated throughout the north and west and was quoted more and argued about more than any journal of its day. Nowhere was this more true than in the West.* [38]

Greeley's biographer, Glyndon G. Van Deusen, summed up his popularity simply: "The West loved Horace Greeley." Accordingly, "the West" was delighted when it learned that he was coming its way, and "the East" delighted in reading about his travels.

Like the mountain men and the wheelbarrow men, A.D.R. epitomizes his generation. Unconventional, still they fairly represent the character and culture of their day. Insightful in and of themselves, segments of society seen through their eyes deepen appreciation for their time and trials. In A.D.R.'s case, how could we even imagine what the 1860 frontier was like without his keen sense of human nature and frailties that made the frontier vibrant? A.D.R. does not disappoint. Writing for an eastern audience, his "letters" paint as rich a picture of frontier life as any accomplished artist could produce. Beginning in May 1860 at Marysville, Marshall County, Kansas Territory, his return to the Front Range and his accounts of his six-month western odyssey fulfill expectations. Through excerpts from the following letters, written to the Editor of the Lawrence *Republican* and edited by Louise Barry, meet the men and women A.D.R. met. Marvel along with A.D.R. over the explosive and troubled growth of the new West. [39]

May 22, 1860
Marysville, Marshall County, Kansas Territory
In company with Thomas W. Knox, Esq., of the Boston Daily Atlas & Bee,
your correspondent left Atchison three days ago, and "thus far into the bowels
of the land, have we progressed without impediment." The difference between
the Pike's Peak emigration of this season and that of last year is obvious to the
most casual observer. In coming to this point (105 miles) we have not seen a
single pedestrian, with his "outfit" on his back; and have passed only one hand-
cart. That was drawn by two enterprising individuals who were harnessed
to it, and were progressing with their load of 500 pounds at the rate of about
twenty-five miles per day. They showed excellent courage, but looked as though
they had already found Jordan a hard road to travel. The road from Atchison
is excellent, and emigrants who intend going by the Platte, find it decidedly for
their advantage, in point of distance, to start from that city.

We have already passed ten quartz-crushing machines, and are informed
here that upwards of fifty have passed this point since the first of April. At
least seventy-five of these machines are now on their way to the mines. Some
months must necessarily elapse before they can all be put in successful opera-
tion; but by the first of August, the receipts of gold in the states will probably
be so heavy as to convince the people that Pike's Peak is a reality after all. The
majority of those who are going to the mines this year seem to be men of intel-
ligence, character, and ample means. Several stocks of goods, ranging in value
from $10,000 to $30,000 are on the way. We pass many families upon the
road, and females in the Gold Region will be much more plenty (sic) than they
were in June last, when we were all in the habit of running to our cabin doors
in Denver, on the arrival of a lady, to gaze at her as earnestly as at any other
rare natural curiosity.

[Two days into their journey, A.D.R. reported the edge of the earth was
in sight — that is, the end of civilization as he knew it. He was crossing into
Nebraska. Noting excellent conditions for all manner of agriculture save for
abundant water, he also was impressed with the absence of waystations, homesteads or communities. Contrasting the view ahead with the Maryville he was
leaving behind, in the year since he last passed this way the town had blossomed
into a megalopolis.]

At that point settlements begin to grow scarce, and the principal signs of
residents along the road consist of cabins and tents of enterprising gentlemen
of a commercial turn who inform the public through very primitive signs that
they are in the grocery business, and sell beer and gingerbread. Though finding
few attractions at their establishments thus far, we cannot expect, because we
are virtuous, that there will be no more cakes and ale. At Ash Point a grocer

seeks to captivate the hearts and purses of emigrants by informing them that he dispenses "Butte Reggs, Flower & Mele." At present he does not seem to be overrun with customers; but how can a reasonable man expect the patronage of Pike's Peakers, when he spells flour with a "w"?

We have passed several large droves of fine cattle, en route for California. The parties taking them through expect to be from five to six months on the way. Two or three forlorn-looking ox trains from Denver have met us on the road. The drivers look as though they had not seen soap, water or clothing stores for several years; and the oxen, whose bones protrude at various points, to whet the appetites of attendant buzzards, trundle mournfully along, as if soliloquizing: "what shadows we are; what shadows we pursue!"

At some points the road is white with the "prairie schooners" of the emigrants for three or four miles; and yet we are assured that the Pike's Peak migration has fallen off greatly, within the last three weeks.

Maryville is improving rapidly, and now claims some fifty houses.

May 30, 1860
Near Fort Kearney, Nebraska
The second evening out from Marysville, while near Rock creek, we crossed the line into Nebraska. There are very few settlers in the vicinity; but a North Carolinian has started a ranch on Rock creek, and, by charging a toll of ten cents per team over a little bridge which he has built across the stream, and furnishing emigrants with corn at one dollar per bushel and milk at a dime a quart, he has struck a richer "lead" than the Pike's Peakers generally will find. . . .

With the exception of the divide last mentioned, all the country along our route from Leavenworth and Atchison to Fort Kearney is susceptible of cultivation, and much of it remarkably fertile. Corn at this point is worth from $2.00 to $2.50 per bushel; sugar, 25 cents per pound, and flour 10 cents.

Fort Kearney, Nebraska. Intended primarily as a supply depot, it nevertheless symbolized American military presence and was a welcome sight to emigrant trains, gold rushers, and journalists like ADR. (*Wikipedia Commons*)

The emigration by the road from Omaha is quite as heavy as that by the route we have followed, and the valley of the Platte, as far as we can see, is white with "prairie schooners." Passengers from Denver by the express coaches state that they have met from 800 to 1,000 wagons per day. They speak of business as somewhat dull in the towns at the Gold Region, as the great majority of the winter population is absent, in the mines.

As yet, we have met less than a dozen wagons of returning emigrants; but there will soon be a backward stampede, though much smaller than that of last year. Immense quantities of goods are being taken out to the mines, and the markets bid fair to be very fully stocked for the next four or five months.

[When A.D.R. and journalists in general used the term "mines," they included placers and scratching the surface of a claim with pick and shovel. Workings that entailed tunnels and shafts were rare in 1859-60. Their day was not far off, but first explosives and mining equipment were required. That required wagon roads and wagons.]

June 5, 1860
Platte Valley, 25 miles above Upper Crossing
Kearney City, two miles west of the fort, is more generally known as "Adobetown." At present it consists of some six or eight wretched-looking houses, mostly of turf; but it is a city of magnificent intentions, and business lots are said to command from $200 to $250.

The intelligence of the killing of several Pony Express riders creates some apprehensions among the emigrants; but thus far all the savages on this route are peaceable toward the whites, though we have met several war parties of the Sioux, on their way to scalp or be scalped among the Pawnees.

We have encountered comparatively few returning Pike's Peakers, as yet, though we occasionally see a party of them, looking like the very last roses of summer, and breathing out all sorts of maledictions against the new El Dorado. The westward bound emigration continues enormous–far surpassing anything ever before witnessed upon the plains. While we were stopping two hours for breakfast, the other morning, more than two hundred wagons passed us; and a short time after, ascending a high bluff, I saw the green valley of the Platte, for many miles both before and behind us, teeming with the busy life of thousands of hopeful pilgrims. Tottering age and unconscious infancy–poverty and wealth–manhood and womanhood–and almost every nation in the world, were represented in the motley throng.

There is something very impressive about this uncontrollable movement westward, which from remotest antiquity has impelled the human race toward the setting sun, and which now, on a great wave of human life, is bearing commerce and American civilization to our farthest frontier, and founding a new empire at the base of the Rocky Mountains.

Among the emigrants whom we have encountered are several delicate, "lily browed" Chicago ladies; an unfortunate lady from Omaha, so reduced by recent rheumatic fever that she cannot walk alone, but is compelled to ride upon a bed; and a baby, who left the Missouri river at the extremely callow age of two weeks! We have passed about a dozen hand-carts, and perhaps half as many emigrants on foot—domestic Atlases with their little worlds upon their shoulders. . . .

The number of families en route for the Peak is quite beyond comprehension. In several instances, extra saddle horses are taken along for the ladies, and the fair travelers seem to find a good deal of enjoyment on the rough journey. The bloomer costume is considerably in vogue, and appears peculiarly adapted to overland travel. We passed a bloomer, a day or two since, who apparently weighed about two hundred and fifty, and who, while her better half was soundly sleeping in the wagon, was walking and driving the oxen. Her huge dimensions gave her the appearance of an ambulatory cotton bale, or a peripatetic haystack.

[Julia Holmes and A.D.R. never had occasion to meet much less discuss "the bloomer costume," but the fashion craze and its social ramifications were well understood by both. By 1860, at least beyond the Missouri frontier, bloomers were far more than a political statement. Their practical nature was undeniable and anyone with a wit of common sense was quick to see their benefits. Often noted in emigrant accounts, descriptions lacked ridicule so often present in years past. In A.D.R.'s case, he was more taken aback by a person's weight than their attire.]

June 12, 1860
Denver City
One train contained an elderly gentleman from Portsmouth, N.H., weighing 350 pounds—a sort of human leviathan. The party taking him out would evidently say, with Caesar: "Let me have men about me that are fat sleek-headed men, and such as sleep o' nights." A day or two after, as a fitting comparison to this huge person, we passed a Missouri lady nearly as heavy; so, if you hear that provisions are scarce at the Peak, attribute it to the arrival of the New Hampshire Fat Boy and Missouri Girl.

Denver is growing like Jonah's gourd, and all the mountains within two-hundred miles of here are literally swarming with people. As the express is just leaving, I must reserve details of news in regard to the mines, trade, &c.(sic) until my next.

[A.D.R. also was awe-struck by the growth along the Front Range, both population and commerce. Unaccustomed to exaggeration, he could not resist describing 1860 Denver City in poetic, superlative terms.]

June 16, 1860
Denver City
The Pike's Peak Gold Region is just now the theater of the grandest and most rapid material development ever witnessed upon the continent. Two years ago, these "mother mountains" as the Spaniards called them, were the abode of almost primeval silence; now, they are teeming with the busy life of fifty thousand people. Twelve months ago Denver was a village of a few rough log cabins with dirt roofs and mud floors, and half of them unoccupied; now it exceeds every city of eastern Kansas except Leavenworth in population, and in point of bustle, activity and that indescribable air which pervades a young metropolis, it is the most live town west of St. Louis.

Old Denver, Auraria and Highland (now consolidated under the name of Denver City), contain upwards of four thousand inhabitants. Many of the buildings are costly and spacious, including several three-story brick edifices now in course of erection. The amount of building going on is unparalleled

Early Denver. Explosive development astounded even ADR and was a clear indication of the scale of the Front Range gold rush and its transformation from prospectors to settlers. *(James F. Gookins, Harper's Weekly, October 13, 1866)*

since the "flush times" in the early days of San Francisco and Sacramento. Two hotels, which claim to be "first class," and a large number of more moderate pretensions, are crowded with people; stages arrive and depart daily for all the different mines; one daily and two weekly newspapers are established; the streets are crowded, and the ground in the vicinity of the city is covered with the tents and wagons of emigrants.

In spite of all these auspicious indications, the Denver merchants say that business is dull and money is tight. Though Hinckley's express brought down $10,000 from the mines, a few evenings since, the amount of dust in circulation here is comparatively small. All the Denver people, however, express the most absolute and growing faith in the mines, and predict that in two months, when the hundred quartz mills here and on the way, are all in operation, and the provisions now in the mountains (brought in by immigrants) are exhausted, business will whirl again.

[Little of this actually happened. Moreover, Denver may have grown into a city, but A.D.R. reminded his readers its landlords were Indian. Crossing the prairie with or without incident was just the beginning of the emigrant adventure. If that was not exciting enough, expect Indian troubles and look forward to frontier justice, ideally as a spectator.]

The "Ute" Indians, who murdered several miners last season, are thus far very peaceable. A large party of Arapahoes (a thousand of whom have been encamped here for some weeks) have just started on a war party against them. Forty miles north of Denver, at the foot of the mountains, the Kiowas, Comanches, Cheyennes, Sioux and Apaches are greatly annoying to settlers, by stealing cattle and other depredations; and as the traders supply them freely with whisky and ammunition, there is reason to anticipate serious trouble before summer is over. The world renowned mountaineer, Kit Carson, is spending a few months here, and manifests the utmost surprise at the wonderful changes which are taking place in the country. . . .

The supreme court of the people, with Judge Lynch on the bench, has just been in session here. Jacob Miller was killed by Marcus Gradier, in camp, about six miles south of Denver, on Wednesday night. . . The people immediately organized a court, with Judge Slaughter on the bench; gave Gradier a full and fair trial on Thursday, and found him guilty of murder. He was executed yesterday in the presence of an immense concourse of citizens.

[For those left wondering how and when tens of thousands of emigrants made their way into the High Country, A.D.R. explained. To the limited extent migration into the mountains occurred in 1859, it required immense courage and determination. By mid-1860, a number of routes were much improved. Just as crossing the prairie was far more reasonable in 1858-60 compared to 1840-1850, so too was chasing rumors (and occasionally truthful reports) of rich gold finds beyond the thin veneer of camps stretching along the Front Range of the Rockies. The so-called Pikes Peak region remained a disappointment, but Ute trails leading west into present-day South Park and the headwaters of the Arkansas River invited exploration. At the end of this trail, California Gulch did not disappoint.]

June 22, 1860
Colorado City, Pike's Peak
The last express for the river [Missouri] carried in $15,000 in dust, and gold begins to circulate freely in the towns, as the result of this season's mining, though many still complain of hard times. A friend who has just returned from the famous "California gulch" informs me that from three to four thousand miners in that locality are realizing all sums, from fair wages to $50 per day. For gulch diggings this is wonderfully rich, but your readers must not forget that at the same time thousands of immigrants through the whole mining region are doing little or nothing, and some are returning home in utter disappointment and disgust.

The five hundred Arapahoe and Apache Indians who went out to fight the Utes, obtained more than they bargained for. At first they surprised a village, killing several squaws and papooses, taking others prisoners, and stealing some sixty horses. But the Utes soon rallied and drove them away, and afterwards surprised and attacked them, while they were camping at night, killing six of their warriors; and causing them to stampede for Denver in great haste. On the way there they grossly insulted several immigrants, compelling them to supply them with provisions, and drew their cocked revolvers and rifles upon a defenseless lady whom they found alone in a log house. Unless the Arapahoes very soon abandon such proceedings, they will soon find a more formidable foe in the field than their Indian enemies. They have now interred their warriors, and are about starting upon another expedition against the Utes. . . .

Colorado City is improving rapidly, and bids fair to be the second town in the Gold Region. Many of the houses are now vacant, the owners being absent in the mountains, designing to return in the fall. Johnson County has just been started, twelve miles distant. Six or seven stores are established, and, now that lumber is to be procured, better buildings than the original log houses are beginning to make their appearance. An excellent field is open here for the establishment of a newspaper and job office, and the company offer a donation of one hundred lots to the party who will first establish one.

[Nor were there limits to the extent entrepreneurs or those quick to seize on a route to a fast buck would go albeit at risk of their own hide.]

A company from eastern Kansas, including Dr. Walters, from Lykins [now Miami] County, and Messrs. King and Dixon, from Lawrence, recently attempted, under a charter from your territorial [Kansas] legislature, to levy toll on the road from this point [present-day Colorado Springs] to the South Park. They did some work on the road, but the Colorado people, who had expended much labor upon it before they commenced, insisted that it should continue a free road, and warned them to desist. They continued to charge toll, however, until a party of Colorado boys visited them one morning, tore down their toll gate, and burned their houses. When last seen they were on the way to Denver, proposing to "sue" the persons through whom they had thus "come to grief," but in a country where there is no law, that procedure would be rather farcical. . . .

Quartz Mill - c. 1860. Unlike placer mining, lodes relied on separating the mineral-bearing quartz in order to make transportation feasible. One common method was crushing the ore with heavy "stamps" driven by animals, water, or steam. *(Fossett, 1879)*

Arrastra. More primitive methods included the horse drawn arrastra. *(Richardson, 1867)*

[More legitimate but not particularly encouraging were enterprises based on freeing fine gold from quartz veins mined from hard rock.]

There are now fifty steam quartz mills in the northern diggings, of which "Gregory's" is the center and nucleus. Only six are yet in operation, and some of these thus far are failures, from imperfect machinery and adulterated quick-silver, which proves utterly worthless for separating the gold from the dirt. In one case, from this cause, a cord of quartz supposed to contain $200 yielded but $2. The only quartz mill from which I have reliable figures, employs twenty-five men, and is yielding from $300 to $400 daily. There are about fifty ar-rastras in the diggings, run by horse, mule and water power, and said to be "netting", on an average, $25 per day. . . .

[And what young journalist could pass up a chance to cover another strug-gling journalist as curious as friend Andrew McGrew.]

You recollect the famous "Wheelbarrow Man" of last season's notoriety? He was shot through the hand a few days since, by the accidental discharge of his revolver, in his pocket. He was a good deal "shot in the neck" at the time, but was not seriously injured by the shot in the hand. Such men seldom are. Your desperadoes who frequent gambling saloons, carry two revolvers and a bowie knife, and are shot at almost every day, always seem to escape uninjured; while your excellent, mild, inoffensive man, who would not harm a kitten for the world, while walking home from market is crushed by a falling brick, or "laid out" by a stray bullet. . . .

[On the more serious matter of Indian troubles, A.D.R. unabashedly shared the attitude of most of his generation and no doubt all at his side who braved the frontier. Nevertheless, it was an uncommon episode of frustration if not a stark departure from how his Quaker upbringing shaped his abolitionist senti-ments and goodwill to all when he was provoked to action. In either case, this frustration also illustrated how high ideals regarding the roiling cauldron of daily frontier life were more sustainable in the comforts of one's own home than on the trail.]

The Indian troubles are attracting considerable attention. A meeting to take the matter into consideration has been held, but resulted in nothing more important than the appointing of a committee to wait upon the Arapahoes, to expostulate with them, and requesting congress to appoint an agent for the tribe. A member of the committee of arrangements for the "Fourth" [of July] suggested that the proper method of honoring that anniversary would be to "wipe out" the Indians altogether; but the humane proposition was rejected.

[That frontier Fourth of July, celebrated with great and daylong exuberance or at least with simple homage to a handmade flag, passed without incident in Denver City. That is not to say there were no shootings or drunken brawls, but neither involved Arapahoes. Falling on a Sunday helped. On a brighter note, 1860 blessed Denver commerce with its own privately held mint. No longer was bartering the only medium of exchange. On March 3, 1863, the Federal Government acquired these private assets for use as the Denver Branch of the U.S. Mint. Even so, entrepreneurs persisted with their own coinage, and A.D.R. continued to root out tales titillating to his eastern audience.]

July 10, 1860
Denver City
Messrs. Clark, Gruber & Co., the well-known Leavenworth bankers, have completed their large brick building, and will commence operations in a few days. In addition to a general banking business, they will issue coin, with their own stamp upon it, in denominations of $20, $10, $5 and $2.50. They have the best of facilities for assaying, and design to have their coin (which will only be alloyed by the silver which is mingled with it) so pure that it will be worth par at the mint. Their machinery for preparing and striking the coin is extensive and excellent, and will enable them to turn out $50,000 per day, should the demands of the country require it. They will manufacture about $10,000 at the first minting, which is expected to be completed this week. On account of its great superiority over gold dust, in point of convenience for circulation, their coin will undoubtedly be largely in demand.

July 19, 1860
Golden City, Pike's Peak
A few days since, a miner in the Gregory diggings erected a cabin on what he supposed the least valuable end of his claim, and covered the roof with poles, hay and dirt. A very violent storm on Thursday caused the frail roof to leak; and, on ascending to repair it, his astonished eyes detected a shining nugget of gold, which had been thrown up in a shovel full of dirt, and washed bare by the rain. On weighing it, it proved to be worth $42.80. . . .

    Denver is growing decidedly lively. A shooting or stabbing affray occurs almost daily. A negro was shot five times, a few evenings since, by another person of color; but, like Webster, he "still lives," and is likely to recover. . . .

The Rock Island quartz mill, in the Gregory diggings, after running twenty-four hours, on "cleaning up" yesterday morning was found to have yielded $2,000. Times are improving, and the gold dust is beginning to flow into the towns. Hinckley's express last evening brought down $2,200 from the Gregory diggings alone, and averages nearly that amount daily. Many trains are starting for the river to bring out winter supplies of goods.

[Frontier survival, mine boosterism, Front Range growing pains including Indian troubles, and the joys of budding civilization were not the only 1860 topics of journalistic interest. Presidential politics increasingly made the list as both the November national election and the Civil War approached. Only the dullest of observers remained hopeful war could be avoided. If Abraham Lincoln became President, he would go to whatever lengths necessary to preserve the Union. A.D.R. reported on an early harbinger of trouble.]

In direct opposition to the popular feeling (which is almost unanimous against making any political issue here at present), two prominent Democrats were announced to address the people upon national politics. The attendance was very large, and the orators made violent Douglas speeches. They then introduced a resolution endorsing the Little Giant, and declaring him the choice of the miners for the Presidency. To their infinite surprise, it was voted down, more than two to one. Their mortification was rendered complete by a call for three cheers for Abe Lincoln, which were given with earnestness and vehemence that made the valleys vocal with their far resounding echoes.

[Toying with the reader, it seemed, perhaps giddy with the opportunity to revisit old stomping grounds shared with his mentor Horace Greeley a year earlier, A.D.R. returned to Gregory Gulch. He drew insightful contrasts worthy of wonderment between 1859 and 1860. Joined by a successful entrepreneur, owner of general stores in Denver, Golden, and Central City, Lewis N. Tappan also was a special correspondent for Horace's *New York Tribune*.]

July 31, 1860
Gregory Diggings, Rocky Mountains
After an absence of more than a year, I am again in the heart of the Rocky Mountains, observing the almost incredible amount of privation and hard labor which men will submit to in searching for gold, and the astonishing rapidity with which a young empire is springing up, six hundred miles west of the recent confines of civilization. But, like David Copperfield, let me begin my story with the beginning of my story.

A few days since, in company with your whilom [erstwhile] townsman, Lewis N. Tappan, Esq., I left Denver, bound for the mountains. A ride of fifteen miles, over sandy, rolling prairies, and in view of the grandest scenery, brought us to the base of the range. The mountains are now entered through the mouth of a narrow canon, whose frowning walls crowned with rocks and studded with pines, often rise almost perpendicularly to the height of five or six hundred feet. The frightful and precipitous hill, up which, in company with Messrs. Greeley and Villard, I climbed wearily a year ago, is now quite abandoned for this more practicable and easy route.

The narrow road through the winding valley is often crossed by a bubbling little stream, ice-cold, and fresh from the mountain snows. Our progress was seriously impeded by long trains of provision and immigrant wagons; huge quartz mills, borne upon wheels, hopelessly imbedded in the fathomless mire, and great loads of hay, which the makers cut and haul eighty miles, over wretched roads, to sell at $80 per ton. Among the novelties upon this thoroughfare may be noted an immigrant with a single ox harnessed into a light cart, and drawing about five hundred pounds of provisions and mining tools. This singular "outfit" has plodded its weary way from Minnesota!

At another point, a philosophic settler was riding upon one of a yoke of oxen which he was taking into the mines. The bovine quadruped was regularly saddled and bridled, and took to his new calling very kindly. Before reaching this point we passed the "Four-Mile House," a popular caravansera kept by Mrs. Hull, from Franklin, Douglas County, Kansas, who is reported to have realized many thousands of dollars from her vocation as a landlady, during the past year. She certainly possesses some of the traits of Crabbe's miraculous heroine "who lost her husband while their loves were young, but kept her farm, her temper and her tongue."

The old Gregory diggings (discovered May 6, 1859) continue the nucleus of the northern mines. Nearly all the gulches in this vicinity are laid out into cities, duly surveyed and platted; and within ten miles of the spot from which I write, there must be a population of twenty-five thousand souls. My first emotions on arriving were those of mingled bewilderment and wonder at the grand development of the past fourteen months, and the astonishing amount of labor which has been performed in erecting spacious and costly buildings, constructing roads, sinking shafts, bringing out and setting up machinery, and excavating the gulches and disemboweling the hills, for scores of miles. Every dollar yet taken out here has cost at least two dollars, and the same amount of work done on the rich prairies of your beautiful territory, would have made them the very garden of the world.

Daily newspapers, and stages from the valley towns, theaters, gambling houses, schools and churches, silver forks at the dining tables of huge hotels, law offices, courts, elections, and the hoarse breath and shrill whistle of scores of steam engines echoing through the gulches, are now some of the salient features of life, where, less than two years ago, reigned almost primeval silence, and the wild elk and grizzly bear held undisputed sway.

[No less a spectacle to behold, A.D.R. revisited the city he called home.]

August 2, 1860
Denver City
On returning home, I find Denver in a state of intense excitement. The gamblers and desperadoes have attempted to overawe the community, and the people have risen, almost as one man, to put a stop to the reign of terror. One of the gamblers has been killed; two more are undergoing trial before the vigilance committee, with the probability of their summary conviction and punishment; the city is guarded at night by over two hundred patrolmen, standing upon every corner and challenging all suspicious parties to give the countersign; and the most intense feeling prevails.

August 7, 1860
Denver City
Want of space in my last letter compelled me to omit several incidents illustrative of life in the mines. In a gold region, the pursuits of many of the settlers differ materially from those they followed in the East. A gentleman who has for many years been engaged in the practice of the law in New York City, and who still keeps an office in that metropolis, is now running a quartz mill in the Gregory diggings. An ex-banker from one of the river towns in Kansas is also there, engaged in selling pies! He was formerly a deacon in the Presbyterian Church, but now retails whisky on Sunday. It would be hard to find on record a more melancholy falling-off, both from dignity and devotion.

General William Larimer. Staking a claim to what he named "Denver" in honor of the governor of the Kansas Territory, and declaring that "I am Denver City," the General became a successful purveyor of city lots and instrumental in the formation of the Colorado Territory in 1861. *(Wikipedia Commons)*

August 25, 1860
Denver City
Notwithstanding a feeling of depression, which prevails in certain locali-
ties, the gold from the mines begins to come out in considerable quantities.
Messrs. Clark, Gruber & Co. receive about $2,000 per day at their banking
house. Hinckley & Co.'s express brought down $10,000 from the Gregory
diggings, night before last. The express which left for Leavenworth and St.
Joseph on Thursday morning, carried out $20,000 by the messenger, and
nearly as much more in the hands of passengers. At least sixty thousand
dollars per week is now sent East by the express. Two or three weeks since,
Mr. John Warner started for the river with $50,000; and since that time,
Messrs. Earl & Thomas, from California gulch, have left for the states, tak-
ing with them, respectively, $50,000 and $20,000.

On the brink of returning to his family, and ever mindful of his obliga-
tion to address the human condition of a friend, A.D.R. deviated from his
frontier beat to update his readers on the Wheelbarrow Man. Along with
a half-dozen others, Andrew McGrew had announced his candidacy for a
seat in Congress. In A.D.R.'s opinion his fellow journalist, with considerable
name recognition accompanying his likable character, would poll well. Sadly
for McGrew, General William Larimer, formerly of Leavenworth along with
so many other pilgrims, polled better. Obviously not a prophet, A.D.R. did
fare better at foreseeing the birth of Colorado's mining industry, a development predicated on "wimmin," preservation of the Union, and Welsh Cousin
Jacks. The completion of the transcontinental railroad and America's industrial
revolution would help.

Notes—Chapter Six: Rapscallions, Nincompoops and Ninnies

[1] Twain, Mark, *Roughing It*, Mark Twain.

[2] Gehling, Richard, "F–The Mountaineers," *The Pikes Peak Gold Rush*, pg. 6. [Uncle Dick Wootton
is an excellent and sad example of the rapid transformation of the Colorado frontier. By 1858,
his mountain man days were long gone and his freight company days were about to end. His
wife died birthing their fourth child, he became disillusioned with freighting and the mountains, and his planned move of family including new wife back to the States never happened. The
final chapters of his life were far rosier, beginning with successful businesses in booming Denver
and ending with a ranch and a toll road/railroad right-of-way over Raton Pass. See: *Uncle Dick
Wootton*, as told to Howard Louis Conard, ed. M.M. Quaife *The Pioneer Frontiersman of the
Rocky Mountains*, Richens Lacy Wootton; "Green Russell, Colonizer," *Herald Democrat*, January
1, 1906, Leadville, Colorado, "J. H. Pierce letter to Mr. Fen G. Barker, Society of Leadville
Pioneers."]

George Jackson found the placer mines at Idaho Springs, and John Gregory found the
Gregory lode at Black Hawk, all before Green Russell returned from his 1858-1859 win-
tering in Dahlonega and staked Russell gulch in Gilpin County. According to Cousin J. H.
Pierce, "there must have been 300 men here (Front Range) before Russell arrived in 1859." And

because the Lawrence Party dallied, naively chased false reports, and otherwise squandered their opportunity to join the elite Midas club, instead of gold they also found upwards of 300 men in the region. Too crowded for even the naïve, they again dallied, founded a couple settlements that went as bust as Pike's Peak, fragmented and went home. At home they soon discovered that the reputations of their competitors and the region had preceded them. Journalists and statured editors like Horace Greeley and rat-finks like John Cantrell torched the imaginations of a gullible nation desperate for a reprieve from a prolonged economic recession and the prospect of an almost certain civil war.

3   Smith, Duane A., *Trail of Gold and Silver*, pg. 48. [See: Ovando J. Hollister, *The Mines of Colorado*, pgs. 106-107.]

4   Paul, Rodman W., *The Far West and the Great Plains in Transition, 1859-1900*, pgs. 30-31.

5   Brown, Robert L., *An Empire of Silver*, pgs. 91-93.

6   Richardson, Albert D., *Beyond the Mississippi*, pg. 185.

7   Hafen, LeRoy R., *Colorado Gold Rush*, pgs. 34-35.

8   Ibid., pgs. 36-37.

9   Richardson, pgs. 157-158.

10 Ibid., p. 158.

11 Spring, Agnes Wright, "Rush to the Rockies, 1859," pgs. 109-113.

12 Richardson, pgs. 159-160. [Reference is made to William H. Russell, "the chief freighter of the plains." An idea of the scale of the conquest of the plains is gleaned from the scale of Russell's freighting operations: "Last year [1858] he employed twenty-five thousand oxen and two thousand wagons, chiefly in transporting supplies for our army in Utah. He stipulates that any one of his teamsters who whips cattle unmercifully or utters an oath, shall forfeit his wages. Of course the precaution proves ineffective, for there is a logical connection between mud-holes and profanity."

13 Spring, pg. 114.

14 Garrard, Lewis H., *Wah-to-yah and the Taos Trail*, pgs. ix- 7.

15 Hafen, "Pike's Peak Gold Rush Guidebooks of 1859," pg. 93.

16 Hafen, "Pike's Peak Gold Rush Guidebooks of 1859," pgs. 99-100.

17 Ibid., pg. 99 FN: etc.

18 Ibid., pgs. 131-132.

19 "Gandy-dancer" was a term used for railroad section-hands. Some suggest the term was coined to describe the "dancing" motion of workers as they man-handled heavy rails onto ties and aligned them with their lining and claw bars, or "waddled like ganders" trying to step from tie to tie.

20 Spring, pg. 114 FN:. [See Hafen, *Colorado and Its People* (New York: Lewis Historical Pub. Co., 1918), Vol. I, pg. 188.]

21 Smith, pg. 25. [See: Horace Greeley, *An Overland Journey from New York to San Francisco in the Summer of 1859*, New York, Alfred A. Knopf, 1964, pgs. 98-106.]

22 Ibid.

23 Ibid., pg. 26.

24 "Central City, Colorado – Boom & Bust," *Legends of America*, pg. 2.

25 Bagley, *With Golden Visions Bright Before Them*, Vol. II, pg. 263.

26 Ibid., pg. 252.

27 Ibid., pgs. 256, 259-261.

28 Ibid., pgs. 259-261,

29 Zamonski and Keller, *The Fifty-Niners*, pg. 19.

30 Ibid., pg. 20.

31 Hafen, *Colorado Gold Rush: Contemporary Letters and Reports, 1858-1859*, pg. 198.

32 Zamonski & Keller, pg. 20.

[33] Gehling, "H–The Fifty-Niners," pg. 9.

[34] Ibid., pg. 11.

[35] Ibid., pgs. 3-6.

[36] Ibid., pg. 7.

[37] Barry, Louise, Editor, "Albert D. Richardson's Letters on the Pike's Peak Gold Region," pgs. 14-57.

[38] Paul, pg. 7. [See: Van Deusen, Glyndon G., *Horace Greeley: Nineteenth Century Crusader*, Philadelphia, 1953.]

[39] Barry, pgs. 2-21.

CHAPTER 7

Wimmin, War, and Cousin Jacks

We cross the prairies as of old
Our fathers crossed the sea,
To make the West, as they the East,
The empire of the free. [1]

L ittle more than rumored at the beginning of 1858, Colorado gold fields warranted a full-on rush by early 1859 and experienced a resurgence of better provisioned emigres in 1860. By most accounts, somewhere in the range
of 100,000 to 140,000 so-called Fifty-Niners slogged across the prairie to the
Front Range. Within months of arrival nearly the same number returned home.
Of the 10,000 to 30,000 who reportedly wintered over, their whereabouts were
a mystery. According to Andrew McGrew, perhaps a few hundred Denverites
enjoyed Uncle Dick's Christmas festivities. The balance of the "stay-behinds"
probably hunkered down along the Front Range wherever weather and weakness deposited them. Unlike the previous year, 1860 brought women, machinery,
technology, and the makings of a great city. Common sense accompanied hun-
ger for gold. A.D.R. foresaw it. He also foresaw 1861 ushering in the Nation's
Civil War.

The end of the 1860 spring mud season marked the resumption of heavy
prairie traffic, but it would be the tail end of the Nation's final mass migration
west. Families outnumbered loners and heavy freighters replaced most farm
wagons, handcarts and wheelbarrows. Prospecting was beginning to transition
into mining, and treasure-seekers were giving way to ranchers, tradesmen, and
shopkeepers. Both developments augured well for the growth of settlements
which in turn necessitated a corresponding increase in all the means of production and sustenance populations needed to survive. On balance, entrepreneurial souls intending to sink roots brought households. Households brought
household goods and the nature and composition of the trail parades changed
accordingly. Hardships abounded, but nowhere to the extent encountered even
a year earlier.

END OF AN ERA

The makeup of the Fifty-Niners rush to the Colorado gold fields differed greatly in 1859 compared to 1860, but collectively the Fifty-Niners were the third and last of America's mass migrations west. Under normal circumstances, the onset of the 1860 winter would have only temporarily disrupted such a migration, expectations being that some degree of travel would resume the following spring. Under 1860 circumstances—the November election of Abraham Lincoln and the subsequent secession of eleven southern states from the Union—the winter disruption would be prolonged. Forty-eight months of civil war, painful reconstruction, and the American industrial revolution would divert America's attention to economic growth and unfamiliar roles on the world stage. Mad rushes to populate western mining camps and homesteads gave way to shrewder calculations and better prepared risk-takers.

In 1860 the foolhardy treasure-seeking class gave place to the entrepreneurial class, men with families prepared to invest in shops, factories and farms. Those contemplating westering, thanks to the honesty of the A.D.R. school of journalism, better appreciated what they needed to survive. They were a teachable lot, although not universally so, and they enjoyed advantages not afforded their predecessors. Denver improved weekly in its ability to replenish depleted provisions—commercial freight and passenger lines established services to and from the Front Range. There also was heavy military traffic east and west. Manufacturers of mining equipment were quick to respond to the call for all manner of steam-powered machinery. Larger and larger boilers and mills arrived. Historian Gehling sums up the improvements in just a year.

> Unlike the Fifty-Niners, the gold seekers of 1860 seemed to have grown somewhat in sophistication. Most seemed to realize that gold in the new El Dorado could not be scooped off the ground; the pick and the pan might provide a little color, but most of the gold lay locked up in rock and could be freed only with the help of machinery. To answer this need, quartz crushers would have to be shipped west to the mountains. John D. Young met such a train of "twenty wagons loaded with a crusher and machinery steam engine boiler, etc." The crusher brought west by Samuel Mallory was but one of more than 150 that had left the Leavenworth-St. Joseph area by June 1. John D. Young on his return east in early July counted forty-one quartz crushers on the road between Denver City and Fort Kearney. [2]

In fact, this second season of emigrants had yet another advantage over their predecessors. Perhaps as many as fifteen hundred who wintered over along the Front Range had filled their days improving roads and buildings. Instead of virgin forests and mountain gulches scarcely marred by animal trails, critical infrastructure and the makings of a rudimentary mining community greeted the 1860 crowd. According to Hollister,

> *The owners of lodes were busy getting out dirt and quartz for the expected mills in the spring…Very fair roads had been made into the Mountains—one via Golden Gate, one via Bradford. They were not so perfect as now, but were a vast improvement upon the first hill-road, over which in places twenty yoke of oxen were required to climb, without dragging anything worth mentioning, perhaps a wagon containing a sack of flour. A road from Denver to the South Park, via Mt. Vernon and Bergen's Ranch, had been projected and was vigorously pushed through the winter. So also was the St. Vrain, Golden City and Colorado Wagon Road, which avoided Denver entirely. A fair wagon road ran from Canon City into the south Park, also one from Colorado City. There were trails from the South Park to the Middle Park, and one from Gregory. On 1 March 1860, Kehler & Montgomery's express coach arrived in the mines from Denver, the first ever run on the line.* [3]

Colorado Territory was locally organized as a state but never acknowledged by the Federal government, perhaps in part because it would have absorbed large surrounding territories. The U.S. Congress approved a territory with present-day Colorado boundaries on February 28, 1861. *(Wikipedia Commons)*

But make no mistake, despite vastly more welcoming conditions along the Front Range and well into the High Country, the civilization that emigrants were accustomed to experiencing was nowhere to be found. Nor did it seem to matter. To Hollister's way of thinking, "never did spring open on a more hopeful people than the inhabitants of the Territory of Jefferson in 1860." The extraordinary improvements made during a single winter explained why.

The richness and great extent of the new gold fields were considered proven. The pioneers had penetrated the previous season from (sic) Taylor's Park, away south of the Arkansas and a hundred miles in the mountains, to the Cache-a-la-Poudre, northwest of Long's Peak, and the Black Hills. Between was a bewildering scope of country, scratched indeed, but not prospected thoroughly; and in view of the unparalleled richness of the lodes and gulches in the Gregory District, the most sanguine expectations were not unreasonable. Under the greatest disadvantages, mining had been prosecuted there with the most

THE RENEGADE STATE
THAT ALMOST REPLACED COLORADO

"On an April night in 1859, a raucous gathering took place at the saloon and gambling hall owned by Denver pioneer 'Uncle' Dick Wootton. The purpose of the gathering was to garner support for a radical idea: creating a new territory known as Jefferson Territory, which would pull the Pikes Peak gold mining region into its own independent state. To the surprise of many, the idea actually caught on and within a few months, the Jefferson Territory was a functional political entity," wrote Brian K. Trembath in the June 24, 2020 edition of the Denver Public Library *Research News*. Historians of all stripes have tried to settle accounts on the details attending this subject with limited success. Herewith is the briefest of summaries, the heart of the matter.

Declaring the region first a territory rather than a state had the practical value of avoiding a military response and securing Federal funding. Neither of these consequences was likely, but who was going to challenge the reasoning of a raucous saloon crowd. By October 24, 1859, by a reasonably democratic process, the "citizens" of the Pike Peak's region (more accurately the Cherry Creek region) had organized what would become the Territory of Jefferson. In November 1859, Hiram J. Graham and Albert Steinberger were sent to Washington with a petition to "effect this object." Graham was from New York, but came to the Front Range by way of Pacific City, Iowa. Steinberger was "a young man, and dropped out of the delegation at Omaha. He was afterward king of a group of islands in the Pacific, but was deposed by a British man-of-war." [4]

gratifying success. Now they were to have the benefit of experience; of machinery, sawmills, cheap provisions, implements and supplies; of established laws and regulations; of roads and means of transportation; of postal facilities; of a great influx of people, many of them women, many of them bringing more or less capital, and coming at least prepared for the emergencies of the season. The agricultural capacities of the country had been found much greater than was at first expected, and the settlers were better prepared to make use of them ....

By the first of May immigrants were arriving from the States at a rate of a hundred a day. "It was estimated that up to that time eleven thousand wagons had passed Plum Creek, bound for Pike's Peak. The Platte Route may be said to have contained, for a full month, but a single train, extending from the mountains to the Missouri River." [5]

Three main routes led west. For tens of thousands the best choice was the "Denver Road," [6] testimony to the Arapahoe village that became a viable city

Also in November during the first territorial legislative session in Denver, delegates appointed Robert Williamson Steele, a Nebraska attorney, Governor. For the next sixteen months the Territory of Jefferson operated as an independent albeit renegade jurisdiction with its own ("miner-style") court system and other features of a legitimate political entity. The Territory was left to its own devices until the U.S. Senate approved the Wyandotte Constitution which admitted Kansas into the Union as a free state on January 21, 1861. On February 28, President Buchanan signed into law the Colorado Territory. Both measures were undertaken in the midst of southern states seceding from the Union to form the Confederate States of America. In light of imminent civil war, both measures were designed to better secure for the Union the mineral resources of the Rocky Mountains. Both measures also spelled the end of any Front Range interests in pursuing Jefferson Territory or statehood status.

Named after Thomas Jefferson, the territory embraced land officially part of the Kansas and Nebraska Territories. Its raucous founders had contemplated a region that also included portions of New Mexico, Utah, and Washington Territories, expanding the borders of present-day Colorado by upwards of seventy percent, but that was a bridge too far. Remote from the seat of Kansas government, a fact of geography that worked to everyone's advantage, Front Range chicanery was largely ignored by Kansas and Federal authorities preoccupied with slavery and dissolution of the Union. With official territorial status granted by the U.S. Congress, the renegade Territory of Jefferson transitioned into Jefferson County. Golden City was the territorial seat, later becoming the Jefferson County seat. On November 1, 1861, a duly authorized Colorado General Assembly organized seventeen counties that included Jefferson County, albeit far smaller in area than first proposed. [7]

and a trail that became a wagon road. It was favored because it offered the greatest assurance of water and grass. This was the northern route, sometimes called the River Road. The Santa Fe Trail was the southern route, also a river route (Arkansas) but never called that. The Smoky Hills Trail was the mid-course, shorter but riskier. Water was scarce and Native American war parties were plentiful.

The Denver Road included numerous branches crossing the Missouri River, all leading to Fort Kearny in central Nebraska Territory, gateway to the Rockies. West of Fort Kearney the road followed the south fork of the Platte to the mouth of Cherry Creek and struggling Denver perched uncomfortably at the base of the formidable Front Range. Although South Park was a relatively easy destination for southern route travelers, the preferred destination was the Gregory District fifteen miles west of Denver. Sadly, for newcomers, braver pilgrims had claimed the best Gregory District prospects the previous season. Happily, for gullible newcomers with cash, every claim was for sale. For newcomers without cash, day jobs abounded in someone else's mine. If trying one's hand in "a deep, wet gulch" no one else thought worth examining was out of the question, returning home was always an option.

At first, warm greetings did not await newcomers. They were unwelcome competition for scarce resources, natural and manmade. The "old-timers"–old defined as a year or even a few months before arrival of the newcomer–felt they paid their dues in privation and hard work and the new crowd should fare no better. "Surely, [they said], all these strangers cannot expect employment here on our ground; let them branch out and find mines for themselves, or if not, go back." Soon labor would be in short supply, choked off by demands of civil war, but in the frenzy of their treasure quest no one was thinking beyond the next day. Hollister captured the heat of the moment.

> *So the dwellers in wagons, in tents, in booths, prospected—which is a discouraging business except to the prospector by nature, who must have the faith of a martyr—made continual purchases of claims which they knew not how to work, gold washing being a nice business, and were obliged to throw up; cut saw-logs or cord-wood, or engaged in such other work incidental to mining, as the case admitted; or finally, laid round and consumed the grub they had brought with them. The whole district was full of tents and camp-wagons; it was overrun with people.* [8]

Still they came, men without a plan, but also entrepreneurs with vision. All manner of infrastructure and services sprang up in and among the camps. Sowers & Company started a coach line between Denver and the mountains. The Western Stage Company did the same–even two lines could not satisfy the demand. When Green Russell and his brothers returned from wintering in

Georgia, they were horrified at what they found. The discovery of California Gulch near present-day Leadville [meet Abe Lee below], very rich and five or six miles long, and a half dozen other less considerable gulches on the Arkansas, Blue and Swan watersheds, would relieve some pressure, but not quickly.

Gregory encountered similar crowds, but they were less a bother for him. As promised, he returned from Missouri with a quartz mill and a plan that did not involve prospecting. His mill was "erected in a few days, ran awhile, taking out two hundred dollars a day, and sold for six times its cost. John H. Gregory not only knew how to find mines, but it appears he knew how to sell out at the right moment." [9]

WELLS FARGO — PONY EXPRESS

In 1860 military freight wagons, very large freight wagons, escorted by well-armed troopers often accompanied second-season travelers. Seemingly non-ending military freight wagons, in Gehling's words, "were immense affairs, usually drawn by eight or ten yoke of oxen and accompanied by a reserve herd of cattle driven along near the train. To William Hedges, the appearance of such a train in the distance reminded him of 'a line of white elephants lumbering along.'" In addition, private freighters shared the road, supplying the increasing number of Denver merchants with all manner of goods. Generally left unsaid, traffic was two-way, comprised not only of "go-backers" but also freighters and coaches engaged in lively commerce. [10]

Emigrants in 1860 were not only wiser than their erstwhile predecessors, as a whole they themselves were better prepared, better provisioned, and better equipped. They even had commercial transportation available to them. The *Central Overland California and Pike's Peak (COCPP) Express*, was the first management firm of the better known Pony Express. Wells Fargo later took charge and operated stagecoaches between St. Joseph and Denver. For a fraction of the cost of outfitting oneself for the journey, a COCPP ticket purchased a jolting if not certain trip to the mines. [11]

Perhaps the starkest contrast to the first season of Colorado gold-seekers— the clearest indication that settlers vastly outnumbered speculators—was the second wave of emigrants brought their "wimmin." How often they heard warnings from "go-backers" they passed heading east is not known, but one Gehling account is probably a fair sampling: "My dear wimmin, you'll rue to your dyin' day ever havin' set your feet on that thar miserable Pike's Peak." [12] Too late, warnings of this nature fell on deaf ears. The *Rocky Mountain News* carried a traveler's report that settled the matter. Apparently bored enough to start counting,

Gehling writes, "on 20 June Wilk Defree reported to the *News* that on his trip from Denver to Fort Kearney he had met 4,925 teams."

At an average of five persons to a wagon, he figured the total to be at least 24,625 emigrants. He also noted: "I think we must have met from eight to ten hundred ladies on the route, most of whom were ladies accompanying their husbands for the purpose of permanent settlement." [13]

COLORADO HIGH COUNTRY

The Colorado Mineral Belt, a region rich in valuable metal-bearing deposits, stretched from the San Juan Mountains to the approaches to Wyoming. Prospecting along Colorado's Front Range was challenging, but the High Country was horrifying. Nevertheless, the sheer mass of humanity elbowing its way into the foothills ensured no mountain region would evade prospectors for long. Soon after Jackson's and Gregory's discoveries, Green Russell and his party had returned from Georgia, arriving in Denver on May 10, 1858. Learning of numerous rich discoveries and that the mountains were filling with eager prospectors, they determined to leave the next morning for the Gregory diggings. At Gregory Gulch, Russell was alarmed by the scene that greeted him. In his own words, "Finding an immense crowd of people in that narrow locality, we did not tarry long, but pushed on to the adjoining gulches." One of those neighboring gulches, soon named Russell's Gulch, proved well worth the effort required to free its gold. Staking off a number of claims, his party of six pitched their tents and went to work. Russell reported, "For nearly four months we have worked from eight to thirteen hands, and averaged $25 worth of gold a hand, per day…the value of our average daily yield I would put at one hundred and fifty dollars." [14]

Likewise, during this season hundreds of other diggings of varying richness made for close and often contentious quarters. Newcomers, of which there were now hundreds, had little choice but to purchase claims if they could afford to do so, or move farther afield which was the choice of most. They followed game trails and Ute trails to South Park and settled Jefferson, Tarryall and Fairplay. They ranged up and down the Arkansas River between California Gulch (Leadville) to the north and Cañon and Colorado Cities to the south. They pushed up Clear Creek to its headwaters, founding Georgetown and Elizabethtown. And so it went, little by little, exploration and exploitation of mountain minerals began. At the dawn of 1860, it is fair to say that the Colorado Mineral Belt east of the San Juan Mountains from New Mexico to Wyoming was home to our emigrants. Where two or more gathered, a mining district and miner's court soon followed. Organization of towns and a statutory Territory if not a legislated State was not far behind.

Contrary to 1859 circumstances that left behind the homemakers, clearly a "bum's rush," 1860 parties and every train thereafter looked more like family Sunday outings. And supporting the notion that the "go-backers" were not uniformly disgruntled, many left only for the winter with every intention of returning in the spring with wives and children, a sure sign that civilization was about to transform the Denver camp into a city.

Two years worth of newcomers elbowed more and more brave-hearts farther into the mountains. Of course, they prospected as they went, first on the cheap with pan and shovel, but knowing now from experience that float should lead to gold-bearing quartz veins they really needed to find. Only the Continental Divide limited their gaze and that not for long. Quartz veins did abound with the bonanza waiting for them at present-day Leadville. Similar to early Front Range motherlodes, it took a California Forty-Niner to find them. Abe Lee earned that bragging right. An unintended but probably inevitable consequence, scrappy Denver also earned bragging rights as the premier regional supply depot and commercial queen of the plains.

Some historians consider Abe Lee one of the founding fathers of hardrock mining in Colorado. Clearly, Abe merits at least partial credit along with Green Russell, John Gregory, and George Jackson. Lee's find in Leadville demonstrated

High Country Brave-hearts. High Country prospecting was a natural consequence of far too many newcomers pressing into far too confining Front Range gold fields. Experienced Georgians and Californians knew how to find motherlodes – California Gulch/ Leadville beckon despite dangers getting there. *(Frank Leslie's Illustrated Newspaper, April 12, 1879)*

Colorado's mineral belt was not confined to lower elevations. If the significance of quartz veins was not universally appreciated after a year or two of Front Range experience, Abe Lee drove the lesson home in California Gulch. As important, Lee laid the groundwork for Leadville growing from a camp to a mill town. In turn, that laid the groundwork for looking beyond gold to silver, a far more common Colorado treasure. [15]

Among the newcomers crowding into Gregory Gulch and the lower elevations, Abe and a small number of pathfinders preferred challenging the isolation and harsher conditions of the High Country. Abe's party reached the Arkansas headwaters by working its way upriver from South Park, the backdoor into Leadville and California Gulch. Others squeezed out of the lower reaches of Clear Creek worked their way west through Georgetown, over the Continental Divide, past present day Frisco to Leadville's front door. Advanced in years, Abe still had gold fever, as well as experience in rooting it out. In April 1860, he did just that.

According to Rodney Paul, "Old Californians" were admired as "wise old fellows" who knew indications of mineral deposits, how to locate and register claims, and how to build and use "rockers," "long toms," and sluices necessary for placer mining. They also appreciated the value of stamp mills and arrastras that were basic to hardrock, vein mines. Perhaps equally important, "Old Californians" knew how to organize a mining district and draft a code of self-imposed conduct complete with a popularly chosen judge or court to settle disputes over claims and try men accused of crimes. Lawless and overcrowded frontier camps desperately needed as many Abe Lee's as they could find.

In fact, "Old Californians" were not hard to find. They were an emerging frontier type, a nomadic, resourceful, hardy, and experienced species that relocated quickly, and did the first prospecting, mining, and organizing of new districts. Their only possible rivals in these matters were the Georgians. Abe Lee fitted this profile.

April in the future Leadville was still winter. In a frigid stream struggling to feed the mighty Arkansas, according to Will Bagley, Abe shouted, "By God, I've got California in this here pan!" Factual or apocryphal matters not. A mining district named "California Gulch" quickly followed. Whether a sop to Abe's excitement or "a tribute to the Golden State's enduring impact on the creation of the mining West" is anyone's guess. Bagley writes:

> *"California was more than the Mother Lode country," observed Duane Smith, dean of hard-rock historians. It "was the mother of western and to a lesser degree, world mining." The state earned the title "Mother Lode for the West" from the ubiquitous veterans of the Sierra mines, for "the 'old Californians,' went everywhere carrying with them their craft of mining," recreating the State's "materialistic, boisterous, transient" ways in camps across the Far West.* [16]

Georgian Cherokees probably deserved a fair share of Smith's tribute, but his point is powerful regardless. As noted, California and Colorado gold rushes had much in common. More importantly, no longer if ever it was the case would placer gold mines signal victory and the end of a hunt. Placer discoveries marked the leading edge of gold's tortured migration downstream from its hardrock source. Of course the source could be exhausted, but more likely not. In either case, the mother lode was the ultimate goal. Determining its worth meant "pans would not do." Russell, Ralston, Gregory, and Jackson on the Front Range and now Lee in the High Country set the standard and secured the start of hardrock mining in the Colorado Rockies. With typical insight, Will Bagley explains.

> *A new American vagabond, the prospector, led the way. Cut from the same cloth in California gold country as Abe Lee, they had known the thrill of discovery, that singular moment when a flash of auriferous color in a pan or the dull glint of a silver vein in a rocky ledge called down visions of instant wealth. They became hopelessly addicted to the ecstasy of standing atop a new fortune, and when it was squandered there was always a new one to be found just over the next ridge in an unexplored creek. As much as the gold-rush trail and the eternal quest to get rich quick changed the American West, the exhaustion and exhilaration of such singular experiences transformed the men and women who struggle to cross a continent in search of a better life. They had seen the elephant and stared him down.* [17]

California Gulch, and the scarcely explored Middle and South Parks, absorbed thousands of gold seekers. A vanguard of stout-hearts even breached Fortress San Juan's upper Animas River valley for a season. Yet, no different than in 1859, by mid-1860 thousands faced "homeward with a dejected air, as if under conviction for sin, or convinced that gold mining was very hard work." [18] Nevertheless, still more came, not less than five thousand a week for months, staying at least until the grub they brought with them ran out. According to Hollister,

> *[T]hey wandered around, joined every stampede–of which there were many– in short, didn't think of returning to the States till fall. Ere that time quartz-mills had sprung up like mushrooms in every gulch in the Gregory District, and a vast deal of labor was called for to keep them running–for run they would, pay or no pay, to keep up appearances.* [19]

Keeping up appearances could be translated "in order to attract investors." Selling shares or the entire claim for a handsome profit was far superior to back-breaking mining, especially if there was any suggestion assays or reserves were going to disappoint. Once again, Hollister's shrewd eye captured the essence of the moment. Commenting on the influx of quartz mills and other techniques such as arrastras to extract gold, he quotes an unnamed "writer of the time:"

> *"There is not attention enough given to mining. Everyone seems to think there is an easier way to make money than by digging, so that all other enterprises than mining are being overcrowded. I think they will find out to their sorrow that the gold has to be dug out of the ground before it can get into their pockets."* The inclination to neglect mining, [Hollister concludes] and trade, speculate, do anything but mine, is also an evil as old as the country, and doubtless destined to outlast it.[20]

"In search of a better life" was a common theme, as was "knowing no other means of earning a living." "Overnight wealth" was a common dream. A sure sign that reality was dawning was the transformation of mining camps into frontier settlements. That transformation was not seamless, but it usually was quick. Mining camps, even most frontier settlements, also had a way of reshaping character, too often for the worse. Their remoteness and the scarcity of the feminine features of hearth and home fomented a culture that in turn shaped expectations. In the end, poor nutrition, poor sanitation, and poor choices explained the demise of many a camp occupant. For many others, camp life provided an opportunity to disappear from a former life including family, friends, and especially creditors and the law. Will Bagley sums up the matter this way:

> *"The old California miners had long since shaken off the shackles of an effete civilization, and had been living for many years free from the trammels and restraints of Sunday-school influences,"* recalled William Goulder, an Oregon pioneer of 1845 who had spent years in the mines of the new El Dorado [Colorado] and joined the rush to Idaho in 1861. These transformed souls were devoted to "the larger liberty that comes from a wild, free life lived so far away in remote mountain regions."
>
> [When pickings got thin in one district, the choices for most were return home or follow rumors and reports to the next gold field. Bad habits acquired in camp generally ruled out any option involving a return home. Besides, their hard-earned knowledge of prospecting and mining provided a competitive advantage in any new gold camp. Abe Lee is a good example.]
>
> As California's golden wealth became harder to get at, many veterans turned back to the country they had already walked across. Some had actually found gold in the Rockies and Great Basin on their way west, but never in sufficient quantity to convince them they had gone far enough or distract them from seeking the end of the California rainbow. But as they drifted back over the trail during the next two decades, they ironically ignited rushes to the very rivers they had crossed on their way west... [21]

THE PROSPECTOR CLASS

Prospecting fed the restless soul. The restless soul thrived on camp life, or in many cases, on solitary camp life. Out of the mass migration to the 1849 California gold fields came a sizeable proportion of the mass migration to the Colorado mineral belt a decade later. Word of gold discoveries on the South Platte, near where Lewis Ralston located it, seeped west as well as east. From time to time, there had been reports of earlier discoveries dating to Spanish times. By the late 1850s tales of gold finds spilled off the lips of practically every mountain man. Bagley writes:

> *Indians came to Fort Laramie in 1857 "with a lot of gold dust and nuggets to trade for such articles as they wanted: and this was not the first time they had done it," Charles Morehead recalled. The Cheyennes had always refused to say where they got the gold, but this time someone sweetened the pot. After demanding ponies, sugar, coffee, flour, tobacco, and blankets, the Natives struck a deal. They took their client up the South Platte, and when he returned, Morehead recalled, "there was a great rush to Pikes Peak." A year later the news of the discovery attracted 60,000 fortune seekers to the mines, Merle Mattes estimated, and the serious settlement of Colorado began.* [22]

Merle probably missed the 1859-60 headcount by a factor of two or three, but he got the consequences right. Forty-Niners circling back from California to the Colorado Front Range, Cherokee Nation forays up the Arkansas and along the Front Range to the Platte, and pathfinders willing to push beyond the prairie into the foothills and High Country discovered enough gold to inflame a nation. Placer deposits led to lode deposits, Abe Lee's California Gulch, and the launching of Colorado's hard rock mining industry. Had it not been for the Civil War, resurgence of Indian troubles, and tempting discoveries in Idaho and elsewhere, the prospector class could have breached Fortress San Juans years before they did.

Rodney Paul, quoting a pioneer that prospected in California Gulch, gives us a sense of what it looked like then:

> *The Camp of Colorado. It was strung along through the gulch...There were a great many tents in the road and on the side of the ridge, and the wagons were backed up, the people living right in the wagons. Some of them were used as hotels; they had their grub under the wagons, piled the dishes there, and the man of the house and his wife would sleep in the wagons nights. They would get some rough boards and make tables where the boarders took their meals, and those who did not want to board did their own cooking. The gamblers would have tables strung along the wayside to take in the cheerful but unwary miner.* [23]

Gold was a coquette. Yes, sizeable quantities of gold made its way from the camps to Denver and beyond, but not because of rich deposits, rather because of many hands working many placers over many seasons. The longer the deposits were worked, the lesser were the rewards–until the real treasure was uncovered. Regarding gold, the real treasure was gold quartz, the mother lode. But there was another treasure. At first thought to be a bothersome gangue, the black sand cast aside as waste was in fact silver-ladened ore. Elsewhere, veins of silver-bearing ores plainly visible on the surface of granite formations caught the eye of those who had an eye to see.

California Gulch. Front Range lode discoveries followed by Abe Lee's discoveries in California Gulch confirmed Colorado gold (and soon silver) was worth the risks of finding it. Far from the pristine condition in which Lee found the gulch, the area was soon crowded with prospectors and ultimately aggressive recovery techniques including hydraulic mining. *(W. G. Chamberlain, c. 1878)*

Unlike panning pure gold from streambeds, freeing gold and silver from quartz veins required equipment and explosives. To be efficient and therefore profitable, it also required smelters. All of this, starting to take on the look of an industry, required investors. Investors inevitably led to speculators and flim-flam artists. The most capital intensive part of this new industry was the smelter, which of course was the focal point of most speculation. Unfortunately, even honest attempts to perfect a workable separation process defeated existing technology and exhausted readily available capital.

Nathaniel P. Hill's Clear Creek Canyon facility epitomized the problem. While achieving some success, his Blackhawk site was "badly cramped, the air unbearably polluted, and fuel increasingly scarce and expensive." To Blackhawk's credit, the city fathers and mercantile class did encourage further development of Denver as an industrial as well as commercial oasis in the western wasteland. This selfless initiative eventually gained traction, in large part due to the absence

of sufficient room to expand necessary facilities. In the meantime,
despite the inefficiencies of existing
smelter capacity that left a high per-
centage of gold on the waste dump,
the district soldiered on. Blackhawk
shipped a high volume of gold,
never mind the volume left behind.

*Ultimately Hill made the crucial
decision to move down to the open
plains outside Denver, where there
was ample space, more chance to
scatter the acrid fumes, and, above
all, access to Denver's growing
network of railroads. The railroads
could bring him Colorado coal and
coke and could enable him to buy
ores from widely separated mines,
both in Colorado and throughout the west, so as to get the right
mix of types of ores and the right
quantity necessary for large-scale
smelting. When other companies
followed his example, Denver
became a major smelting center*

Nathaniel Hill, Metallurgist. The complexity
and composition of Colorado ores greatly
limited their value. Hill devised a solution and
in 1868 built the first smelter in Blackhawk,
Colorado Territory. Partially effective,
nevertheless it and others succeeded
in attracting widespread investment in
Colorado mining. *(Harper's, May 1888)*

*and an expanding city. More than a hundred miles south of Denver, Pueblo,
situated at the point where the Arkansas River emerges from the mountains,
proved to be comparably well situated for smelting, with good rail connections
and access to coking coals.* [24]

Thus began a new phase of Denver's development that resulted in a city worthy of the title "Queen of the Prairie." Not only was it on the cusp of becoming a
regional supply depot, it was on the cusp of becoming an industrial powerhouse
and future railroad hub. Sadly, it also was on the cusp of civil war.

Denver and Colorado as a whole did not escape the repercussions of Abraham
Lincoln's election. The compromises reached on a national scale that included
Kansas becoming a Free State and Colorado becoming a "Free Territory" were just
the beginning. Sadly, no compromises capable of abolishing slavery and averting
war were forthcoming. As a result, the development of Denver as a robust supply depot and the Colorado Mineral Belt as a major source of the nation's gold
and silver shifted into low gear despite an abundance of ingredients for success.

Locating gold- and silver-bearing quartz lodes was almost a daily occurrence. Mills, boilers and all manner of mining equipment were included in every wagon train. Scheduled transportation by coach and heavy freight wagons was routine. All that was missing were eastern entrepreneurs with access to British capital riding railroads westward in search of investment opportunities. That day was not far in the distance, but restoring confidence in western adventures sufficient to overcome the dampening effects of civil war would take time.

SILVER

Frustrations in refining gold ores yielded a crucial unintended consequence. In conjunction with the realization that Colorado was flush with silver-bearing ores, Hill's smelter technology was found to also work reasonably well with silver. Leadville at an altitude of 10,000 ft., and the decaying placer camp Abe Lee inaugurated in 1860 in California Gulch, earned the right to host a smelting industry of its own when it was realized large dumps of mine waste actually contained a fortune in silver reserves. August R. Meyer, a metallurgist, discovered that the ores frustrating mine owners for years were actually valuable silver-lead carbonates.

Meyer secured financial backing from St. Louis and built Leadville's first smelter. Awash in silver-lead carbonates, other Leadville smelters followed.

> *From a few log huts in 1877, Leadville boomed into a city of 14,820 people in 1880, with gaslights, a waterworks, schools, churches, hospitals, and, of crucial importance, railroad service to the outer world. Like most "hard-rock" centers, its labor force included Irish, Cornish, Canadians, and Germans. More than a third of its population was of foreign birth. Its silver output, while not the equal of the Comstock's bonanza years, was large and came into production just in time to compensate for the loss of the Comstock's big yield.* [25]

The Leadville community supplied more than local enterprises with skilled labor. When California Gulch and nearby Leadville could neither accommodate nor compensate its 1860s Argonauts, the newcomers and more adventuresome moved farther into the mountains, the San Juans included. With the establishment of Lake City and the development of scores of Henson Canyon silver lodes, Leadville again provided its fair share of emigrants to that region. In due course, Henson Canyon mines eventually shipped considerable quantities of ore to Leadville as well as Pueblo and Denver for processing. Sadly, mill returns were disappointing everywhere. The best refractory technology of the day was no match for the complex, low-grade San Juan ores. Even under foot of the conquering prospector and miner, Fortress San Juans yielded its treasures begrudgingly.

In the false-dawn of civil war, lawlessness also was a problem that grew with the population. At the same time mining districts were getting a grip on managing their frontier, Denver's City Fathers struggled to do the same. Secession from the Union of eleven southern states escalated the stakes. The outbreak of deadly warfare in neighboring New Mexico Territory and the direct threat Confederate forces posed to Denver and the Front Range alarmed even the polyannas.

Most in Colorado were Union sympathizers, but no one was sure how many were not. As it turned out, there were enough Southerners to organize a guerrilla band, terrorize outlying mining camps, and threaten Denver. If that was not worrisome enough, Texas had fielded a militia, and attacked Union forces in Arizona and New Mexico. The stated goal of the campaign was seizing California and Colorado mines to finance the Confederacy.

The Army of New Mexico, better known as the Sibley Brigade, was formed by Brigadier General Henry Hopkins Sibley during the summer of 1861. Originally, he had planned to use local Texas militia, but finding them unreliable, he recruited his regiments from eastern Texan counties. Three regiments were under his command. The 4th and 5th Mounted Rifles, both with a battery of howitzers, and the 7th Mounted Rifles to garrison Fort Thorn in New Mexico Territory. The volunteers provided their own weapons, horses, and blankets. Weapons were a problem. They included muskets, squirrel guns, and double barreled shotguns. Sufficient provisions also was a problem.

Sibley's forces began operations in mid-February 1862. His brigade got the best of Union forces commanded by Colonel E.R.S. Canby on February 20-21 at the Battle of Valverde [also known as Valverde Ford], but suffered heavy losses and failed to capture Fort Craig. Bypassing this stronghold, Sibley continued north to capture Albuquerque on March 2, and Santa Fe on March 13, but failed to capture Union supplies. Forced to live off the land, Sibley's forces alienated the local population as it slowly advanced northward. On March 28, Confederate forces under the command of Colonel William R. Scurry engaged Union Colonel John P. Slough's troops moving south from Fort Union. The outcome of the ensuing Battle of Glorieta Pass was a narrow Confederate victory in the field, but a Union victory strategically. A Union detachment had out-flanked the Confederate line and succeeded in burning Scurry's meager supply train. Already woefully short of provisions, what remained of the Sibley Brigade retreated first to Albuquerque, then back to Texas where Sibley was relieved of his command. The remnant of his brigade redeployed eastward to reinforce Confederate units in Louisiana engaged in the Red River Campaign. [26]

Denverites did not need the outbreak of lethal conflict and mass casualties at their doorsteps to unnerve the average citizen. The city already was an armed camp at war with itself, southern and northern sympathizers in the midst of those just alarmed by the displaced Indian Nations that were not a bit happy about it. If the constant threat of partisan violence or attack by one war party or another was not

Gettysburg of the West. Fought to a draw in pure military terms, strategically it was a Union victory. The battle of Glorieta Pass ended Confederate hopes of occupying western gold fields that would have helped fund southern seccession from the Union. *(Wikipedia)*

enough to keep everyone on edge, the rowdy pathfinder or the criminal element never let a quiet night pass. Early in 1861, Union supporters acted. They organized the First Colorado Cavalry, better known by the less-than-fearsome name *"Pet Lambs."* In Texas, Confederate forces organized their own militia for the avowed purpose of forcing Colorado and California into the Confederacy. In honor of Lieutenant-Colonel John R. Baylor, victor in one of the first if not most significant engagements west of the Mississippi, they called themselves no less threatening a name than *"Baylor's Babes."* Baylor, acting largely on his own initiative, had proclaimed the Confederate Territory of Arizona after the First Battle of Mesilla fought on July 25, 1861 in present-day New Mexico.

Whimsical names soon gave way to first-hand death and destruction. Battlefield engagements ended at Glorieta Pass, but not the risk of southern mischief. A well-armed secret society, the *Knights of the Golden Circle*, lurked in the shadows waiting for an opportune moment to strike a mortal blow. Not only did the *Knights* threaten Denver and all of Colorado throughout the Civil War, their reach extended across the Nation and persisted for decades after the war ended.

Unsettling to the Unionists, Confederacy-leaning Coloradans were vocal about their beliefs that if the entire south joined South Carolina in seceding from the Union, the West would join the new nation as well. Their conviction, after all, was consistent with widespread discontent concerning Federal Government neglect of western interests including rebuffing Jefferson Territory efforts to be officially recognized as a territory and future state. Not surprisingly, they also aroused considerable support among the rougher elements of society, men who by their very nature found it difficult to accept authority regardless of its origin, who came to the frontier to take advantage of its freedoms. These were the "gamblers, bummers, and transient troublemakers...who knew that rebellion would

---

KNIGHTS OF THE GOLDEN CIRCLE

In January 1861, word reached Denver that South Carolina forces opened fire on the Union steamships *Star of the West*, and *Brooklyn* attempting to reinforce Fort Sumter. What was young Denver to do? Largely Unionist in nature, the first initiative was forming and equipping a military unit. Adequate men and arms were available, but powder was in short supply. The City Fathers ordered the curtailment of needless usage. *Company A, First Regimental Cavalry of Jefferson Territory* was organized, its men to be uniformed and drilled in the event of an emergency. A second unit, *The Denver Guards*, was able to muster a hundred men with two hours' notice. "Within a week a third military unit was organized." At the same time, southern sympathizers either began making their way home to join the Confederate Army, or began organizing tactical militias in the mountains. Highway robbery and small-scale confrontations resulted. Dedication and loyalty to what this fraternity of activists stood for reached far afield and for years to come. The assassination of Abraham Lincoln was the most audacious, albeit never confirmed, act attributed by many to the *Knights of the Golden Circle.* [27]

---

upset law enforcement, communications, and even morals, giving them a rare opportunity for quick and easy profits." [28]

The majority of Denverites and Front Range adventurers stood with the Union. They also were inclined to remain as neutral as possible and let eastern politics stay in the East. There were enough problems in western backyards to consume their time and resources. To begin with, there were the hungry and the homeless. The year 1860 brought pilgrims and entrepreneurs much better provisioned than the year before, but the Front Range was nowhere near self-sustaining. Furthermore, the long and raging winter drove many from outlying mining camps to a city already struggling to shelter its huddling masses. They were a pitiful lot based on A.D.R's first-hand account.

> *The stampeders, turning homeward, convinced that gold digging was hard and unremunerative, left their picks and shovels behind, and trudged mechanically with downcast, woe-begone faces.* [29]

High prices and scant work awaited them in Denver. Too destitute to go on, too destitute to stay on, men and families needed assistance. Not far from finding themselves in similar straits, the more fortunate still shared what they could. When that was insufficient, they organized fund-raisers. When that was insufficient, Alexander McGrew, the wheelbarrow man, and compatriots stepped in.

Generous as usual, the sporting fraternity came to the rescue. Proprietors turned over their houses to theatrical ventures and donated all proceeds to the charitable campaign. These events drew the usual patrons plus the moneyed crowd, and turned over sizeable sums to the poor. When the professional entertainers succeeded, though, the amateurs had to try. Surprisingly, the amateur theatricals unearthed some quite respectable talent. Alexander McGrew performed a hilarious skit called "The Wheelbarrow Man." [30]

Denver pilgrims had heart, but sadly, harsh weather, destitute go-backers, and charitable entertainment were imperfect bulwarks against the raging hatred and rising carnage of the war in the East. Denver and the outlying camps escaped horrific battlefield casualties, [31] but not violence.

Local ill feeling mounted, prompting brawls and knife fights, splitting the town more and more sharply into two camps. The inaugural address by Jefferson Davis gave both Northerners and Southerners something new to talk about. "The declared compact," Mr. Davis said, "of the Union from which we have withdrawn was to establish justice, insure domestic tranquility, provide for the common defense, promote the general welfare, and secure the blessings of liberty to ourselves and our posterity… When in the judgment of the Confederated States now comprising this Confederacy for which it was ordained, [the Union] ceased to answer the ends for which it was established. A peaceful appeal to the ballot box declared that, so far as they were concerned, the government created by that compact should cease to exist." [32]

Confederate exuberance was short-lived even if violence was not. Somewhat ominous, during the first week of March 1861 word reached Denver that Congress approved a bill providing for Kansas statehood and the new Colorado Territory. *The Rocky Mountain News*, piloted by Unionist Editor Byers, did not hesitate endorsing this sought after action. "This is a consummation long desired," the *News* editorialized in saluting the event, "which will send a thrill of joy to every city, village and hamlet through the Rocky Mountains." [33]

More ominous, on March 4, Abraham Lincoln delivered his inaugural address in the midst of a nation already mobilizing for war with itself. A week later, the stage lines delivered the news to the Front Range. To some it was a sincere appeal for national unity and peaceful compromise. To others it was a calculated rebuke of Jefferson Davis' inaugural address. A month later, on the pre-dawn morning of April 12, 1861, the South Carolina militia began an artillery bombardment that forced the surrender the next day of the Union's Fort Sumter. The American Civil War irreversibly began.

Insulated by the Great Plains, Denver and outlying settlements were not immune for long. Family heritage and regional loyalties led many to act out and ultimately move out in response to Union and Confederate calls for volunteers. "Gettysburg of the West" would soon be fought at Glorieta Pass, in the meantime lesser skirmishes abounded.

Singly and in bunches, Southern agents slipped into town to converge... with the small but militant clique of rabid Secessionists. They came and went at all hours. Such goings-on became acutely sinister in the local view when the entire region was gripped with general unrest. Troubles broke out in the mining camps. Horse thieves, cattle rustlers, and highwaymen went into action all across the territory. The turbulence of a nation at war spread its contagion to the frontier to breed a plague of crime and violence. To make matters worse, migrating bands of Indians stirred new fears. Rumors reported that the Confederates were hiring redskins to attack Union sympathizers in the gold fields. Other rumors said that, with the whites warring against each other, the Indians were preparing to strike for themselves and wrest back their lands....

[Confederate ambitions aside, in fact it would be two more decades before Denver and High Country settlements were comfortable among the Indian Nations. In 1861, citizens of the newly established Colorado Territory were anything but comfortable. Rumors from the mountains of Indian hostilities repeatedly trickled into Denver. As spring waned, local alarm increased when a band of well armed, well supplied, and well painted "savages moved in."]

Indians from not too friendly tribes pitched camp south of the city along Cherry Creek. Arapahoes moved back into their camp at the edge of town. A few of the bolder red brethren located along the town's boardwalks. By mid-April nearly seven hundred Indians had bivouacked in or near Denver. Anxious citizens found temporary relief in the rumor that the warriors only planned to leave their women and children in camp while they sent war parties against the Utes, believed to be encamped some thirty miles from town. But as days stretched to weeks, anxiety mounted to a brittle tension. [34]

Out of desperation and in the midst of too many Native Americans with access to too much illicit whiskey, Denver City Fathers sought the help of two accomplished Indian agents, mountain man Jim Beckworth and Colonel Albert G. Boone, grandson of famous frontiersman Daniel Boone. Just months earlier Boone helped Chiefs Left Hand and Little Raven negotiate the Fort Wise Treaty that transferred practical ownership of eastern Colorado from the Arapahoes and Cheyennes to the emigrants. In discussions with Left Hand and Little Raven, Boone and Beckworth learned that the purpose of the gathering of the tribes was to revisit the Treaty they had just signed. Concerning Native American hostilities in the mountains, the two Chiefs pleaded "ignorance and innocence." While a promising start, routine emigrant-Native American skirmishes continued for years—both parties had legit-imate grievances, illicit whiskey sales to the Native Americans persisted, and the good people of Denver remained on edge. To the credit of the negotiators, and Arapahoe and Cheyenne indifference concerning white man troubles, an alliance of the tribes and southern sympathizers never materialized.

Native American indifference to the white man's war notwithstanding, south-erners tried their best to provoke Native American attacks on the Unionists. At the same time, Confederates in St. Joseph sent word they would pay forty dol-lars for every Navy Colt, fifty dollars for every Dragoon pistol, and "unspecified amounts for every rifle." The Unionists in turn urged everyone not to sell, but the southerners achieved some success. As an example, on May 23, "a group of known Southern sympathizers boarded the Statesbound express coach to depart this land forever. Their many pieces of luggage were extremely heavy—heavy enough to be full of pistols and rifles." [35]

In one respect, Colorado Territory pilgrims were no different from pioneers everywhere–if they ignored a problem long enough they expected it to go away. The war did not go away. To the east, partisan raiders bloodied Kansas towns. Parts of New Mexico and Arizona to the south aligned with the Confederacy and would be garrisoned by Confederate forces. Texas adopted "an ordinance of secession and proceeded to recruit troops and supplies in preparation for the occu-pation of Federal forts." Colonel Loring, commander of Federal troops in New Mexico with headquarters in Santa Fe, resigned his command and joined the

Texas militia. A native of North Carolina, he urged his Texas compatriots to invade Colorado. In his place, Lincoln's War Department appointed Colonel Edward Canby, a West Point graduate. Colonel Canby distinguished himself well given his tenuous circumstances, but at the time of his appointment his selection

Knights of the Golden Circle. A pro-slavery secret society founded in 1854 for the purpose of creating a new country comprised of the southern United States, Mexico, and Caribbean islands, thus forming a "circle." A Colorado contingent was organized to fight alongside Confederate regulars expected to invade Colorado. The Battle of Glorieta Pass dampened that hope, but the Knights remained a threat throughout the Civil War. (Wikipedia)

offered little consolation to Colorado unionists. Canby was a native of Kentucky "and therefore suspect." Zamonski and Keller capture the drama well. [36]

There was the *Knights of the Golden Circle* threat. In addition to Confederate activists leavening Union bread in Denver, also active were these Southern sympathizers in the Arkansas Valley. Headquartered near Pueblo, the "*Knights*" maintained relay stations for arms, ammunition, and supplies smuggled south to the Confederacy. Southwest of town, Colonel John Heffinger raised a Rebel regiment in *Maces' Hole* with upwards of six hundred men who hid out there "waiting to join the forces which would march from Arkansas and Texas to seize Denver City." [37]

Federal authorities were slow to respond, but finally did. In July 1861, Colonel Canby commanding the Fort Garland garrison "requisitioned" two companies of volunteer infantry from Governor Gilpin to reinforce Federal troops at the fort. Indicative of the sickly nature of government resources and authority, the Governor's ability to comply was limited to Sam Cook's "personal army."

> *Samuel Cook was [the] restless and far-sighted gentleman who had recruited a detachment of volunteers in the hills. His men were mostly those who had prospected unsuccessfully. These sons of the frontier were a gay, tempestuous lot. Hard drinkers and hard fighters, they were a gang of undisciplined individualists, each looking out for himself. Under Captain Sam Cook's command, they had moved into Denver, expecting to head for the States by the middle of August.* [38]

By August the Governor's uneasiness concerning the security of his territory and his capital, and local failed attempts to create a viable local militia, had led him to Sam Cook. In deference to the Governor, Sam changed his plans to continue east. Instead, the majority of his men marched to Fort Garland to support Canby. Sam and his senior command remained in Denver to recruit a full regiment, the "*First Colorado Volunteers.*"

> *Now through the pall of dust and heat, Denver folks became acquainted with the sounds of a training army. They heard a dissonant cacophony, a kind of Military Suite, with the clang of hammer on anvil, the crackle of gunfire from the practice range, shouted commands, grumbled curses, and the rattle of gear all played endlessly to the monotonous rhythm of tramping feet. And the townspeople watched with growing distress as the volunteers strode the streets as arrogant conquerors instead of defenders. Runaways, castoffs, and strays, the recruits chose the army's security of eleven dollars a month and miserable rations. . . .*

[Denver had troops, but Denverites were not exactly sure on whom their weapons would be trained.]

A tainted air of uncertainty, of scorn, pervaded the public places, the stores, even the homes. The new soldiers were as ill-fed and ill-clothed as they were undisciplined and drunk. They looted hen roosts and smoke houses. They broke into saloons to get whiskey. In the presence of protesting storekeepers, they helped themselves to clothing and hardware and food and anything that happened to strike their fancy. [39]

In response, Governor Gilpin took matters into his own hands. The Territory had few funds, but out of concern for a southern reaction, he sent out secret agents to buy up all the weapons they could find. His goal was as much to deny their use to southern sympathizers as to arm his own unruly forces.

The agents bought lead from the mines and secured three loads of gunpowder from a friendly John Burke in Topeka. The desperately needed supplies of food, clothing, and blankets were purchased periodically from local merchants and paid for with drafts drawn on the Treasury of the United States. [40]

Commendable leadership, however the Governor had no authority to issue U.S. Treasury drafts. When they eventually reached Washington, a total of $375,000 worth [serious money in the day], the Treasury refused to honor them. Infuriated merchants squealed loud and long enough to have the Governor eventually removed from office. Worse still, despite Gilpin's efforts to acquire weapons secretly, his southern adversaries had found out. The arms race that ensued, already emboldened by Confederate actions in Texas and New Mexico, was impossible to keep secret. To the contrary, brazen Denver secessionists posted handbills all over town offering high prices for rifles, shotguns, pistols, powder, and percussion caps. Nevertheless, they too suffered setbacks. "Many guns they procured were obsolete in size, caliber, or action and unfit for military duty." [41]

There were additional challenges for authorities interested in remaining loyal to the Union. Confederate sympathizers staged drunken brawls to disrupt Union recruitment rallies. Finances and equipment remained inadequate, and from Utah came word that 10,000 Mormons pledged their support to the South. The Mormons, still smarting over their treatment while living mostly among northerners, also saw similarity of interests between owning slaves and having multiple wives. Fortunately for Colorado, a Confederate-leaning Mormon army was an unfounded rumor. Its existence was contrary at its core to Mormon leadership policy, like that of the Plains Indians, who had decided to "sit out the Civil War." [42]

By mid-August 1861 Denver appeared deeper in crisis than ever. Union troops, still idle, also remained too often drunk, undisciplined, and prone to daily outrages against the public. Rumors continued to circulate routinely about

Confederate forces on the march from the south. Taunts from Southern-leaning civilians became more pronounced. Even loyal townspeople labeled the local Yanks "chicken thieves and a disgrace to themselves and the country." The inactive troops became even more unruly.

They were reluctant to fall in, they refused to stand guard, and they handled their weapons so carelessly that they often shot each other and even succeeded in killing off a few volunteers. Daily the men grew apprehensive that their military service might never get beyond police duty in Denver. They had enlisted

---

10,000 SOUTHERN SYMPATHIZERS

As the Nation moved ever-closer to civil war, the U.S. Government and the Utah Mormons worked at finding accommodations for their differences. An uneasy truce of sorts was in play when the North and South took up arms on the battlefields of the country and southern forces threatened Colorado. Rumors circulated that a Mormon battalion 10,000 strong was prepared to invade Colorado Territory on behalf of the Confederacy. The March 1862 Battle of Glorieta Pass came and went without Mormon involvement. To the contrary, on May 1, 1862 a Mormon cavalry company rode east into the mountains to help the Union Army guard the overland mail route and telegraph line in northern Utah and what is now southwestern Wyoming against Indian attack. Brigham Young had decided that the Mormons would remain neutral throughout

Brigham Young. Undisputed leader of the "Mormon Nation" possessing a well-organized and equipped army, Young's decision to remain neutral during the Civil War comforted Colorado Territory authorities. *(Richardson, 1867)*

the Civil War. He saw the conflict as God's punishment of the United States for its past mistreatment of his church, especially its failure to protect Joseph Smith, the Mormons' founder who was murdered by an Illinois mob in 1844. In Young's view, the war was a prelude to the "winding-up scene," the end-times in which American society would collapse under the weight of divine judgment. Mormons would save the Constitution, welcome the return of Jesus Christ, and participate in His millennial reign. Neither pro-Union nor pro-Confederacy, Brigham Young in his capacity as Mormon President maintained that he and his church were simply pro-Mormon. [43]

to win fame at the front lines. Anything less was unbearable. Grain, blankets, guns, and any company property that could be bartered for liquor began to disappear. Desertions were reported almost daily. Many deserters enlisted in the Confederate army. [44]

The demeanor of these unsuccessful emigrant miners now expected to be disciplined troopers was typical of their kind and the age in which they lived. They needed purpose in their daily walk–they signed up to fight and fight they would even if it was among themselves. The sheer magnitude of battlefield carnage during the Civil War testified to this facet of human nature in the Nineteenth Century.

At the same time, some aspects of life in war-time Colorado seemed to track a steady, predictable and even hopeful course. Newcomers still dreamed of new opportunities and a bounteous future. Old-timers—meaning anyone who had survived the hardships of a winter—still looked for ways to improve their prospects. "Go-Backers" still looked for handouts and received them in quantities sufficient to motivate their journey east. With the 1862 arrival of spring came the northern victory at the Battle of Glorieta Pass and the end of Confederate initiatives to seize Front Range gold mines. Mountain Man Wootton, now more a homesteader, offers insight into this mosaic of conflicting pursuits including the benefits of an increased U.S. Army presence.

> *For three years I plowed and planted and harvested my grain, leading almost as quiet a life as the average eastern farmer. The markets were good for everything in the way of farm produce because the troops which the government kept stationed in Colorado and New Mexico required supplies, and everything that could be raised on the small amount of land under cultivation was taken at handsome prices.* [45]

Nevertheless, on a day-to-day basis, life had to go on. Gold and silver lodes still beckoned from the High Country. Lodes still required skilled labor, heavy equipment, and capital that Denver and Front Range settlements could not supply. In the final analysis, the eastern war was of little concern to men and women struggling to survive the hardships of frontier life. Recalling the words of Dick Wootton who lived it, a Virginian by birth and of southern persuasion:

> *We soon made up our minds that the War of the Rebellion wasn't to be fought out in Colorado and that there was no occasion for us to get greatly excited over it out here. After we had gotten into this frame of mine, Northern and Southern men got along very comfortably together, notwithstanding their differences of opinion.* [46]

General Lee's Appomattox Courthouse surrender of horse, saber, and the Confederate Army of Northern Virginia on April 9, 1865, ended the Civil War. It began another cross-plains movement of humanity. this time more measured and better prepared for the hardships that awaited them. Transcontinental railroad companies resumed laying track. Shipments of heavy equipment to Colorado's Front Range increased in proportion to the resumption of eastern and foreign capital. Shortages of labor at the mines and mountain camps dwindled as war veterans and new immigrants sought a fresh start on the frontier. Survivors of the war, hardened by the greatest of privations and ever-present risk of death, did not flinch at the prospect of Spartan rations, Native American hostilities, and backbreaking work. In fact, laborers from all backgrounds and origins were valued, Italian and Chinese possible exceptions, and few were more welcome than hardworking, mine-savvy Cousin Jacks. [47]

Driven from their Welsh and Cornish homelands by harsh living conditions, large numbers of Cousin Jacks did not wait until war's end to make their way to Colorado mining camps. Not only did they reinforce the labor pool, they provided skills rarely found among Americans willing to work underground. They also became the human face of the best science and technology America's industrial revolution offered Colorado's mining industry. They recognized avoidable risks when they saw them. They embraced innovation when presented the opportunity. Whether from Wales or Cornwall, as a social class the Cousin Jacks earned a reputation as the world's premier miners. Despite their nearly unintelligible accents, superstitions, and invariable ability to persuade their superintendents to flesh out a crew with one of their own "cousins," these emigrants quickly demonstrated their worth:

Transcontinental Railroad -- Sierra Nevada Branch. Completion of the transcontinental railroad was in doubt from the beginning of its Sacramento start. The Sierra Nevada's were a nearly insurmountable barrier, overcome only by a newly invented explosive and Chinese immigrants. *(Richardson, 1867)*

Englishman Maurice Morris, visiting Colorado in 1863, noted "the large influx of Cornish miners," who were expected to "improve the practice, if not the theory, of mining here." The Cornishmen complained almost immediately about the "rude way many of the shafts are constructed" and the great "risk consequently run working them." [48]

Just as prospectors and miners were not the same, neither were superintendents, engineers and miners the same. Yet, in general they all were referred to as "miners." In practice, especially in small operations, an individual could fulfill more than one role. A superintendent could also drill, blast, and muck alongside laborers he supervised. An engineer could maintain and operate boilers and compressors in addition to directing the installation of timber sets and the location of drifts, shafts and winzes. Engineers usually earned a higher hourly or daily wage than other crafts, sometimes even higher than the superintendent who might be compensated in part by owning shares of profits. In the end, teamwork and multi-tasking were essential elements for safety and success. That said, the "labor class" naturally resented "authority figures." The less hands-on labor an engineer or superintendent performed, the less they were respected. If they were trained in universities, European institutes or came from a "privileged class," they were likely to be ignored if not held in outright contempt.

Superintendents and engineers that had earned their way up from mucker and trammer working in shafts and tunnels were more accepted. Cousin Jacks were more accepted still. Centuries of hard rock mining and hard knocks had trained the Cousin Jacks well and anyone working beside them soon understood why. Said to have a "nose for ore," they also had a gift for "hand-drilling, timbering, dewatering, hoisting, and blasting." They also were familiar with better equipment than that found in western mines and insisted on their owners getting it, notably steam-powered tools and the Cornish pump. They also insisted on

Transcontinental Railroad — Prairies Route. Building westward was aided by favorable terrain, but hindered by harassing war parties. *(Richardson, 1867)*

respect for their colorful superstitions, respect easily earned in the face of great misfortunes otherwise. Duane Smith warns:

> *"Tommy Knockers," those invisible folk who inhabited mines, for instance, needed to be treated carefully and considerately, to ensure that they gave warnings before a mine disaster or help in finding ore bodies. Proper consideration might include leaving part of one's lunch for them; after all, if one did not, tools might mysteriously disappear, rocks might fall on miners' heads, and leads to good ore might vanish.*
>
> *The Cornish might have been some of the best miners around, but they also had occasional lapses from virtue. Some owners suspected that they "high-graded" ore, or stole to supplement their income. It was said that a "mine could not be successfully worked without them or make a profit with them." *[49]

Tommyknockers were mythical underground gnome-like characters found in many European cultures. They influenced Cornish and Welsh behavior in Colorado mines in the 1860s. Superstitions were more fact than fiction that mining superintendents learned to respect. *(Wikipedia Commons)*

An unexpected outcome of the Civil War was increased investment capital that was sorely needed to finance transportation, mining equipment, and mills capable of processing complex hardrock ores. Successful marketing of Colorado mines attracted eastern and eventually British capital. British investors had waited out the war and early reconstruction, instead testing their judgment on railroad projects they expected to provide better returns. Northerners, having experienced war-stimulated economic prosperity, also had experienced the effects of insufficient currency to support available sales and trade. Unlike foreign investors, many of them entered the post-war reconstruction era more comfortable putting their resources to work in Colorado mining ventures. According to Duane Smith, many

> *began to worry about inflation and the government's turning to paper currency rather than continuing to use gold and silver coins, the "money of the Bible." In short, Easterners were seeking an investment, and what was better than gold? Nothing seemed safer or more dependable as a foundation for one's wealth. *[50]

But not only were there typical risks, there was typical fraud and typical foolish-ness. Duane Smith writes that staked claims were sold as bonanza mines. New Yorkers and Bostonians invested in claims "staked in the snow," and "nonexistent holes in the ground owned by liars." He also writes that there were warnings.

Frank Hall, from his office in the *Daily Mining Journal*, cautioned: "Those who have the true interest of Colorado at heart, will uniformly frown on all attempts to swindle parties in the East by selling at enormous figures property which has no known existence, outside of the Recorder's Office."

On April 6, 1864, he [Hall] returned to the subject: "Never in the history of the country did the excitement of mining speculation run so high as at present. Men are every day receiving windfalls in the shape of receipts from the sales of claims to Eastern capitalists. Demand increases rather than diminishes....This state of things is unhealthy, and therefore can not (sic) be permanent." [51]

For a variety of reasons, some of them legitimate, by the end of the Civil War what had developed into Colorado's "gold bubble" popped. The largely reckless albeit limited infusion of capital into any venture pertaining to gold ebbed, but its negative effects on the territory and on investor confidence persisted for a decade. Even the master of boosterism was alarmed. Duane Smith reports that William Byers, in his December 11, 1864 *Rocky Mountain News*,

> *fretted about there having been so many failures in Colorado mining that "people are now afraid" to invest. The wealth was there, he assured his read-ers, "but the territory has not fulfilled its glittering promise of two years ago." Despite forecasting a bright future with the new "separation processes" being built, Byers vacillated; eleven days later, he headlined an article, "The Curse of Colorado,"* pleading with mine owners to stop running other mining properties down "to build up" their own. [52]

The 1859-1861 boom period had had its busts, but in a more damaging way the 1864-1865 bursting of the gold bubble had far more lasting effects. Despite Byers' best efforts, "migratory, restless men" headed for new gold discoveries and speculators with capital were close behind. Byers was not easily discouraged. He pivoted from boosting gold to boosting silver. In their wake, Duane Smith also observed, fickle men did not leave silver for long. Silver, "that alluring coquette that had teased men for decades in these mountains, finally materialized from fleeting hopes and dreams into a reality." [53] In fact, silver-bearing ores were far more common in the Colorado Rockies than gold-bearing ores, and thought [mistakenly] to be far more likely to be profitable ventures. Rich samples appeared on the Front Range and eventually on the outskirts of the San Juans. The Cousin Jacks were on it.

All that a rebirth of good times required was better transportation and a return of loose money. Otto Mears and a few others would take care of the former

NEW MONEY

Hollister reported little Colorado emigration and little Colorado investment beginning in 1861, no doubt a function of the state of hostilities between North and
South. By mid-decade with the end of hostilities began an infusion of "new money"
and a season of renewed optimism. "The forepart of the season was very dull in the
quartz mines."

> *Still, everything steadily improved. New towns in all the mining districts sprang
> into being, and the old ones replaced log houses with stone or brick, or sub-
> stantial frames, and extended their area. There has never been wanting to
> Colorado the cry of "hard times," nor has her improvement in every respect
> ever ceased for a moment. It should be borne in mind that dull times in a
> mining country would be considered flush times anywhere else. If a thousand
> people are not coming and going every day; if towns of tents and booths and
> cabins do not spring up in a night; if mining does not pay one hundred dollars
> a day to the hand, and if this money is not in vigorous circulation, it is called
> "hard times."* [54]

Again, Colorado treasure hopes ebbed and flowed. Capital came and went.
Investors funded mills and idled them, sometimes without a day of operations.
Technology improved equipment and smelter performance, but smelters continued
to lose money. Quartz mines in the hands of Colorado emigrants found their way
into the hands of New York and Boston moneyed men. The Denver Mint opened
for business in 1863. In April the heart of Denver burned to the ground. By the end
of the year it was rebuilt so much better than before "that good citizens audibly
wished the balance of the town might be burned over once."

> *Their wish was and was not granted, for in the spring of 1864, Cherry Creek,
> which is normally a wide bed of dry, hot sand, rose suddenly one evening about
> twenty feet, and washed a good portion of the town clear of all encumbrances,
> goods and chattels, houses and lands, legal fictions and lawsuits; so that, as
> General Bowen remarked in a pensive manner, "it flowed unvexed to the sea."* [55]

The year 1865 began with more reports of Union advances in Confederate
states, and then General Lee's capitulation. Western migration started afresh.
Steadily, the transcontinental railroad advanced on the interior mountain west from
both east and west. Colorado mines, bereft of everything needed to make a profit,
began to revive with the infusion of men, materiel, and capital.

within a decade. Separating loose money from a new generation of speculators required less time. [57]

As the effects direct and indirect of the Civil War dimmed, and the capitalization of America brightened, another transformation was quietly underway. Subtle at first, by the end of the decade it was unmistakable. The sale of Colorado mines to eastern interests was both a transfer of wealth and a regional fraud. For their part, Colorado prospectors and miners harbored few illusions about the vagaries and hardships of their endeavors. Most would never look back when they traded their claims and indebtedness for hard cash, or even just a promise of it. If their take was sufficient to tide them over at least for another winter, they were the better for it. If they were covered for the balance of their lives, they were blessed and wise. When buying and selling among themselves quickly ran its course, selling to "moneyed newcomers" would do fine.

As for the capitalist accustomed to their money doing all their work—best of all, other people's money—multiplying the value of their newest acquisition was only a question of equipment, time, and promotion. The prospector located the vein. The prospector or pioneer miner demonstrated its value. Their muscle and courage did fine close to the surface, but labor alone had serious limits. The capitalist was needed to invest in the powder and machinery to sink shafts and drive tunnels to richer and richer deposits. Failing this, a good publicist could save the day, which explained how Colorado mines ended up in eastern hands. Hollister explained how the game began.

An Honest Miner. Recognizing the role capitalists would have to play in making a mine a paying proposition, ADR mocked them nevertheless. Grubstaking a prospector was a small matter, funding a mine once surface deposits were exhausted required investors. Many investors found working stock trades was easier and more lucrative than working mines. (*Richardson, 1867*)

The mines worked easy on the surface; windlasses and horse-whims answered for hoisting; there was but a slight accumulation of water to be drawn off; the gold was coarse and free in the quartz, from long exposure to the elements; fuel was cheap; there were considerable placer mines, which made money plenty and times easy, and everything therefore went on swimmingly.

But as the mines grew deeper and filled with water, increasing the labor of hoisting and compelling the use of steam for that purpose; as fuel and timber became scarce and dear, and the ores more difficult of treatment—in short, as the curtailing of facilities and the increase of expense incident to the necessary expansion of the business were beyond both the means and ability of mine operators as a class, they become badly involved and embarrassed. Observe how natural and unavoidable was all this. [56]

Miners profited from placers but could not afford to develop quartz mines. Eastern interests came to their aid, purchased shares and eventually owned the mines. The expenses associated with deep mining, processing complex ores, and generally high living expenses soon persuaded investors there were better returns trading mine shares than mining silver or gold. Even more lucrative and far easier was buying and selling the mines themselves, especially when fraudulent behavior often went undetected or unpunished.

With diplomacy and grace, Rodman W. Paul characterized this phase of Colorado's mining legacy.

The anxious Colorado mining and milling men of the early 1860s understood neither the nature of their difficulties nor the possible solutions to them. Most of the miners were as short on capital as on experience. As their expenses mounted, they had to borrow from the bankers who handled their gold shipments. Continued bad luck brought a transfer of ownership from debtor to creditor. The banks, in turn, exploited their business relationships with Eastern financial interests to secure the incorporation and sale of the foreclosed mines to Eastern speculators.

Thus introduced to Colorado, Easterners proved unexpectedly eager to risk their money, and in 1863 and 1864 capital was raised with comparative ease in New York, Boston, Philadelphia, and other large cities. These were the wartime days when the speculative impulse was strong throughout America. For Coloradans the resort to Eastern capital was caused in part by the justifiable conviction that additional funds were necessary for further development. Presently the further discovery was made that it was easier to work Eastern "suckers" than Colorado ores. [57]

Surprising, was it not, that at the same time the Nation was destroying itself on one battlefield after another, there was a vibrant economy capable of raising large sums of money seemingly oblivious to the risk of a national collapse? Geography and the thrill of discovery sheltered Colorado prospectors and miners from these concerns, but New York money-men, too? It can only be avarice and someone else's money that explains such matters.

Of course someone else's money did not assure success. It did assure expensive buildings and experimental equipment of far greater capacity than available ores justified. Invested funds could not set idle lest they be transferred elsewhere. Thus, expenses of all sorts exploded. Along with the new money came a new class of industrialist, the "scientist," to spend it. Always lurking somewhere in the background, Merlin's alchemists and academics rode the wave of nineteenth century discovery including innovations only wars seemed to produce. They eventually stepped to the forefront. They did not distinguish themselves.

> *Worst of all, Colorado became infested with a race of pseudo scientists, charlatans who bestowed upon themselves the title of "professor," and talked learned nonsense about patented processes and ingenious gadgets that they had invented to conquer the "refractory ores."* [58]

Who *were* the "suckers?"

The citizens of Colorado did not see the 1864-1865 economic collapse and ensuing recession coming, but in hindsight it was inevitable. As if business conditions could not worsen, they did. Winter storms, spring floods, and increasing Native American attacks greatly handicapped freighting services across the plains. Midwestern foundries and machine shops gave priority to government wartime requisitions and post-war reconstruction. Delayed deliveries coupled with short mountain seasons spelled financial disaster for many. The arrival of rail service would improve matters, but it was still years away.

Nevertheless, the 1860s were good to Colorado–even the war years took a light toll save for the mines. Denver recovered from fire and flood, shrugged off occasional civil disturbances and Native American skirmishes, and welcomed development as fraudulent as it sometimes was. Unappreciated at the time, English capitalists always on the lookout for new investment fields, satisfied at last that the Union would prevail, were poised to rediscover America. A.D.R. saw it coming in another insightful assessment based on his post-war return to the Front Range. Published in 1867, *Beyond the Mississippi* reports his 1865 astonishment at the change in so few years highlighted in the series of excerpts on the following four pages. [59]

> *[Richardson:] We passed much heavy quartz machinery, including a boiler drawn by sixteen oxen. The ranches forty or fifty miles apart where passengers take meals, are termed "home stations," those where the coach only stops to exchange teams, "swing stations." By a droll conceit, the drivers call the pebbles which they gather in these treeless regions, to fling at their lazy mules, "stone whiplashes."*
>
> *The daily coaches [serving Denver], each carrying several passengers and about half a ton of mail, now made the trip from Atchison and Omaha to the Placerville railway in California (Shingle Springs station) in less than three weeks.*
>
> *To the weary, way-worn emigrant, journeying with slow teams through these dreary wastes, the mail coach coming in sight imparts new life. It is the*

connecting link between the desert and the world. To him it represents home, government, civilization, Saratoga, Bunker Hill, the American Flag, and the Fourth of July!" emigrants and ranchmen besieged us for papers. One night, when we rolled up to a lonely station miles from any other human habitation, the stock-tender, ragged, shaggy, sunburnt and unkempt, put his lantern up to our coach window and implored: "Gentlemen, can you spare me a newspaper? I have not seen one for a week and can't endure it much longer. I will give a dollar for any newspaper in the United States not more than ten days old." He was a representative American. No other nation so subsists upon the daily journals as our own.

The soldiers who accompanied us and guarded the stations were all rebel prisoners or deserters who had taken the oath of allegiance and enlisted in the United States service. They styled themselves "galvanized" Yankees; were faithful prompt and well-disciplined.

[At first blush, the inhospitable prairie was now tame, but thinking so was a mistake. Transportation, amenities along the way, and accommodations at journey's end were much improved, but Indian troubles were not. For the balance of the decade and well into the next, matters worsened. Nor would weather and environment be a friend. Still, Denver was growing up, already a Queen.]

[Richardson:] In four days and a half from Atchison we reached Denver. Scourged by war and fire and blood, the city has grown up through great tribulation. Repeatedly, hostile Indians have cut off communication with the States for months at a time. The early settlers erected excellent brick and frame buildings on the dry bed of Cherry Creek; and for two or three years it remained

quite innocent of water. But at midnight, on the nineteenth of May 1864, without any warning,

Mail From Home. The timeless yearning for news from hearth and home remained frustrated by Plains Indian troubles well after the end of the Civil War and the introduction of the telegraph and "regularly" scheduled coach service into the foothills. *(Richardson, 1867)*

a great storm on the plains changed the creek from a sand-bed to a deluge. An immense torrent came plunging down, sweeping away every building like gossamer. Not a vestige remained. Not a relic was ever found even of the six printing presses of the News office, or the great iron safe which contained the archives of the city. Several lives were lost. The next morning the creek-bed was again dry; but real estate there, in great demand before, has not since possessed any marketable value.

For two or three early seasons the crops in the valleys were utterly destroyed by grasshoppers. These plagues of the frontier seem to visit all new States. Again and again they passed through Utah like hungry armies, eating every green thing. At last enormous flocks of birds came upon their track and devoured the grasshoppers themselves, which never afterward troubled the Mormons. The Saints thought the deliverance a special interposition of Providence on behalf of their prophet and the Lord's chosen people. Colorado had no Brigham; but this year the grasshoppers were harmless, and we found the valley abounding in flourishing ranches—the universal term for farms...home crops supplied the population of the Territory with every farm product except corn.

FRUITS AND VEGETABLES
(1861 – 1865)

Local sources of food were not as promising even a year or two earlier, but neither were they limited to beasts of the field and "fishes of the seas." As Uncle Dick demonstrated when he saved the Denver pilgrims, provisions could be procured from the old Hispanic settlements in the upper Rio Grande Valley of New Mexico, and from their offshoots in the southern valleys of Colorado, notably the San Luis Valley. Flour, melons, and vegetables cultivated for American military outputs did not escape the attention of entrepreneurs like Wootton capable of freighting them to market. In fact, the military was the best customer in the West for supplies and services. It was a major consumer of flour, beef, buffalo, grains, and livestock when at peace, and an enormous buyer when at war. Likewise, the Mormons were well positioned to ship flour, vegetables, fruit, eggs, and butter. Both Salt Lake City and Denver, the "overnight creation of the misnamed Pikes Peak rush," were destined to become supply hubs, but that state of affairs was nearly beyond even the imagination of a visionary like A.D.R. In any event, he would not have considered Denver an "overnight" creation. [60]

At my last visit, five years before, civilization had barely extended to these wilds the tips of her gracious fingers. Now Denver boasted a population of five thousand, and many imposing buildings. The hotel bills-of-fare did not differ materially from those in New York or Chicago. Single building lots had commanded twelve thousand dollars. One firm had sold half a million dollars' worth of goods in eight months.

With fresh memories of the log-cabins, plank tables, tin cups and plates, and fatal whisky of 1859, I did not readily recover from my surprise on seeing libraries and pictures, rich carpets and pianos, silver and wine–on meeting families with the habits, dress and surroundings of the older States...Western emigration makes men larger and riper, more liberal and more fraternal.

Within a decade, the handful of 1859 campsites strewn along the Front Range had grown into vibrant Colorado Territory cities bristling with opportunities. Another decade and a half and the Territory would become a State. Gold and silver production, a few thousand dollars in 1860, increased from $2.9 million in 1870 to $19.5 million in 1880. In less than twenty years, Colorado would be the largest precious metals producer of any state in the country. Transcontinental railroads and narrow gauge lines they spawned pushed deeper into the High Country to retrieve newfound treasures. Another rush was in the making, this time into Colorado's final frontier. Fortress San Juans, always formidable, would not easily fall. Denver was a mighty ally, Leadville a welcoming waystation, but the Ute still commanded the highlands and were far from inclined to relinquish control. Remedying this reality was yet another precondition standing in the way of unearthing the fortress treasures secured in its castle-keep.

Notes—Chapter Seven: Wimmin, War and Cousin Jacks

1   John Greenleaf Whittier.
2   Gehling, Richard, "J–The Diarists of 1860," *The Pikes Peak Gold Rush*, pg. 13.
3   Hollister, Ovando, *The Mines of Colorado*, pgs. 104-105.
4   Bancroft, Hubert Howe, *History of Colorado*, pg. 403.
5   Hollister, pgs. 106-107.
6   Gehling, "J–The Diarists of 1860," pg. 2. [Accurately or not, the "Denver Road" also was considered "The Mormon Road," and also referred to as the "government trail" and Oregon Trail. The point here is that the Platte River routes were not unknown or uncharted, just lightly traveled between a few episodes of mass migration.]
7   Trembath, Brian K., "Jefferson Territory: The Renegade State That Almost Replaced Colorado," June 24, 2020.
8   Hollister, pg. 108.
9   Ibid., pg. 109.
10 Gehling, "J–The Diarists of 1860," pg. 13.
11 Frajola, Richard. https://www.rfrajola.com/pony/page 1_1.htm .
12 Gehling, "J–The Diarists of 1860," pg. 12.
13 Ibid., pg. 10.
14 Spring, Agnes Wright, "Rush to the Rockies, 1859," pg. 115.

[15] Paul, Rodney W., *Mining Frontiers of the Far West 1848-1880*, pgs. 109-117.

[16] Bagley, *With Golden Visions Bright Before Them*, Vol. II, pg. 390.

[17] Ibid.

[18] Hollister, pgs. 109-110.

[19] Ibid., pg. 110.

[20] Ibid., pg. 111.

[21] Bagley, pgs. 390-391.

[22] Ibid., pgs. 391-392.

[23] Paul, *Mining Frontiers of the Far West 1848-1880* pg. 117. [Reports that in 1860 a third of Colorado's total population was in South Park.]

[24] Paul, *The Far West and the Great Plains in Transition 1859-1900*, pg. 265.

[25] Ibid., pg. 266.

[26] "Army of New Mexico," *Wikipedia*; Zamonski & Keller, *The Fifty-Niners*, pgs. 255-265.

[27] Zamonski & Keller, pgs. 225, 256.

[28] Ibid., pg. 226.

[29] Ibid.

[30] Ibid.

[31] The Battle of Glorieta Pass,(which included an initial skirmish at Apache Canyon),the largest fought in Colorado, pitted 1,100 Confederates against 1,300 Union troops and Colorado militia. A total of Union killed was 51. Confederate dead numbered 50.

[32] Zamonski & Keller, pg. 228.

[33] Ibid.

[34] Ibid., pgs., 241-242.

[35] Ibid., pgs., 242-247.

[36] Zamonski & Keller, pg. 255.

[37] Ibid., pg. 256.

[38] Ibid., pg.257.

[39] Ibid., pgs., 257-258.

[40] Ibid., pg. 258.

[41] Ibid.

[42] Turner, John G., "The Mormons Sit Out the Civil War," *The New York Times*, May 1, 2012.

[43] Ibid.

[44] Zamonski & Keller, pgs. 264-265.

[45] Wootton, pg. 263.

[46] Ibid.

[47] Decker, Sarah Platt, Vol. II, "Charlie Griffith's Story," pg. 143.

[48] Revise citation to: Smith, Duane A., *The Trail of Gold and Silver*, pg. 60.

[49] Ibid., pg. 90.

[50] Ibid., pg. 60.

[51] Ibid., pg. 61.

[52] Ibid., pg. 64.

[53] Ibid.

[54] Hollister, pgs. 115-116.

[55] Ibid., pg. 129.

[56] Ibid., pgs. 131-132.

[57] Paul, *Mining Frontiers of the Far West 1848-1880*, pg. 120.

[58] Ibid.

[59] Richardson, Albert D., *Beyond the Mississippi*, pgs. 330-333.

[60] Paul, *The Far West and the Great Plains in Transition, 1859-1900*, pgs. 47, 49.

CHAPTER 8

No Laughing Matter

Have ever you heard of the Land of Beyond,
That dreams at the gates of the day?
Alluring it lies at the skirts of the skies,
And ever so far away;
Alluring it calls: O ye the yoke galls,
And ye of the trail overfond,
With saddle and pack, by paddle and track,
Let's go to the Land of Beyond!

Have ever you stood where the silences brood,
And vast the horizons begin,
At the dawn of the day to behold far away
The goal you would strive for and win?
Yet ah! In the night when you gain to the height,
With the vast pool of heaven star-spawned,
Afar and agleam, like a valley of dream,
Still mocks you a Land of Beyond.

Thank God! There is always a Land of Beyond
For us who are true to the trail;
A vision to seek, a beckoning peak,
A fairness that never will fail;
A pride in our soul that mocks at a goal,
A manhood that irks at a bond,
And try how we will, unattainable still,
Behold it, our Land of Beyond! [1]
— Robert Service —

For Nineteenth Century Americans the "land of beyond" was all frontier territory west of the Mississippi and Missouri Rivers. Just a half-century earlier, to the citizens of the first thirteen states, the "land of beyond" was all territory west of the Appalachian Mountains. By 1800—irrespective of Spain claiming sovereignty over the southwest and California—Texas, the Arkansas watershed, the Pacific coast, and the Rocky Mountains, all shielded by the fearsome Great Plains or great distances over vast seas, beckoned to anyone brave enough to leave behind the security of their homes. The Spanish invited Americans to settle what became east Texas, more concerned about French ambitions spilling out of Louisiana than American adventurism. Within three decades the Spanish did not need to concern themselves with either. Spain ceded a vast swath of territory to the French to calm European troubles, the French sold this and more [Louisiana Purchase] to the United States to settle European debts, and revolution leading to the remainder of Mexico emerging victorious as an independent Republic ended Spanish sovereignty in North America.

Exploring and settling this frontier was the high water mark of "westering." Distant European powers had claimed it for a season, but explorers prepared to settle it would own it, albeit at a price. Sometimes that price was paid by the United States government through negotiation or war. Often enough, the price was death at the hands of current occupants. This possibility, persisting throughout most of the century, was nothing to take lightly, and was no laughing matter.

In the case of the San Juan Mountains, mastering this natural fortress and exploiting Henson Canyon, its natural castle-keep, came late in this transformation. The country had extended its borders to the Pacific. It

1877 Lake City. Strategically located at the confluence of the Lake Fork of the Gunnison and Henson Creek, Lake City boomed from camp to "Queen of the San Juans" in a handful of years. *(Fossett, 1879)*

had survived and even prospered from civil war. It had opened the interior with the aid of the transcontinental railroad system, and it was sparing no effort meeting the requirements of the industrial revolution. All this stimulated renewed interest in western mineral resources. Prospectors, miners and investors returned in force to Colorado's High Country. The San Juans, rich in metal-bearing ores, attracted its fair share of attention, and in due course so did a new boomtown. Lake City, situated at the confluence of the upper Lake Fork of the Gunnison River and Henson Creek, was well situated to support the discovery and development of scores of Henson Canyon silver mines. As the 1870s unfurled, only two challenges remained: overcoming the difficulty of getting there, and Ute who were not excited about welcoming new arrivals to their sacred homeland.

CASTLE-KEEP

The San Juans was not a fortress built by human hands. The mountain range was a volcanic natural granite citadel almost too formidable even for the likes of the early Spaniards and a dozen generations that followed. The Conquistadors were no strangers to castle fortresses, but the frightful barrier to their treasure hunts posed by ridgeline upon ridgeline gave them pause. Try as they may, their seasons of fair weather were never long enough to probe much beyond its outer walls, and the Sangre de Cristo and Sierra de la Plata ranges. Nor was there a great need to do so. Ute traders, responding to annual Spanish trade fairs known as "rescates," journeyed to Abiquiu, Taos, and lesser colony outposts.

More importantly, Spaniards knew from trader's tales that not far beyond the outer walls, fierce Ute would certainly challenge their approach. Whether acknowledged or not we cannot say, but the practical effect was clear. The San Juans loomed large, a natural fortress hindering passage for centuries to all but its Ute landlords ever watchful from its parapet walls. By the 1870s the San Juans were familiar territory to encroaching Americans, many areas comfortably settled, others probed and left behind perhaps for another day. Henson Canyon with its El Paso Gulch had been left behind for another day.

Like Old World castles, narrow and difficult gates broke the San Juan's walls only sparingly. Within the outer walls, more high walls with narrow and more difficult gates bound San Juan's courtyards of narrow valleys and alpine meadows. Cached beyond these inner walls and gates, imagined and real treasures waited in the castle-keep, the refuge of last resort. Henson Canyon was just such a refuge. With its El Paso Gulch, it would eventually echo day and night with blasts from scores of mine portals, but not until the Ute threat was laid to rest.

Lorded over by the fierce Ute, fearsome to superstitious trespassers, a promising albeit foreboding treasure trove to the earliest Argonauts, the San Juan Mountains were never a laughing matter. Remote rugged terrain was enough to forestall exploitation long after the Spanish and the Fifty-Niners dulled their picks on its hardened flanks, but the Ute were an even more formidable deterrent. By reputation and hostilities, the ever-protective Ute did not relinquish their sovereignty gracefully or in haste. Whether thwarting "foreign" [plains tribes and white men] aggression with its towering buttresses or harassing them with its horrific weather, the San Juans were a natural fortress boasting a natural castle-keep. Within this natural fortress, so dreamers dreamed, quartz veins impregnated with silver and gold awaited any soul hardy enough to breach its granite walls, and risk Ute revenge.

The Ute creation story, as told by Alden B. Naranjo, a tribal historian, and Monica Lujan, held as self-evident truths that the Ute people always inhabited their mountain homeland. The practical consequence of this belief was sovereignty defended to the death.

> *In the days even before the ancient times, only Sinawav, the creator, and Coyote inhabited the earth. They had come out of the light so long ago that no one remembered when or how. The earth was young and the time had not come to increase the people. Sinawav gave a bag of sticks to Coyote and said, 'Carry these over the far hills to the valleys beyond.' He gave specific directions Coyote was to follow and told him what to do when he got there. 'You must remember, this is a great responsibility. The bag must not be opened under any circumstances until you reach the sacred grounds,' he told him." Once out of sight, Coyote disobeyed Sinawav. He peeked in the bag. To his surprise, out rushed people speaking many different languages. He tried to catch them, but only caught a few. These, now known as the Utes, he dumped out in the sacred valley. He returned to Sinawav and soon confessed what he had done. Sinawav first explained that those who escaped would forever be enemies of the people released in the sacred valley. Then Sinawav cursed Coyote "to wander this earth on all fours forever as a night crawler.* [2]

Ute called themselves "Nueche" [spelled "nutc" by some Ute writers] meaning "the people" or "we the people." Ute creation accounts explained that no one inhabited the San Juans before them. The Ute say they did not migrate from anywhere else. The "Two-Legged," the name they gave the Spanish, first found them where they had always been, in the mountains of northern New Mexico and Colorado. The Spaniards were the first Two-Legged to encounter the Nueche. They called them "Yutas." Plains Indians roaming Colorado's Front Range, notably the Cheyenne, called them "Black People." Omaha and Ponca tribes called them "Rabbit Skin Robes." The Zuni knew them as "Deer Hunting Men," and neighboring Pueblos simply referred to them as the "Mountain People." All such names accurately described the Nueche. By the time American treasure-seekers and settlers darkened their horizons, the Nueche were known in mixed company as the Ute. [3]

THE TWO-LEGGED

From the earliest encounter with the Spanish conquistador, the Ute referred to the White Man as "the two-legged." This was neither a title of dignity nor respect. While not timid about debasing the White Man, the Ute were quick to respect and value his horse, the Spanish "Magpie" that sat upon it was another matter. The horse was regal and useful, the rider unworthy of equal grace. The Ute accorded the Spaniards neither the stature of a human nor the dignity of four-legged animals. Of course, the Ute quickly learned they also were no laughing matter—after all, they killed or enslaved with impunity. Nevertheless, in the Ute domain the Spaniard would never rise to even the level of other dangerous wildlife. Those with four legs clothed and fed them well. Quite the opposite, the Two-Legged, encased in their armor, and accustomed to all manner of behavior unbecoming a Ute, merited no respect.

The Two-Legged also demonstrated inferiority by carelessly allowing their most impressive weapon, their horses, to be stolen by Ute raiders, and worse yet, eventually trading them and their firearms as well. Not even the Plains Indians were this foolish. Should it be any surprise that the Ute reduced Europeans to the lowest common denominator, the number of legs? For further proof of Ute superiority if needed, look no further than the San Juan grandeur of which the Ute was one. The Shaman could easily have reinforced this truth around every campfire, no offense intended, no respect due.

The San Juan Mountains' most formidable allies were ruggedness and weather—next in line were the Ute. Marvin Opler writing in "*The Southern Ute of Colorado*" explained that the Ute nation amounted to a loose confederation of "bands" further dispersed into family units owing to the scarcity of food supplies. The Southern and Tabeguache Ute claimed the San Juans and were committed to its defense. Totaling perhaps one thousand people, their ability to police their vast domain depended on great mobility and skillful hunting parties prepared to transform themselves overnight into fierce war parties. The Gunnison River more or less served as a physical boundary between the "southern" and "northern" Ute. It did not hinder cultural or linguistic homogeneity, but it did contribute to the lack of any mutual political or military unity.

While the Southern Ute fully realizes that his northern neighbor speaks the same language and "thinks as he does," nevertheless he sees no need for greater tribal solidarity than is expressed in the term applied to all his tribesmen – nutc, or "The People." [4]

[Topography further divided the Southern Ute into three sub-groups. West of the Continental Divide below the Gunnison south to Navajo country lived the "Weminutc,"]

. . . a band who pitched their summer camps in the La Plata and San Miguel ranges, or less often, on the western slopes of the San Juan mountains around Pagosa Springs. To the east of them, on the other side of the Divide, lived the Kapota, occupying the region around the Sangre de Cristo and San Juan ranges in the warmer seasons. Still farther to the east lived the Mowatsi, who occupied the territory between the Sangre de Cristo and Culebra ranges on the west over as far east as the present sites of Denver, Colorado Springs, Pueblo, Raton, and Trinidad. These three groups, bound together by geographic proximity and occasional intermarriage, are known as the Southern Ute bands. [5]

The eastern frontier was the most troublesome to the early Ute, before the 1800s the southern frontier the most tempting. To the east were aggressive Plains Indians, Kiowa, Cheyenne, and Arapaho who considered raids into the mountains sport and a right-of-passage. To the south were the Spanish, the "Two-Legged" to the ancients. Their outposts and settlements were far enough south to pose no threat of encroachment to the Ute, but possessed marvelous trade goods and poorly secured livestock "free for the taking." Particularly tempting to the Ute was the Spanish horse, at the top of every warrior's trade list. If the Spanish owner was not interested in taking animal skins in trade, the Ute may have reasoned, who would notice if from time to time a few went missing. The Spanish also possessed fearsome weapons of war, but given Ute poverty when it came to gold and silver, the Spaniard was rarely motivated to unleash them. [6]

Exactly how and when horses and Ute became inseparable is unclear. Whether directly from Spaniard to Ute or from Spaniard through Pueblos or Apache to Ute, there is no doubt the exchange began with the Spaniard. New Mexico Governor Otermin is on record as entering into treaties with the Ute around 1675, but Opler assures us that the Ute were well acquainted with horses long before then, perhaps a generation before then. There also is no doubt that Ute proficiency with regard to mountain mobility and warfare with their enemies molded them into a much feared adversary well able to preserve their mountain redoubt for themselves, and well able to hunt buffalo and raid enemies on the Plains with near impunity. Without mastery of the horse, none of this would have been possible. Because they did not possess gold and silver metal [ore rich in silver was another matter], the Spanish viewed them rather as likely allies and a buffer against more aggressive tribes. Conquistadors were not miners, not moles that nosed out underground treasures. They were conquerors that seized booty. Possessing no booty, the Ute homeland was of little interest to the Conquistador, stark contrast to Spanish colonizers including prospectors that would follow. The Ute were not offended. After all, the Spaniard was not even human by Ute reckoning. For their part, the Ute benefited from Spanish respect for their mountain prowess. [6]

Conquistador Expeditions. Even Conquistador treasure-hunts faced natural and native resistance that limited their curiosity. Convinced there were no gold caches similar to Aztec and Inca caches, they left colonization and mine development to others. (Courtesy of Western Reflections Publishing)

In less than fifty years from Christopher Columbus sighting land in the Caribbean, the Spanish occupied present-day Mexico, mapped the Gulf, and dispatched expeditions north into present-day New Mexico, Colorado, Utah, Kansas, Arizona and California. In 1540, seven decades before the English settled Jamestown or the Pilgrims set foot on Plymouth Rock, the Spanish layed claim to the Southwest. Francisco Vasques de Coronado sent home to the Royals dispatches on his expedition across northern New Mexico and southern Colorado from Arizona to Kansas. A half-century later Juan de Oñate began the colonization of New Mexico, founding Santa Fe in 1598. While the Spanish grip on the region was tenuous, they survived and ruled until defeated by their subjects in 1821. [7]

"Tenuous" probably does not do justice to just how weak Spanish dominance of their New Mexico colony actually was.

In 1752 the Spaniards and Spanish-speaking residents of the Abiquiu District had only twenty-two arms-bearing men, forty horses, ten muskets, seven lances, four cueras (leather-armored jackets), four pistols, and one sword with which to defend themselves. By the time of Rivera's expeditions, these settlers of the Abiquiu area probably did not have significantly more or better armaments.

By 1752 Santo Tomas de Abiquiu was home to 108 genizaros (Spanish-speaking former slaves). This number included thirty-four heads of families, forty-four children, and some thirty women. They were even more poorly armed than the Spaniards and had only six horses and thirty-nine arms-bearing men who were equipped with 1,113 arrows, two lances, no swords, and no leather jackets. No firearms were listed among any of the genizaros of the colony. By 1760 approximately 166 genizaros from fifty-seven families and 617 Spaniards and "castas" (mixed-blood people) from 104 families were living in the Abiquiu settlements. By 1776 only forty-six families were still living at the pueblo. [8]

The first recorded Spanish intrusion into the San Juans was 1765. Juan Maria de Rivera seeking gold, and the truth about bearded men who might be European

THE CLAVO DE PLATA

Spanish exploration of New Spain was not the sole domain of armor-clad Conquistadors. By 1765, Juan Maria Rivera is better characterized as the first Colorado mountain man and possibly the best-known, earliest prospector. In the place of armor he wore a leather vest and wide-brimmed hat. Like the conquistadors, Rivera and his men did depend on mules and horses, the latter for transportation and trade. By 1765, friendly ties with Ute and Paiute Captains securely tucked away in the San Juans, and persistent rumors of European-looking men and silver treasure cities to the north and northwest, warranted an expedition. Failing apprehension of trespassers, or discovery of treasure, fur trade would do.

The catalyst for Rivera's expedition into the Ute homeland was a "clavo de plata," a "silver nail," brought to Abiquiu by a Moache Ute trader from north of the Animas River. The single specimen was high-grade silver ore the trader dug from a soft surface deposit in the La Plata Mountains. He sold his specimen to Jose Manuel Trujillo, an Abiquiu blacksmith, who smelted it into enough pure silver to cast two rosaries and a crucifix. If there was any doubt the San Juans harbored valuable minerals, Jose's handiwork dispelled them. Had the Ute brought silver metal instead of ore, the aftermath of the matter would have been far different. Absent the means to exploit a distant mine if in fact one existed, this account soon became just another rumor.

Steven Baker explains that mineralogists refer to the Ute's specimen as a pseudomorph of silver chloride (chlorargyrite) that

trespassers, ventured into the La Plata Mountains. His expedition turned west-ward and then up the Dolores River, followed the San Miguel River, and crossed the Uncompahgre Plateau to the Uncompahgre Valley near present-day Delta. Eleven years later an expedition led by Fray Francisco Atanasio Dominquez and documented by his subordinate, Fray Silvestre Velez de Escalante, followed Juan's route to some extent and ended up just south of present-day Montrose. Later forays were more about treasure than trespassers, but in none of them was there mention of attempts at entering the San Juans despite Ute indifference to their presence at the time. Not surprising, these later journeys were by prospectors and miners, later still, traders and fur trappers, who had every reason to remain silent. Noting the absence of jewelry, they also had every reason to discount tales of treasure troves free for the taking, but they were intrigued by a "clavo de plata."

Ute culture dating back to ancestral times did not honor status ornaments, blazed lodge-poles, or monuments of stone. Those were symbolic of property rights of Europeans and other tribes considered inferior. Among the Ute, status

---

chemically replaced an elongated, nail-shaped crystal of the silver sulfide mineral, argentite. Prior to the advent of large-scale mining, many virgin silver deposits were capped by a surface crust-like zone of chlorargyrite. In such contexts, the original silver mineral, including argentite, had weathered and reacted with chlorine in meteoric water to form silver chloride (AgCl). Such replacement reaction can create these pseudomorphs with the chlorargyrite retaining the exact form of the former argentite crystals. Chlorargyrite has long been known as horn silver to prospectors because of its mottled off-white-gray-yellow-green-brown color, which is reminiscent of the colors in cow horns. [9]

Of greater significance than motivating 1765 Spaniards to hazard a journey north-ward along the western wall of Fortress San Juan, this account of the Ute's silver nail suggested that knowledgeable Ute "miners" were engaged in silver trade despite their lack of interest in adorning themselves with it. At a time when the economy of Spain's New Mexico frontier struggled to support settlement, the prospect of silver deposits nearby warranted investigation. During the summer and fall of 1765, Rivera led two expeditions northward. Exhausted horses and men ended both quests short of accomplishing any of their primary missions. Rivera journeyed as far north as the confluence of the Gunnison and Uncompahgre Rivers at present-day Delta, Colorado. He never penetrated the San Juans taunting him from his east. He never found bearded European-looking trespassers although he heard accounts of them from many Ute and Paiute along the way. And he never reached rumored treasure cities, the seven cities of Cibola in some accounts, the land of Copala in others. Nor were more silver nails found, although mineral veins observed along the way held promise for another day.

befell skillful hunters and gatherers conferred by superstition and by force of arms. Deeded possession of a particular territory was unthinkable—mastery of everything that that territory offered governed the social order. Neither Plains Indians to the east nor Pueblos to the south would change that. Not even the mighty Spanish emboldened by conquest of Aztec, Inca and Pueblos mattered much. Indeed the Conquistadors scarcely tried—why should they bother with a trackless wilderness devoid of treasure. Far more dignified, they reasoned, to content oneself with claiming, naming, and leaving the hard work of colonizing to others.

Fortunately, for the seventeenth century Spaniards, claiming, naming and returning to Santa Fe in time for the fall and winter festivals was wisdom in disguise. Wintering over in the San Juans was not child's play. Neglecting to adopt Ute names for topographical features surrounding them also was understandable. Arrogance aside, neither Spaniard nor Ute were inclined to spend much time trying to understand each other. Without malice of forethought, before wheeling back south the Spaniard took the liberty of naming the Ute homeland the "Sierra de la Grulla [Mountains of the Cranes] Mountains." These petulant discoverers also christened the outer San Juan ramparts east across today's San Luis Valley the "Sangre de Cristo [Blood of Christ] Range." In similar fashion, they baptized ramparts to the west the "Sierra de la Plata (Mountains of Silver)." To the Spaniard, including "silver" in the name struck them as prudent and prophetic. There were many local rumors of silver somewhere in that region. Reportedly Rivera noted likely silver-bearing veins that he did not take time to examine. And in any case, referring to "silver" whenever possible in official reports was in keeping with the dreams and expectations of their overlords in Mexico City and Spain that authorized and funded their exploits. [10]

The Spaniard, who thought no more of the Ute than the Ute thought of the Spaniard, nevertheless was wary of Ute mountain prowess, and equally wary of the mountains themselves. These early Spanish expeditions were few in number and far from friendly reinforcements. They also were superstitious. Hard-pressed to find the high mountain passes threaded through ridgelines limiting passage to the San Juan interior, they faltered. Beyond cautious marches up the Rio Grande watershed [and eventually, the Animas and Uncompahgre rivers], their resolve usually waned. Reaching the soft underbelly of the interior Rockies, the present-day San Luis Valley, was significant progress toward penetrating the San Juan Range, but not progress enough. Their early visits were short-lived and their intended returns always uncertain. The San Luis Valley stretched along the eastern flank of the San Juans. Getting there from the eastern plains, through the Sangre de Cristo range, was far more difficult than trudging up the Rio Grande. Likewise, reaching the San Juan interior even from the headwaters of the Rio Grande, Animas and Uncompahgre Rivers required ferreting out passes through rugged ridges to the east and north, tasks happily left to others.

Passes leading into the San Juan interior were not easily discernible. Their whereabouts and safest routes to them were well-known to the Ute, one of their strategic advantages, but not well-understood by the intruder. Likewise, trails leading to them, well-worn over the ages by man and beast, nevertheless had many branches and many dead-ends. Wilderness signposts were few and far between. The Ute did not need signposts, nor did they share obscure trails with the Spaniard.

Despite the early Spaniard's insatiable appetite for gold and silver, he also had concluded there would be no repeat of Aztec and Inca finds. The Ute had little apparent knowledge or interest in silver or gold, certainly not reduced to ornaments and idols. Silver-rich minerals were another matter, but largely impractical in their semi-nomadic lifestyle and trade. Occasionally exchanged in Spanish outposts for manufactured goods, the "clavo de plata" was not tempting enough to encourage searching out their Ute sources. Empire builders claimed territory and carried off cached booty. Not only could someone else to the colonizing, someone else could prospect and mine.

The "someone else," in the case of colonial Spain, would be a small number of unauthorized prospectors and adventurers willing to risk imprisonment at the hands of Spanish magistrates committed to respecting the Ute homeland, and possible death at the hands of offended Ute. [11] The "someone else" would not be

Trespassers Beware. There was a time when prospectors could be tolerated. Short-lived, prospectors along with settlers and miners became trespassers subject to harassment and death. *(Harper's Weekly, October 25, 1879)*

Spanish settlers. Their struggles to establish communities in Mexico's northern districts consumed their time and energy, and in any event ended with 1821 Mexican independence. Additional settlements would be left to newly emancipated Republic of Mexico adventurers who would put down roots in the San Luis Valley and prospect the mountains surrounding it. Americans would not be far behind.

With the exception of early 1800s Texas, Americans [meaning anyone no matter where they originated from or how recently they had arrived in the United States] were never welcome in territories claimed by Spain. Learning of the Lewis and Clark expedition, Spanish authorities dispatched unsuccessful patrols to intercept it both coming and going. Early United States Army surveying parties were harassed and in one instance imprisoned. Spanish authorities did not even welcome American traders despite a citizenry desperate for their goods. The Mexican Republic was different. Mexican revolutionaries, or more specifically the Santa Fe and Taos mercantile class, were not as finicky. The Santa Fe Trail quickly became a predictable wagon road. Bent's Old Fort became a

RIVER ROUTES

Time ran out for the proud inheritors of the Conquistador legacy. Mexicans—indigenous peoples and multi-generational Spaniards quite over pledging allegiance and sending their wealth abroad to a Spain they did not know—achieved independence in 1821. They escaped Spanish rule, but soon ceded a sizeable portion of their new country north of the Rio Grande to Texans whom also prized independence.

Scarcely appreciated at the time, access to the San Juans' heartland prior to the mid-1800s had to rise from the south. Beginning with Spanish expeditions that had the provisions and endurance to wander far from the security of their northern New Mexico outposts, outflanking the imposing San Juans to the east or the west was best achieved by following rivers. Following the Rio Grande was an obvious first choice. Not many days journey upriver, they could easily have journeyed north through the San Luis Valley, but that route would never lead west. Instead they stayed with the river on its journey west. They also found their way farther west to the Animas River and routes north to the Uncompahgre, Gunnison and Colorado Rivers—they would be promising, too, but exploration would have to wait. As it was, troubles closer to home dampened curiosity. Spanish expeditions struck their colors by 1821 and Mexican sovereignty lost out to Texas independence in 1836 and superior American military forces by 1848. Conquest of the San Juans would require another three decades of probes and pauses.

destination, a supply depot, and a jumping off place for mountain men braver than the Conquistador. Gradually mountain animal trails were worn into horse trails then wagon roads that led to "gates," high passes through treeless ridges. Gradually the mountains surrendered ancestral Ute secrets. The lowly Two-Legged were no longer an occasional nuisance. They were becoming a serious threat to Ute sovereignty.

To everything there was a season. For the Spanish friars and settlers, the early nineteenth century was the end of their season. In retrospect, encouraging trade utilizing the Santa Fe Trail marked the beginning of America's season. Ute mastery of the mountains—knowledge of passes, obscure trails and deep snow in winter unchallenged for centuries—slowly yielded in the face of American advances. Perhaps as important, unlike previous trespassers and superstitious enemies who believed the Ute enlisted vicious allies both real and supernatural, Americans were less superstitious. In this regard, the prospect of gold and silver helped a lot.

The Ute homeland was immense. It spanned half a summer's journey on foot from the Utah valley in the west to a hundred miles out on the endless eastern plains. The northern mountains seemed endless, as well. A vicious gash long and deep, Gunnison's Black Canyon, served as a natural San Juan's boundary and severely hindered interactions between the northern and southern Ute. The southern boundary of Ute-dominated territory was defined more by hostile tribes stationed along the present-day New Mexico-Colorado border than by topography. The Ute ranged widely over their domain, hunting and foraging familiar grounds. They camped mostly in milder western valleys in winter and in the San Juan Range in summer. They braved the rugged interior of their domain to forage, and to traverse the mountains to hunt buffalo or punish their tribal enemies on the eastern plains. Of course, Plains Tribes could be counted on to return the honor. To the Ute way of thinking, not every intruder was a threat. Mountain men were trespassers but worthy of respect. Prospectors, originally few in number, were harmless visitors. When prospectors multiplied, and mining began, prospectors and miners were trespassers worthy of attack. When mining camps spawned towns, farms and ranches, settlers became invaders to be dealt with like any other tribal enemy. Fortunately for both the Ute and the Two-Legged, this level of hostility was both sporadic and short-lived.

Farms and ranches were not only a foreign culture to the Ute, they along with mines defaced the sacred homeland. Every Ute was a nomad, breaking camp and relocating when conditions required it. Camp was populated with family units, men, women, and children of all ages. But not every Ute was master of the hunt. Only those who were deemed mountain-savvy and fearless were invited to join the nimble hunting parties. When stakes were especially high, for favorable weather, bountiful provisions, decisive victory in forthcoming battle, and divine favor matter most, the faithful shaman could be counted on for wise counsel and inspiration. When Ute leaders decided it was time to relocate the camp, the women took charge. In the absence of dogs or horses, they were responsible for pulling the Travois'. [12]

THE POO-GAT

Bravest of all among the Ute was the Poo-gat, for when the survival of the tribe was at risk and he felt compelled to seek out the Creator, alone he abandoned familiar trails and threaded a way known only to him and his forefathers to Uncompahgre Mountain. At the top of the sacred mountain, he entered the white clouds, home to the eagle, and the Creator. Getting there was more than a grueling climb. Part of the mystique of the San Juans homeland, the part that fueled superstitions bolstering its defense, was the "spirit world" the Poo-gat also had to navigate. With care, he avoided the underworld, black haven of the rattlesnake. Likewise, the center earth haunted by wolves was a problem. But the mountains, the "upper earth," ruled by the lion and patrolled by perpetual wind and snow, here even the Poo-gat hesitated to go.

According to Ute accounts, "shaman" was the name most often used by the Spanish, but "shaman" sadly diminished understanding the place such a leader held among his people. "Poo-gat" was the name answered to among the Ute. Poo-gat is best translated "one that knows the way," far richer in meaning because it was understood as knowing both the obscure trails throughout the mountains, as well as knowing the way and ways of the Creator.

The White Man had little appreciation for the power of the Poo-gat and no fear regarding spiritual or mountain matters that the lure of silver and gold could not overcome. The White Man did respect Ute willingness to repel intruders, more than an annoying problem to be sure. Imagine, Uncompahgre, the same mountain sacred to the Ute also beckoned to thousands of irreverent prospectors. Central to the Ute way of thinking was the belief that their cradle of existence was the San Juans. They were not wanderers migrating from elsewhere. Their duty to their deity was good stewardship of not only all life encountered there, but the very mountains and valleys that sustained all life. To the extent ownership was a consideration, they and the mountains were one. If one must choose, the mountains possessed them, they did not possess the mountains. If any matter sent the Poo-gat to the mountaintop, the slightest loss or desecration of the homeland was it.

Herein resided unavoidable conflict between Ute and the Two-Legged. Resolution required dismantling the Ute San Juans heritage. Dismantling Ute San Juan heritage was a precondition for exploring the mineral wealth of Fortress San Juans. Exploring the San Juans for mineral wealth was a precondition for unearthing Henson Canyon mines, for breaching the castle-keep. Fortress San Juans' castle-keep sat at the knee of sacred Uncompahgre. [13]

Whether the Ute had any interest or knowledge of gold and silver during the Spanish era or beyond is debatable. If the Ute valued precious minerals or treasure troves ever existed, these matters remain a mystery. There were, however, mountain trails familiar only to the Utes that traversed ranges and watercourses salted with rewards. Unlike in tamer terrain, these Ute trails stealthily departed from raging watercourses or alpine tundra. The San Juans is the product of upheavals, volcanoes and glaciers, heavy rain and snowfalls that resulted in gulch upon gulch gouged out of sheer canyon walls and second-growth forest amidst fallen virgin timber choking every canyon. Through this maze of mountain range and ancestral forest, more accurately in spite of it, Ute traders, hunters, war parties, and shaman knew their way. Trails above tree line and on narrow ledges across talus slopes and eroded into jagged cliff walls were barely visible save to the trained Ute eye. Along with changing almost everything else in the West, Ute acquisition of the horse further improved this advantage. [14]

In profound ways, introduction of the horse to indigenous peoples influenced not only cultural norms but also the balance of power among bands and nations. What the horse could not change was topography, which of course is the simplest way of explaining why the San Juan Mountains was the fortress homeland of the Utes. Limited and rugged foot trails leading from the surrounding low lands was challenging enough—trails suitable for horses were even harder to find and navigate. Steven Baker explains:

> *Prior to the introduction of the horse, the aboriginal landscape of all of North America, including its western mountains and deserts, was crisscrossed by an intricate network of long-enduring pedestrian trails as well as navigable water routes. Like modern roads and highways, this system contained major arterials and junctions, as well as a maze of more local routes. These trails connected every Indian nation and individual settlement on the continent. The people who used these trails commonly shared them with large animals such as deer and elk.*
>
> *People could travel anywhere their lungs and legs could carry them so long as the geography permitted, and the occupants of various areas were amenable to receiving visitors. By means of this system, Indian traders, messengers, and war parties traveled far and wide, typically by running. Running allowed them to cover great distances with impressive speed. Trails were usually established in keeping with the dictates of topography and followed the most easily traveled routes, such as along natural ridgelines, valley bottoms, and the heads of canyons. Side slope contours of valleys were often utilized when the bottoms were choked with beaver ponds and heavy vegetation, as was commonly the case. People traveling on foot could still traverse some deep canyons and other rugged terrain that horses could not.*
>
> *Spanish conquistadors introduced horses into the continent's aboriginal landscape in the sixteenth century. In the seventeenth century, some Native*

Americans began to use horses, and by the eighteenth century, equine stock was increasingly common among some Indian groups. By the latter nineteenth century, horses had become the primary means of transportation for many American Indians who came to be stereotyped as equestrian cultures, such as the peoples of the Great Plains. [15]

Another indicator of the fragmented nature of the Ute bands, and the ability of topography to isolate them from one another, was the scarcity of horses on the western slope. Spanish Conquistadors introduced the Ute to horses on the New Mexico frontier in the late sixteenth century. A hundred and fifty years later horses were still an anomaly Juan Rivera experienced in 1765 during his trek along the base of what he described as the "great wall" of the San Juans to his east. The labyrinth of deep, sheer-walled canyons guarding the eastern, western and northern approaches to the San Juans that he navigated clearly account for the absence of even crude trails suitable for mounted riders.

The Utes and Paiutes Rivera encountered in 1765 do not appear to have been equestrian. Various entries in his account suggest that horses were then still not widely dispersed among them…On Colorado's western slope, Rivera traveled in a landscape that was still largely characterized by old, pedestrian Indian trails. [16]

The Ute preferred conducting trade in neighboring regions rather in their San Juan's heartland. They packed elk, deer, and colorful jewelry made from river rock on their backs, or on travois' pulled by dogs, to the Pueblos, Cheyenne, Apache and Arapahoe. On occasion, some Western Slope Utes packed high-grade silver ore literally hacked out of surface deposits. They returned with buffalo meat and hides to get them through the winter. For the Spanish, they traded for knowledge of ancient routes to mines that they hoped delivered treasure to cities just like ones they found in Mexico and Peru. The Ute quickly learned treasure tales were fair exchange for Two-Legged wares. Since they had no mines or treasure cities, they also quickly learned to lie.

They also quickly grasped that the value of the horse was far superior to a dog or a squaw when it came to transporting lodging or provisions through the mountains, or hauling trade goods to and fro. With horses, the Ute transported more provisions and shelter far greater distances much faster than on foot or with travois' alone. They ventured farther from their beloved western valleys to hunt bison. They intimidated or when necessary killed more plains enemies. The horse provided its rider a strategic advantage in battle and in flight. The Ute could blunt the advance of war parties with a small number of mounted warriors. In the mountains, the Ute raided and fought with near impunity until confronted with the American military and America's mass migration.

The Ultimate Strategic Weapon. Columbus is credited with introducing a number of strategic weapons to the western hemisphere. Among them were twenty Spanish Jennet war horses which were bred and relied upon wherever the Spaniard ventured. By the mid-1600s Jennets were being traded or stolen among indigenous peoples living in northern New Mexico settlements. They quickly became a Ute strategic weapon. *(Wikipedia)*

The horse also was well-appreciated by Christopher Columbus. He not only knew his way around ships and seamen, he knew the New World needed horses. Observing no horses on his first voyage of discovery, he introduced Iberian stock to the West Indies on his second of four voyages in 1493. Twenty-five years later Cortes conquered the vastly superior Aztecs and claimed Mexico and most of the southwestern United States with the invaluable aid of perhaps four-score cavalry. A hundred years later mounted Spanish dandies in the service of the Royals impressed northern New Mexico Pueblos and Ute traders in the southern and western foothills of the San Juan Mountains.

By 1684, the Pueblo people had relieved the Spaniards of the trouble of caring for many of their finest mares and stallions, doing quite well at avoiding trading for most of them in the process. How they explained their acquisitions to their Spanish overlords is a mystery. Like Columbus, Cortes, and the Pueblos, the value of a horse was not lost on the Ute. They too were adept at liberating them from their owners, both by tedious trades with the Pueblos and chicanery among the Spanish. They had little to explain, instead disappearing into the mountains from which they came. With every addition to their herd came additional power—with additional power came a gradual shift in the regional balance of power. In less than a generation, the Ute were skillful breeders and rightfully boasted of commanding slightly more than their fair share of regional stock. Quite naturally, with horses came status and wealth. The number of mink furs, baskets, and bison hides measured the value of a horse. Within Ute ranks, the number of horses owned by warriors signaled who were the bravest and most desirable mates.

The Ute became feared mountain people, mobile beyond belief on horses bred to the treacherous terrain. The mountain horse transformed the Ute from hunter-gatherers living in small family groups to a military force best not trifled with. Eventually Ute prowess spilled over to the Plains Indians who also became

master riders, but the Ute never lost their mountain edge. For all practical purposes, the San Juans were off-limits, plain and simple, and the expectation among
those who tested this notion was that the penalty for trespassing could be death.

Of course the Two-Legged tested this notion. Loss of the advantages of
the horse was taken in stride. Tempted to probe and patrol beginning with the
thrill of discovery, not until evidence of great mineral wealth, the end of the War
Between the States, and the pressure of renewed emigration were adventurers
willing to become settlers and miners. Even then, there was a precondition. The
Ute must go. By force or by negotiation, it mattered little to the emigrants eager
to press farther into the High Country and alpine valleys. The Ute must go, that
was a given, that was a precondition. When they did, Fortress San Juans would
fall. Until then, if for no other reasons than ruggedness and remoteness, this
mountain range would be given a wide birth. [17]

Little wonder. The San Juans stand among the most foreboding terrain
anywhere in the Rocky Mountain chain. Fourteen of the fifty-four peaks in
Colorado over 14,000 feet are in the San Juans. The Lake Fork of the Gunnison
and Henson Creek area alone accounts for five "fourteeners," Uncompahgre the
highest at 14,309 feet. Hundreds of "thirteeners" contribute to the saw-toothed
and usually year-round snow-capped skyline. Their sheer, serpentine granite cliffs
lock arms and fold back upon themselves giving the appearance of bowels of a
giant beast laid open to dry. Complementing this foreboding terrain is plentiful
precipitation and low nightly temperatures even in the summer. Blizzards, snow-
pack and drifts dozens of feet deep are typical from late fall through spring. Hail
and earth-scorching lightening are possible always, including the dead of winter.
The mountain ranges and their storm allies formed such daunting barriers surrounding the headwaters of the Rio Grande, Animas, Uncompahgre, and Lake
Fork of the Gunnison rivers that there were no good reason to enter the region
until discovery of gold. Finding little gold, silver would do. Josie Moore Crum, an
early settler, described the challenge from a firsthand perspective.

> The term, "San Juan Country," in early days meant the northern and eastern or
> Uncompahgre, Gunnison and Rio Grande slopes of the San Juan Mountains
> as well as those to the west and south. The term, "San Juan Basin," means
> the San Juan River drainage which is the territory west of the San Juan
> Mountains to the Colorado River and south of them to include northeastern
> Arizona and northwestern New Mexico. The Rocky Mountains in Colorado
> generally trend north and south except in the southwest where they break into
> several ranges [sub-ranges] as the San Juans, San Miguels and La Platas and
> run in all directions. The San Juan area is the highest in the United States,
> possibly in North America, containing hundreds of peaks over 13,000 feet, and
> fourteen or nearly one-sixth of all the peaks in North America over 14,000
> feet. The Needle Mountains in the San Juans, are the most precipitous not only

of Colorado but of the United States. The San Juans have been the bane of explorers. Fremont called them, "the highest, most rugged, most impracticable and inaccessible of the Rocky Mountains." Drainage on the north, west and south is toward the Colorado River, on the east toward the Mississippi and on the southeast toward the Rio Grande.

In the San Juan Mountain region is to be found one of the most complete geologic records [although Cambrian, Ordovician and Silurian outcrops are quite rare] in the United States from the earliest Pre-Cambrian granites and schists thru all eras and most periods to recent times—a rare distinction indeed...Volcanic flows and intrusions by the thousands...are the common thing besides all kinds of metamorphic formations. In the recent Pleistocene Period three different glaciers, called the Cerro, Durango and Wisconsin, of different size and extent have either filled all valleys or have covered the region so that only the highest peaks and ranges stood above the ice. The small hills down the valley from Animas City to Durango constitute the terminal moraine of a glacier, and Durango is built on glacial deposit. [18]

The Ute harbored no illusions about the risks to their way of life posed by the Two-Legged. A thousand miles to the east American patriots would draft their Declaration of Independence from British rule, and would fight their Civil War, but in the San Juans neither Spaniard nor Mexican nor Ute knew or would have much cared. The Spanish preoccupation in the summer of 1776 was leading a party in search of a direct route from Santa Fe to the Spanish mission in Monterey. Failing that, a worthy secondary goal was equally elusive silver and gold. The Mexican preoccupation in the 1860s continued to be defending their new Republic against further loss of territory to an expansionist America. The Ute concern mimicked the Mexicans—how best to preserve their San Juan's sovereignty already eroded by intrusions and sloppy treaties. For all intents and purposes, sovereignty was mortally wounded in 1873 with the Brunot Treaty, and laid to rest with the Ute expulsion from Colorado in response to the 1879 Meeker Massacre.

Fortresses built by human hands have gates, prominent and boldly constructed, but the intended route to the interior. The San Juans fortress also has gates, *passes* by another name. They are rugged, convoluted and obscure, and the only routes to the interior. Finding what looked like a pass in a San Juans rampart was an occasion of great joy for the Two-Legged. What discoveries must lie on the far side? Yet, Spanish writings tell us the joy of navigating one breach usually gave way to frustration over the need to ferret out still another breach. For the San Juans was a textbook example of defense in depth. Beyond one ridgeline, one range, one bench rose another and another. More ramparts, more snow-capped pickets, more alluring discoveries, but never enough time and provisions to get to the land beyond. Gradually over two centuries the Two-Legged, petulant always, ferreted out the perimeter gates. Sadly, in journaling their progress they failed to

SPANISH LEGACY

In Spanish times, surveying a fast track to California probably was not the sole mission of friars, maybe not even the primary mission. The mysterious mountain fortress rising to their east, its outer defenses sometimes dry rounded foothills, sometimes sheer granite-walled mesas, was barely a half-days ride away. Unseen mysteries lying beyond had to evoke their curiosity despite the risk of Ute attack. Friars, far from being caricatured plump parish priests, were as accustomed to wielding Toledo steel as wielding the Word of God. At the very least, surely they dispatched small scouting patrols—if so, to no end they dared record. Any report of treasure would have to await later forays by prospectors and miners who had even more reason to remain silent. Successfully avoiding Ute confrontations was a daily requirement, running afoul of Spanish law was no less a threat once home.

Nevertheless, there was evidence rumored throughout the San Juans of Spanish presence—Spanish prospectors who defied their authorities and risked provoking the Ute—where there should have been none. Because the San Juans were off-limits to all but the Utes, and trespassing even by friars was punishable under Spanish law, written records of these adventures are scarce. Yet, evidence of Spanish prospecting and remnants of their equipment and weapons greeted the first American mountain-men and military expeditions a full two centuries later. The easy routes east-west and north-south gave wide berth to the headwaters of the Rio Grande, Animas and Lake Fork of the Gunnison, but little wonder adventurers suspected the greatest treasurers rested in just such places, a hundred miles north to south and a hundred miles east to west.

And little wonder the lure of treasure eventually overcame any fear of just such places, of superstitions, of the wilderness or the law, or of hostile Ute. Had there been tales of ancient riches so common to other Spanish conquests in New Spain, or with more Spanish perseverance, it would have become clear far sooner that the San Juans were rich in mineral deposits. In fact, the San Juans encompassed some of the most mineralized terrain anywhere in the world. The area between the headwaters of the Animas River and the Lake Fork— the boney-ribbed southern flanks of Uncompahgre Peak that help form the Henson Canyon drainage below Engineer Pass showed early signs—are particularly rich in outcrops of quartz and other promising mineral veins. Fortunes in gold, silver, lead, copper and even zinc awaited the courageous and industrious "young Americans" willing to assault these inner fortress walls. [19]

FORTRESS SAN JUANS

Deep moats, towering granite walls, and a natural maze defended Fortress San Juans. Winter snows, spring run-off, and the Ute were reliable allies. "Gates," passes by another name, are few and far between. Many of them are ill-suited for horses, none of them in their natural state would tolerate wagons.

In addition to dominating the southwest quadrant of Colorado, the San Juans are a natural 17,000 square mile oblong maze bordered on all compass-points by towering granite walls or moat-like river canyons as much as three thousand feet deep. The Rocky Mountain Front Range blunts approaches from the Great Plains, six hundred miles of defenses in its own right. Guarding approaches from the south and southwest are the V-shaped, sheer-walled canyons of the Animas, San Miguel, and Dolores Rivers up to a thousand feet deep, with "entrenched meanders" to the geologist. Escalante and Dominquez Canyons, equally foreboding, shepherds the Uncompahgre and Gunnison Rivers to the Colorado River and its youthful canyons above and below present-day Grand Junction, effectively barring access from the northwest and north. East of its confluence with the Uncompahgre, the Gunnison roars from its headwaters along the Continental Divide through the 3,000 ft. deep Black Canyon of the Gunnison to Delta, Colorado, ensuring the Fortress San Juans moat fulfills its purpose to this day.

The maze is constructed of hundreds of 13,000 foot and fourteen 14,000 foot peaks thrust up and worn down into scared hogback ridges and twisted serpentine ranges. For there to be highlands there must also be lowlands that present their own challenges—marshes and fallen timber seemingly braided together by a giant weaver. Broad throated canyons, often carved out by glaciers, all too soon pinch out or turn back upon their own contorted spines. Complicating approaches from all directions are equally daunting ranges with their own fourteeners, the Sangre de Cristo, Sawatch, Ten Mile, Central and Southern Front, and Elk by name. If this topography was not challenging enough, all too often hidden from view are obscure passes over or through the maze walls separating one watershed from another—all too often, a short-lived gulley atop a wall masquerades as a pass.

The fortress spans sixty to one hundred miles from the San Luis Valley west to Utah, and as much as one hundred to one hundred and fifty miles from New Mexico north to central Colorado's Uncompahgre plateau. Getting into the San Luis Valley was no easy chore. Even the Continental Divide is subject to the fickleness of the maze, tracing a serpentine path, generally trending north-south, in the heart of the San Juans bulging east-west. Headwaters of major western watersheds tumble from its flanks, but none defeat the maze. They flow their separate ways to the Mississippi River, to the Gulf of Mexico, to the Sea of Cortez. Retracing their courses does not reveal the way across the San Juans, through the maze. Retracing their courses leads to their headwaters seeping weakly from the flanks of their respective maze walls.

note they barely began navigating what we understand today to be the San Juans maze. Had there been more promise of gold, or more days in mild seasons, there may have been more Spanish pluck. Required "pluck" came with the American mountain men, motivated not by gold but by beaver.

San Juans contours could be mistaken for an enormous platter of noodles or the field-dressed entrails of an elk. Like any cleverly designed maze, the San Juans falsely encourages travel up cascading drainages along promising game trails only to confound the pilgrim with headwaters pinched out by sheer canyon walls. An adventurer might eye along the way an obscure breach in a ridgeline, albeit treacherous and wholly unsuited to all but nimble foot travel, but merit forgiveness for considering it a pass. Too often such an opportunity affords passage out of one mountain defile, yet sadly descends into another. In tracing the probable 1765 Abiquiu to Delta route of Juan Rivera, Steven Baker paints an unforgettable word picture of his ordeal that is only slightly less trying today.

New Mexico is a harsh and generally dry land of vast deserts and deep rocky canyons. Although impressive, these local features are dwarfed by a great mass of lofty mountains. While some of these, like the Sangre de Cristo Range, extend southward into New Mexico, most are located in Colorado with their east to west leading edge commencing about one-hundred miles to the northwest of Santa Fe. This virtual sea of towering snow-capped peaks comprises the San Juan Range of the Southern Rocky Mountains.

Gulch and Canyon Defenses. If sheer walls were not intimidating enough, marshes and eons of tree-falls clogged most watershed approaches to the High Country. The Ute knew to get above tree-line whenever possible, leaving breaking lowland trails to the impetuous Two-Legged. (*Crofutt's Grip-Sack Guide*)

This range combines with other mountain ranges; the great escarpments of the Colorado Plateau; and the Colorado, San Juan, and other deep tributary river canyons to form a bold and essentially unbroken, natural wall-like barrier that stretches nearly 500 miles from east to west…These mountains and canyons, as well as others on northward beyond them, cover some 120,000 square miles…Even if the great mountain wall could be penetrated, a second natural barrier still stood between the New Mexicans and the distant Teguayo [Colorado River]. This was formed by the deeply incised canyons of the Colorado River and its Gunnison River tributary. These truly great chasms … combined to form an effective moat. This extended westerly from near the Continental Divide in Colorado for some 250 miles before it became the truly ominous Glen and Grand Canyons of the Colorado in Utah and Arizona. Horsemen headed north could readily breach this moat at only two places where Mother Nature momentarily eased the topography just enough to allow for narrow gateways to the legendary province and even more remote Native American territories. These critical gateways were on the Colorado River near today's Moab, Utah, and the Gunnison River near Delta, Colorado. [20]

Mastering the San Juans defensives required perseverance, and purpose–and centuries-long patience.

Perseverance and purpose, therein lay the key. Spanish-era incursions, American military journeys of discovery, and an elite cadre of mountain men notwithstanding, forays deeper and deeper into the western mountains did not reach a new milestone until the summer of 1860. That July, and into the following summer, Charles Baker–to this day credited with far more than he achieved–popularized the notion that the upper Animas River valley was a gold-rich region Even then, the outbreak of the Civil War and of course the Ute spared the San Juans serious degradations a considerable while longer.

Notes—Chapter Eight: No Laughing Matter

[1] Service, Robert, "The Land of Beyond," *The Best of Robert Service*, pg. 69.

[2] Wroth, William, ed., *Ute Indian Arts & Culture from Pre-History to the New Millennium*, "The Ute Creation Story" as told by Alden B. Naranjo and Monica Lujan, "Traditional Cosmology, Ecology and Language of the Ute Indian," interview of James N. Goss (linguist), pgs. 7-8. [Jan Pettit provides a similar version of the Ute creation story featuring Coyote, *Utes, the Mountain People*, pg. 5.]

[3] Pettit, Jan, *Utes, The Mountain People*, "Introduction by Eddie Box," pgs. ix, 1. [These arrogant interlopers, Spaniards probing northward from their camps in northern New Mexico, would be called "Two –Legged" according to "Red Ute" Eddie Box, Sr., from the Moache and Capota band.]

[4] Linton, Ralph, ed., *The Southern Ute of Colorado*, "Acculturation in Seven American Indian Tribes," by Marvin Opler, pg. 126.

[5] Ibid., pgs. 126-127.

[6] Ibid., pg. 157. [Concerning Ute acquiring Spanish horses, Marvin Opler writes: "According to

Ute tradition, the horse was borrowed from the Spaniards."]

[7] [Pope's Rebellion or "Pueblo Revolt" in 1680 did force a retreat south—not until 1692 were the Spanish back in Santa Fe.]

[8] Baker, pg. 38.

[9] Ibid., pg. 73.

[10] [The Spanish were accustomed to naming every sub-range of the San Juans they encountered, but Anglo-Americans were accustomed to call all sub-ranges the San Juans. In fact, the La Plata's were rich in silver.]

[11] Nossaman, Allen, *Many More Mountains*, Vol. I, pgs. 33-76,17.

[12] Wroth, "Traditional Cosmology, Ecology and Language of the Ute Indian," from an Interview with James A. Goss, pgs. 1-10, 48.

[13] Ibid.

[14] *TRUEWEST MAGAZINE.*

[15] Baker, pg. 61.

[16] Ibid.

[17] In 1874 the Utes had sold the San Juans, but this action was never fully accepted by many tribal leaders. In September 1879 hostilities erupted. The Northern Utes massacred Nathan Meeker and all eight male employees at the Ute agency. Three women were taken hostage. The catalyst was plowing up the Ute horseracing track to plant vegetables. On September 29, 1879, the Milk Creek Massacre in which a U.S. cavalry rescue party was attacked by the Utes. Thirteen soldiers were killed, forty-three wounded. Thirty-seven Utes died. [See: Smith, P. David, *The Story of Lake City*, pg. 178.] Ute mastery of the mountains, aided by the vast and rugged wilderness, would slip away for the same reasons. While skillful and mobile, the Ute were disorganized and few in number. Dominance quickly eroded with the 1873 Brunot Treaty, and ended with expulsion to reservations after the 1879 Meeker massacre.

[18] Crum, Josie Moore, "The San Juan Country," *Pioneers of the San Juan Country*, Vol. I, pg. 7. [Left unsaid is reference to the "great curve" in the Rocky Mountain spine that helps define the San Juans.]

[19] On a positive note, during this period transcontinental railroads were constructed which greatly facilitated development of the western United States and the Rocky Mountains in particular.

[20] Baker, pgs. 52-53.

CHAPTER 9

The Last Great Gate

I wandered today to the hill, Maggie,
To watch the scene below.
The creek and the creaking old mill, Maggie,
As we used to long ago.

They say I am feeble with age, Maggie,
My steps are less sprightly than then,
My face is a well written page, Maggie,
But time alone was the pen. [1]

Tom Ashley had a soothing tenor voice. Every night, with the only song he knew, Tom calmed the nerves of his parties' livestock as well as his fellow watchmen as they made their way across the hostile Native American prairie to their new frontier homesteads. The devastation of Civil War had ended, Tom had done his duty, and now his personal reconstruction was about to be birthed in the San Luis Valley. His journey and new life was emblematic of another wave of westering. Charles Baker was old school, but he had succumbed to post-war thinking similar to Tom Ashley's with the exception that his destination was the familiar upper Animas Valley and his purpose was picking up his prospecting interests where he had left them in 1861.

On the cusp of the outbreak of the war, Baker had undertaken a bold expedition underwritten by California Gulch adventurers including Abe Lee, Stephen Kellogg, Thomas Pollock, and Adnah French. Like the Front Range camps, what had quickly grown into an overcrowded present-day Leadville was no place Baker, Kellogg, Pollock and French could tolerate. Unlike Abe Lee, who was content to work his profitable California Gulch placers and bask in the knowledge that he was the source of the gulch's name, Baker and the others were not similarly inclined. Clearly, age had something to do with their frame of mind. Lee was flush with cash, willing to risk some of it on Baker's dreams, but he was old. Baker was late to the Leadville game, financially insecure, but full of himself. Kellogg,

Pollock and French had done well on the Front Range and in California Gulch, but were confident they could do better in more remote regions. Friends Baker and French, more impatient than the others, were ready to go in July. Kellogg and Pollock needed more time. From their Denver base, they would recruit a large number of like-minded adventurers and prepare to join Baker in "short order." "Short-order" turned out to be five months before leaving on a very slow journey. It also turned out that the entire venture would be short-lived and involve more than one Denver visit. Between July 1860 and July 1861, Baker cycled in and out of the Animas Valley probably not twice, but numerous times. Apparently the others did too.

In July of 1860, Baker and French departed California Gulch for the San Juans with twenty others. French was a lot like Baker. Besides being friends, they shared similar interests and had common traits that included impatience and recklessness. Adnah French also had a habit of showing up when gold was the issue. By contrast, Kellogg and Pollock would not show up until December, but for good reason. Concerned from the outset that Baker's July party was danger-ously undermanned, they had worked to recruit a much larger party. Successful in that regard, and apparently unconcerned about entering the mountains in December, they packed up not only grubstakes but families and proceeded to join Baker somewhere between Denver and the heart of the Ute homeland.

Baker and his party of discontents panned their way among the towering ridgelines, down the upper Arkansas River, over Poncha Pass into the upper San Luis Valley, over Cochetopa Pass on the new but crude wagon road built in 1858 by the Loring expedition, down the Gunnison River a short distance, up the Lake Fork of the Gunnison River, and over Cinnamon Pass to the upper Animas River. [2] The upper Animas valley would be the future home of Howardsville, Silverton to the south and Animas Forks to the north. The area came to be called "Baker's Park." Coddled deep within the San Juans maze, pristine and deathly still, it was a fortress courtyard nearly impossible to reach. In Marshall Sprague's words:

> *What Baker and his men gazed on beyond Cinnamon was the secret heart of the San Juan Range, technically the San Juan Uplift, and they were the first whites to tell the world about it.* [3]

Allen Nossaman took issue with "the first whites" statement. In his incred-ibly thorough *Many More Mountains* published in 2006, he writes that Baker did not discover the

> *...park which bears his name nor the fact that it contained gold-bearing ma-terials, it must also be acknowledged that this mysterious—and near legend-ary—man was, indeed, the first person to view the park on the Animas as a*

destination in itself and to proceed in an organized fashion to prospect it and to promote it as the metal-rich region it is now known to be. [4]

Much is disputed in the many accounts of Charles Baker and the upper Animas Valley region in general, probably least of which who got there first. The purpose here is not to resolve these matters. Far more manageable, the purpose here is four-fold: (1) to further illustrate the awesome majesty and remoteness of the San Juans that accounted for their fortress-like nature; (2) to further document that the Ute landlord, and to a lesser extent the Navajo and other neighboring tribes, helped hold the Whites at bay through violence as well as accommodation; (3) because of (1) and (2), Engineer Pass—Henson Canyon was the last major east-west route opened for gold and silver exploration in the San Juans; and (4) to highlight the grit and willingness to endure hardship of yet another class of pioneer.

Working their way down the Gunnison River, Baker's original party of twenty-one began to lose heart. Panning for gold was hard work and they were not finding much. Somewhere between present-day Gunnison and the Black Canyon, the party decided to split up. Fifteen retraced their path and returned to California Gulch and the Front Range. The remaining six of Baker's party, to their credit, reached Eureka Gulch on the upper Animas River. In addition to a host of gulches draining towering mountains on every flank, the upper Animas also anchored a faint Ute trail that threaded its way up the west face of Engineer Mountain and over present-day Engineer Pass. Had any of Baker's remnant

Baker's Rebuff. Charles Baker's party of twenty-one dwindled to six after a hard go from 1860 California Gulch/Leadville to the upper Black Canyon. Intimidated by their surroundings but resolute in their quest for gold, Baker's remnant of six turned south and followed the Lake Fork of the Gunnison to present-day Lake City, Cinnamon Pass, and the upper Animas Valley. *(Courtesy of Ethan Marsh)*

found their way to that pass and stood in its saddle, looking eastward and below, they could have seen upper Henson Creek cutting a deep canyon downward some twenty-plus miles through the castle-keep. But no one in the Baker party had any awareness of this, nor was the remnant inclined to explore farther. If any one did, they did not gossip about it.

Baker's goal, according to Marshall Sprague, "was to follow the Divide southward until it qualified to be part of the South, to find diggings for Southerners, and to use Santa Fe as a Southern supply center rivaling Denver."[5] Points east were of no interest; besides, the season was too short to explore rabbit trails. Knowledge of the castle-keep was safe for another decade. So was knowledge of Engineer Pass, the last of the great gates. Baker's motives are one of those debatable matters left to others to unravel. Important to note here is that Baker and company, while inclined to rely on established southern routes to and from New Mexico settlements like Abiquiu and Santa Fe for supplies and winter quarters, were eager to pan for gold,

---

GREAT GATES

The southern Spanish outposts in the New Mexico highlands—Santa Fe, Abiquiu, Taos and outlying settlements—now lorded over by Americans, continued to serve purposes similar to those later served by Leadville and its spawn. Century's earlier Spanish patrols ventured north along the Rio Grande, but always turned east or west to skirt the ominous San Juans. Juan Bautista De Anza thought otherwise, but he too wavered out of an abundance of caution. He determined in 1778 to eradicate terrorist Comanches "through regions different from those which have been followed," but failed his primary mission. His strategy was to outflank his enemy by way of a route never before taken, meaning finding a way east through the mountains and attacking the Comanches from the plains. De Anza did succeed in being the first European to penetrate the outermost defensive ramparts of Fortress San Juans through its "most useful southern gates." La Glorieta, Sangre de Cristo, and Raton passes opened the southern flanks of the Rockies to the Great Plains to the east and the interior San Luis Valley to the west. Cochetopa and Poncha passes opened the northern San Luis Valley to the Gunnison River watershed to the west and the Arkansas River watershed to the north. Still undiscovered and unconquered were seven inner gates: Marshall, Monarch, Slumgullion, Spring Creek, Stoney, Cinnamon, and lastly Engineer. From the north, Charles Baker's party breeched Cinnamon Pass during the summer of 1860. Neighboring Engineer Pass would be overlooked until 1871. From the south, Stony Pass would grant access to the upper Animas watershed from the headwaters of the Rio Grande throughout the 1860s and beyond. [6]

not climb mountainsides. On subsequent trips in and out of the Animas watershed they continued to prefer the old, southern Spanish trails, or cross the Divide and follow the upper Rio Grande to the New Mexico settlements.

Baker found a small quantity of gold in Eureka Gulch in August, 1860, near present-day Silverton, and the party spread out to prospect neighboring gulches. They panned with poor results through July, August and most of September. According to Nossaman, during this first season Baker traveled more than he prospected, to the New Mexico settlements and Front Range outposts all the way to Denver. In early October he journeyed to Abiquiu by way of the Animas River along the old Spanish trials in search of supplies. In mid-October he returned to the upper Animas Valley and staked claim to a town site, the future Baker City. In November 1860, he and at least some of his party returned to Abiquiu in advance of approaching heavy snows. According to Marshall Sprague's account, with a slightly different timeline, Baker avoided Animas Canyon by way of Molas Divide and Coalbank Pass, crested Horse Lake Pass in New Mexico, and arrived in Abiquiu in late October. For Charles Baker, wintering over in northern New Mexico did not mean laying about. Whether by letters and interviews with local newspapers, or another trip or more to Denver, Baker was credited with stoking the "San Juans excitement." Sprague writes that he:

> *began promoting his Southern kind of Gregory Gulch in Santa Fe [as an aside, Gregory reportedly claimed that his diggings belonged to the slave states by right of discovery.] The news of fabulous San Juan riches flew to Denver, and several parties set out for the region over Sangre de Cristo Pass and through Fort Garland. Some planned to get in by Cochetopa and Cinnamon passes.*

[Indicative of the degree of emotion that boosterism could elicit, William Byers puffed up like a banty rooster guarding its henhouse. According to Sprague, in defense of the local business community, the *Rocky Mountain News* unleashed a series of attacks on the San Juans region and Baker himself.]

> *He charged Baker with being fifty different kinds of humbug, and a traitor besides. He warned that those foolish enough to quit the home camps which Denver merchants toiled so nobly to supply were risking their lives to reach those fake diggings away down there in–his contemptuous designation–"Mexico."*[7]

Cynthia Becker and P. David Smith paint a somewhat kinder picture of Baker's 1860s activities.

> *By the end of 1859, Colorado mining men and prospectors had already de-duced that there was a rich "Mineral Belt" in the future Colorado that ran from Boulder southwest to the new discoveries in California Gulch, and that*

it evidently continued southwest into the San Juan Mountains. A few successful Colorado mining men in the future Leadville area put together a small party to explore the region under the leadership of Charles Baker.

If anything was found, Baker was to file claims (although the San Juans were in Ute country and the claims would not be legal), establish a toll road into the "diggings" (they too were looking for placer gold, panning the streams for nuggets), locate a town site in the best place possible near the diggings, and sell lots in the new town. All of these activities were illegal and the minerals were in the heart of the rugged San Juan Mountains with no easy access and in the heart of Tabeguache Ute territory. [8]

According to Becker and Smith, the Baker party found signs of gold and silver in July of 1860 along the Lake Fork and the Animas Rivers, "but nothing spectacular."

However, when Baker returned to Denver in the fall of 1860, he reported that a major discovery had been made in what came to be called "Baker's Park," and that the men had recovered twenty-five cents per pan in gold, which would be about ten dollars a day when wages were about a third of that amount. He also wrote to the Santa Fe Gazette *predicting that "there will be no less than 25,000 Americans engaged in mining and agricultural pursuits (in the San Juans)… within a year, perhaps double that number." The* Rocky Mountain News *also printed Baker's letter, in which he stated he was unhappy to learn that some people were going to come into the area from the north.*

Baker himself then went to Denver, had an interview with William N. Byers of the Rocky Mountain News *in which he gave the proposed new route, and set off from Denver with a much larger party, which varied in size as people gave up, joined the group, stopped because of problems, or rode ahead of the main group trying to get to the "diggings" first.* [9]

Neither Sprague nor Nossaman speak to a Byers-Baker meeting. Moreover, accounts differ concerning what most agree was a mid-December departure of a large party [Kellogg-Pollock] of Animas-bound gold-seekers. What the exact nature was of Byers and Baker's conversation if it occurred at all is lost to history. Under any circumstance, it is likely Baker did not share his goal of securing the San Juans for the Confederacy if in fact there was any truth to that. And Byers probably managed to restrain himself from calling Baker a lying traitor to his face, probably just as tempted to shoot him dead on the spot. The likelihood in that day and time that such language could quickly lead to gun-play was high, an outcome Byers had already experienced more than once in his quest for journalistic excellence. Older and wiser, he left labeling Baker a liar and traitor to his *Rocky Mountain News,* and hoped for the best.

Baker's whereabouts and activities, as well as unrelated parties, between the 1860 and 1861 prospecting seasons are other matters with differing understandings. Reportedly when Baker left Denver in December 1860, he did so leading a second, larger party to the Animas River prospects. Among the more notable members were two of his financial backers, Stephen Kellogg with family, and a prominent new convert with a colorful history of adventure, Thomas Pollock. Almost certainly, however, Baker was not in this party, but would join it probably when it arrived at its destination. This may not have been Baker's and Kellogg's original plan, but Nossaman makes a good argument that it was the case.

Kellogg, according to Nossaman, concerned that he could neither winter over without his family nor wait until spring to travel to the diggings, organized his winter expedition knowing that numerous newspaper accounts had already motivated Denver prospectors to head for the San Juans as early as October 1860. On December 14, 1860, Kellogg and family were packed and ready to go. The large December party, more appropriately called the "Kellogg-Pollock Party," was actually two parties led by each man but traveling together for safety. The route Kellogg and Pollock took along with perhaps 200-300 men, women and children, and the difficulties encountered along their way, in Allen Nossaman's studied judgment, "further highlighted the remoteness of the new discoveries, and proved an undertaking of that scope was a dozen years ahead of its time." [10]

The so-called "second Baker Party" route to the San Juans did not involve the Lake Fork [northern] or even the Rio Grande [southern] route known to prospectors since the 1850s. Instead, December 1860 parties, Kellogg-Pollock and others, in part hopefully to avoid the worst of winter weather, in part to avoid the Ute, plotted a course down the Front Range and over Sangre de Cristo and La Veta Passes to Fort Garland and west to Animas City. Charles Baker, based on Sprague's writings, probably was in one of the New Mexico settlements gathering provisions, recruiting adherents, and promoting the mineral wealth of Baker's Park. According to Sprague, in the spring of 1861 he led

> *a hundred men, women and children from Santa Fe over Horse Lake Pass to Animas River and the San Juan diggings. On the way, Baker platted the town of Animas City below Engineer Mountain in the charming lower Animas Valley fifteen miles north of present Durango.* [11]

Also on the way he began building a toll road between Abiquiu and Baker's Park that had been authorized by the New Mexico Territorial legislature and signed into law by the Governor on December 28, 1860. Nossaman is uncertain about the depth of Baker's southern leanings, but it is clear that Baker was more hopeful of good returns from his *Abiquiu, Pagosa and Baker City Road Company* toll road and town-sites, devoting more time to them than to his prospects. [12]

Baker's Ace-In-The-Hole. Charles Baker's vision extended well beyond finding gold. He established a town-site (Animas City), promoted lots and cabins, built a bridge across the Animas, and obtained a charter from New Mexico authorities for the Abiquiu, Pagosa and Baker City Toll Road. *(Wikipedia)*

Historian Hall, with evidence to support his view, adds further details to Nossaman's account. If accurate, it is also further proof that Baker spent more time journeying and promoting than he did prospecting, and if he was going to have anything to do with the Kellogg-Pollock Party he would either leave it early enroute to Animas City to recruit a Santa Fe Party, or he would rendezvous along with his Santa Fe Party with the so-called "second Baker Party" in the Animas Valley. According to Hall, Baker and his party were hunkered down in "brush shanties" in present-day Silverton when Kellogg and several others caught up with them.

Hall's Santa Fe account includes a number of other interesting and compatible details. As artfully critical as William Byers was, still the clouds he cast over what came to be known as *Baker's Park* did not deter Baker from leading a spring 1861 party of upwards of several hundred men, women and children from Santa Fe over Horse Lake Pass to the Animas River Valley. They settled in at what became known as Animas City north of present-day Durango. By July, in the face of plentiful hardship including lack of food, and pitiful quantities of gold, the discouraged party came to two conclusions. First, they should abandon the valley and return east to avoid starvation and scalping if not to fight for the Confederacy. Second, before they departed they should lynch Baker. With or without a miner's court, he needed to be held accountable for getting them into such a mess.

Baker was spared [Nossaman believes he was never in real danger], but the campers including Baker did abandon partially-built Animas City. According to Sprague, Baker scurried to Missouri and joined the Confederate Army as a captain. Frank Hall has Baker returning to his home state of Virginia. Nossaman discredits both accounts, and flight to Georgia as well, instead noting that if Baker ever served in the Confederate army it was not in Virginia, Missouri, or Georgia regiments. If at all, Baker may have served in a frontier Texas Legion or New Mexico unit. Regardless, no one with the possible exception of Allen

Nossaman disputes his Confederate leanings and absence from the San Juans region until 1867. Moreover, Baker and a few others did not leave the valley until late fall, instead continuing to pan in Baker's Park before crossing the Divide and following the Rio Grande route to Fort Garland. [13]

Hall joins most others in stating that "Captain Baker" and Stephen Kellogg bonded in 1860 California Gulch where life-long ties with Lee, French, and Pollock took root.

In 1860 California Gulch was swarming with placer miners; among them were S. B. Kellogg & Company., who owned some of the rich ground and took out large amounts of gold, and Charles Baker, a restless, adventurous, impecunious man who was always in search of something new. He entertained extravagant opinions of the richness of the country beyond, and at last prevailed upon Mr. Kellogg and F. R. Rice to outfit him for a prospecting expedition. He set out in July 1860, to explore the San Juan country—meaning the country along the San Juan River. [14]

Five months later Stephen Kellogg and Thomas Pollock were prepared to lead their own parties. They traveled south through Colorado City and Pueblo and over Sangre de Cristo Pass. Fourteen miserable wintry days later they entered "San Luis Park" where they were buffeted by "a terrific storm of wind and snow that scattered their stock and caused intense suffering to many of the people." [15]

Wagon boxes and other property were burned for fuel. On the 4th of March they passed Conejos and traveled thence via Abiquiu, Chama River and Pagosa Springs. April 1st they reached Cascade Creek, a branch of the Animas River about twenty-five miles south of where Silverton was subsequently located, where they went into camp. Kellogg and several others went in search of Baker and found him and his party in Baker's Park, now Silverton. They were living in brush shanties where they had wintered. Their diggings were nine miles up the river, at the point later known as Eureka. They had cut out lumber with whip-saws and made some sluices, but had collected very little gold . . . . Men passed back and forth constantly between the camp at Cascade Creek and Baker's Park. Kellogg, Baker and Rice explored the country east, north and west, passing over the high mountains to the headwaters of the Gunnison, Uncompahgre and San Miguel Rivers, prospecting all their head tributaries and gulches, but they were searching only for gulch, or placer gold diggings, knowing nothing about lodes or quartz veins. [16]

Baker, Kellogg, Pollock and scores of others had no sooner returned to their Animas River encampments when pressures to leave approached a breaking point. By the fourth of July, 1861, the San Juans excitement would end as unpredictably as it had begun. Seemingly overnight, Animas City and upriver outposts were empty. The reasons why were easy to understand. The prospecting seasons were not only too short, they were too disappointing. The ever-present threat of Ute attack in the valley, and Navajo attacks coming and going, were "a source of constant concern." Supplies, especially basic foods, were scarce. And the unknown effects the Civil War could have on southerner and northerner confined in close, austere quarters could only be imagined. Oddly enough, at the same time eager treasure-seekers were entering the valley, the brave citizens who had endured so much were homeward bound, all but a few die-hards, that is. In this environment, Charles Baker continued prospecting his beloved Eureka Gulch, and Thomas Pollock managed to return from seeking badly needed provisions in the New Mexico settlements to rescue his wife.

END OF THE SAN JUAN EXCITEMENT

Camped along the upper Animas in a remote wilderness separated from even a semblance of civilization by some of the highest mountain ranges in North America, surrounded by aggrieved Ute, and often nearly starved, still 1860-61 prospectors falsely boasted of their good fortunes. Reports of their discoveries found their way back to the mining camps of the upper Arkansas, California Gulch and beyond, throughout South Park, and ultimately to the Front Range and the States. Even in the midst of the sudden July 1861 abandonment of camps throughout the upper Animas Valley, newcomers continued to arrive. By Frank Halls reckoning,

> one stampede followed another, until hundreds of men were scattered all through the mountains and valleys of Southwestern Colorado. Between the 5th and 10th of July several hundred men left California Gulch alone, stealing away by night, one party followed by another, in the belief that the leaders had secret information of Baker's fabulous discoveries of gold. Many of them never crossed the mountains, but winter caught hundreds scattered through that inhospitable region. All through the fall and winter they came straggling in to the military posts, and to the towns and settlements of New Mexico and Colorado. Some were almost naked, or clothed in the skins of animals; others nearly starved, and doubtless never returned at all, perishing by the wayside. [17]

Hall's reckoning may overstate the situation, but his word-pictures are valid. As for the sweep of history, we can rely on Nossaman to flesh out the rest of Baker and Pollock's story and in the process prophesy the future of the San Juans for the decade to come.

According to Nossaman, while the Ute were pleased that the Whites were retreating from one of their prized summer encampments, and thus content to let them depart in peace, the Navajos were not of like mind. They did not hesitate to attack vulnerable contingents before the mass exodus and they did not hesitate attacking the defeated stragglers as they worked their way back to New Mexico settlements and Fort Garland. The larger the departing party, the safer the journey could be, but even numbers were no guarantee. Both the Ute and the Whites considered the Navajo vengeful by nature. An especially aggressive Navajo band led by a chief named Ceyetano gave them ample reason to believe so. Ceyetano had kept Whites out of the Animas Valley, and challenged Ute sovereignty there, until 1859 when the Ute succeeded in driving his band south across the San Juan River. [18]

As for Baker, French, and Pollock, their strength of character and self-confidence seemed to be the only security they needed. As noted earlier, Baker and a few of his loyalists were probably the last to leave the Animas Valley. Adnah French, in the words of Allen Nossaman, "we will hear again," meaning there is no information regarding how or when he returned to the Front Range, but his story is far from over. More is known about Thomas Pollock's exodus, and Charles Baker's ultimate fate, as well. Better understanding each of these men contributes much to appreciating the struggle to conquer Fortress San Juans.

Thomas Pollock staked the most on Charles Baker's San Juans dream, and was "a legend before the Baker's Park rush ever began, who ultimately became its humanitarian and one of its many heros," according to Allen Nossaman. [19] Pollock was one of present-day Denver's first settlers, arriving December 26, 1858 with Uncle Dick Wootton. By mid-January 1859, he had opened the first blacksmith shop. He soon operated a ferry across the South Platte River, started a carpentry and cabinet making business, and performed undertaker duties. He produced a crop of early radishes and was credited with the first locally grown produce in the region. He built the first two-story building, the Pollock House, which hotel was also the site of the first Presbyterian church service in Denver. He also built the frame house in which the first female school teacher held class on May 7, 1860.

Pollock's unsolicited claim to fame, however, was as one of the new camp's leading advocates of law and order during a crucial two-year period when literal control of the Cherry Creek settlements was the subject of a bloody tug-o-war between desperados and permanent settlers. Pollock was handy with firearms, and was captain of an ad hoc militia group called the "South Platte Rangers." He was executioner for the settlements' first hanging, and when he, the minister and the prisoner were driven under a cottonwood tree in a wagon to conclude the business at hand, Pollock and the minister knelt down. When the prisoner didn't, Pollock poked the condemned man in the ribs until he did. [20]

Lawlessness in Denver City and Auraria reached its most threatening dimensions early in 1859. A group of desperados, self-styled as the "Bummers," advanced from harassment and petty theft to firing upon the sheriff in the center of town. Sheriff W.H. Middaugh... was not injured by two separate shots, but when the "South Park Rangers" appeared on the scene to disperse the "Bummers," the latter group threatened to burn the town to the ground that night. The citizens group stood guard, but the trouble was curtailed when a man named McCarty, who had taken one of the shots at Middaugh, walked up to Pollock and threatened him with a bowie knife. Pollock cracked the rowdy's skull with a blow from his riffle barrel. [21]

William Byers' earned a role in the fight with articles he published in his *Rocky Mountain News* that the Bummers found offensive.

It culminated when George Steele, one of the desperados, rode by the News office on horseback and actually fired into the building, which had been barricaded by Byers and his employees. Steele was slightly wounded by return fire, and galloped crazily up the street, across the Platte River, and back again. Citizens armed themselves and prepared for the worst, but Tom Pollock jumped on his horse, intercepted Steele at the intersection of Sixteenth and Blake, rode up alongside him, and emptied a shotgun into his head. [22]

Pollock owned the first buggy in Denver, and among the young ladies he shared it with that summer of 1860 was Sarah Ann Chivington, daughter of the newly arrived first presiding elder of the Methodist Episcopal church, John M. Chivington. John would later refuse a chaplain's commission and distinguish

Newsroom Neutrality. Editor Byers believed the pen was mightier than the sword, but there were times he had to resort to gunplay. Like most pilgrims, it was always prudent to be prepared. *(Richardson, 1867)*

THOMAS POLLOCK

Pollock remained in Denver for most of the 1860s. In 1868, he prospected in Moreno, New Mexico. In 1870, he was known to be operating a successful "placer workings" in Elizabethtown, New Mexico. He returned to Colorado in 1873 and moved his family to Del Norte. He opened a blacksmith shop in Loma and operated pack trains up the Rio Grande and into the Animas Valley. 1874 was not a good year for Thomas. In a February incident he had been shot at. In April his blacksmith shop was burglarized. In May a fire in Central City destroyed $6,800 of his property. The bright spot in the midst of such gloom was his early entry into the 1874 San Juans boom. In 1874, Pollock's summer residence—he wintered in Del Norte with his family—was Eureka, and at the first La Plata County Republican convention he was nominated for county coroner and took office that fall, garnering 297 of the 301 votes cast. His coroner duties were minimal if any. Instead, his many entrepreneurial ventures and mercantilism occupied most of his time.

Thomas Pollock was born January 9, 1829, in Greene County, Pennsylvania. He died July 14, 1877, aged 48, in Howardsville, San Juan County, Colorado.

himself with the Colorado volunteers during the Civil War. [Sadly, four years later he was credited with engineering the Sand Creek Massacre on the plains east of Denver.] Sarah, on September 16, 1860, five months after the Chivington's arrival in the new Cherry Creek settlements, married Thomas. Four months after that, Thomas bundled his sixteen-year-old bride into a "spring wagon" to be "whisked into an adventure that was to put the Rio de las Animas and the majestic San Juans in her blood for the rest of her life." [23] Accompanying Sarah and Thomas were eleven sturdy army wagons fitted out with $50,000 worth of provisions pulled by six to eight yoke of oxen per wagon, and two hundred head of beef cattle. Nine months later, Sarah and Thomas returned to Denver with one light wagon, one new-born baby girl, Jesse Fremont Pollock, and two young Navajo boys, one of whom the Pollock's would raise. Two young Navajo girls also in the care of the Pollocks had been placed in loving homes in Santa Fe during Thomas' ill-fated attempt to resupply the Animas camp that spring.

Thomas Pollock was a man of action, a man of means, and a man with a big heart. He was a shop-keeper by all outward indications, but a shop-keeper with firearms he was well-versed in using. These traits were evident when he accompanied Uncle Dick Wootton on his humanitarian mission to spare early Denver from starvation, and they resurfaced during that frigid 1860 December journey to the Animas Valley where he found his advance party destitute. Both Hall and Nossaman have something to say on the matter. First, Hall:

[Pollock] had taken from Denver eleven wagons loaded with provisions and goods, and nearly a hundred head of oxen, mules and horses. There was no money among the adventurers, and he had to feed many of them. When they reached the Animas Valley the Utes flocked around them and threatened hostilities, which were averted only by Pollock's furnishing them such provisions and goods as they demanded. In exchange, however, he purchased four Navajo children who were held as captives, and for whom he gave $1,500 worth of goods. When his stock became exhausted Pollock set out for Santa Fe for another supply, and was absent two months. On his return [early 1861], war had broken out between the Mexican and Utes, which impelled him to turn the train back, he finally making his way through to Animas City alone [July 1861]. Of the white settlers, only his wife and an invalid prospector remained, and they were surrounded by a camp of Ute Indians. Soon after the savages warned all the white people out of the country. Pollock and his wife took the direction of Denver, where they arrived in September. Baker, Perdee, with a few others, remained at Eureka Gulch until late in the fall, when they passed out to Fort Garland, where they received the first intelligence that had come to them of the War of the Rebellion. Baker at once started for his native State, Virginia, where he entered the Confederate army and served during the war. [24]

While possibly misstating that Virginia was Baker's native state, less forgivable was Hall's cavalier account of the four Navajo children. Nossaman is far more sensitive to the risks Pollock faced. Since there was neither currency nor sufficient gold in the hands of the Whites or the Ute to pay Pollock for his goods, he "sold" them for IOUs until he could no longer do so. When he finally had to demand payment, the Ute presented him with the four Navajo children who they insisted were worth about $1,500 worth of goods. The alternative, they made clear to Pollock, was confiscating what they wanted. Nossaman writes:

While of doubtful value to Pollock, the four children were highly prized by the Utes, who saw them as future slaves, and thus more valuable than the metal the white man traded with. Pollock consulted with his young bride and with the leading men in the camp at the time and, although the Pollocks were the only ones with anything materially at stake, counsel favored making the trade to avoid any hostilities. Thus, Thomas Pollock became the owner of the four Navajo children—two girls and two boys. [25]

With his trade goods nearly depleted, Pollock entrusted his bride to those in camp and started what would turn out to be a tortured journey to Santa Fe to restock his wagons. The weather was mild but Indian encounters were heated. Usually the Navajo were the culprits, but the Ute were not above suspicion.

At one point, for a period of 16 days, not a single traveler over the road made it to Animas City. A long train of animals, carrying principally flour, was the first safe arrival after this period. It was designed to replenish the stock of Manuel Armijo [the only other mercantilist in the Animas camp], and had been heavily guarded en route. In one day's travel over the route by one party, the bodies of 16 men were found.

Indian agent Lafayette Head, who was to become the first lieutenant governor of Colorado 16 years later, reported to the government that the Navajos had compelled the virtual abandonment of the San Juan and Rio de las Animas mines, having killed 40 Americans and 15 Mexicans on the road to the mines. [26]

Pollock was big-hearted, but he also was no one to trifle with, as the Bummers had discovered the hard way. Nossaman speculated that men like Pollock, and he included Kit Carson and Lafayette Head as further examples, had an aire about them that usually fended off trouble. "The Indians perceived this as readily as animals perceive humans who are frightened of them," determining in the process that attacking such men would result in more harm that it was worth. [25] With respect to the Ute, they also remembered Pollock's kindness regarding needed provisions. When Pollock finally made it back to Animas City to find only his wife and an old man left in her care, he also found that the Ute had ordered all Whites out of their country. In his case, however, they

furnished this last small party safe conduct to Conejos, fighting on more than one occasion with the Navajos and losing one of their number in the process. The Pollocks [presumably with the children] arrived in Denver in September 1861, two yoke of oxen the only remainder of the once-mammoth wagon and stock train Thomas Pollock had assembled to duplicate his Auraria pioneering feat deep in the land of many more mountains. [27]

As for the four Navajo children the Ute "traded" him, Nossaman reports that he took the two girls with him in 1861 when he traveled to Santa Fe for supplies. One girl was adopted by a German family in Santa Fe, and by all accounts remained with them. The other girl, placed with Col. Pffieffer also in Santa Fe, was murdered with the rest of his family in 1863 by Apaches near present-day Truth or Consequences, New Mexico. When the Pollocks reached Denver in the fall of 1861, two boys were with them. Thomas

presented one of the two Navajo boys to Richard E. Whitsitt, an energetic gentleman who had become the virtual kingpin of the Denver Town Company, had been one of the founders of Colorado City, and who had participated in–and survived–the first duel in Denver. Whitsitt intended to raise and educate the boy, but the child died within a few years. The other boy was raised by Pollock, and named John Milton Pollock. [28]

Charles Baker's exodus from the Animas Valley is not only a mystery, so is his service to the Confederacy. According to Frank Hall, he probably achieved the rank of Captain and settled in Virginia at war's end. Allen Nossaman simply states that,

Charles Baker's career temporarily vanished–into the Confederate ranks of the Civil War–his ultimate fate was ironically linked to his haunting preoccupation with the search for specks of gold in the waters of the river named for John the Baptist. [29]

Three years after Appomattox, having lost heart in efforts to start afresh in Virginia, Baker returned to Colorado in the summer of 1868. For many war veterans, Colorado and the western frontier in general was therapeutic, a land begging for emigrants and not caring a wit about why they came. Baker camped for a short time in familiar territory, the upper Arkansas, but perhaps for the same reasons he left there in 1861 he did so again. With several other men who Nossaman identifies he trekked south-southwest through the mountains, prospecting the Gunnison, Animas, San Juan and La Plata Rivers. By the time he reached the La Plata, his only companions were a man named White [and Strole]. Ignoring signs of likely Native American attack, they continued on to the Colorado River of the West not far from the mouth of the Colorado Chiquito (Little Colorado).

The Indians had followed and harassed them constantly, and they were reduced almost to the last extremity. On the river bank where they had clambered down to the water, there was a quantity of driftwood, from which they constructed a raft upon which they intended to risk their lives and float down the turbulent and dangerous stream. All was ready for the start, when a volley poured down upon them from the cliffs. Baker fell, crying out to his companions, "Boys, I'm killed! Look out for yourselves." [30]

Nossaman's account of Baker's last days is more detailed. He found Baker after the war in Atchison, Kansas, where he had met James White, a stagecoach driver on the Santa Fe Trail, George Strole, an old Mississippi River boatman, and Joe Goodfellow.

Indians had reportedly stolen Baker's horses, and the foursome, deciding it may be time to move on, stole 14 head of Indian horses and eluded the tribesmen across the plains, crossing the river at Cimarron, Kansas, and going to

Colorado City, which is part of present-day Colorado Springs. At this point, Baker proposed a prospecting expedition to some country with which he had a degree of familiarity–the land along the San Juan River and its tributaries, particularly the Animas. [31]

In agreement, beginning on May 20,1867, the four men departed Colorado Springs and passed through South Park. During an argument between White and Goodfellow, Goodfellow was shot in the foot and left behind. The remaining three entered the San Juans by way of the upper Rio Grande, perhaps the first "Whites" to re-enter the valley since 1861, and began prospecting in Baker's beloved Eureka Gulch. With no better outcome than in 1861, the men followed the Animas River south, crossed the La Plata to the Mancos, and followed the Mancos to the San Juan. Approaching the Colorado River near its juncture with the Green River, according to White, Charles Baker was killed by Native Americans. White and Strole escaped on a hastily built raft down the Colorado. Passing through the Grand Canyon, Strole drowned, White emerged to tell the disputed tale. [32]

Undisputed, Baker was dead. Some considered him a charlatan, some a patriot, some an aimless visionary. Historian Hall wrote a balanced obituary, truthful even, with the likely exception of his last accolade:

Such was the untimely end of Capt. Baker, who has been credited with much romantic heroism, but really accomplished very little; who has also been censured for much of the sorrow and suffering that befell his associates, was threatened with shooting and hanging for leading men upon "fool's errands," but actually never intentionally deceived any one. [33]

The post-Civil War San Juans adventure of Baker is a stark reminder of the deadly elegance of the San Juans Fortress, its defensive maze, the murderous diligence of its Ute landlord and neighboring tribes, and the fact that little had changed since his 1860-61 expeditions. In fact, after the failed 1860-61 expeditions, the San Juans country was ignored—"left to its primeval solitude" in the words of Hall—for a number of years largely due to the direct and indirect effects of the Civil War. Clearly this was too conservative an assessment—it also neglected to mention both Baker's 1867 return for a short season, and the "rest of Adnah French's story." Still, Hall had a point. With emphasis on "well planned and systematically," the next exploration "to that distant and almost inaccessible region that was well planned and systematically prosecuted" occurred in 1869. Once again Henson Canyon would escape attention. As usual, its isolation in large part was a function of coping with hostile landlords. Once again success or failure would rely on the determination and courage of our adventurous veteran Adnah French.

The rest of French's story begins in Arizona Territory.

On the first day of August 1869, a party of twenty-two prospectors and miners was organized at Prescott, Arizona, with Calvin Jackson for leader and captain. Jackson was a Californian with a varied and adventurous experience—conspicuously in Indian warfare, which was fortunate, as many conflicts of this kind were to be met in the course of their travels. The party expected to join Capt. Cooley's expedition, a similar company of twenty-eight men that had been organized at Forts Goodwin and Reno, in Arizona, for the same purpose...

The prospectors now numbered fifty men, well mounted and equipped, and armed with breech-loading guns and revolvers. The command was shared equally by Jackson and Cooley, who were alike devoted to the common good of their respective companies. Hostile Indians [Apaches] swarmed over the country, intent upon preventing the white men from effecting a lodgment in their favorite hunting grounds. At night signal fires were seen on the lofty mountain peaks; during the day columns of smoke exchanged messages between the savage bands. Alarms and surprises were constant and wearing. A third of the force was required to guard the camps, as many more to care for and protect the stock, while the remainder were prospecting and exploring, though never daring to stray very far from the others. [34]

Apaches—Western Slope Risks. Like the Ute in their mountain redoubts, the Apaches to the southwest did not welcome others, especially prospectors. Primitive-looking by American standards, nevertheless they were a fierce foe when they chose to be. Adnah French and his party of prospectors were willing to risk their ire to reach the Animas Valley from the west. French earned their friendship instead. The greatest threat to the party was the early onset of San Juans winter weather. *(Wikipedia Commons)*

Circumstances deteriorated, according to Hall. The men held a "council," at which time a majority concluded that the party was undermanned and should retreat to Prescott. Eight men disagreed and prepared to press northeastward toward the San Juans. The eight were Adnah French, J. C. Dunn, Dempsey Reese, N. Marsh, David Ring, Wood Dood, A. Loomis, and "Old Boston" Graves. All had been compatriots in Prescott. French, by virtue of having accompanied Baker in 1860-61, earned the honor of "captain" of the group. Without explaining the details of what transpired next, French and the Apache chief leading the Coyotero band that was harassing them found a way to exchange words instead of gunfire. Frank Hall shares the rest of the story on the following three pages.

Negotiations were opened by them [French party] with the Coyotero band of Apaches, who had grown tired of war. Their chief, Miguel, was inclined to be friendly, and the result of the negotiation was a treaty, by the terms of which the white men were to be permitted to travel as rapidly as possible across the country, without stopping to dig holes in the ground or search for gold in any way. In return, Capt. French was to use his influence with the "great Father" at Washington in behalf of the Coyoteros, for their good. An escort of nine

---

ADNAH FRENCH

Born in 1833 in Brandon, Vermont, Adnah French was a member of the Lawrence Party characterized. In 1858-59, French was "instrumental in the founding and earliest growth of the Mile High City." He was a trusted confidante of Charles Baker and an eager participant in Baker's July 1860 trek into the San Juans. French applied his Denver experience to the task of establishing Baker City and organizing Baker's toll road company in Santa Fe. There is no reliable record of Adnah French during the Civil War. Nossaman states that he was pro-slavery in Kansas prior to joining the Lawrence Party, which probably made for interesting campfire discussions given that the majority of the Lawrence emigrants were of abolitionist persuasions.

At age thirty-six, having drifted throughout the west on one prospecting venture after another, French joined Jackson and Cooley's 1869 Prescott, Arizona party intent on entering the San Juans from the southwest. Most of the party abandoned the quest—French and seven others did not. Successfully negotiating safe passage with two Apache bands, French's remnant reached the Animas River Valley in time for an early winter storm. Barely surviving the ordeal, they retreated south and wintered over in New Mexico. Undeterred, Adnah returned to the Animas Valley in 1870 with a number of men who would have a great deal to do with making Baker's Park the site of the first settlements in the rugged San Juans labyrinth. [35]

braves was furnished them, and the little band of eight white men turned their faces northward." [36]

What either White man or Apache chief truly expected was anyone's guess. It was fairly certain Capt. French would have little success in conveying anything to the "Great Father" in Washington, and it was equally doubtful Chief Miguel had authority sufficient to guarantee Capt. French safe passage beyond the near horizon if that far. One day's travel demonstrated reasons for concern.

The first night's encampment of the French party was on a stream called Carissa, in the midst of a great number of Indians who were engaged in a drunken revel. The liquor they drank was called <u>tswin</u>, made from corn and vegetable roots. They were holding war dances, decked out in all the savage finery of war paint, feathers and war dresses, whooping and shouting like fiends, and making the mountains echo and re-echo with their hideous yells. [37]

The French Party did not sleep well. Nor did the dawn comfort them, according to Hall. For reasons unknown, Chief Miguel's escort refused to break camp. The day passed, but early the next morning the march resumed and brought them to the camp of another Coyotero chief named Juaro and his band of warriors. To French's wary delight, they were welcomed by the surprised chief, well fed, and invited to rest a short time. When the tortuous journey resumed, Juaro and his band insisted on accompanying the French party.

In the afternoon they crossed several large and fresh Indian trails which caused them much anxiety, but the young chief assured them there was no danger, — that he would protect them at the cost of his own life, if necessary. They traveled in this manner for several days, without serious adventure, but with frequent new causes of alarm. At length they ventured to talk with Juaro about the object of their journey, and inquired if he knew where gold could be found. He replied that he did, but dared not reveal such knowledge, because if he did, his life would be taken by his people.

Several long night marches ensured for want of water that taxed the strength of men and animals to the utmost. One morning after the severest of all their nocturnal rides, as they were building fires to cook breakfast, a large party of Indians armed with guns, swept down upon them, creating the greatest alarm, but the presence of their dusky escort disarmed hostile intent, and the white men explained that they only came to trade. In the evening they reached one of the Zuni villages, where they were most hospitably treated, and there rested for some time. They found the Zunis to be a peaceful, industrious, agricultural people, whose proudest boast was that none of their race had ever shed the blood of a white man. [38]

In due course French and company [with no further mention of their Apache escorts] made their way through Navajo territory to the Rio Mancos and the base of the San Juans. It was now mid-October. Their provisions were adequate, their attire was not.

> *Just as they approached the mineral region, the goal of their ambition, and for which they had endured so many hardships and encountered so many dangers, they went into camp one delightful October evening, and after supper lay down under the clear starlit sky. Next morning they awoke to find themselves covered with twelve inches of snow which had fallen during the night. The storm prevailed for five days, when French ordered a retreat to a lower altitude.... When the party set out from Arizona they were provided only with such clothing and blankets as were necessary in that warm climate, hence, being unprepared for such severe weather they suffered intensely from the cold. The direction of their retreat was south, across the Dolores Range, shoveling their way through the drifting snow. They reached the valley of the Animas, a distance of about sixty miles, in the course of ten days of hard work and most laborious travel...*[39]

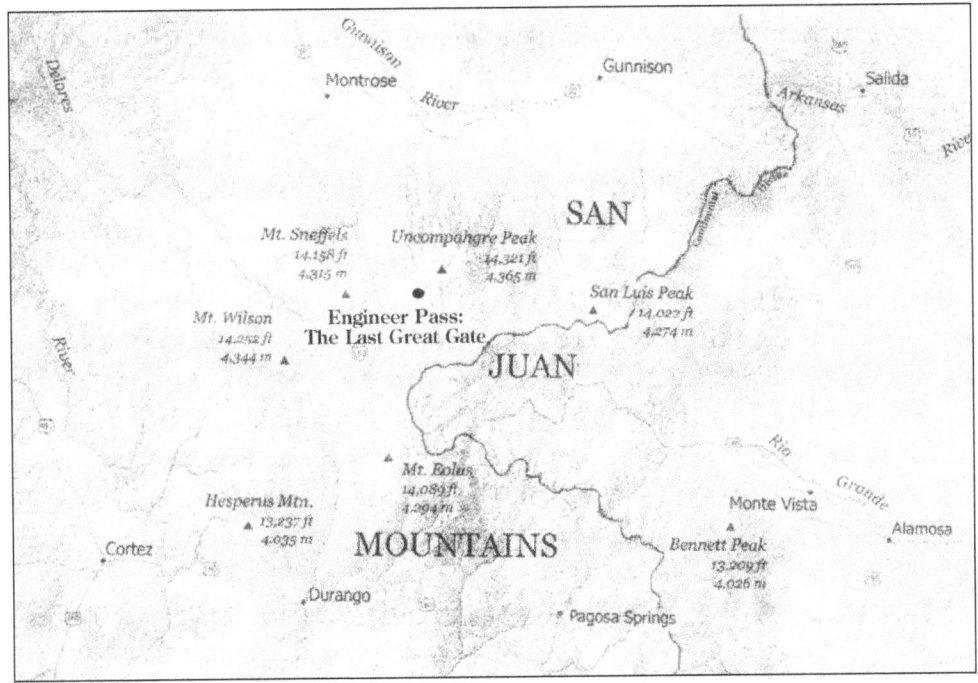

Last Great Gate. Engineer Pass, located a short distance north of Cinnamon and Stony Passes, somehow escaped exploration despite four near-misses. Not even Animas Fork developments spawned curiosity. That would come not from its spring-fed headwaters of Henson Creek that flowed to Lake City, but instead from the creek's Lake City confluence with the Lake Fork of the Gunnison, site of the 1874-75 gold rush that quickly morphed into a silver rush. *(Author)*

French and friends eventually made their way back to civilization and took refuge in Santa Fe and Tierra Amarilla northeast of Abiquiu. Replenishing supplies including tools, guns and ammunition, they prepared for a spring return to the San Juans.

So, too, did a number of other parties planning on prospecting the Animas Valley no longer deemed too risky or too remote to explore. "By late February, 1870 Tierra Amarilla resembled the starting gate at a race track." [40] April 1870 found Adnah and two long-time friends [Johnson and Reese] back in Baker's Park where they had an epiphany that changed everything. According to Nossaman,

> *French and Johnson reminded each other of the potential for vein deposits, and it is almost as if a mutation had occurred in the species overnight. As Bruns [unpublished manuscript] pointed out in one of his more clever passages, the three men were suddenly walking around with their heads up, instead of proceeding "bug-like" to pursue the sparse placer offerings which directed them to keep their heads down. The San Juan was born as a mining district with that mutation.* [41]

With quartz outcrops in plain sight, claims were staked in what became known as Cunningham Gulch and throughout Baker's Park. Notably, the *Little Giant* was one of them. At the end of a short season, all but the hardiest and probably most foolish returned to more hospitable surroundings. French wintered over in Abiquiu where he recruited additional partners with financial resources, and where word of his good fortunes spread quickly. By spring 1871 the rush to the Animas Valley was again in high gear. French with five partners left Santa Fe in May 1871 for Ute territory still considered hostile by way of the upper Rio Grande and across the Divide. To avoid "Indian trouble," the trespassing miners started out "in ceded territory in the San Luis Valley and taking what seemed to be a back door into the high mountain realm not particularly cherished by the Utes." [42] Cresting present-day Stony Pass, French and partners entered Cunningham Gulch June 16, 1871, relocated the *Little Giant*, and on June 20, 1871 began the "first work of lode or vein mining in the upper Animas country." Returning to familiar New Mexico haunts for the winter with impressive ore samples and equally impressive stories, French and partners had little difficulty attracting investors. Another season of development would bring the introduction of steam-powered equipment. It also brought offers for the *Little Giant* that Adnah could not refuse.

On July 19, 1873, the Animas Valley awoke to the shrill scream of the *Little Giant* steam whistle blowing in its steam plant for the first time. Adnah French, fearless and shrewd, a central figure in bringing it and hundreds of pilgrims to the district, "never heard that whistle blow."

The moving force linking the 1860 and 1870 explorations of Baker's Park, French never got out of Santa Fe in the spring of 1873. His reward for years of toil had been too long in coming for an impatient man, and French used his proceeds from the Little Giant sale to drink himself to death, passing away in obscurity and poverty at the residence of a man named Torres in the New Mexican capital on June 19, 1873. [43]

The Ute landlord did not need a steam whistle to wake them up to the impending loss of their homeland. Pre-Civil War concerns gave way to outright alarm as the war-years lull became a distant memory. A council of Ute chiefs along with Native American agent Major Henson had attempted to confront the interlopers in Abiquiu and nip the invasion in the bud. All seemed to end well. Chiefs Ignacio and Sopatah among others could not have been more clear:

They objected to prospecting in the country, but finally gave permission to dig for gold and silver, provided they would not plow up the ground, build cabins nor make fences, and furthermore, they were never to forget that the country belonged to them – the Utes. [44]

But it was too late, even before news of the *Little Giant* spread it was too late. It was too late regarding prospectors, and it was way too late regarding homesteader plows, cabins, and fences. Regarding the Animas watershed, by 1872 hundreds of hardy souls had poured into the region. By 1873, numerous mining districts were organized, three or four hundred prospectors and miners often with families settled in, and thousands of claims were filed. In 1874, after another severe winter, reports of the extent and richness of Animas watershed lodes spread farther afield. Baker's Park, about to become bustling Silverton, was gaining recognition as a bonafide treasure chest. Long-deceased Charles Baker may have been a "hum-bug," but the Park that went by his name was not. Still, as late as 1874-75, getting there was challenging and Henson Canyon remained undefiled despite a number of near-misses.

While routes into the San Juans varied, southern access was the norm until Otto Mears' toll roads opened the upper Lake Fork of the Gunnison valley and Lake City, and the removal of Ute from most of western Colorado opened access through the Gunnison valley from the north. Until then, settlements in New Mexico and the San Luis Valley, and Fort Garland, served as supply depots for expeditions up the Rio Grande and across the Continental Divide at Stony Pass. The upper Lake Fork of the Gunnison valley and Henson Canyon would remain inhospitable and unexplored a while longer.

But Fortress San Juans was losing ground. Its defensive maze was giving up its secrets, and the Ute were giving up their sovereignty. By 1873 yet another treaty would cede their San Juans homeland to the Whites. The upper Animas

NEAR MISSES

Baker's 1860 and 1861 expeditions to the upper Animas River valley, as did all others then and for another decade, bypassed the Henson Creek watershed and Engineer Pass. The 1860-61 "excitement" was the first of four near misses for prospecting Henson Canyon and El Paso Gulch. The second near miss, a decade later in 1871, this time from the west, could have been Adnah French choosing nearby Stony Pass. Instead, it was J. K. Mullins clawing his way over Engineer Pass and struggling down Henson Creek Canyon to the future site of Lake City and points east without sparking further interest in exploration. Reportedly, his journey required weeks to scramble over and around centuries of fallen timber and dense willows. In the process, his prospector instincts probably led him to outcrops worth returning to when better prepared to linger and the Ute were not as threatening, but he failed to follow up on this matter. The third near miss, again from the west, was in 1873 when Eugene Barthoff with two brothers and five others, on a prospecting odyssey beginning in present day Silverton and leading to Lake City, decided on Cinnamon Pass to descend the Lake Fork of the Gunnison instead of following Mullins' track through Henson Creek Canyon. The fourth near miss, again from the east, was Otto Mears' decision to choose the Lake Fork of the Gunnison/Cinnamon Pass route for his Saguache-San Juan Toll Road to Animas Forks and Silverton. Begun in 1873 with investments by Isaac Gotthelf and Enos Hotchkiss, Mears completed a rough road the following year with additional investment from others. Further improvements in 1875 addressed "the excrations [sic] of nearly every teamster who drove over it." [45]

River Valley, once their exclusive summer camp, was quickly becoming home to the dreaded miner and settler equipped with boilers and mills and all manner of provisions. High above the valley floor, Mears' toll road over Cinnamon Pass would soon rival the so-called wagon road over Stony Pass. Still, Engineer Pass was ignored. Granted, it was undiscernible from the valley floor, scarcely a shadow along the ridgeline, and barely accessible from east or west by the faintest of Ute trails. Why contend with rugged Henson Canyon when Cinnamon Pass and Otto Mears' Lake Fork toll road, a short distance to the south, could "comfortably" accommodate wagons and coaches? And not to be underestimated, treaties not withstanding, anxieties still lingered regarding renegade Ute. Why risk that?

The San Luis and Gunnison Valleys were another matter. They were easier to access, and in the case of the San Luis, easier to settle. Beginning with the Spanish, inroads were made. In the post-Civil War era, which coincided with one of several "Ute-accommodation" eras, both valleys were ripe for development. While Charles Baker, Adnah French and men of their ilk hurried back to Colorado's mountains in search of treasure, homesteaders like Tom Ashley and his ilk drove cattle and family wagons into Colorado valleys in search of a new homeland of their own.

Plows, cabins, and fences—"homesteader" in graphic terms—depicted the face of the greater enemy to Ignacio and Sopatah. Unmistakable even then, the post-Civil War resumption of westering included more homesteaders than treasure-seekers. Unlike treasure-seekers, they were not inclined to move on. The prairie was filling with them. Colorado's Front Range was filling with them. The mountain valleys were filling with them, the Tom Ashley family a case in point.

According to Daisy Ashley, his daughter-in-law writing from Saguache, Colorado in 1944, the family journey west had its fair share of trail drama. Tom Ashley had a good tenor voice and was the official song leader until the others got tired of "When You and I Were Young, Maggie." When their train reached the present site of Denver, remembered as a settlement and trading post of some two dozen log cabins and tents, Tom herded their work oxen and other livestock on what is now the State Capitol grounds.

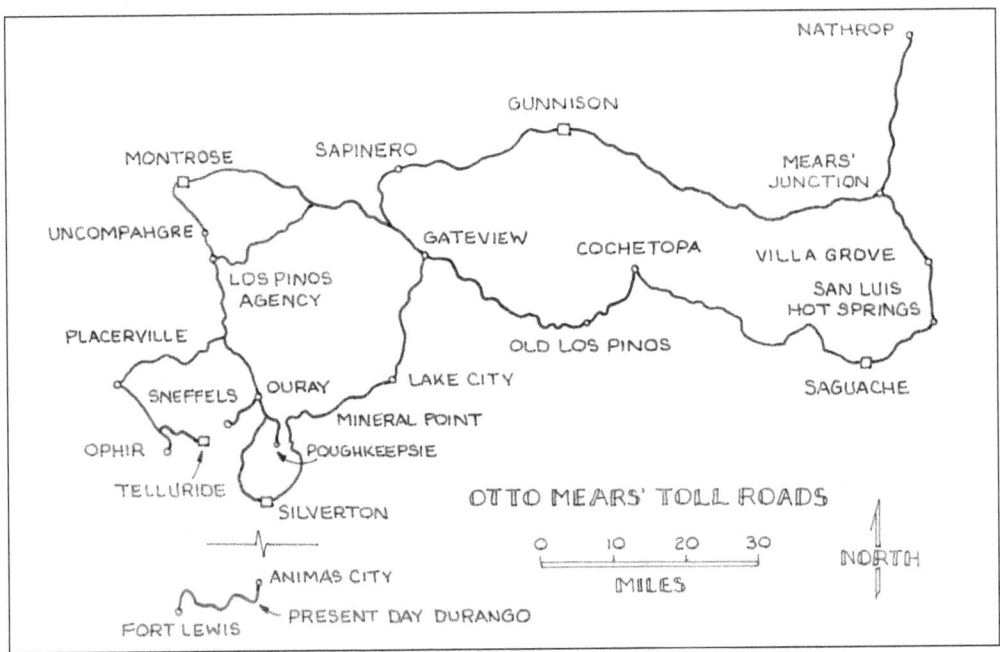

Otto Mears' Toll Roads. Improving access to mines and mining camps throughout the San Juans was critical to the vitality of the region. Mears' toll roads followed by narrow gauge railroads helped improve mine profits and the sustainability of supply depots. Even so, low-grade ores doomed most mines and mining towns alike. *(Courtesy of Western Reflections Publishing)*

TOM ASHLEY [46]

Native American hostilities, in particular war among the Plains Indians and mountain skirmishes with the Ute, always taken seriously, boiled over once again in the wake of the Civil War and in the midst of a new surge of westering. Daisy H. Ashley, in 1944 Saguache, Colorado, wrote about her father-in-law's journey from Kentucky to the San Luis Valley, and his life as a nineteenth century emigrant. Tom Ashley's colorful story is especially rich with the authenticity that embraced an entire generation of San Juans pioneers. Imagine the sense of adventure, savor the fresh dreams of the American and foreign emigres eager to leave European serfdom and Civil War battlefields behind.

Smoke of the Civil War had hardly cleared away in the spring of 1865, when long and slowly moving wagon trains headed westward across the plains from St. Joseph, Missouri, and in one of them was the Samuel Ashley family. There were seven hundred men, women and children and three hundred and sixty-five vehicles in this train, and although it was attacked by Indians several times, it escaped serious mishap during the three months trip. This train, like all the others at that time, was guarded day and night by a company of soldiers. When they camped at night, the settlers' vehicles formed a circle, then the extra heavy and very large freight wagons encircled these, thus affording considerable protection to the people. Their livestock grazed nearby and the younger men and boys took turns helping the soldiers guard them against the Indians' frequent attempts to stampede the herds, and thus make off with fine horses and cattle. During the night-herding the men sang almost continually in order to keep the cattle quiet and also to scare away wild beasts as well as the Indians.

The Samuel Ashley family was moving to the San Luis Valley because of the glowing account of the Valley given them by a son-in-law who, with many others, came through here on his return to Missouri from the California gold rush. Driving ox teams, they entered the Valley over Mosca Pass and settled at Fort Garland where a company of soldiers guarded the settlers against raiding parties. During the ensuing three years Tom farmed at Fort Garland and San Luis and also worked at a saw mill; then in the fall of 1868 the family moved to Saguache.

Tom Ashley and Daisy's command of details concerning his early years in Colorado may be fuzzy, but the overall picture they paint is clear. Saguache was as frontier a settlement as one could imagine. Daisy reports that the first houses built were adobe bricks with walls three to four feet thick. Equally thick circular walls also surrounded some homesteads for additional protection. Chief Ouray, friendly toward Whites, guaranteed their safety against attacks

I wandered today to the hills Maggie
To watch the scene below
The creek and the creaking old mill Maggie
Where we used to long long ago.

The green growth is gone from the hills Maggie
Where first the daisies spring
The creaking old mill is still Maggie
Since you and I were young.

Oh they say that I'm feeble with age Maggie
My steps are much slower than then
My face is a well written page Maggie
And time all along was the pen.

Oh they say we have outlived our time Maggie
As dated as songs that we've sung
But to me, you're as fair as you were Maggie
When you and I were young.

Comfort to Man and Beast. Emigrants crossing the post-Civil War prairie continued to face many dangers not least of which were hostile war parties. Standing guard over wagons and livestock, Tom Ashley for one sang these melancholy verses to sooth the nerves of his compatriots and his cattle. (*Wikipedia Commons*)

by roving hostile bands. Tom the Tenor—he did have a good voice and remained fond of singing—homesteaded a short distance east of Saguache with wife and children for the remainder of his life. Described by those who knew him as a generous and lively "box dinners" bidder at church picnics, and "the Prince of the San Luis Valley" for reasons never shared, he died of measles on June 26, 1921 after a four-day illness. From a few adobe citadels to Otto Mears supply depot for the Lake City excitement in 1875, from the still possible danger of Ute attack to their Colorado expulsion a decade later, Tom Ashley weathered it all.

Ovando Hollister, usually as sharp a contemporary eyewitness as one can hope to find, explains well the battlefield the Ashley family was pleased to leave behind, and the battlefield they endured ahead. He compares the clash of northerner and southerner to the clash of White man and Red man yet to run its course.

In large measure, the economic collapse of 1857 ignited the fuse on both clashes by setting "many adventurous spirits in the then West peering into the obscurity beyond them for a new field of enterprise."[47] The competing passions of the Civil War that erupted and the battle over the Plains that followed fundamentally shaped the nature of Western development for the next two decades. Writing from personal experience what in present times are harsh words, Hollister's 1867 vernacular expressed the westering sentiment and sense of "manifest destiny" of Americans and foreign emigres alike:

> *Thus was the last dreadful struggle between the white and red man boldly braved by this handful of pioneers, for what? For the* <u>chance</u> *of finding an habitable land further west. That struggle we have just fairly begun, and no one doubts that it must go on to the extinction of the savages, involving great sufferings on our part, of course. Grant beat the rebellion with hard knocks, and perhaps gave man for man; having more men he was enabled to wear it out. It is not a bad illustration of our conflict with the savages. Both were inevitable, and both must end in the same way. The Government and the rebellion were incompatible on the same ground; so are our people and the savages. That was a life and death struggle, ended by the death of the rebellion: this is a life and death struggle, to be ended by the death of the savage—and the sooner it can be finished the better.*[48]

By most accounts, out of all the mining regions in Colorado, the San Juans held the greatest promise. Part of this sentiment was based on decades of rumors, myths, and occasional evidence of actual gold and silver. Part of this sentiment was based on the allure of the unknown and wishful thinking. The Civil War siphoned off labor and interest. The Plains Indians disrupted mass migration, transportation and Front Range development. Ute war parties, despite the efforts of Chief Ouray, threatened safe access to their Fortress San Juans homeland, otherwise considered by emigrants a treasure trove free for the taking. The Colorado "treasure trove" birthed as a gold district would mature into a silver region, but not without further conflict, notwithstanding several thousand settlers like Tom Ashley in the San Luis Valley.

Despite ridicule from critics who remembered the 1860-61 fiascos, by 1870 mining and permanent settlement had gained a toehold in the upper Animas Valley. William Byers, *Rocky Mountain News* booster-in-chief, who had written in 1870 that the San Juans was a "hoax or worse," was an enthusiastic convert by 1872. In his customary style, he praised the region. "Possibilities point to a busy and exciting season," he crowed in his May 18 edition. "All will be bustle, hurry, noise, excitement and confusion."[49] Not even Byers could have imagined what the Animas would look like two or three years later.

Territorial Defense. Nomadic peoples were no less territorial than settlers. Nor was the end of the Civil War the end of disrupting westering. Mass migration to the mountain west eventually led to increased violence and open warfare with indigenous peoples including the mountain Ute. *(Dunn, 1886)*

Herein lay the root cause of the "Ute question." Little by little, the more prospectors and miners encroached on Ute treaty lands, the more restless Ute dissidents became. The U.S. Indian Bureau took up for the Utes. Colorado newspapers took up for "oncoming Whites." "We can but regret that this decision is adverse to the development of so desirable a region," reported the *Central City Register*. "Our opinion exactly!" added the April 20, 1870 *Rocky Mountain News*.

The classic colonist/indigenous peoples conflict was rejoined. Colorado newspapers "demanded" that the region be opened for development that benefited the state and the nation. The Ute, and for the most part the Federal Government in Washington, thought otherwise. In 1872, the U.S. Congress created a commission to negotiate a settlement. Failing the task, a second commission in September 1873 succeeded. The Utes agreed to sell four million acres of mountain in exchange for $25,000 a year. Congress slow-walked ratifying the agreement until early summer of the following year. A resumption in hostilities did not take that long.

The Utes believed they had the right to hunt in the mountains, as they had for centuries, and the Whites believed otherwise. Furthermore, Ute land

TRADE GOODS [AND BADS]

Indian troubles pre-date Christopher Columbus's arrival in a world new to him. New to the Indian at that time were White Man diseases and technologies, both deadly and death dealing. South and Central America aside, North American indigenous populations had no natural defenses against the likes of measles, cholera and small-pox which swept across the country mid-century. [No respecter of persons, disease also killed President Polk shortly after leaving office.] Nor did the indigenous popula-tions harbor natural inhibitions regarding the White Man's alcohol, tobacco and all manner of weaponry [especially the horse] and domestic goods. The consequences of these circumstances played out over the next 400 years with the annihilation of one indigenous culture after another. In many cases, the final desperate act was a futile war resulting in Indian reservations for those who survived and open lands for pioneers and settlers. In the case of the American experiment, the seaboard tribes were first to be rolled back to the interior, the Rocky Mountain Ute among the last to be removed to reservations. Leapfrogging both were pathfinders to the Pacific.

In 1775, reportedly the Spanish explorer Bruno Heceta brought the curse of smallpox to Oregon. Epidemics swept the Pacific Northwest in 1781 and 1830. According to Will Bagley citing John McLoughlin, before the mass overland emigra-tion in the 1840s and 1850s ran their course, an estimated ninety percent of the Native American population "had been swept away. For some groups, the destruc-tion was total, or nearly so." [50]

Similar accounts of death-dealing diseases commonly accompanied American expansion from the Atlantic seaboard across the Appalachians, Ohio and Mississippi river valleys, and the Great Plains. At the same time, other White Man gifts, as was the case with their own handicrafts, were gladly accepted and traded coast-to-coast along a network of trails whose origins were lost in the ancient past. Curses accom-panying commerce were unavoidable. Will Bagley explains:

> For centuries, Pacific Coast dentalium shells had moved far inland from one tribe to another. Southwestern turquoise made its way north, west, and east, and skillfully crafted baskets and pottery were appreciated in villages far from the peoples who made them. Traders brought salt to those who had none in their lands, and buffalo hunters exchanged fine robes and meat with tribes that raised squash, beans, and maize. . . .

> "We did not know there were other people besides the Indian until about one hundred winters ago, when some men with white faces came to our country," Chief Joseph of the Nez Perce said of his people's first encounter with French traders. "They brought many things with them to trade for furs and skins. They brought tobacco, which was new to us. They brought guns with flint stones on them, which frightened our women and children. Our people could not talk with these white-face men, but they used signs which all people understand." [51]

still surrounded much of the San Juans. Neither side was truly satisfied, and the racial conflict that underlay much of the conflict still festered. The Rocky Mountain News *warned in a bold headline: "NOTICE TO ALL PERSONS GOING TO THE SAN JUAN MINES:" do not "trespass upon any portion of the Ute Reservation by passing over or settling upon same." (April 23, 1874)* [52]

With notable exceptions, trade as opposed to warfare characterized relationships among Native American nations and Europeans well into the nineteenth century. Often the best response of prospectors accosted by Ute warriors—assuming they had an opportunity to speak at all—was claiming they were there to trade. By the mid-1860s, this dynamic had changed. The preservation of the Union unleashed a surge of investment, westward migration of dispirited and dislocated Yankees and Confederates, and a renewed flood of European and Asian immigrants. Railroad construction across the plains and interior western mountains resumed, first "standard" and then "narrow gauge," and along their right-of-ways, new pioneer farms and villages spread outward from every section station.

Plains Indian culture was not threatened by war parties or U.S. Army troopers as much as by buffalo hunters and railroad agents eager to profit from the millions of acres the U.S. Government awarded them along with their transcontinental rights-of-way. Enough was enough. Détente in the interests of trade, facilitated by an ill-defined balance of power among tribes and White men, no longer could be sustained. Decimated by disease, disenfranchised by development, millennial cultures in disarray, open warfare on the plains and in the Fortress San Juans mineral belt was unavoidable. Uncle Dick Wootton remembered those post-Civil War years: "The influx of Whites into the Territory [in the 1860s] led the Indians to believe that their country would soon be overrun and they looked upon every immigrant as a trespasser. The Cheyennes, a band which the mountain men had generally been on good terms with, became for some reason or other particularly incensed against the settlers." [53]

Other tribes in the region followed suit. Those who once were friendly to the emigrant or warred with neighboring tribes over ancestral hunting grounds formed a most effective albeit informal, fluid alliance and strategy. The Comanche, Cheyenne, Kiowa, Arapahoe, Apache, and Shoshone took turns befriending or battling the Whites. While one band marauded, the others traded, and so it went. Passage from the States across the "Great American Desert" to the Southwest, and Colorado was increasingly hazardous at best. For those who survived and chose to pursue their fortunes in the mountains, in the ancestral homeland of the Ute, their lives were no less at risk into the 1880s.

Much is made of the peaceful Ute relinquishing ever more of their mountain redoubts even as the nature of the White invasion changed from

WORTH FIGHTING FOR

The survival of the North American bison herd, therefore the survival of the Plains Indians, was a major determining factor in Native American decisions to cast aside peaceful coexistence with the Whites. Will Bagley paints a grim picture: The bison

> ... once ranged from Pennsylvania to Florida, west to Oregon and California, and from Mexico north to the Yukon. Not long before overland emigration began, the range of Bison bison extended from the valleys of the Great Salt Lake and the Snake River to the Missouri. Weather and predators exterminated them west of the Sierra Nevadas and the Cascade Range, while hunting and farming had the same effect east of the Missouri River. During the 1830s or early 1840s, the bison disappeared from the Salt Lake Valley and the Snake River plain shortly after the arrival of firearms, or perhaps following a devastating winter storm. The diminishing range of the great beasts was a harbinger of changes to come. By 1840 few Americans had ever seen a bison, whose range was now reduced to the plains between the Missouri River and the Rocky Mountains. [54]

Plains Indians took notice. Even the mountain Ute lifestyle included buffalo hunting and trade on the plains.

Worth Fighting Over. The transcontinental railroad not only brought more emigrants west, it hastened the near extinction of the buffalo and the Plains Indians' way of life. The unmistakable consequence was the outbreak of western Indian Wars. *(Library of Congress)*

explorer to trapper to trader to prospector, miner and settler. "Peaceful Ute" was a misnomer. Reluctant to surrender their High Country, the Ute were adamant concerning their more temperate pastoral valleys. They had accommodated for a time trapping beaver, searching for valuable minerals, even surveying routes for wagons and railroads, but there was little doubt that these developments were leading to Ute displacement. Despite treaties, the first in 1868 followed by the Brunot Treaty [Agreement] ratified in 1874, and Federal Government Indian Agencies administering allotments and mediating disputes, risk of Indian attack persisted. Almost certainly, Tom Ashley continued singing "When You and I Were Young, Maggie" long after he settled his family on the outskirts of Saguache. It would be long after his arrival there that the risk of Indian attack was a distant memory. In fact, it would not be until well after the end of war with the Plains Indians and the 1879 Meeker Massacre, no laughing matters for sure, that the contested prairies and Colorado frontier could rest in peace.

Notes—Chapter Nine: The Last Great Gate

1 Ashley, Daisy H., "William Thomas Ashley," *Pioneers of the San Juan Country*, Vol. II,, pgs. 32-36, [Tom Ashley sang the only song he knew, "When You and I were Young, Maggie," to calm nerves of livestock and men as they crossed the post-Civil War prairie under threat of Indian attacks, and settled in the Ute threatened San Luis Valley.]

2 Probably the most accurate and complete account of Charles Baker and his adventures in the San Juans is found in Allen Nossaman's *Many More Mountains*, Vol. I, Chapter 3.

3 Sprague, Marshall, *The Great Gates*, pg. 178.

4 Nossaman, Allen, *Many More Mountains*, Vol. I, pg. 37.

5 Sprague, pg. 177. [Southern sentiments, especially among Georgians, were strong. John Gregory, for example, reportedly claimed that his diggings belonged to the slave states by right of discovery.] [Also see: Decker, Sarah Platt, *Pioneers of the San Juan Country*, Volume III, pg. 134.]

6 Sprague, pgs. 18-23. [Nineteenth century trappers and traders were certainly courageous and industrious, and they may have been alert to gold float, but gold float and the furs they sought rarely shared habitats. Likewise, American military expeditions would have been keen to map mineral finds were it not for higher priorities such as finding feasible routes through the Rocky Mountains for military wagon roads and eventually the nation's transcontinental railroads. Both of these groups were adventurers, but it would take a bonafide gold rush to qualify men to be Argonauts.]

7 Ibid., pgs. 179-180.

8 Becker, Cynthia S. and P. David Smith, *The Life and Times of Lafayette Head*, pg. 125.

9 Ibid., pgs. 133-134.

10 Nossaman, pg. 42.

11 Sprague, pg. 180.

12 Nossaman, pg. 42.

13 Ibid., pgs. 69-70.

14 Hall, Frank, *History of the State of Colorado*, Vol. II, pgs. 192-193. [Hall credits Kellogg for this account: "The true story of the Baker expedition is about as follows, as gleaned mainly from S. B. Kellogg of Lake City."]

15 Ibid., pg. 193.

16 Ibid., pgs. 193-194.

[17] Ibid., pg. 195.

[18] Nossaman, pg. 70.

[19] Ibid., pg. 46. [Refer to pgs. 46-74 for comprehensive treatment of this topic.]

[20] Ibid.

[21] Ibid., pgs. 46-47.

[22] Ibid., pg. 47.

[23] Ibid.

[24] Hall, pgs. 194-195.

[25] Nossaman, pg. 61.

[26] Ibid.

[27] Ibid., pg. 69.

[28] Ibid., pgs. 73-74.

[29] Ibid., pg. 74.

[30] Hall, pg. 196. [According to Hall, White and the other man escaped on the raft, but only White survived the tumultuous trip through the canyon. Washed ashore in southwest Utah, White was nursed to health and turned up in Lake City in May 1877. He later took up residence somewhere in southwest Colorado. Hall states "he was then about thirty-five years of age, a plain, matter-of-fact, practical and adventurous man. There is not a shadow of doubt about his wonderful adventures and his marvelous escape through the awful canons of the Colorado."]

[31] Nossaman, pg. 74.

[32] Ibid., pgs. 74-75.

[33] Hall, pg. 196.

[34] Ibid., pgs. 197-198.

[35] Nossaman, pg. 81.

[36] Hall, pg. 199.

[37] Ibid., pgs. 199-200.

[38] Ibid., pg. 200.

[39] Ibid., pgs. 201-202.

[40] Nossaman, pg. 84.

[41] Ibid., pg. 89.

[42] Ibid., pg. 95. [Further testimony to natural San Juan's defenses is Nossaman's description of the 1871 route from New Mexico settlements to Baker's Park: "It cannot be said with absolute certainty, but it appears that this was the first time the Rio Grande was used as an avenue to or from the San Juan Mountains by a party of white men who were neither lost nor trying to get somewhere in desperation. In this context, Bruns implies in his manuscript that this party named the key landmarks along the route....Certainly this party, or members of one of the half-dozen other groups assumed to have taken this same route in 1871, were responsible for most, if not all, of the names we associate with this relatively isolate area today." "The first 60 miles of the Spaniards' Great River of the North is an enticing gateway into the complex mountains from which it gathers its waters—a seductive pathway that lures the traveler farther and farther west with gentle country only to confront that same traveler with the ultimate reality that he still must cross the Continental Divide on one of the most punishing summits along its entire course." "The men were passing through country that was highly familiar to the Utes, and well traveled by them. The significant difference was that the white men were traveling in a direction the Indians seldom traveled, toward a destination that had been of little interest to them."]

[43] Ibid., pg. 127.

[44] Hall, pg. 202.

[45] Tucker, E. F., *Otto Mears and the San Juans*, pg. 34.

[46] Ashley, pgs. 32-33.

[47] Hollister, Ovando J., *The Mines of Colorado*, pg. 7.

[48] Ibid., pg. 11.

[49] *Rocky Mountain News*, May 18, 1872.

[50] Bagley, Will, *Overland West*, Vol. I, pg. 19. [Cites Lawrence, "The Indian Council in the Valley of the Walla-Walla, 1855"; and Parker, "Journal of an Exploring Tour, 1778."]

[51] Ibid., pg. 20.

[52] Smith, Duane A., *The Trail of Gold and Silver*, pg. 85.

[53] Wootton, Richens, *Uncle Dick Wootton*, pg. 263.

[54] Hollister, Ovando J., *The Mines of Colorado*, pg. 7.

CHAPTER 10

No Man's Land

Land, water, and grass. It always came down to that. On the prairie the
health of the buffalo herds were at stake, thus the health of the prairie
tribes. In the Colorado mountains and valleys, particularly the San Juans,
the health of the deer and elk herds were at stake, thus the health of
the Ute. Always contested, first among tribes and then with the Two-
Legged, the matter was settled once and for all by 1880. By 1880 the
routes west and Colorado's mountains and valleys welcomed all comers.
Neither Red nor White, no man could claim eminent domain.[1]

Robert Edmund Strahorn's generation fought the final battles over contested
prairies and mountains and his calling was telling others about it. He was a
savvy, self-made journalist. Of equal interest was Strahorn himself. In some ways
he was another Wheelbarrow McGrew or A.D. Richardson when it came to
humble beginnings and living what he wrote. Like their colorful lives and writings, Strahorn conveyed meaning far deeper than the scenes and circumstances
he described. He deserves heightened attention.

Gifted in this way despite dropping out of school at age ten, at eighteen he
was a journalist first in Denver, then a roaming correspondent serving large eastern newspapers as well as the *Rocky Mountain News*. In 1877, he was filing dispatches from battles with the Sioux he participated in with rifle in hand alongside
U.S. Army troopers. In 1880, he was filing dispatches from Gunnison, at that time
a late-blooming boomtown on the San Juans frontier. With the "Ute expulsion"
underway, Strahorn's journalistic instincts persuaded him that *Silver World* claims
that Lake City was the heart of the "San Juans excitement" needed to be challenged.
In explaining why Gunnison was late to the party, he unwittingly fulfilled a broader
purpose. He documented more of the character traits that helped both Lake City
and Gunnison thrive, traits that helped the San Juans and the greater West thrive.

By the 1870s, the mineral wealth of the Ute San Juans homeland was both
irrefutable and irresistible. Nevertheless, unlike the Lake City region, more remote
but quickly occupied, settling the Gunnison Valley sixty miles to the north was
more challenging. The coveted site was an ancestral Ute hunting ground, one

of their best and last seasonal camps, sure to be more fiercely contested than San Luis camps long-ago lost and Animas camps about to be. Despite straddling established routes linking both sides of the Continental Divide, within easy travel from Abe Lee's California Gulch, thriving Leadville, and Denver, the large number of Ute that camped there each summer was dangerous if not outright deadly for the White Man. Prospectors and especially settlers tended to give the valley a wide berth, and roadbuilders like Mears engineered less troublesome albeit more rugged southerly routes to the upper Animas Valley.

The Ute considered Lake City little more than a remote mining camp, more or less within the Ute tolerance zone for interlopers, but nascent Gunnison was another matter. It had the makings of a major commercial center, and the certain demise of another Ute tradition. The Brunot Treaty did not help much in this regard. It's critical "line in the sand" expressed as a "meridian" ran a few miles west of present-day Gunnison. Latitude and longitude meant nothing to the Ute—the Continental Divide was a boundary they understood well. Correspondent Strahorn explains the contested "no man's land" in the following series of excerpts:

Eyewitness. Self-taught western journalist, Robert Strahorn did his best work while immersed in his subject matter. He fought and wrote about the Plains Indian wars, and about the San Juans' Ute resistance to "Two-Legged" incursions until they were expelled from Colorado in 1880. He exemplified his "young America" generation. *(Wikipedia)*

> [Strahorn:] *In the early days of Rocky Mountain exploration this whole region was vaguely defined as "the Grand River Country," its noblest stream, now called Gunnison, being then known as the South Fork of the Grand. Our earliest tangible knowledge of the geography and probable utility comes from Governor Wm. Gilpin, who in 1845, a mere stripling, returned from Oregon to St. Louis, crossing its entire length from west to east. Crossing Southern Utah by one of the old Spanish trails, his course then lay through the valleys of the South Fork of the Grand and Uncompahgre rivers, thence over Cochetopa Pass, at the southeastern rim of the Gunnison country, and thence to Bent's Old Fort on the Arkansas. He was enthusiastic in his description of the valleys and the country generally ... [despite being] pursued at intervals for 100 miles by savages...*

The interval between 1845 and 1853 only records vague stories from trap-
pers and Mormons, the former boasting of the region as an ideal game-field
and of the riches in certain inaccessible gulches, and the latter taking care to
let the world know only what dangers were threatened by savages. This last
claim was well supported, or the Mormon crime speciously covered, when in
1853 Captain Gunnison's name was given the region at the expense of his
life.

While exploring in this vicinity that year for a Pacific railroad route he
was killed; history says by Indians, but subsequent developments point to the
Mormons as the murderers. In 1854 the indomitable old "Pathfinder," General
Fremont, passed over nearly the same country from east to west [on his fifth
expedition], but even his glowing tributes to the beauty and richness of the
region did not serve to bridge the seven-year gap which ensued with talks of
genuine pioneering. [2]

ROBERT EDMUND STRAHORN [3]

Robert Edmund Strahorn was born near Bellefonte, Centre County, Pennsylvania, on May 15, 1852. He spent the first four years of his life in Pennsylvania, and was then taken by his parents to a farm in northern Illinois. Strahorn's school opportunities ended at age ten. Instead, he sold papers on the streets, and for five years worked at learning the printer's trade in Sedalia, Missouri. At age eighteen he was advised by a doctor to move to the Rocky Mountains for his health. In 1870, he moved to Denver. He tried working as a cowboy until a bucking bronco inflicted a lifelong injury. In 1871, he secured a position on the *Rocky Mountain News*, working as a reporter, editor and correspondent until 1877.

At the age of twenty-four, Strahorn signed on with General George Crook's "Big Horn and Yellowstone Expedition" as a war correspondent for the *New York Times*, *Chicago Tribune*, and the *Rocky Mountain News*. Embedded among the troopers, Strahorn fought and reported for over a year on the events of the war with the Sioux. "I insisted that I was going in to fight. It was my business as a correspondent to get the news, and I couldn't think of getting it from the rear." According to General Crook, "Strahorn worked as well with his rifle as with his pen." He was commended for distinguished bravery and gallantry in action against hostile Indians during the Great Sioux War at the "Horsemeat March, Battle of Powder River, Battle of the Rosebud, Battle of Slim Buttes, Dull Knife Fight, and Battle of Wolf Mountain." He also reported the "Battle of the Little Big Horn" and witnessed the surrender of Crazy Horse at Fort Robinson on May 6, 1877. Strahorn summarized his role in the "Great Sioux War" this way:

In a dozen engagements in which I participated there were only a couple of weeks

Prospecting parties spilling over from California Gulch did pass through the Elk and Collegiate ranges. They named Washington Gulch, Taylor Park, Rentz's Gulch, and Union Park near the head of the Slate River. Prospecting was profitable, and under normal circumstances would have spawned a stampede, but sadly for twelve Argonauts in particular this did not occur. Riding along the Washington Gulch they were killed in 1860 by Ute. In the following few pages of lengthy Strahorn quotes we glean a sense of why the Gunnison valley would be late to the San Juans rush.

[Strahorn:] This wholesale massacre, which gave the gloomy side defile the name of Dead Man's Gulch, sent a thrill of terror through every incoming prospector. The outrage was magnified each time its story was repeated, and the result was an almost entire abandonment of the country by the Whites. Not even the stories of "pound diggings," of golden bullets that the Indians used, and of the famous "Snow-Blind Gulch" along the Cochetopa where it

of real fighting, while the pursuit of the Indians to gain that result involved over a year of continuous and most arduous hunting for them, the various marches totaling about 4,000 miles. Much of this was accomplished in blizzards, in far below-zero temperatures, without tents or adequate bedding, alternating with blistering and famishing lack of water. Most of it was fatiguing and monotonous in the extreme, and a lot of it on half and quarter rations, some of it only horse meat, supplied by our worn-out and dying horses. [4]

Robert married Carrie Adell "Dell" Green, the daughter of a prominent Illinois physician and surgeon, on September 19, 1877. Within a week Jay Gould offered him a job promoting the interests of his Union Pacific Railroad. Strahorn accepted with the understanding that his new bride could accompany him on all his travels. His "Indian-fighter" days were over, but risk taking was not. Both journalists and adventurers, Dell and "Pard," her name for Robert, traveled the West for six years by stage, train, steamboat, horseback, and pack train writing books and newspaper articles extolling the attractions and opportunities "Out West." It was during this phase of his very long and productive life that Strahorn's attention was drawn to the San Juans and the Gunnison country.

Strahorn made and lost at least three fortunes. He did well with business ventures in the Northwest, but at age seventy-five had lost his real estate investments in San Francisco in the Great Depression. In the late 1930s and early 1940s, still an adventurer with undying faith in the "New West," pursued mining ventures in Oregon and Idaho. On March 31, 1944, he died at the age of ninety-two in San Francisco. His Spokane newspaper obituary read in part, Robert E. Strahorn "was a colorful figure of the Old West, remembered here as a railroad and town builder and early-day newspaperman." [5]

was currently believed two miners whip-sawed boards for flumes and washed out a pound of gold each per day, and finally, when the snows of 1862 fell, becoming snow-blind they perished an easy prey to savages or storm, not even these lured the most daring in the then populous gulches of Central Colorado to exploration.

[According to young Strahorn, in fact contradicting himself, others did risk the landlord's wrath.]

[Strahorn:] A few other faithful ones, however, remained, fortified themselves in Washington Gulch, living almost wholly for months at a time on game and fish, and were harassed as probably intruders deserved to be, by renegade Utes. In 1863 three men, whose names, I am sorry to say, have passed from history, still "held the fort," and with such rude sluice-boxes as they could fashion by hand, made from $0 to $20 per day. These placers have been worked almost constantly, under all sorts of discouragements, with fair results ever since. Rifle went hand in hand with the shovel, and the skeletons often exhumed in these days of peace indicate many a thrilling chapter of unwritten history.

Developments in quartz mining [not to be confused with placer "mining"] date back to the summer of 1872 when George and Lewis Waite, two old California Gulch miners, crossed the mountains to see what could be found on the western slope. They passed over 60 miles of mineral country, failing to detect what have since developed into some of the finest gold and silver quartz districts of the Gunnison, and hardly called a halt until they reached Rock Creek, an important tributary of Roaring Fork of Grand River. They were encouraged by long-since abandoned surface-diggings, and soon discovered an enormous vein of gold and silver bearing quartz...

A small band of prospectors from Denver and Golden, headed by Jim Brennon, also entered the Rock Creek district in 1872, and their reports resulted in the first organized attempt at occupying the land in 1873, when Dr. John Parsons, Professor Sylvester Richardson and thirty picked mountaineers, including an assayer, smelter, geologist and botanist, entered from Denver. Machinery for testing and reducing ore on a small scale, was taken along. This necessitated wagon transportation, and the only practicable route was via Sagauche and Los Pinos Agency, at the southeastern boundary of the Gunnison country. The Utes had some ten years before exchanged San Luis Valley for about all of Colorado lying west of the 107th meridian, and had the Whites been protected in their rights no trouble would have ensued from their going as far west as the present site of Gunnison City. The agency itself was located twenty miles east of Indian soil, but General Charles Adams, then in charge, said the expedition could only go by permission of the Utes. A heated controversy and a tie vote were finally settled by Ouray in favor of the Whites. This was undoubtedly the turning point in Gunnison's history, all praise to Ouray for remnants of the expedition made valuable discoveries of gold, silver, coal, iron, copper, lead, & c. (sic), and more than this, let the outside world know of their success.

In March, 1874, a colony was formed in Denver to settle upon agricultural lands in the Valley, and in the winter following twenty persons, all told, were scattered for thirty miles along Gunnison and Tomichi valleys, while the mining districts contained a still smaller showing on account of the San Juan stampede…The county and town of Gunnison were organized in 1876, but not until late in 1879, when prospectors fresh from Leadville and San Juan found rich gold and silver ores, and what they called carbonates at the Head of Quartz Creek, near the present site of Pitkin, at the head of Tomichi River, and in other localities, did the region attract the attention it deserved. In the spring of 1879 the grand influx began…At the height of these developments last fall came the Ute outbreak, the Thornburgh and Meeker massacres, and for weeks during the last working season at these great altitudes scarcely a day passed that did not witness some act of Indian deviltry in sight of the various mining camps, such as setting fire to the valuable forests, stealing horses or even killing a straggling prospector. Scarcely a man was to be found at many of the best camps when winter set in, and there were not adequate supplies for even the few who had the courage to remain.

[Not exactly out of an abundance of caution, development of Gunnison country resources languished until the Ute matter was resolved. Lake City labored under no such concerns. Some sixty miles from future Gunnison up the Lake Fork of the Gunnison River, Lake City sprouted almost overnight from a few dozen 1874 prospectors to a mining camp to a bustling settlement by 1875. Unlike Gunnison, the Ute were not particularly fond of the Lake Fork routes into the upper valley, preferring instead more southerly passes and trails leading to their Los Pinos Agency. Relinquishing the upper Lake Fork watershed did not come without isolated bloodshed, but Lake City became a formidable foe overnight, and in any event, the mountain ranges to the west would check further advances. No doubt the "formidable foe" rationale was persuasive, in any event after spring 1874 it was too late to act. As for reliance on their natural allies, San Juan's weather and terrain, to stem the tide, that too was a miscalculation. The Lake City basecamp soon shrank the San Juans Fortress to its final redoubt, the Henson Canyon castle-keep, and within a year that was no longer sacrosanct. Gunnison was another matter, a matter the 1875 Ute clearly understood and Strahorn's 1880 observations confirmed. At stake in the Gunnison Valley was the utter annihilation of the Ute way of life.]

[Strahorn:] A strong force of Uncompahgre Utes camped last summer [1879] on the site of Gunnison, their tepees now being replaced by some 300 houses, with a population of 1,200 or more. A number of these structures are now occupied with stocks of goods worth $40,000 to $85,000 each, from which sales are made to the extent of $10,000 to $30,000 per month each.... A $15,000 courthouse, $20,000 hotel and $7,000 public schoolhouse, besides several churches and excellent business blocks in course of erection, are a few of the surprises in this three-months-old town; but the strangest of all are real estate values. The lot occupied by the Bank of Gunnison, which cost $100 last fall, is now worth $1,500...Late last fall, the Gunnison post office was the unimportant occupant of a dry-goods box. It now handles some 3,000 letters daily, and receives regularly 200 different publications. [6]

[Strahorn was not finished. He explained how easy—and in that day how efficient and affordable—it was to reach this newest gateway to the San Juans. Ignoring Otto Mears' roadbuilding into the region and beyond, he dutifully

Ute Intemperance — No Laughing Matter. The eastern view of docile Ute bands was not shared on the Western Slope. Raids on their Native American enemies aside, they also attacked "white trespassers." Development of the Gunnison watershed, prime real estate in the early 1870s, had to await the 1879 White River Agency (Meeker) massacre and the expulsion from Colorado of most of the Ute nation. In 1880 Robert Strahorn documented the incredible Gunnison City growth unleashed by the removal of the Ute threat. *(Frank Leslie's Illustrated Newspaper, December 6, 1879)*

focused on the progress and potential of railroads. The rate of change from pristine ancestral hunting ground to commercial powerhouse on a transcontinental rail system had stunned even him, seasoned booster that he was.]

[Strahorn:] How to get here and the cost, as well as the facilities for travel in the Gunnison country, are questions no doubt daily asked in the outside world. Gunnison is as easily reached as was Leadville a year ago, and railways are approaching so rapidly that the travel of another season will mainly come by rail right to this site of the principal Ute camp of a year ago. From the Eastern seaboard to the Missouri River in these days of elaborate railway advertising the route is plain, and thence to Denver one cannot well go amiss. If the traveler reaches the Missouri at Kansas City or Leavenworth he takes the old Kansas Pacific Line; if he comes by the more northerly belt and lands at Omaha, the Union Pacific is the open sesame. By either of these routes he comes from the Missouri River to Denver in about thirty-one hours; there connecting with trains of either the Denver, South Park and Pacific, or Denver and Rio Grande railways, he journeys through some of Colorado's grandest scenery some ten hours to those common points, Alpine (present terminus D., S. P. & P. Railway), and Poncha Springs (on the D. & R.G. Railway), from where Concord coaches of the Sanderson line convey him through to Gunnison City in ten or twelve hours more. Time from either Kansas City, Leavenworth or Omaha to Gunnison, about fifty-one hours; fares from either of these points rule about as follows: To Gunnison or Pitkin, first class, $46.70; emigrant (which on these lines means second-class passage on express trains), $39.70; to Irwin, Ruby Camp and Gothic, first-class, $52.70. Holders of emigrant tickets on the Kansas and Union Pacific line allowed 150-200 pounds of baggage free.

From Gunnison there are daily stage lines to Irwin, Gothic, Crested Butte, Pitkin, and all other prominent points. Distances and rates from Gunnison are as follows: Irwin, Ruby Camp, 30 miles, fare $5; to Pitkin, 26 miles, faire $4; to Gothic, 36 miles, fare $5; to Pitkin, 26 miles, fare $4; to Ohio City, 18 miles, $3.25; to Jack's Cabin, 17 miles, fare $2.50; to Lake City, 60 miles, $8,50; to Ouray, 110 miles, $16.50. It may interest those who are coming in conveyances of their own to know that nearly all roads in the Gunnison country are toll roads, and that the tolls for each ten miles will average about as follows: For two-horse team and wagon, $1; each additional team, 50 cents; saddle animals, 25 cents; one horse and carriage, 50 cents. Occasionally we strike a toll bridge, or rather the toll bridge strikes us with wonderment when the rates are announced, which are all the way from 10 cents for a footman to $1 for teams. A bridge costing $500, across the Gunnison River near here, has had average receipts of $65 per day all this summer. [7]

[Remembering that Strahorn was in the employ of Jay Gould's Union Pacific Railroad adds deeper perspective to his noting the costs and inconveniences of traveling by other means. Clearly a promoter in general of the "New West," he completes his lengthy narrative with a prophecy.]

[Strahorn:] The San Juan country will in two years be penetrated from end to end by at least two lines of railway. It contains every element desired to build up several of the richest mining communities in the world, and has only lacked this advance of the iron horse. Its climate, though rigorous, cannot prevent underground operations the year round. Its smelting facilities of fuel, lime, water, and all varieties and grades of ore, are unexcelled. To say that some of the largest smelting works in the world will now soon spring up in the San Juan Mountains, and that they will turn out millions of dollars where thousands are found now, is entirely reasonable. That thousands of poor prospectors will in this great wilderness yet "strike it rich," and that thousands of capitalists will by making judicious investments reap still greater rewards, is in such a country simply inevitable. The time will soon come when Gunnison and San Juan will be regarded as the bulwarks of the mining industry not only of Colorado, but of the whole southwest. It now only remains for us to see who will be the fortunate participants in the work which will attain this gratifying end. [8]

Strahorn's hindsight may have been perfect, but Ute foresight was not bad. Frank Hall sheds light on their point of view. They imagined with the first shabby prospector bobbing into their homeland where it all would lead. The 1873 Brunot Treaty [really a territorial sales agreement] was an unmistakable milestone. The Ute begrudgingly had retreated from the San Luis Valley, from the Upper Animas, and by 1874-75 even the Upper Lake Fork. Their instinctive responses—warfare—always successful with previous interlopers from the plains and the south did not prevail for long with these pesky Americans from the north. The Brunot Treaty opened the San Juan Mountains to mineral exploration, but did not eliminate the risk and actual occurrences of Ute attacks. Chief Ouray predicted as much in a letter to Colorado Governor Elbert that he dictated to Felix Brunot:

We want you should tell Governor Elbert and the people in the Territory that we are well pleased and perfectly satisfied with everything that has been done. Perhaps some of the people will not like it because we did not wish to sell our valley and farming lands, but we think we had good reasons for not doing so. We expect to occupy them ourselves before long for farming and stock raising. About eighty of our tribe are now raising corn and wheat, and we know not how soon we shall have to depend on ourselves for our bread. We do not want to sell our valley and farming lands for another reason. We know if we should

Peace-Keepers. Despite notable exceptions, Ouray the Southern Ute Chief, and Otto Mears, the Colorado toll road king, managed to lead their respective segments of western society to peaceful outcomes during tumultuous times. Ironically, Mears roads (and railroads) would exacerbate the challenge. The 1879 Meeker massacre changed everything. Peaceful coexistence was assured, but largely due to dispatching most Ute to an out-of-state reservation. *(Wikipedia Commons)*

the Whites would go on them, build their cabins and drive in their stock, which would of course stray upon our lands, and then the Whites themselves would crowd upon us till there would be trouble. We have many friends among the people, and want to live at peace and on good terms with them, and we feel that it would be better for all parties for a mountain range to be between us. We are perfectly willing to sell our mountain lands, and hope the miners will find heaps of gold and silver. We have no wish to molest or make them any trouble. We do not want they should go down into our valleys, however, and kill or scare away our game. We expect there will be much talk among the people and in the papers, about what we have done, and we hope you will let the people know how we feel about it. Truly your friend, Ouray. [9]

Of course, the Chief was right. Of course, the San Juan Mountains witnessed a steady inflow of prospectors and camp followers, and of course "renegade" Utes rebelled despite the best intentions of Chief Ouray. Where minerals were located, settlements arose. Within the year, the upper Lake Fork of the Gunnison valley, Lake City in particular, began hosting the "White crowd." The Gunnison valley enjoyed no such grace. In fact, the San Juans as a whole were not free of Ute "molestations." That had to wait until 1881 when the U.S. military expelled the

Ute, save for Chief Ouray's southwest cohorts, the Southern Utes, from Colorado. With the threat of isolated attacks seemingly lifted, unhindered pursuit of mineral development of the San Juans was unleashed. Gunnison sprang to life and grew into a bustling rail hub and supply depot for all points south and west. The Lake Fork Valley and its very own frontier canyon, with the shameless help of the Lake City *Silver World*, boasted of incalculable mineral wealth.

Chief Ouray was friend and ally of Colorado Whites when most other Ute Chiefs and the majority of his people were their mortal enemies. Whether out of wisdom or due to avarice [even bribes], historians argue for both, on many occasions he came to the aid of emigrant and settler alike. Frank Hall described him as short of stature, characteristic of the Ute in contrast to the Plains Indians, but long on charm. He was a wise leader in tune with his times. The following series of excerpts summarizes Hall's views of Ouray.

> *[Hall:] He stood about five feet seven inches high, and became quite portly in the latter years. His head was strikingly large, and well-shaped, with regular features, and bearing an expression of great dignity in repose, but lighting up pleasantly in conversation. In his ordinary bearing his manner was courtly and gentle, and he was extremely fond of meeting and conversing with cultivated white men, with whom he was a genial companion, compelling their respect and favor by the broad enlightenment of his views. In his habits he was a model; never using tobacco, abhorring whisky, and only taking a sip of wine when in company of those who were indulging, and then only as a matter of courtesy to them. He never swore nor used obscene or vulgar language, was a firm believer in the Christian religion, and about two years before his death united with the Methodist Church. His name, Ouray, or more properly U-re, was simply a pet name given by his father, and, so far as he knew, had no particular significance.*

[Ouray along with Kit Carson averted open Ute warfare during the earliest days of White emigration and settlement in the San Luis valley. Kaneache, chief of the Muache Utes, initiated hostilities on the Rio Las Animas that prompted a U.S. Army counter attack. Kaneache sought Ouray's help in making war on the Whites. Rebuffing the invitation, Ouray seized Kaneache's runner and sent out loyal messengers to warn the Whites on the Huerfano of the impending attack. Often portrayed as a beloved benefactor of his people, Ouray also was a strong leader quite capable of killing them.]

> *[Hall:] When in active command of his men his word was law, and disobedience death. In the autumn of 1874, at Bijou, while returning from Denver to their camp in the South, one of his men desiring to build a fire, started to cut some wood for that purpose within the enclosure of a white*

settler. Ouray discovering his intention, ordered him back, reminding him that they must not trespass upon the property of white men. The obstinate Ute replied that he must have firewood, and he would cut it anyway. Ouray answered that if he did he would kill him, where at the other fellow observed that two could play at that game. Instantly both started for their guns, reaching them about the same time, but Ouray was quicker than his adversary, and promptly shot him.

[On another occasion Ouray shot and broke the arm of another member of his tribe, a man named Johnson. Indicative of his overall rebelliousness, Johnson later was at the center of trouble at the White River Agency and Meeker Massacre.]

[Hall:] Johnson was given to gambling, horse racing, lying and trickery of all kinds. In the present case he had stolen some horses from white men and refused to return them when commanded, thereby in Ouray's opinion, bringing disgrace upon the Ute nation, for which he ought to be punished.

[Historian Hall wraps up his character sketch of the Chief with the following salute:]

[Hall:] The foregoing incidents serve to illustrate the sterling honesty and the general character of this remarkable chief, the statesman of his nation, and the only man worthy of that high distinction in the history of that people. Though a warrior of renown, brave to rashness in battle against the natural enemy, he comprehended that the Caucasian had come to stay and to overspread the land; that resistance would be useless, and only result in the extermination of the red men... The nature of the Ute is much like that of the wild Apache—bloodthirsty and cruel. There have been many occasions when the strong, restraining hand of Ouray has prevented his people from taking the war path in force against the isolated settlers in the mountain regions. In looking back over the past it is a matter for wonder that we escaped with so few murders, depredations and outbreaks, when the causes and opportunities were so numerous. [10]

That's how historian Hall pictured the Chief. Lest misperceptions linger concerning why the Ute was no laughing matter among White and Red alike, Otto Mears shared one of his personal experiences also with friend Ouray. Mears' story also belied conventional wisdom that the Utes were peaceable by nature and Chief Ouray was a stately father figure. Concerning a trip he and wife Mary made to visit Chief Ouray after the agency relocated to the Uncompahgre River area in 1875, E. F. Tucker shares Otto's account:

I made the trip to the Uncompahgre Agency, where the city of Montrose now stands. Ouray was head chief then and I wanted to see him. The distance was 150 miles, and I went by buggy with my wife and baby. When we were nearly at the place, we found that the river was badly flooded and we could not ford it. We had to get across for we could not stay where we were. Finally I thought of a plan. I had two empty oat sacks, for of course we had to carry all our provisions and fodder for the horses with us. I filled these sacks with rocks and tied one on each end of the back axle, and I drove my rig full speed. The horses swam, dragging the buggy after them. The buggy could not upset, because the two loaded sacks held it down, just as two anchors would. The water rose as we sat in the buggy. My wife held the baby up in her arms. I tried to guide the ponies.

When we reached the other side I heard the firing of guns and an Indian ran past me. Ouray came out and called me to come into the house as quickly as I could. He lived in a 'doby' house and after we went in, he barred the doors and windows. He said that the Indian we had seen had been sent out by the Northern Utes to try to induce his Indians to rebel and join with them in an insurrection against Ouray as Chief. [Ouray was Tabeguache] When Ouray heard this he ordered the Indian shot. He told us that there would be trouble during the night. We did not sleep much, but kept on the lookout as Ouray felt that the Northern Utes would come down on him. We were not particularly comfortable in between these two fires, the Northern Utes on the one hand and Ouray with his Indians on the other. The next morning, all being quiet, I hitched up and drove on to the government agency ten miles away. On the road we passed the dead body of the Indian we had seen shot the night before. We stayed at the agency ten days and when we came back, the body still lay as we had seen it. It was badly decayed and covered with buzzards, who were eating the flesh, but not one of Ouray's Indians could be induced to bury it. [11]

With the Brunot Treaty as a framework for peaceful Ute-White Man coexistence, and Chief Ouray more or less firmly in power, overcoming the last barrier to an unrestrained assault on Fortress San Juans was at hand. Otto Mears was building a toll road up the Lake Fork and over Cinnamon Pass to Silverton. Discovered along the right-of-way was gold. If there was gold up the Lake Fork, surely there was gold up adjacent Henson Creek. By late 1874, pathfinders had established the Lake City base camp at the confluence of Henson Creek and the Lake Fork of the Gunnison River. When winter weather broke early the following year, the rush up Henson Canyon would break with it. There would be back-sliding but no retreat. Finally, Fortress San Juans' castle-keep would be breached, but from the east, from the canyon floor. Lofty Engineer Pass, the last great gate lording over the descending canyon to the east and the upper Animas valley to the west would no longer matter.

Nor is it likely that the impending San Juans gold rush would matter to Strahorn. If it did, he would have to read about it and subsequent Henson Canyon developments in the upstart Lake City *Silver World*. For his part, he would be kept busy fighting and filing dispatches in the Sioux homelands, and covering stories of interest elsewhere in the West. By the time his curiosity returned to the San Juans, thousands of claims would be located, Lake City would be bursting with gold-seekers and camp followers, and the Gunnison valley would no longer be a contested no man's land. Less apparent, the San Juans fortress legacy would be dead, its obituary written by a new generation of dreamers hard at work on a legacy of their own.

Notes—Chapter Ten: No Man's Land

[1] Author.

[2] Strahorn, Robert Edmund, *Gunnison and San Juan*, pgs. 5-6.

[3] Strahorn, "Ninety Years of Boyhood", *Autobiography Online*. [hereafter cited as "Strahorn Autobiography."]

[4] Strahorn Autobiography, pg. 1.

[5] Ibid., FN 156.

[6] Strahorn, pgs. 6-9, 14.

[7] Ibid., pgs. 67-68.

[8] Ibid., pg. 79.

[9] Hall, Frank, *History of the State of Colorado*, Vol. II, pg. 191.

[10] Ibid., pgs. 501-512.

[11] Tucker, E.F., *Otto Mears and the San Juans*, pgs. 57-58.

Bibliography

Bagley, Will, *Overland West* Series, Vol. I, "So Rugged and Mountainous," University of Oklahoma Press, Norman, 2010.

Bagley, Will, *Overland West* Series, Vol. II, "With Golden Visions Bright Before Them," University of Oklahoma Press, Norman, 2012.

Baker, Steven G, *Juan Rivera's Colorado, 1765: The First Spaniards Among the Ute and Paiute Indians on the Trails to Teguayo*, Western Reflections Publishing Company, Lake City, CO, 2015.

Bancroft, Hubert Howe, *History of Colorado*, Western Reflections Publishing Company, Lake City, Colorado, 2008.

Barry, John M., *The Great Influenza*, Penguin Books, 2005.

Barry, Louise, Editor, "Albert D. Richardson's Letters on the Pike's Peak Gold Region" written to the Editor of the *Lawrence Republican, The Kansas Historical Quarterly*, February 1943 (Vol. 12, No. 1). [https:www.kshs.org/p/albert-d-richardson-s-letters-on-the-pike-s-peak-gold-region/12926]

Brittner, Lynn, "The People of the Horse, TRUEWEST, History of the American Frontier, August, 2012. [https://truewestmagazine.com/article/the-people-of-the-horse/.]

Brown, Robert L., *An Empire of Silver*, Caxton Printers, Ltd. Caldwell, ID, 1968.

Bruns, Robert J. *The First We Know: Pioneer History of the San Juan*, unpublished manuscript first cited in Nossaman, Vol. I., pg. 37. San Juan County Historical Society Archival Collections, Silverton, CO.

Burke, Marril Lee, *Ghosts of the Lake Fork Region*, Western Reflections Publishing Company, Lake City, CO, 2009.

Carey, Alex, *Memories, Scenes and Humorous High Lights of Lake City*, handwritten notes, unpublished.

"Central City—Black Hawk Historic District," *Colorado Encyclopedia*, December 14, 2019, [https://coloradoencyclopedia.org/article/central-city.]

"Central City, Colorado—Boom & Bust," *Legends of America*, [https://www.legendsofamerica.com/co-centralcity/]

Chamberlin, Rollin T., "Memorial to William Frank Eugene Gurley," *Proceedings Volume of the Geological Society of America*, Annual Report for 1943, April 1944.

Curry, Thomas Sherrod III, "San Juan Scenery the Result of Successive Eruptions, Erosion," *Silver Thread Scenic & Historic Byway*, Summer, 2007

Darley, George M., *Pioneering in the San Juan*, Fleming H. Revell Company, 1899. [Community Presbyterian Church of Lake City, CO reprint, 1986.]

Ellis, Richard N., "The Spanish," *The Western San Juan Mountains*, ed. Rob Blair, University Press of Colorado, Niwot, CO, 1996.

Everhart, William C. Ed., *The Mining Frontier*, U.S. Department of the Interior, National Park Service, Region Four, San Francisco, CA, 1959.

Field, *Crossing the Plains*, 16 June 1845, Oregon Historical Society.

Fletcher, Patricia K. A. and Dr. Jack Earl Fletcher, "Cherokee Trail Diaries." Fletcher Family Foundation, Sequim, WA.

Frajola, R., "Transcontinental Pony Express: April 1860 to October 1861," May 2006. [https://rfrajola.com/pony/page1_1.htm.]

Franklin, George Cory, "Major M.V.B. Wasson," Vol. II, *Pioneers of the San Juan Country*, Sarah Platt Decker Chapter, D.A.R., Durango, Colorado, The Out West Printing and Stationary Company, Colorado Springs, CO, 1942.

Garrard, Lewis H., *Wah-to-yah*, University of Oklahoma Press, Norman, OK, 1955.

Gehling, Richard, *The Pikes Peak Gold Rush* Online:[https://sites.google.com/site/pikespeakgoldrush/a,] 2009.

Genealogy Trails History Group, "Jefferson County, Colorado, Genealogy and History." [https://genealogytrails.com/colo/jefferson/]

Georgia INFO, "This Day in Georgia History." [https://georgiainfor.galileo.usg.edu/thisday/gahistory/10/27/gold-discovered-in-georgia]

Gibbons, Rev. J. J., *In the San Juan, 1898 Sketches*, Calumet Book & Engraving Co., Chicago, IL, 1898 [St. Patrick's Parish, Telluride, CO, 1972].

Greeley, Horace, *An Overland Journey from New York to San Francisco in the Summer of 1859*, Alfred A. Knopf, New York, 1964.

"Gregory's Discovery of Gold Opened New Era In Colorado," *Steamboat Pilot*, February 11, 1943, [https://www.coloradohistoricnewspapers.org/]

Hafen, LeRoy R., ed. "Pike's Peak Gold Rush Guidebooks of 1859," Vol. IX, Porcupine Press, Philadelphia, PA, 1974.

Hafen, LeRoy R., ed. "Colorado Gold Rush, 1858-1859," Vol. X, Porcupine Press, Philadelphia, PA, 1974.

Hafen, LeRoy R., Editor, *The Colorado Magazine*, "Western Mountaineer," Golden, Colorado, December 14, 1859 cited in "George A. Jackson's Diary, 1858-1859," Denver, CO, Vol. XII, No. 6, November 1935.

Hafen, LeRoy R. and Ann W. Hafen, *The Diaries of William Henry Jackson*, The Arthur H. Clark Company, Glendale, CA, 1959.

Hall, Frank, *History of the State of Colorado*, Vol. II and IV. Western Reflections Publishing Company, Lake City, Colorado, reprint of The Blakely Printing Company, Chicago, IL, 1895.

Hannibal Messenger, "The Gold Seeker's Song," Anon., April 28, 1859.

Herald Democrat, "Green Russell, Colonizer," January 1, 1906, Leadville, Colorado. J.H. Pierce letter to Mr. Fen G. Barker, Society of Leadville Pioneers.

History Colorado Library, Reynolds Collection (MSS 1220), Denver, CO.

Hollister, Ovando. James, *The Mines of Colorado*, Promontory Press, New York, 1974. Original: Samuel Bowles & Company, Springfield, Mass., 1867. [Ovando J. Hollister, *The Mines of Colorado*, Samuel Bowles, Springfield, MA, 1867.]

Ingham, G. Thomas, *Digging Gold Among the Rockies*, Western Reflections Publishing Company, Lake City, CO 2008.

Irving, John Duer, *Geology and Ore Deposits Near Lake City*, CO, USGS Bulletin 478, GPO Washington, D.C. 1911.

James Jefferson, Robert W. Delaney, and Gregory C. Thompson, *The Southern Utes, A Tribal History*, edited by Floyd A. O'Neil, Southern Ute Tribe, Ignacio, Colorado, University of Utah Printing Service, Salt Lake City, UT, 1972.

Kendall, George Wilkins, *Texan Santa Fe Expedition*, Harper & Bros., New York, 1844, referenced in Wikipedia "Prairie Dogs."

Lake City Phonograph, numerous citations.

Lake City Silver World, numerous citations.

Legends of America, "Central City, Colorado–Boom & Bust." [https://www.legendso-famerica.com/co-centralcity/.]

Lillard, *Desert Challenge*, 186 ff. quoted in *The Mining Frontier*, Benjamin F. Gilbert, edited by William C. Everhart, United States Department of the Interior, National Park Service, 1959.

Linstrom, Lois C., *Ralston's Gold*, unpublished manuscript, 1986.

Linton, Ralph, Editor, Marvin Opler *"The Southern Ute of Colorado," Acculturation in Seven American Indian Tribes*, D. Appleton-Century Company, Inc., 1940. (reprinted by Peter Smith, Gloucester, MA., 1963.)

Morse, Milo and Fay Bielser, *A Brief History of Mining in Hinsdale County*, B&B Printers, Gunnison, CO 2000.

New Georgia Encyclopedia, "Gold Rush," [https://www.georgiaencyclopedia.org/articles/history-archaeology/gold-rush.]

North, Pam, "Glimpses of Past & Present: John H. Gregory, Man Behind the Mystery," Central City, *The Mountain Ear*, September 10, 2014. [https://themtnear.com/2014/09/glimpses-of-past-present.]

Nossaman, Allen, *Many More Mountains*, Vol. 1, Sundance Books, Durango, CO, 2006.

Owens, Kenneth N., ed., *John Sutter and a Wider West*, University of Nebraska Press, Lincoln, NE, 2002.

Paul, Rodman W., *The California Gold Discovery*, The Talisman Press, Georgetown, CA, 1966.

Paul, Rodman W., *The Far West and the Great Plains in Transition 1859-1900*, Harper & Row, New York, 1988.

Paul, Rodman W., *Mining Frontiers of the Far West 1848-1880*, Holt, Rinehart and Winston, New York, 1963.

Pettit, Jan, with Introduction by Eddie Box, *Utes, The Mountain People*, Johnson Books, Boulder, CO, 1990.

Pielou, E.C., *After the Ice Age: The Return of Life to Glaciated North America*, University of Chicago Press, Chicago and London, 1991.

Pioneers of the San Juan Country, Vols. I-III, Sarah Platt Decker Chapter, D.A.R., Durango, Colorado, The Out West Printing and Stationary Company, Colorado Springs, CO, 1942. [Searcy, Helen M., "Otto Mears," Pioneers of the San Juan Country]

Poxson, Ben, *A Reminiscence*, Chronicles Publishing Company, October 1988. [History Colorado Library], Denver, CO.

Reck, Jamie and Kevin Alexander, Ph.D., *Henson Creek Watershed Analysis*, United States Environmental Protection Agency, Denver, CO, 2007.

Richardson, Albert D., *Beyond the Mississippi*, American Publishing Company, Hartford, Connecticut, 1867.

Rickard, T. A., *Across the San Juan Mountains*, Bear Creek Publishing Company, Ouray, CO, 1980.

Scamehorn, Lee, *Albert Eugene Reynolds, Colorado's Mining King*, University of Oklahoma Press, Norman, OK, 1995.

Service, Robert, *The Best of Robert Service*, Perigee Books, NY, 1953.

Smith, Duane A., *San Juan Gold: A Mining Engineer's Adventures, 1879-1881*, Western Reflections Publishing Company, Montrose, CO, 2002.

Smith, Duane A., *Song of the Hammer and Drill*, University Press of Colorado Press, Boulder, CO, 2000.

Smith, Duane A., *The Trail of Gold and Silver*, University Press of Colorado, Boulder, CO, 2009.

Smith, P. David, *Early Colorado Gold Prospectors*, unpublished manuscript, 2022.

Smith, P. David, *Mountains of Silver*, Western Reflections Publishing Company, Montrose, CO, 2004.

Smith, P. David, *The Story of Lake City*, Western Reflections Publishing Company, Lake City, CO, 2016.

Spring, Agnes Wright, "Rush to the Rockies, 1859," *Colorado Magazine*, April 1959, p. 105, History Colorado.

Sprague, Marshall, The Great Gates, Little, Brown & Company (Canada) Limited, Toronto, 1964.

Steele, Joe M, *Guide to Lake City Geology*, B&B Printers, Gunnison, CO, 2002.

Strahorn, Robert Edmund, *Gunnison and San Juan*, Western Reflections Publishing Company, Lake City, CO, 2012. [Also see: https://military-history.fandom.com.]

Trembath, Brian K., "Jefferson Territory: The Renegade State That Almost Replaced Colorado," June 24, 2020, *Research News*, Denver Public Library, Denver, CO.

Tucker, E.F., *Otto Mears and the San Juans*, Western Reflections Publishing Company, Montrose, CO, 2003.

Turner, John G., "The Mormons Sit Out the Civil War," *The New York Times*, May 1, 2012.

Twitty, Eric, *Basins of Silver*, Western Reflections Publishing Company, Lake City, CO, 2008.

Twitty, Eric, "Hinsdale County Study, Ocean Wave Mine, Site 5HN1082 [on file in Hinsdale County office]."

Twitty, Eric, *Riches to Rust*, Western Reflections Publishing Company, Montrose, CO, 2002.

Unruh, John D. Jr., *The Plains Across*, University of Illinois Press, Chicago, IL, 1979.

West, Elliott, *The Contested Plains: Indians, Goldseekers and the Rush to Colorado*, University of Kansas Press, Lawrence, KS, 1998.

Western Mining History Online "The Colorado Gold Rush." [https://westernmininghistory.com/articles/11/page 1.]

Wickersheim, Laurel M. and Rawlene LeBaron, Mine Owners and Mines of the Colorado Gold Rush, Heritage Books, Inc., Berwyn Heights, MD, 2011.

Wikipedia, multiple dates and titles.

Williams, Joseph, *Narrative of a Tour From the State of Indiana to the Oregon Territory in the Years 1841-2*, Cadmus Book Shop, New York, 1921.

Wootton, Richens Lacy, *Uncle Dick Wootton, The Pioneer Frontiersman of the Rocky Mountains*, as told to Howard Louis Conard, ed. M.M. Quaife, The Narrative Press, Santa Barbara, CA, 2001.

Wright, Carolyn and Clarence, *Tiny Hinsdale of the Silvery San Juan*, Big Mountain Press, 1964.

Wroth, William, ed., *Ute Indian Arts & Culture from Pre-History to the New Millennium*, "Traditional Cosmology, Ecology and Language of the Ute Indian," Interview of James N. Goss (linguist), Taylor Museum of the Colorado Springs Fine Arts Center, 2000.

Zamonski, Stanley W. and Teddy Keller, *The Fifty-Niners*, Sage Books, Denver, CO 1961.

Zollinger, James Peter, *Sutter, The Man and His Empire*, Oxford University Press, New York, 1939.

Index

www.ingramcontent.com/pod-product-compliance
Lightning Source LLC
Chambersburg PA
CBHW080900120626
46555CB00008B/2891